P9-DGY-287

CRITICAL INSIGHTS

James Baldwin

CRITICAL INSIGHTS

James Baldwin

Editor
Morris Dickstein
Graduate Center of the City University of New York

Salem Press
Pasadena, California Hackensack, New Jersey

Cover photo: Ulf Andersen/Getty Images

Published by Salem Press

∞ The paper used in these volumes conforms to the American National Standard for Permanence of Paper for Printed Library Materials, Z39.48-1992 (R1997).

Library of Congress Cataloging-in-Publication Data

James Baldwin / editor, Morris Dickstein.
p. cm. — (Critical insights)
Includes bibliographical references and index.
ISBN 978-1-58765-701-6 (vol. 1 : alk. paper)
1. Baldwin, James, 1924-1987—Criticism and interpretation. 2. African Americans in literature. I. Dickstein, Morris.
PS3552.A45Z72355 2011
818'.5409—dc22

2010030192

PRINTED IN CANADA

Contents

Career, Life, and Influence

Critical Contexts

Critical Readings

Resources

About This Volume

Morris Dickstein

James Baldwin is one of the best-known writers to emerge in America in the early 1950s. In addition to gaining the respect of exacting critics, his books became best sellers with the 1962 publication of his third novel, *Another Country*, and Baldwin's subtle yet incendiary sermon "Letter from a Region in My Mind" caused a sensation when it appeared in *The New Yorker* a few months later and was collected the following year in *The Fire Next Time*. He also became one of the leading figures identified with the civil rights movement. But as the prerogatives of celebrity, along with his frustrations about the slow progress of change, pushed Baldwin to take an increasingly militant stance, his literary output and reputation began to wane.

Unexpectedly, the rise of cultural studies and gender theory after Baldwin's death in 1987 gave his work a new currency, at least among academics, and this has led to a reassessment of his neglected later work. In his overview of Baldwin's critical reception in this volume, D. Quentin Miller describes this as "a willingness to evaluate Baldwin thematically rather than strictly aesthetically," something earlier critics were loath to do. This willingness enabled scholars, rightly or wrongly, "to shed light on some of the works that had been critically dismissed," says Miller, "and to explore a plurality of contexts in order to recognize fully the accomplishments of this complex writer."

The present volume, which includes both reprinted essays and newly commissioned pieces, covers a wide range of both aesthetic criticism and contextual discussion, some of it driven by new approaches in cultural theory. Following overviews by myself, Barry Mann, and Richard Beck (writing for *The Paris Review*), the "Critical Contexts" section opens with Douglas Field's examination of Baldwin's position in his own time, stressing his "dislike of sexual classification," which would undoubtedly have led him to recoil from recent commentaries stressing the intersections of race and sexuality in his work. "Those terms, homosexual, bisexual, heterosexual, are 20th century terms which, for me, have very little meaning," Field quotes him as saying, and he notes that Baldwin also felt that sexual orientation was a private matter, which may explain why he dealt with homosexuality far more in his fiction than in his essays, where he spoke for himself more directly.

Field's piece is followed by James Campbell's account of a key moment in Baldwin's young life, his arrival in Paris in 1948 and his earliest writing there, including his seminal essay "Everybody's Protest Novel" and his parallel piece on homosexuality, "Preservation of Innocence," which he never reprinted. Horace A. Porter then explores Baldwin's relation to the two chief figures of the former essay, Harriet Beecher Stowe and Richard Wright, writers so close to him that he needed to free himself from their influence. Like Stowe but unlike Wright, Baldwin was deeply influenced by the biblical tradition. Mildred R. Mickle compares the role of faith in Baldwin's first novel, *Go Tell It on the Mountain*, with its treatment in the works of three writers seemingly remote from him, the eighteenth-century black poet Phillis Wheatley and two allegorical science-fiction writers, Tananarive Due and Octavia E. Butler. This section concludes with D. Quentin Miller's account of scholarly literature on Baldwin and the ups and downs of his critical reputation up to the present.

Another essay by Douglas Field leads off the "Critical Readings" section. Field documents Baldwin's complex interaction with the black nationalism that developed in the 1960s and shows how his sexuality, especially his determination "to challenge and demystify myths of black sexual prowess," was undone by the attacks of militant blacks such as Eldridge Cleaver and then by his own adoption of their militant rhetoric. It did little to pacify his critics, who continued to dismiss him, but did much to suppress his own inner voice, and especially to discourage any discussion of homosexuality, since this was a special object of derision for black nationalists. Baldwin was effectively deprived of his greatest strength as a writer, the social meaning he could draw from his own lyrical introspection and richly nuanced ambivalence. This point becomes clear in Charles Scruggs's intricate study of the interplay of the characters and voices of *Go Tell It on the Mountain*, all of them shot through with regret and recollection and all of them partly speaking for Baldwin himself. Peter Kerry Powers takes this further in "The Treacherous Body," as essay on the relations among body, community, and confession in the same novel. Discussing the ecstatic rituals of the kind portrayed in the book, such as speaking in tongues and being possessed or "saved," which vary dramatically from sect to sect and from church to church, he says that "the hidden truth of the inward self is only possible through rituals of the body that a community not only recognizes but also demands." Powers argues that, in Baldwin's vision, "this hidden self must be revealed through confession, displacing the false social self imprinted on the body." This confession in turn becomes a bond when it is received by the community, as it is for Baldwin's protagonist, the fourteen-year-old John Grimes. Indeed, the retrospective character of the whole novel, its reckoning with the past, could be seen as confessional.

Taking a different, more political tack on some of the same issues, Geraldine Murphy places Baldwin in the context of the Cold War liberalism and anti-Stalinism of the New York Intellectuals, such as Lionel Trilling, who sponsored his early work. She sees these writers, along with Baldwin, displacing the social concerns that drove writers of the 1930s toward issues of personality, subjectivity, and autonomy that were less threatening to the status quo. But she also argues that Baldwin, by focusing on race, gave a radical turn to the subjectivity and the antitotalitarianism of the Intellectuals, since his concern with identity, as a black person, made an especially strong case for racial equality. Baldwin's own position shifted by the mid-1960s, as can be seen in the essays by John M. Reilly and Tiffany Gilbert on two strikingly different short stories. Reilly emphasizes the communal themes of "Sonny's Blues," an artist fable that first appeared in *Partisan Review* in 1957 and that remains Baldwin's best-known story. It describes the stiff mid-

dle-class narrator's growing understanding of and sympathy for his musician brother, a victim of the drug culture of the Harlem streets and the jazz scene. Hearing his brother play when he himself has grown vulnerable, he hears the language of community, the timbre and rhythm of its soul, as if for the first time. In Gilbert's surprising reading of the much-criticized 1965 story "Going to Meet the Man," we see Baldwin deploying a familiar theme of nostalgia, not to fathom his black characters but to probe the mind of a racist and impotent white sheriff, who is sexually excited by his graphic memory of a lynching he witnessed as a boy.

All critics agree that the mid-1960s were a turning point for Baldwin, as we can see in three pieces written at the time by Lionel Trilling, F. W. Dupee, and C. W. E. Bigsby. Each of them deals apprehensively with Baldwin's rhetorical shift from a private role to a more public one. Dupee wonders whether Baldwin, in *The Fire Next Time*, "has exchanged prophecy for criticism" and provided an insufficiently "solid base for the speculative fireworks the book abounds in." As a result, he fears, Baldwin "manifestly weakens his grasp of his role, his style, and his great theme itself." Trilling is more sympathetic to *Another Country*, although, in his judgment, the novel lacks the gift of style and the "delicacy of perception" he admired in Baldwin's earlier books. He, too, wonders, "how, in the extravagant publicness in which Mr. Baldwin lives, is he to find the inwardness which we take to be the condition of truth in the writer? How is he to make sure that he remains a person and a writer and does not become merely a figure and a representative?" The response to these queries, which augured a major shift in Baldwin's later work, comes in Bigsby's account of *Blues for Mr. Charlie*. "Baldwin's play," he says, "matches with disturbing precision his own definition of sterile protest literature." He adds, "The rage which he had felt at the death of his friend [Medgar Evers] has betrayed him into the oversimplifications of a sociological literature which he had always consciously avoided," an accusatory literature in which black people are wholly good and white people wholly evil.

Such sentiments can be seen in two neglected books from the early 1970s, the book-length essay *No Name in the Street* (1971) and the novel *If Beale Street Could Talk* (1974), which are the subjects of two essays by Yoshinobu Hakutani and Trudier Harris. Hakutani lays bare the close relationship between these two works, and Harris, a leading Baldwin scholar, offers an unusually detailed and sympathetic reading of the novel, describing Baldwin's shift of focus from the Negro church to the nuclear family as a source of security and solidarity, perhaps reflecting the older Baldwin's deepening ties to his own family, first forged in a unified resistance to their difficult father. It was during this period that Henry Louis Gates, Jr., as a twenty-two-year-old journalist, visited Baldwin in the south of France in 1973. For Baldwin, the visit became the basis for one of his last works, a play called "The Welcome Table," and Gates offers a luminous personal account of both the visit and Baldwin's writing in his 1992 essay.

The volume concludes with two virtuoso essays by Darryl Pinckney. Written in response to the publication of the landmark 1998 Library of America editions of Baldwin's collected essays and his early novels and stories, Pinckney's essays provide both a thematic summary and a fresh assessment of every one of Baldwin's major works and many minor ones as well. These two pieces clearly arise out of a reflective personal engagement that parallels the best qualities of Baldwin's own essays. They show that despite the unevenness of his work, which many have seen as a precipitous decline, Baldwin survives as a key figure in the constellation of postwar writing and in our comprehension of the traumas of race in America.

CAREER, LIFE, AND INFLUENCE

On James Baldwin

Morris Dickstein

Along with Richard Wright and Ralph Ellison, James Baldwin was not only one of the powerful black novelists who emerged in the middle decades of the twentieth century but also one of the key American writers. Wright, who began publishing in the last years of the Great Depression, was a social novelist whose work combined strands of naturalism and modernism, the circumstantial realism of Theodore Dreiser with the almost hallucinatory psychological intensity of Fyodor Dostoevski. He was a man with a mission—to deploy fiction to awaken the nation to the cancer of racism and its effects on the lives and minds of black people, both in the North and in the South. His work exposed the psychological toll this system took on those who grew up in it and warned of the dangers it posed to those who allowed it to continue.

Wright's early protégés, Ellison and Baldwin, shared his goals but backed off from his literary influence. They developed other techniques to give readers a visceral sense of the challenges that confronted young black men coming of age in America. Like Zora Neale Hurston, Wright's early rival, they focused on the relations of black people to one another, not simply to the white world. Ellison was a modernist whose only completed novel, the picaresque *Invisible Man* (1952), marshaled a Joycean anthology of styles to refract much of his own experience, from his boyhood in Oklahoma to his schooling in the Deep South and his arrival in Harlem in the mid-1930s. Baldwin, who broke with Wright more dramatically after following him to Paris in 1948, was a more directly autobiographical writer both in his eloquent essays and in his first and best novel, *Go Tell It on the Mountain* (1953). His work foreshadowed the autobiographical turn in American writing that soon would extend to Norman Mailer and Jack Kerouac in prose and Allen Ginsberg and Robert Lowell in poetry. Making more direct use of their own experience, energized by the confessional personas they created in their work, these writers turned their backs on the social muse of the Depression years and the ironic, distancing forms of modernism that dominated the postwar period.

Baldwin's essays, at once keenly observant and acutely introspective, set the stage for the New Journalism of the 1960s. His approach differed sharply from the self-projecting egotism of Mailer or the seemingly spontaneous flow of recollection in Kerouac. Like the Holocaust survivors who began speaking out long after World War II, Baldwin saw himself less as a lone individual and more as a solemn witness who had lived through a historical cataclysm of epic proportions, someone who could convey its day-to-day sensations in personal terms. While others had studied the conditions of blacks in poor families, menial jobs, and urban ghettoes, Baldwin could show what it felt like to grow up in Harlem, then later to encounter vicious discrimination while working among whites, learning to curb his temper for fear of getting himself killed. He could explore what it was like to escape uneasily into the bohemian life in Greenwich Village or the expatriate life in Europe.

As the sexually ambivalent, emotionally confused son of a single mother, and then as the stepson of a preacher whose paranoid fears and humiliations gradually took over his life, as a teenage preacher who took refuge in the church from the patriarchal authority of his stepfather and the temptations of the streets, as an exceptional student singled out and encouraged by his teachers, Baldwin channeled his early adventures into stories at once unique to him and yet typical of their time and place. He worked for years on a novel and a long essay that would do justice to his embattled relationship with David Baldwin, the fierce stepfather who died in 1943 when Baldwin was nineteen. The novel was first called "Crying Holy," and Baldwin hoped it would serve as a kind of exorcism. When he felt he could stop hating his stepfather and tried instead to understand him, this book turned into *Go Tell It on the Mountain*, a study of two black generations. Its frame story centers on the ecstatic religious conversion of John Grimes on his fourteenth birthday, but the body of the novel is made up of three long flashbacks, almost separate novellas, that fill in the earlier lives of his stepfather, his bitter, dying aunt, and his mother, all of whom migrated to the North. While there is something stiff and inhibiting about the form of the novel, its cadenced biblical prose can be surpassingly beautiful.

Baldwin himself had not yet seen the South, and he fills in the older generation's memories with tales of lust and betrayal, death and abandonment. Like every other Baldwin novel, its subject is love and hate—the troubled relations between parents and children, between husbands and wives, between lovers trapped in a world that barely lets them breathe. Each character experiences rejection, loss, and disappointment, a bad omen for the young protagonist, who is himself physically drawn to an older adolescent who received the call before him. Yet, in his forays into the city, he also feels an attraction to the wider world outside Harlem, outside the church, away from his family. Somehow Baldwin kept this heady brew of race, religion, and sexuality under control. His conflicts over homosexuality he would save for his second novel, set in expatriate Paris, *Giovanni's Room* (1956), which concentrates on the failure of love as the consequence of a cowardly failure of emotional honesty.

The young Baldwin's flight from Harlem and his worldly aspirations would give his books and essays a double consciousness, anchored in his condition as a Negro yet determined to reach beyond color, toward a more universal sense of humanity. In his introduction to his second collection of essays, *Nobody Knows My Name* (1961), Baldwin writes, "I still believe that the unexamined life is not worth living. . . . the question of color, especially in this country, operates to hide the graver questions of the self" (12). The early Baldwin focused as much on issues of identity and sexuality as on race. He was influenced by the tragic realism and liberalism that dominated American intellectual life in the decades after World War II. His work was first published by New York editors and intellectuals, many of them Jewish, in journals such as *The New Leader, Commentary*, and *Partisan Review*. These modernist intellectuals welcomed Baldwin's introspective approach to cultural criticism, stressing less the sociology than the psychology of race, the almost unbearable tensions, the deep inner wounds. They also helped form his view of the novel as an aesthetic construct, a layered exploration of the mysteries of personality and the paradoxes of consciousness. Their idol in fiction, Henry James, became his model as well. As much as Baldwin's early training in the pulpit, James was the inspiration for the rolling periods of his style, its riot of subordinate clauses, its inexorable building energy.

The same impulse to transcend the stereotypes of race took him abroad. "I left America," he says in *Nobody Knows My Name*, "because I doubted my ability to survive the fury of the color problem here. (Sometimes I still do.) I wanted to prevent myself from becoming *merely* a Negro; or, even, merely a Negro writer" (17). But taking refuge in the mountains of Switzerland, "in that absolutely alabaster landscape, armed with two Bessie Smith records and a typewriter, I began to try to re-create the life that I had first known as a child and from which I had spent so many years in flight." He had never listened to Bessie Smith in America, "but in Europe she helped reconcile me to being a 'nigger'" (18). Fleeing first to Greenwich Village, then to Europe in search of a color-blind human identity, he rediscovered the people and places he came from as well as the fuller person he could become. The essay is called "The Discovery of What It Means to Be an American."

It is axiomatic for the early Baldwin that every black person, because of how he is treated in white society, feels a burning rage that he cannot let loose, since it would either get him killed or, worse still, eat him up alive. Baldwin develops this not only in *Go Tell It on the Mountain* but also in parallel essays on his own father, David Baldwin, and his literary father, Richard Wright. These declarations of independence provided him with some of his richest literary material. "Notes of a Native Son," one of the greatest essays ever written by an American, juxtaposes his father's death, just as his last child is being born, with the Harlem race riot that occurred in the same week. Baldwin's two initial essays on Wright, "Everybody's Protest Novel" and "Many Thousands Gone," also collected in *Notes of a Native Son* (1955), were far more than salvos in a drama of Oedipal conflict, with a son trying to establish his own identity by slaying his forebear. They represented key moments in his struggle for self-definition.

In all three essays, Baldwin aims to disclose and transcend the legacy of anger he inherited from the older generation, though it also spoke to his own experience. He was determined to avoid becoming merely a Negro writer while dramatizing the dark truth about how Negroes lived and felt. He saw how they were unmanned, most of all psychologically, by the limits and pressures that hemmed them in. Such pressure, in Baldwin's view, led Wright to become a protest writer, coarsening the protagonist of *Native Son* into a hapless victim and violent aggressor, a menacing challenge to white readers, but not someone with any real relationship with the people around him, black or white. A similar pressure drove the paranoia and cold fury that took over the life of Baldwin's father, effectively destroying him and making life difficult, at times unbearable, for his children. Passive toward the white world he feared and loathed, he took out his anger on his own family.

Linking private pain with public trauma, Baldwin connects his father's emotional torment with the littered streets through which the funeral procession must pass, the scene of destruction where Harlem and history had sent a message:

> He had lived and died in an intolerable bitterness of spirit and it frightened me, as we drive him to the graveyard through those unquiet, ruined streets, to see how powerful and overflowing this bitterness could be and to realize that this bitterness now was mine. (*Notes of a Native Son*, 84)

This bitterness, which he had resisted, now threatens him as well. "There is not a Negro alive who does not have this rage in his blood—one has the choice, merely, of living with it consciously or surrendering to it" (92). "I saw nothing very clearly but I did see this: that my life, my *real* life, was in danger, and not from anything other people might do but from the hatred I carried in my own heart" (95). He concludes that

> it was necessary to hold on to the things that mattered. The dead man mattered, the new life mattered; blackness and whiteness did not matter; to believe that they did was to acquiesce in one's own destruction. Hatred, which could destroy so much, never failed to destroy the man who hated and this was an immutable law. (108)

In vowing "to keep my own heart free of hatred and despair" (109), however, Baldwin was making a promise he could not keep, however satisfying it could be to white liberals, many of whom had been his friends and mentors. Baldwin's renunciation of hatred, violence, and despair not only fueled his eloquence but also served as the verbal music of the early civil rights years, which were focused on integration and nonviolent resistance. At the heart of this movement was an alliance between blacks and the liberal whites who supported their quest for legal remedies and joined in their dignified and courageous protest marches, rallies, and sit-ins. Reporting from the South for the first time, Baldwin, though hardly political, was drawn in. With the publication of his third novel, *Another Country* (1962), and his longest, most impassioned essay, *The Fire Next Time* (1963), in the same year as the great March on Washington, Baldwin became the most famous writer in the United States. With his face blazoned on the cover of *Time* magazine, he was transformed into a spokesman as well as a writer.

Yet Baldwin was unable to maintain this humanist stance that his white readers so much admired. The passage of the Civil Rights Act and the Voting Rights Act in 1964 and 1965 proved to be the high-water mark of the civil rights movement. As the Vietnam War escalated, as American cities erupted in race riots, a more militant mood was in the air. Faith in integration and black-white cooperation gave way to black nationalism, separatism, and racial pride. "Black Power" and "Black Is Beautiful" became the slogans of the day. Baldwin caught some of this mood, especially as younger black writers such as Eldridge Cleaver began attacking him as white man in blackface. His public activities, his new role as a celebrity, left him less freedom to write, and the atmosphere of the times, combined with his own growing impatience and frustrations, changed what he did write.

The first half of *The Fire Next Time* brought him back with renewed energy to the autobiographical material of *Go Tell It on the Mountain* and "Notes of a Native Son"—growing up in Harlem, his father, the church, his conversion and preaching, a background that became almost palpable in the book's prose:

> The church was very exciting. It took long time for me to disengage myself from this excitement, and on the blindest, most visceral level, I never really have, and never will. . . . Nothing that has happened to me since equals the power and the glory that I sometimes felt when, in the middle of a sermon, I knew that I was somehow, by some miracle, really carrying, as they say, "the Word"—when the church and I were one. (49, 50)

But Baldwin's renewed sense of his own calling, not in the church but in a political pulpit, combined with his growing resentment toward white privilege, could be dangerous to him as a writer. Intoxicated at moments by its own rhetoric, the book gradually turns into a sermon, a jeremiad about the power of black anger "to precipitate chaos and ring down the curtain on the American dream" (119). "Black has *become* a beautiful color—not because it is loved but because it is feared" (105). Blacks have discovered their "power to intimidate" (115). This is prophetic of the racial polarization that developed in the 1960s, but it also shows how Baldwin allowed the destructive rage he diagnosed in his father and in Wright's work to possess him. Enveloped by a sense of impending apocalypse, fearing a black Holocaust, he would deliver screeds against white racism and forecast doom for American society.

This shrill note could be heard in his play *Blues for Mr. Charlie*

(1964) and in the title story of his collection *Going to Meet the Man* (1965), whose protagonist, an impotent white lawman who brutalizes blacks, can muster an erection with his wife only by recalling a lynching he had witnessed as a boy in which the victim was graphically emasculated. With this psychosexual take on racial violence, Baldwin sinks back into the lurid clichés of protest fiction that he had attacked as a young writer. His fiction suffered from a loss of complexity.

As essayist, Baldwin could still on occasion reach into a well of personal reminiscence and achieve real power, as in the opening pages of *No Name in the Street* (1971) and in one of his last essays, "Freaks and the American Ideal of Manhood" (also called "Here Be Dragons," 1985). This was one of his rare discussions of homosexuality outside his fiction; he vividly recalled his early conflicts, when he was abused or abused himself, and affirmed how much he hated to be typed, categorized. More and more, however, the writer disappeared into the public personality, the memoirist and storyteller evaporated into the finger-pointing accuser. His influence waned; his books were ignored. But some five thousand people, myself included, were drawn to his 1987 funeral in the Cathedral of St. John the Divine, on the cusp between Harlem and the academic world of Morningside Heights. An epoch in our lives had ended. It was one last tribute to the writer he had been and the striking cultural figure he became.

Works Cited

Baldwin, James. *Another Country*. New York: Dial Press, 1962.

___________. *The Fire Next Time*. 1963. New York: Dell, 1964.

___________. *Giovanni's Room*. New York: Dial Press, 1956.

___________. *Going to Meet the Man*. New York: Dial Press, 1965.

___________. "Here Be Dragons." *The Price of the Ticket: Collected Nonfiction, 1948-1985*. New York: St. Martin's/Marek, 1985.

___________. *No Name in the Street*. New York: Dial Press, 1971.

___________. *Nobody Knows My Name: More Notes of a Native Son*. 1961. New York: Dell, 1963.

___________. *Notes of a Native Son*. 1955. London: Michael Joseph, 1964.

Biography of James Baldwin

Barry Mann

James Baldwin was born in New York City on August 2, 1924. His mother, Emma Berdis Jones, was unmarried at the time, and his illegitimacy would haunt him throughout his life. In 1927, Emma married David Baldwin, a former slave's son who had come north from New Orleans. David worked in factories, preached on weekends, and raised his nine children with iron discipline and little warmth.

James grew to hate his father for constantly criticizing and teasing him. As a teenager, he rebelled in many ways, first by becoming a young minister at a rival congregation, then by rejecting the church to pursue writing. At the same time, he watched his father slowly descend into a mental illness. Days before Baldwin's nineteenth birthday, his father succumbed to tuberculosis.

From the first, Baldwin loved to read, and by the time he graduated from the prestigious DeWitt Clinton High School in the Bronx, he had written essays for his school and church papers and made friends, black and white, who later became important professional contacts. In 1942, to help support his family, he went to work laying railroad track for the Army in New Jersey. It was his first experience outside New York, and the bigotry he faced there infuriated him. He spent several years moving from job to job, exploring his sexuality in brief affairs with other men and writing his first novel.

In 1945, novelist Richard Wright helped Baldwin secure a Eugene F. Saxton Fellowship for a manuscript he was working on, titled "In My Father's House," but its rejection by publishers devastated him: he went into hiding and started a lifetime career of heavy drinking. He turned to writing smaller pieces—stories, articles, reviews—and by 1948, he was regularly publishing book reviews and essays in periodicals such as *New Leader*, *Commentary*, and *Partisan Review.* When the strains of being a black among whites and a homosexual among heterosexuals (he was at one point engaged to be married) became too much,

Baldwin left the United States to join friends in exile in Paris. For the rest of his life, he would frequently cross the Atlantic Ocean.

In Paris he lived a penniless, bohemian life and met such writers as Truman Capote, Saul Bellow, and Jean Genet. Richard Wright was also in Paris, though a rift began to grow between him and Baldwin as the latter began to chafe against his mentor and his tremendous reputation. An article by Baldwin criticizing Wright's *Native Son* (1940) was published simultaneously in Paris and New York and attracted much attention.

Baldwin became great friends with a Swiss national named Lucien Happersbarger, and it was in Lucien's Alpine village that he completed *Go Tell It on the Mountain* (1953), his first published novel. Returning to New York, he found readjustment difficult, again facing the racism he had crossed the ocean to escape. He wrote steadily, compiling topical essays into a collection called *Notes of a Native Son* (1955). His second novel, *Giovanni's Room*, published in England in 1955 and a year later in the United States, established his literary standing and identified him as an openly homosexual novelist.

With his mounting success, Baldwin remained deeply sensitive to the plight of blacks. In 1956, he covered a conference of black writers and artists in Paris and made his first trip into the Deep South, where he met the Reverend Martin Luther King, Jr., Rosa Parks, and other civil rights activists. These experiences confirmed his commitment to civil rights and led to a second volume of essays, *Nobody Knows My Name: More Notes of a Native Son* (1961). Two years later, he published *The Fire Next Time*, a piece about the extremist Black Muslims and Baldwin's own more moderate views. By virtue of his essays, he came to be considered a spokesman for his race. In 1963, Attorney General Robert Kennedy invited Baldwin and other prominent blacks to discuss the nation's racial situation. Despite goodwill on both sides, no common language could be found, and the meeting reminded Baldwin how far the nation still had to go.

Baldwin continued writing fiction. *Another Country*, his most candid and ambitious novel, appeared in 1962 to mixed reviews; his plays *Blues for Mister Charlie* (1964) and *The Amen Corner* (1954) were recognized for their vivid passion but faulted for poor structure; his sole volume of short stories, *Going to Meet the Man* (1965), and the novel *Tell Me How Long the Train's Been Gone* (1968) met with harsh criticism and reviewers began to wonder if Baldwin was getting stale. He was accused by activist and writer Eldridge Cleaver of race hatred in *Soul on Ice* (1967), and he pulled no punches in an ongoing rivalry with novelist Norman Mailer. In many ways, he was caught on the fence separating art and politics, and his eloquence and artistic vision were waning.

The final straw was the assassination of King on April 4, 1968. The loss, on both personal and political levels, profoundly affected Baldwin. Years of hope and struggle had only brought him back to the bitterness that had infected his father. In 1970, at the age of forty-six, he settled permanently in southern France. He still returned frequently to the United States, was still as devoted to friends and family as he had always been, and still wrote. None of his later works, however—*No Name in the Street* (1971), further essays on race; *If Beale Street Could Talk* (1974), a novel; *The Devil Finds Work* (1976), essays on film; *Just Above My Head* (1979), his last novel; *Jimmy's Blues: Selected Poems* (1983), a book of poetry; and other articles, collections, and collaborations—garnered the praise his earlier works had received. While he had myriad projects in mind, it became more and more difficult to write. He lectured and taught widely, but decades of liquor, cigarettes, constant travel, casual romance, publicity, and loneliness were taking their toll.

Baldwin developed cancer of the esophagus, and it claimed his life on December 1, 1987, in his home in France. His brother David, who had always been a close friend and supporter, was at his bedside when he died. A week later, more than five thousand people attended the funeral service held for him at New York's Cathedral of St. John the Divine, on the edge of his native Harlem.

From *Magill's Survey of American Literature*. Rev. ed. Pasadena, CA: Salem Press, 2007.

Bibliography

Balfour, Lawrie Lawrence, and Katherine Lawrence Balfour. *The Evidence of Things Not Said: James Baldwin and the Promise of American Democracy*. Ithaca, N.Y.: Cornell University Press, 2001. Explores the political dimension of Baldwin's essays, stressing the politics of race in American democracy.

Campbell, James. *Talking at the Gates: A Life of James Baldwin*. New York: Viking Press, 1991. Biography describes the events of Baldwin's life and places his works within context.

Fabre, Michel. "James Baldwin in Paris: Love and Self-Discovery." *From Harlem to Paris: Black American Writers in France, 1840-1980*. Chicago: University of Illinois Press, 1991. Discusses Baldwin's Paris experiences. Brings biographical details to the European experiences of the bicontinental playwright, who owed France "his own spiritual growth, through the existential discovery of love as a key to life." The notes offer interview sources of quotations for further study.

Harris, Trudier, ed. *New Essays on "Go Tell It on the Mountain."* New York: Cambridge University Press, 1996. Collection of essays examines the composition, themes, publication history, public reception, and contemporary interpretations of Baldwin's first novel.

Kinnamon, Keneth, ed. *James Baldwin: A Collection of Critical Essays*. Englewood Cliffs, N.J.: Prentice-Hall, 1974. A good introduction to Baldwin's early work featuring a collection of diverse essays by such well-known figures as Irving Howe, Langston Hughes, Sherley Anne Williams, and Eldridge Cleaver. Includes a chronology of important dates, notes on the contributors, and a select bibliography.

Leeming, David. *James Baldwin: A Biography*. New York: Alfred A. Knopf, 1994. A biography of Baldwin written by one who knew him and worked with him for the last quarter century of his life. Provides extensive literary analysis of Baldwin's work and relates his work to his life.

McBride, Dwight A. *James Baldwin Now*. New York: New York University Press, 1999. Stresses the usefulness of recent interdisciplinary approaches in understanding Baldwin's appeal, political thought and work, and legacy.

Miller, D. Quentin, ed. *Re-Viewing James Baldwin: Things Not Seen*. Philadelphia: Temple University Press, 2000. Explores the way in which Baldwin's writing touched on issues that confront all people, including race, identity, sexuality, and religious ideology.

O'Daniel, Therman B., ed. *James Baldwin: A Critical Evaluation*. Washington, D.C.: Howard University Press, 1981. This useful introduction to Baldwin groups essays in six categories such as "Baldwin as Novelist," "Baldwin as Essayist," and "Baldwin as Playwright." Supplemented by a detailed bibliography, notes on contributors, and an index.

Porter, Horace A. *Stealing the Fire: The Art and Protest of James Baldwin*. Middletown, Conn.: Wesleyan University Press, 1989. Originally a doctoral dissertation; the author expanded his original material and published it following Baldwin's death. Porter attempts to relate Baldwin to the larger African American tradition of social protest.

Pratt, Louis H. *James Baldwin*. Boston: Twayne, 1978. This well-balanced evaluation of Baldwin emphasizes the artist and his literary art. Pratt firmly believes that Baldwin's major contribution to American letters is in the essay form. Complemented by a chronology, a select bibliography, and an index.

Romanet, Jerome de. "Revisiting *Madeleine* and 'The Outing': James Baldwin's Revision of Gide's Sexual Politics." *MELUS* 22 (Spring, 1997): 3-14. A discussion of Baldwin's story "The Outing" in terms of its contrast with Gide's Calvinist guilt. Discusses sexual identity in this story and other Baldwin fictions. Argues that Baldwin's exile in France was as concerned with racial identity as with sexual emancipation.

Sanderson, Jim. "Grace in 'Sonny's Blues.'" *Short Story* 6 (Fall, 1998): 85-95. Argues that Baldwin's most famous story illustrates his integration of the personal with the social in terms of his residual evangelical Christianity. Argues that at the end of the story when the narrator offers Sonny a drink, he puts himself in the role of Lord, and Sonny accepts the cup of wrath; the two brothers thus regain grace by means of the power of love.

Scott, Lynn Orilla. *James Baldwin's Later Fiction: Witness to the Journey*. East Lansing: Michigan State University Press, 2002. Analyzes the decline of Baldwin's reputation after the 1960's, the ways in which critics have often undervalued his work, and the interconnected themes in his body of work.

Sherard, Tracey. "Sonny's Bebop: Baldwin's 'Blues Text' as Intracultural Critique." *African American Review* 32 (Winter, 1998): 691-705. A discussion of Houston Baker's notion of the "blues matrix" in Baldwin's story; examines the story's treatment of black culture in America as reflected by jazz and the blues. Discusses how the "blues text" of the story represents how intracultural narratives have influenced the destinies of African Americans.

Standley, Fred L., and Nancy V. Burt, eds. *Critical Essays on James Baldwin*. Boston: G. K. Hall, 1988. An attempt to anthologize the important criticism on Baldwin in one definitive volume. More than thirty-five articles focus on Baldwin's essays, fiction, nonfiction, and drama.

Sylvander, Carolyn Wedin. *James Baldwin*. New York: Frederick Ungar, 1980. This good overview of Baldwin's work provides an aesthetic perspective, a bibliographical summary, and an analysis of individual works, with greater emphasis given to Baldwin's plays, novels, and short stories.

Tomlinson, Robert. "'Payin' One's Dues': Expatriation as Personal Experience and Paradigm in the Works of James Baldwin." *African American Review* 33 (Spring, 1999): 135-148. A discussion of the effect life as an exile in Paris had on Baldwin. Argues that the experience internalized the conflicts he experienced in America. Suggests that Baldwin used his homosexuality and exile as a metaphor for the experience of the African American.

Troupe, Quincy, ed. *James Baldwin: The Legacy*. New York: Simon & Schuster, 1989. Contains eighteen essays by and about Baldwin, five of which were written for this collection, and homage and celebration from many who were profoundly influenced by him, including Pat Mikell's account of Baldwin's last days in St. Paul de Vence. With a foreword by Wole Soyinka.

Tsomondo, Thorell. "No Other Tale to Tell: 'Sonny's Blues' and 'Waiting for the Rain.'" *Critique* 36 (Spring, 1995): 195-209. Examines how art and history are related in "Sonny's Blues." Discusses the story as one in which a young musician replays tribal history in music. Argues that the story represents how African American writers try to reconstruct an invalidated tradition.

Weatherby, W. J. *James Baldwin: Artist on Fire*. New York: Donald I. Fine, 1989. A lengthy personal reminiscence of Baldwin by a close friend who calls his biography a portrait. Rich in intimate detail and based on conversations with more than one hundred people who knew Baldwin. Reveals the man behind the words.

The *Paris Review* Perspective

Richard Beck for *The Paris Review*

"Every writer has only one tale to tell," said James Baldwin; for better or worse, his own life and work proved him right. The novels, plays and (most of all) essays that made him the most famous black writer in the world for three decades are variations on a single theme, telling the story of a country deformed by an idea of blackness that white people had invented. "What white people have to do is try to figure out in their own hearts why it was necessary to have a nigger in the first place," he told the psychologist Kenneth Clark in 1963. "Because I'm not a nigger. I'm a man. But if you think I'm a nigger, that means you need it."

Baldwin always thought of himself as an American, but his life can be read as a study in different kinds of homelessness. He spent more than a decade expatriated in Paris without ever involving himself with French intellectuals. He went to Istanbul for most of the 1960s but never learned Turkish. And back in the United States, the all-but-official spokesman for the Negro race faced his harshest criticism from other black writers. Some of the attacks had to do with identity: macho black nationalists referred to the homosexual Baldwin as "Martin Luther Queen." But other, more substantial critiques were made as well. Baldwin's subject may have been American blackness, but the audiences that packed his lecture halls were white, and this made his contemporaries suspicious. Langston Hughes called *Notes from a Native Son,* Baldwin's excellent first collection of essays, "the *Uncle Tom's Cabin* of today."

Yet it is this same sense of homelessness that shaped Baldwin's literary identity. He frequently told interviewers that one of the main difficulties facing an African American writer was the hostility embedded in the language itself and wrote, in his essay "Stranger in the Village," that "the most illiterate [white person] is related, in a way I am not, to Dante, Shakespeare, Michelangelo." In the twentieth century, many black writers responded to this knowledge by abandoning Europe, drawing their influence instead from jazz, blues, and the sermons and spirituals that emerged out of southern slavery. And while Baldwin certainly did not divorce his writing from black culture, his style, with its long, winding, sentences (Norman Mailer uncharitably called them "perfumed"), owed as much of a debt to Henry James as Richard Wright. It is possible to call this racial betrayal. It is possible to call this accommodation. It is also possible to call it using the master's tools to dismantle the master's house.

Baldwin did much of his dismantling with a 1962 *New Yorker* essay called "Letter from a Region in My Mind," subsequently published in book form as *The Fire Next Time*. The essay's first half is an autobiographical meditation on black American Christianity. Almost all of Baldwin's work is autobiographical to some degree. In his first novel, *Go Tell It on the Mountain,* a Harlem teenager named John begins preaching at his church, in part to defy and upstage his abusive father, who is also a preacher. In *The Fire Next Time*, Baldwin, who started preaching at the age of fourteen, describes the climax of one of his own sermons:

> Their pain and their joy were mine, and mine were theirs—they surrendered their pain and joy to me, "I surrendered mine to them—and their cries of "Amen!" and "Hallelujah!" and "Yes, Lord!" and "Praise His name!" and "Preach it, brother!" sustained and whipped on my solos until we all became equal, wringing wet, singing and dancing, in anguish and rejoicing, at the foot of the altar.

Yet Baldwin eventually found that "the blood of the Lamb had not cleansed me in any way whatever. I was just as black as I had been the day I was born." He believed that American blacks—especially in the North—were making the same discovery, and that Martin Luther King's nonviolent activism was outliving its usefulness. "There are lots of black people who don't go to church no more," writes Baldwin. He knew. He was one of them.

What marked the key turning point in *The Fire Next Time* is also, eventually, what marked the turning point in Baldwin's career: the rise of Elijah Muhammad's Nation of Islam. In the essay's second half, Baldwin describes a visit he made to Muhammad's Chicago headquarters. There, he heard that God was black. "All black men belong to Islam; they have been chosen. And Islam shall rule the world." Though Baldwin criticized these beliefs as old fantasies of domination dressed up in new skin tones, he could not find anyone who spoke with more credibility on black daily life than Malcolm X. Baldwin understood the message's seductiveness by allowing himself to be partially seduced: "The real reason that non-violence is considered to be a virtue in Negroes," he wrote, "is that white men do not want their lives, their self-image, or their property threatened."

The essay produced the kind of literary sensation that no longer occurs in this country, and it turned an artist into a political activist. Lionel Trilling, reviewing Baldwin's novel *Another Country* that same year, expressed an unfortunately prescient concern: "How, in the extravagant publicness in which Mr. Baldwin lives, is he to find the inwardness which we take to be the condition of truth in the writer?" It was often as much about time as inwardness. For the rest of his life, his schedule packed with television sit-downs, speaking appearances, and political events, Baldwin would have to steal time to write. This had a disastrous effect on his work, which eventually traded intellectual fineness for political use-value. "Nineteen sixty-three," the biographer James Campbell wrote, "was the year his voice broke."

By the time Baldwin was interviewed by *The Paris Review* in 1984, he was in the final years of his life and looking back anxiously at a career that had, in one sense, been over for two decades. His anxiety was caused, in part, by the sense that white Americans still had not confronted the hypocrisies and contradictions embedded in what he called their "sense of reality." For someone who imagined the moment of healing and reconciliation in essentially messianic terms—who thought the transformation would be sudden, sweeping, and glorious—this was perhaps an inevitable disappointment. "In some ways I've changed precisely because America has not," he said. He lamented the fact that, while he had been "schooled in adversity," over the years he had become "skilled in compromise." Today, as a nation with a black president still wrestles with many of the old racial wounds, that statement's double-edged wisdom is plain to see.

Works Cited

Baldwin, James. *Collected Essays.* Ed. Toni Morrison. New York: Library of America, 1998.

___________. *Conversations with James Baldwin.* Ed. Fred L. Standley and Louis H. Pratt. Jackson: UP of Mississippi, 1989.

___________. *Early Novels and Stories.* Ed. Toni Morrison. New York: Library of America, 1998.

___________. "Interview with Kenneth Clark, 1963." Video. 4 May 2010. http://www.youtube.com/watch?v=Rt-WgwFEUNQ&feature=related.

Bloom, Harold, ed. *James Baldwin.* New York: Chelsea House, 1986.

Campbell, James. *Talking at the Gates: A Life of James Baldwin.* Berkeley: U of California P, 1991.

"Debate Between James Baldwin and William F. Buckley at the Cambridge Union, February 1965." Video. 4 May 2010. http://sunsite.berkeley.edu/videodir/asx2/2299.asx.

Zaborowska, Magdalena J. *James Baldwin's Turkish Decade: Erotics of Exile.* Durham, NC: Duke UP, 2009.

CRITICAL CONTEXTS

James Baldwin in His Time

Douglas Field

"What in the world was I by now," James Baldwin asked in his long essay *No Name in the Street*, "but an aging, lonely, sexually dubious, politically outrageous, unspeakably erratic freak?" (458). Published in 1972, four years after the assassination of Martin Luther King, Jr., Baldwin's remarkable essay charts his various roles as artist, celebrity, and political activist. Though much of *No Name* considers the landscape of civil rights politics, from the assassinations of Malcolm X and King to the impact of the Black Panthers, Baldwin's own role as witness and participant in this turbulent period also unfolds throughout the work. Scattered throughout the essay are tantalizing biographical accounts of Baldwin's early years living with his grandmother, a former slave; his reflections on McCarthy and the Cold War; and meditations on the ways in which his sexuality complicated his position as a participant in the arena of black radical politics.

Though Baldwin is often best known as an eloquent and relentless witness to the civil rights movement, *No Name* is a useful reminder that his writing comes out of four turbulent decades, from the 1940s to the 1980s; his childhood began in the 1920s during the Harlem Renaissance and the Great Depression, and his life ended in the south of France during Ronald Reagan's second term in office as U.S. president. During his sixty-three years, Baldwin observed the impacts of World War II, the Cold War, the civil rights movement, the Vietnam War, and the Stonewall riots; he died only two years before the fall of the Berlin Wall. His plays, fiction, and essays bear witness to these momentous changes in American and international life, and Baldwin himself helped shape the literary and political landscapes that he documented in his work.

Baldwin's early left-wing interest may well have been fueled by the poverty he experienced as a child. Growing up with an expanding family in Harlem, Baldwin recalled how "I hit the streets when I was seven. It was the middle of the Depression and I learned how to sing out hard experience" ("Dark Days" 788). Baldwin's childhood was also characterized by his strained relationship with his stepfather, David, a disciplinarian preacher. Although Baldwin's recollections of his father are frequently painful and bitter, it was his early religious experience that formed the backbone of his early writing. Aged fourteen, Baldwin became a Pentecostal preacher, an experience he drew on for his first novel, *Go Tell It on the Mountain* (1953), and his first play, *The Amen Corner* (1954). The impact of the church on Baldwin's writing should not be underestimated: not only is his syncopated prose shot through with the cadenced language of the King James Bible, but also much of his work—not just his early writing—underscores the importance of the church to African American life. By setting his first two works in the church, Baldwin followed a long tradition of African American narratives that unfolded against the backdrop of Christianity. But while Baldwin, at least on the surface, continues this literary tradition, he should also be seen, as Sondra O'Neale notes, "as the last black American writer to exploit as a major theme the black man's relationship with Christianity" (140). By the 1950s, as Trudier Harris has pointed out, religion became less central to African American writing; Harris concludes that Lorraine Hansberry's play *A Raisin in the Sun* (1959) was "Christianity's last stand" in African American literature (21).

This shift toward secularity is most acutely illustrated by the work of Richard Wright, the most famous post-Harlem Renaissance African American writer, who renounced Christianity in favor of communism and, later, existentialism. In his novel *Native Son* (1940), Wright explicitly draws attention to what he sees as the failure of religion, suggesting that the demise of his protagonist, Bigger Thomas, is exacerbated by the black church's lack of support and influence. Bigger, Wright explains, "had become estranged from the religion and the folk culture of his race"; he lived in a world that "contained no spiritual sustenance," an urban hell in which "God no longer existed as a daily focal point of men's lives" (513, 520, 521). By the 1960s and 1970s, in the face of mounting civil rights tensions, Christianity was increasingly viewed as incompatible with radical politics, as can be seen in the growing interest in Islam and in the repudiation of nonviolent action among black radicals.

Like a number of African American writers, Baldwin criticized the church for its lack of political action during the civil rights movement. In his best-selling essay *The Fire Next Time* (1963), Baldwin recalls how he realized early on that "God . . . is white (304)." At the moment of his conversion, Baldwin begins to question the integrity of Christianity: "And if His love was so great, and if He loved all His children, why were we, the blacks, cast down so far? Why?" (304-05). For Baldwin, African Americans have been "taught really to despise themselves from the moment their eyes open on the world," and the white church has done nothing to counter this self-loathing (*Fire* 302). The Bible, Baldwin notes, was written by white men, and "according to many Christians, I was a descendant of Ham, who had been cursed, and that I was therefore predestined to be a slave" (307). For Baldwin, armed with the knowledge of (white) Christianity's dubious history, his position as a minister became increasingly problematic. "It began to take all the strength I had not to stammer, not to curse," Baldwin recalled, "not to tell them [the congregation] to throw away their Bibles and get off their knees and go home and organize, for example, a rent strike" (309). In his second play, *Blues for Mister Charlie* (1964), the conflict between the church and political action is played out explicitly with the unfolding of the revelation that racial injustice will "end with the Bible and the gun," a clear indication of the tensions between Christian tolerance and radical action (120).

Though Baldwin's writing became increasingly critical of the church as an institution, his later work continued to explore the importance of spirituality, often through examinations of music, which has long been associated with the black church, as Baldwin demonstrates by drawing attention to the parallels between the musician and the preacher. Historically there is a close, albeit complex relationship between the Holiness movement and jazz, a point that Baldwin makes in *The Fire Next Time* in his recollections of preaching: "I would improvise from the texts like a jazz musician improvises from a theme. I never wrote a sermon. . . . You have to sense the people you're talking to. You have to respond to what they hear" (*Conversations* 234-35). This connection between spirituality and music, according to James Campbell, became a central theme in Baldwin's later years. Campbell notes that while Baldwin "was not a believer in the sense of subscribing to a particular faith, or belonging to a specific church, his life was based on a faith that can only be called religious. . . . His scripture was the old black gospel music" (281).

Campbell's observation is corroborated by a striking example of Baldwin's love of the church's music that pierces the often acerbic prose of *The Fire Next Time*:

> The church was very exciting. . . . There is no music like that music, no drama like the drama of the saints rejoicing, the sinners moaning, the tambourines racing, and all those voices coming together and crying holy unto the Lord. (35-36)

Much has been written about Baldwin's pioneering use of the blues and jazz in language and his repeated references to himself, not as a writer, but as a blues singer. Consider, for example, the plethora of Baldwin's titles that draw on African American music: *Go Tell It on the Mountain*, *The Amen Corner*, "Sonny's Blues," (1957), *Blues for Mister Charlie*, *If Beale Street Could Talk* (1974), and *Just Above My Head* (1979). Many of Baldwin's fictional characters are musicians, whether blues singers (Ida in *Another Country*), jazz musicians (Rufus, also in *Another Country*), blues instrumentalists (Luke in the play *The Amen Corner* and Frank in *Go Tell It on the Mountain*), or gospel singers (Arthur in *Just Above My Head*). In his essays and interviews, Baldwin often stressed the cultural significance of jazz musicians and female blues singers, in particular Miles Davis, Ray Charles, Billie Holiday, and Bessie Smith.

Like a number of African American writers, including Ralph Ellison and LeRoi Jones (later Amiri Baraka), Baldwin iterated the importance of music in his writing, claiming that he wanted to write the way jazz musicians sound. In a vivid recollection of finishing his first novel, *Go Tell It on the Mountain*, in his essay "The Discovery of What It Means to Be an American," Baldwin acknowledged his debt, not to his literary antecedents of the Harlem Renaissance but to the blues singer Bessie Smith. Baldwin recalled that, as he finished *Go Tell It* in Switzerland, it was Smith's "tone and her cadence" that helped him "dig back to the way I myself must have spoken when I was a pickaninny" (138).

Baldwin's reference to Bessie Smith is significant. In his 1951 article "Many Thousands Gone," Baldwin suggested that music itself was the fundamental expression of black American culture. "It is only in music," Baldwin wrote, "that the Negro in America is able to tell his story" (19). As Baldwin writes in *The Fire Next Time*, "There is something tart and ironic, authoritative and double-edged" in jazz and the blues (311). White Americans, Baldwin avers, "do not understand the depths out of which such an ironic tenacity comes," mistaking happy songs as happy and sad songs as sad (311). Baldwin's writing on music teeters toward the claim that one needs to be black to hear the blues but he stops short of saying this explicitly. Rather, for Baldwin, the blues comes out of suffering and an understanding of that condition, something that excludes most—but not all—white listeners. Here Baldwin seems to anticipate LeRoi Jones's famous 1962 essay "The Myth of a 'Negro Literature,'" in which Jones argues that, since all black American literature up until then had been based on white literary forms, no authentic African American literature had yet been written. It would be only in music, Jones concluded, that the African American could create authentic and original cultural forms.

Baldwin's first novel, *Go Tell It on the Mountain* (1953), remains one of his best-read and critically received works, but he cut his teeth as a writer with a group of literary magazines associated with the New York Intellectuals, a group of editors and writers who worked for anti-Stalinist left-wing publications such as *The Nation* and *Partisan Review.* As Baldwin recalled in the introduction to *The Price of the Ticket*, editors such as Saul Levitas of *New Leader* and Eliot Cohen of *Commentary*, "were all very important to my life. It is not too much to say that they helped to save my life" (xiii). Between 1947 and 1949 Baldwin published a number of book reviews on a wide range of topics, from Russian literature to Brooklyn gangs.

Writing reviews was invaluable experience for a young writer without a university education or any ready-made connections to the literary world, and a number of Baldwin's early pieces read as warm-ups for his more sharply distilled essays. Though few of his reviews in fact focused explicitly on race, Baldwin claimed that he wrote his famous essay "Everybody's Protest Novel" (1949)—which was first published in a small Paris-based magazine, *Zero*, and republished in his first collection of essays, *Notes of a Native Son* (1955)—as "a summation of all the years I was reviewing those 'be kind to niggers' and 'be kind to Jews' books" (*Conversations* 276).

After a short spell as a Trotskyite, which Baldwin stated taught him only that it "may be impossible to indoctrinate him," Baldwin would never again identify with an established political ideology (*Price* xiii). Despite his suspicion of political parties and ideologies his writings illustrate his continued disillusionment with the invasive surveillance of the Central Intelligence Agency (CIA) and Federal Bureau of Investigation (FBI) and the stifling cultural and political climate during the Cold War years of the late 1940s and up to the mid-1960s. When Baldwin moved to Paris in 1948, he escaped the suffocating racism and homophobia of postwar America but was only too aware that his and other writers' movements were monitored by government agencies and that a number of high-profile magazines were sponsored by the CIA. As Baldwin correctly intuited in *No Name*, he covered the first International Conference of Black Writers and Artists in Paris, 1956, "for *Encounter* (or for the CIA)" (475).

With the publication of best-selling works such as *Another Country* (1962) and *The Fire Next Time* (1963), Baldwin was very much in the public eye. When he appeared on the cover of *Time* magazine in 1963, he was the most famous living African American writer. Baldwin's rise to celebrity, however, came at some considerable cost, as is illustrated by his enormous FBI file, which was active between 1960 and 1974. The sheer volume of entries on Baldwin, which total seventeen hundred pages, gives credence to his self-proclaimed role as "disturber of the peace" and also illustrates how the U.S. government, particularly during the Cold War and the civil rights movement, closely monitored writers and artists (*Conversations* 171). For Baldwin, who was not only outspoken and politically attuned but also homosexual, this meant an extended period of surveillance. Although Baldwin had recanted his formal allegiance to left-wing politics, he remained an iconoclast, taking repeating swipes at Senator Joseph McCarthy and the FBI's director, J. Edgar Hoover, whom he describes in his long essay *The Devil Finds Work* (1976) as "history's most highly paid (and most utterly useless) *voyeur*" (162). In 1963, for example, Baldwin contributed to the satirical collection *A Quarter-Century of Un-Americana: A Tragico-comical Memorabilia of HUAC* (House Un-American Activities Committee). Unlike many former left-wing intellectuals, Baldwin spoke unequivocally of HUAC as "one of the most sinister facts of the national life," and he would later dismiss McCarthy as "a coward and a bully" in *No Name in the Street* (in Pomerantz 127; *No Name* 466).

Baldwin is rightly acknowledged as the first major African American writer to be openly homosexual and to discuss homosexuality in his fiction and nonfiction during the McCarthy years, when "deviant" sexuality was considered "un-American" behavior. And yet his position as a gay black writer is anything but straightforward. Despite his importance as a central figure of twentieth-century gay literature,

Baldwin consistently renounced the adjectives "homosexual," "gay," and "bisexual." "The word gay," Baldwin told Richard Goldstein, "has always rubbed me the wrong way. I never understood exactly what is meant by it," a view that he also forcefully echoed in an interview with James Mossman (Goldstein 13): "Those terms, homosexual, bisexual, heterosexual, are 20th century terms which, for me, have very little meaning. I've never, myself, in watching myself and other people, watching life, been able to discern exactly where the barriers were" (*Conversations* 54). Asked by Goldstein whether he considered himself gay, Baldwin replied that he did not: "I didn't have a word for it. The only one I had was homosexual and that didn't quite cover whatever it was I was beginning to feel" (13).

Baldwin's dislike of the terms "gay" and "homosexual" can in part be explained by the fact that he grew up as part of a pre-Stonewall generation. Samuel R. Delany recalls that the Harlem Renaissance writer and artist Bruce Nugent, like Baldwin, stated on numerous occasions during the 1960s, "I just don't see why everyone has to be labeled. I just don't think words like homosexual—or gay—*do* anything for anybody" (204). According to Delany, Nugent felt left behind by the gay activism of the late 1960s and early 1970s, a point implicitly made by Baldwin. The gay world, Baldwin states, is "a world that has very little to do with me, with where I did my growing up," adding that gay life was "a phenomenon that came along much after I was formed" (Goldstein 13).

Baldwin and Nugent's dislike of identity categories was shared, as will be seen, by two notable white homosexual writers. However, in "Go the Way Your Blood Beats," Baldwin deliberately steers Goldstein away from comparing black and white experiences of discrimination on account of homosexuality. On one hand, the gay movement borrowed heavily from the political tactics and experiences of the civil rights movement. Not only that but, as Denis Altman has noted, "the very furtiveness and outlaw status of the gay world has led to its greater integration across colour lines." On the other hand, as Altman also points out, white homosexuals are not necessarily less racist than their white heterosexual counterparts (qtd. in Dollimore 333). Still more important, perhaps, is many homosexual African Americans' perception of the gay movement as predominantly white. Indeed, Baldwin implicitly codes the gay world as white when he rejects Goldstein's claim that white and black homosexuals may feel the same sense of alienation: "The gay world as such is no more prepared to accept black people than anywhere else in society. It's a very hermetically sealed world with very unattractive features, including racism" (14). Baldwin was not alone in his views. A. Billy S. Jones, for example, recalls that, for many blacks, "the gay movement looked like a white trip with a few misguided Blacks tagging along for the ride" (143), a point echoed by Essex Hemphill, who noted that he did not recognize his experience in homosexual literature, concluding, "I could have ignorantly concluded that homosexuality was peculiar to white people" (xvi).

Although there are dangers in conflating white and black experiences of homosexuality, Baldwin's views are also mirrored—at least in part—by arguably the two most influential writers of homosexual fiction this century, Gore Vidal and Jean Genet. Despite the fact that Baldwin was dismissive of Vidal's *The City and the Pillar* (1948), both writers share a resistance to the mainstream rhetoric and ideology of the postwar gay movement. Although Baldwin criticized Vidal's novel, claiming that it is "not concerned with homosexuality but the ever-present danger of sexual activity between men," there are clear parallels between the two authors ("Preservation" 599). As Robert Corber has eloquently argued, Vidal's refusal to locate homosexuality along the axes of catalogued experiences aligns him more with gay liberationists, who questioned the validity of sexual categorization, than with the more prevalent gay rights activists, who sought to align homosexuality with issues of social subordination, such as the plight of ethnic minorities.

Baldwin's dislike of sexual classification also has parallels with the views of Jean Genet. According to Edmund White in his magisterial biography of Genet, “The social world evoked by the phrase ‘homosexual culture’ would have struck Genet as absurd, since he considered his own homosexuality to be something that alienated him from everyone, even other homosexuals” (317). Genet, like Baldwin, rarely lent his name to the causes of gay rights, but Baldwin was considerably more vociferous in his condemnation of public displays of solidarity. Although he spoke in New York on “race, racism and the gay community” in 1982, Baldwin harshly condemned public exhibitions (Leeming 359). “These people are not involved in anything resembling lovemaking,” Baldwin stated, “they're involved in some kind of exhibition of their disaster” (*Conversations* 80). The very negative language here suggests more than a suspicion of labels, illustrating the complexity of Baldwin's views.

Baldwin's insistence that “one's sexual preference is a private matter” sits at odds with his reputation as a key figure in gay literary history, especially as one who used the public forum of the novel to explore homosexuality and bisexuality. And yet Baldwin's insistence on privacy punctuates his commentaries on sexuality. In his essay on Gide, “The Male Prison,” Baldwin reprimanded the French author, insisting that he ought to have kept his sexuality hidden. Baldwin's sexuality, as he recounted to Goldstein, was “very personal, absolutely personal. It was really a matter between me and God” (231).

Leaving aside his intriguing invocation of Christianity for the moment, I want to consider other possible factors for Baldwin's desire for privacy. Jerome de Romanet reaches the reasonable conclusion that Baldwin “reserved the more public voice of spokesman (of the black community as a whole, of writers and artists) for his essays and formal addresses, while he often let his fictional characters discuss the more private issues of sexual politics and preference” (8). In contrast to the paucity of essays explicitly dealing with sexuality—Baldwin published only three, “Preservation of Innocence” (1949), “The Male Prison” (1954), and “Freaks and the American Ideal of Manhood” (1985, also published with the title “Here Be Dragons”)—the author's fiction is replete with depictions of same-sex desire. It explores bisexual and homosexual relationships, hinted at in his first novel and then made explicit in *Giovanni's Room* (1956), one of the most important novels about homosexuality in twentieth-century American literature, and later novels, particularly *Tell Me How Long the Train's Been Gone* and *Just Above My Head*, pioneered depictions of black male homosexuality in fiction.

Why Baldwin chose to circumscribe homosexuality in his essays is a difficult question, though the novel, because of its status as fiction, was arguably a safer genre for exploring such taboo subjects. Baldwin was no doubt aware that readers and critics who were uncomfortable with his fictional depictions of homosexuality and bisexuality were less troubled by the emphasis on race in his essays. While critics are divided over whether Baldwin's foremost strength is as essayist or novelist, Emmanuel Nelson is surely right to suggest that many heterosexist critics felt more comfortable with Baldwin's relative silence on sexuality in his essays. The glaring disparity between discussions of sexuality in his essays and fiction also highlights the ways in which Baldwin was preoccupied by his roles as an artist and as a spokesman. In the mid-1960s in particular, Baldwin came under increasing attack by a new generation of radical black American writers, such as Ishmael Reed and Amiri Baraka, who criticized his writing—and in particular his fiction—for not being sufficiently politically engaged. Baldwin was hounded by charges not only that *Another Country* focused on the individual (at a time when collective solidarity was called for) but also that his work suggested that the power of love could unseat racial oppression. It is important to note that criticism of Baldwin's political ineffectiveness was bound up with the public knowledge of his sexual orientation. As Henry Louis Gates, Jr., notes, "National identity became sexualized in the 1960s, in such a way to engender a curious connection between homophobia and nationalism" (234).

Before focusing on Baldwin's precarious position as an openly homosexual writer during the mid- to late 1960s, it is important to get a sense of the writer's participation in the civil rights movement. Unlike any other major African American writer, such as Ralph Ellison or Richard Wright, Baldwin engaged directly with the movement in his fiction and nonfiction. His long essay *The Fire Next Time* lambasted white liberals and explored the complexity of the "Negro problem," a phenomenon that Baldwin forcefully argued was, in fact, a white problem. In his play *Blues for Mister Charlie*, which was based on the murder of the fifteen-year-old Emmett Till, Baldwin explored the tensions surrounding Christian forgiveness and direct action. In his last novel of the 1960s, *Tell Me How Long the Train's Been Gone*, Baldwin reflected on the role of the artist amid radical black politics, a theme he would return to in another long essay, *No Name in the Street*.

In 1957 Baldwin left Paris to return to America, spurred on by accounts of racial injustice. That year, acting as a reporter for *Partisan Review* and *Harper's* magazine, he visited the South for the first time and met up with Martin Luther King, Jr., and other race leaders. His essays about his experiences, "A Fly in the Buttermilk" (1958) and "A Letter from the South: Nobody Knows My Name" (1959), were reprinted in his second collection of essays, *Nobody Knows My Name: More Notes of a Native Son* (1961), a volume that announced him as a major voice of the civil rights movement. In his essays on the civil rights movement, Baldwin considers the psychological effects of racism and the interracial history of the South. In later visits to the South in 1960, Baldwin would become a witness to and chronicler of the movement, publishing two further essays, "They Can't Turn Back" (*Mademoiselle* 1960) and "The Dangerous Road Before Martin Luther King" (*Harper's* 1961).

With the success of *The Fire Next Time*, Baldwin emerged as a significant spokesman of the civil rights movement. In May 1963 Baldwin met with Robert Kennedy, the U.S. attorney general, bringing with him a group of African Americans, including the actor Harry Belafonte, the playwright Lorraine Hansberry, and Jerome Smith, a young African American from the South who had been badly beaten during the Freedom Rides of 1961. Although the meeting was not a success, it illustrated Baldwin's commitment to and involvement in the civil rights movement. That year, Baldwin also appeared on the cover of *Time* magazine, a rare feat for an African American writer. The accompanying article, however, fed into and anticipated problems that Baldwin would have as a homosexual writer involved in civil rights. Describing the author as a "nervous, slight, almost fragile figure, filled with frets and fears," and then "effeminate in manner," the article tacitly pointed out Baldwin's homosexuality (26). As Morris Dickstein notes, "The argument was that Baldwin's homosexuality, his unconfident masculinity, is the hidden root of all his writing and completely disqualifies him as a representative spokesman" for black Americans (168). Although Baldwin would later explore his problematic role as both writer and spokesman in *Tell Me How Long the Train's Been Gone*, emphatically telling interviewers in 1969 that "I am *not* a public speaker. I *am* an artist," his sexuality crucially explained why other black radicals understated his involvement in the civil rights movement (*Conversations* 81). In 1968, the year that Baldwin published *Tell Me How Long the Train's Been Gone*, Eldridge Cleaver, minister of information for the Black Panther Party, attacked Baldwin in a scabrous essay in his book *Soul on Ice*. Although Baldwin in fact worked with the Black Panther Party, Cleaver tore into Baldwin for his outmoded political views, and, crucially, his homosexuality. For Cleaver, Baldwin had become not only "a reluctant black" but also "a white man in a black body" (99, 102). In Baldwin's writing, Cleaver continues, we find a "total hatred of the blacks," thereby suggesting that Baldwin's sexuality rendered him less authentically black (103).

The attacks that Baldwin received from younger radical writers, including Amiri Baraka and Ishmael Reed, certainly had a profound effect on the author. By the end of the 1960s, Baldwin was middle-aged, and his last book of the 1960s, *Tell Me How Long the Train's Been Gone*, was panned by critics who saw a decline from the finely tuned, syncopated writing of his earlier work. Although Baldwin was a visible presence during the civil rights movement, he was frequently attacked for being out of touch, due in part to his long spells abroad in Paris and the south of France and then Turkey. Many of his critics suggested that Baldwin no longer had his finger on the political pulse.

Although Baldwin's later work did not receive the critical attention that his early work enjoyed, his later essays and interviews continue to be relevant to American society today. First, as the first openly homosexual black American writer, Baldwin's work has been the cornerstone of emerging black queer theory. While earlier criticism of Baldwin seemed unable or ill equipped to deal with Baldwin as a black *and* gay writer, scholarship since the early 1990s has begun to see the author as a major writer of black gay literature. Second, Baldwin's role as a "transatlantic commuter" between Europe and America and his writings on the relationship between Africans and black Americans in Paris contribute to a broader understanding of transnationalism. As Magdalena Zaborowska has argued in *James Baldwin's Turkish Decade: Erotics of Exile*, Baldwin's work is rarely discussed outside of the context of the United States, and yet his writing contributes toward what Zaborowska terms the "transnational dimension of mid-twentieth century black literary culture" (6).

For Zaborowska, Baldwin's ten years in Turkey contribute toward the developing field of transnational African American studies, an area that has grown and expanded since Paul Gilroy's *The Black Atlantic* established his theory of the Black Atlantic cultures. Baldwin repeatedly refused to romanticize the connections between people of African descent, as his essays on the encounters between African and black Americans illustrate. In *Notes of a Native Son* ("Encounter on the Seine: Black Meets Brown") and in *Nobody Knows My Name* ("Princes and Powers"), Baldwin drew attention to the cultural and linguistic differences between black Americans and Africans. As Baldwin iterated in an interview to François Bondy, "To be born in Jamaica, Barbados, or Portugal . . . or to be black, wouldn't seem to me to be enough" to form the basis of a diasporic community (16). Although Baldwin was criticized for refusing to align the experiences of black people around the world, his work anticipates developing theories of the Diaspora that stress the importance of acknowledging cultural and linguistic differences. As Baldwin declared in an early essay, "Autobiographical Notes," "All theories are suspect. . . . One must find, therefore, one's own moral center and move through the world hoping that this center will guide one aright" (16). Throughout his prolific career, Baldwin continued to call attention to complexity and repeatedly questioned terms of identification and ideologies. Baldwin's iconoclastic intellectualism—his refusal to accept theories without challenging them—remains perhaps his most pertinent legacy in and outside of the academy. As a self-confessed "disturber of the peace," Baldwin's keenly inquisitive mind shook up and shaped postwar America.

Works Cited

Baldwin, James. "Autobiographical Notes." 1952. *Collected Essays*. New York: Library of America, 1998. 5-9.

___________. *Blues for Mister Charlie*. 1964. New York: Vintage Books, 1992.

___________. *Conversations with James Baldwin*. Ed. Fred L. Standley and Louis H. Pratt. Jackson: UP of Mississippi, 1989.

___________. "Dark Days." 1980. *Collected Essays*. New York: Library of America, 1998. 788-98.

___________. "The Devil Finds Work." 1976. *The Price of the Ticket: Collected Nonfiction, 1948-1985*. New York: St. Martin's Press, 1985. 557-640.

___________. "The Discovery of What It Means to Be an American." 1959. *Collected Essays*. New York: Library of America, 1998. 137-42.

___________. *The Fire Next Time*. 1963. *Collected Essays*. New York: Library of America, 1998. 291-347.

___________. "James Baldwin, as Interviewed by François Bondy." *Transition* 12 (Jan.-Feb. 1964): 12-19.

___________. "Many Thousands Gone." 1951. *Collected Essays*. New York: Library of America, 1998. 19-34.

___________. "No Name in the Street." 1972. *The Price of the Ticket: Collected Nonfiction, 1948-1985*. New York: St. Martin's Press, 1985. 449-552.

___________. "Preservation of Innocence." 1949. *Collected Essays*. New York: Library of America, 1998. 594-600.

___________. *The Price of the Ticket: Collected Nonfiction, 1948-1985*. New York: St. Martin's Press, 1985.

Campbell, James. *Talking at the Gates: A Life of James Baldwin*. Boston: Faber & Faber, 1991.
Cleaver, Eldridge. *Soul on Ice*. New York: Ramparts, 1968.
Corber, Robert. *Homosexuality in Cold War America: Resistance and the Crisis of Masculinity*. Durham, NC: Duke UP, 1997.
Delany, Samuel R., and Joseph Beam. "Samuel R. Delany: The Possibilities of Possibilities." *In the Life: A Gay Black Anthology*. Ed. Joseph Beam. Boston: Alyson, 1986. 185-208.
Dickstein, Morris. *Gates of Eden: American Culture in the Sixties*. New York: Basic Books, 1977.
Dollimore, Jonathan. *Sexual Dissidence: Augustine to Wilde, Freud to Foucault*. Oxford: Clarendon Press, 1991.
Gates, Henry Louis, Jr. "The Black Man's Burden." *Fear of a Queer Planet: Queer Politics and Social Theory*. Ed. Michael Warner. Minneapolis: U of Minnesota P, 1993. 230-38.
Goldstein, Richard. "Go the Way Your Blood Beats: An Interview with James Baldwin." *Village Voice* 26 June 1984: 13-14, 16. Rpt. in *James Baldwin: The Legacy*. Ed. Quincy Troupe. New York: Simon & Schuster, 1989. 173-85.
Harris, Trudier, ed. *New Essays on "Go Tell It on the Mountain."* New York: Cambridge UP, 1996.
Hemphill, Essex. "Introduction." *Brother to Brother: New Writings by Black Gay Men*. Ed. Essex Hemphill. Boston: Alyson, 1991.
Jones, A. Billy S. "A Father's Need; A Parent's Desire." *In the Life: A Gay Black Anthology*. Ed. Joseph Beam. Boston: Alyson, 1986. 143-51.
Jones, LeRoi [Amiri Baraka]. "The Myth of a 'Negro Literature.'" *Home: Social Essays*. 1966. Hopewell, NJ: Ecco Press, 1998. 105-15.
Leeming, David. *James Baldwin: A Biography*. New York: Alfred A. Knopf, 1994.
Nelson, Emmanuel. "Critical Deviance: Homophobia and the Reception of James Baldwin's Fiction." *Journal of American Culture* 14.3 (1991): 91-96.
O'Neale, Sondra. "Fathers, Gods, and Religion: Perceptions of Christianity and Ethnic Faith in James Baldwin." *Critical Essays on James Baldwin*. Ed. Fred L. Standley and Nancy V. Burt. Boston: G. K. Hall, 1988. 124-43.
Pomerantz, Charlotte, ed. *A Quarter-Century of Un-Americana, 1938-1963: A Tragico-comical Memorabilia of HUAC*. New York: Marzani & Munsell, 1963.
"Races: Freedom—Now." *Time* 17 May 1963. 27 Nov. 2009. http://www.time.com/time/magazine/article/0,9171,830326,00.html.
Romanet, Jerome de. "Revisiting *Madeleine* and 'The Outing:' James Baldwin's Revision of Gide's Sexual Politics. " *MELUS* 22.1 (1997): 3-14.
White, Edmund. *Genet: A Biography*. New York: Alfred A. Knopf, 1993.
Wright, Richard. "How 'Bigger' Was Born." *Native Son*. Ed. Arnold Rampersad. 1940. New York: HarperCollins, 1993. 503-40.
Zaborowska, Magdalena. *James Baldwin's Turkish Decade: Erotics of Exile*. Durham, NC: Duke UP, 2009.

Exiled in Paris:
The Beginnings

James Campbell

Baldwin's reasons for quitting New York were in essence the same as Wright's—in a letter written home he spoke of "a violent anarchic, hostility-breeding" pattern,[1] with race at the bottom of it, which was eroding the fabric of his identity—but the circumstances of his arrival could hardly have been more different. No chauffeur-driven car to meet him, no room reserved at the Trianon-Palace, no Gertrude Stein, no "beautiful, absolutely beautiful" at the revelation of the wide boulevards and the quays. He had holes in his socks and $40 in his pocket. He was a ragamuffin with a big talent. His suitcase held a change of clothes, the manuscript of a half-finished novel, copies of the Bible and the works of Shakespeare, which he carried with him everywhere, and something by each of his more modern heroes, Dostoyevsky and Dickens. He had not an ounce of Wright's success—in New York he had stumbled from one badly paid job to another, trying to help his widowed mother feed a family of eight—nor a cent of his healthy bank balance. His stepfather had died insane, he had lost the Christian faith which had sustained him through every crisis, and had, on the same day, so to speak, accepted the burgeoning of his homosexuality—not welcomed in Harlem, where he lived, nor in the church in which he had served as a young minister. About the only thing of value he carried with him to Paris was the address of Richard Wright.

Baldwin and Wright had met in New York. Too callow to aspire to approach the older writer on equal terms, Baldwin had nevertheless been helped by him to gain a fellowship in order to buy time to go on with his novel. It went under the provisional title "Crying Holy." When Wright saw the first fifty pages in 1944, it was a mess. But Wright was sufficiently convinced of the talent of its author, and of the promise of the work itself, for him to recommend Baldwin for an award from the Eugene F. Saxton Memorial Trust. That was five years earlier; the money had long since been spent and "Crying Holy" was still a mess. One of his reasons for quitting America ("I didn't go to Paris," Baldwin would say later. "I left New York") was to try and turn the mass of pages into a novel. And yet another reason—though he shrank from admitting it—was that Richard Wright was there.

Baldwin arrived, by air, on November 11, 1948. A friend from New York met him off the connecting train and led him straight to St.-Germain, where Hoetis was at the Deux Magots, engaged in the latest phase of the continuing *Zero* editorial meeting which was to last throughout that winter. Hearing of the imminent arrival of Baldwin, whom he knew vaguely from Greenwich Village, he arranged for Wright to be present. When Wright saw his protégé, he rose and welcomed him, as he always did in New York, with a smile and a paternal "Hey, Boy!" These were the first friendly words that Baldwin heard in Paris, and just about the last he would hear from Richard Wright.

* * *

Baldwin was a noticeably tense young man, slight in stature, with extravagant hand gestures and a facial expression that could veer from tragic to comic, encompassing everything in between, in a moment's conversation. Immediately after his arrival, as he put it to a journalist who spoke to him about it later, "he 'went to pieces,' a process begun at home but hastened by his exposure to the chill of Paris. . . . 'I'd gone to pieces before I left New York. But I really did go to pieces when I got to Paris.'"[2] Going to pieces was a part of Baldwin's defense against the world; and also, by now, a part of his style—something which, as a friend meeting him then for the first time noticed, "explained everything and excused everything."[3]

Hoetis settled him into a cheap hotel—and for Baldwin it had to be cheap indeed—on the rue du Dragon, a few doors down, as he surely noticed, from a house in which Victor Hugo had once lived. After a few days, Hoetis returned with some other acquaintances and they parceled Baldwin up and shipped him across the Boulevard St.-Germain to a more agreeable abode on the rue du Verneuil, a pleasant street of ancient houses running parallel to the Seine. This was a small hotel, mainly for students and student types, run by a tolerant Corsican matriarch called Mme. Dumont. The Hôtel du Verneuil was low in comfort—just one or two toilets, of the type that the French call "à la Turque" but which the rest of the world knows as French, serving seven floors—but high in other benefits. It was international, friendly, and Mme. Dumont was relaxed concerning the payment of rent.

She was relaxed about other things, too. Soon Baldwin was using his room—and, when his delay in handing over the rent exceeded even Mme. Dumont's patience, other people's rooms—for a string of seductions, "mostly young French boyfriends," according to Hoetis, "a few of whom were shady characters." He had spent the years between fourteen and seventeen in the pulpit, embracing the morality of the scripture he preached with extreme fervor. And when he broke free of the church, and renounced its Calvinist strictures, he did that with extreme fervor, too. "In some deep, black, stony, and liberating way," he wrote, "my life, in my own eyes, began during that first year in Paris."[4] And he determined to stay there until he had made himself a writer—or nothing at all. "Go for broke" was Baldwin's motto; he virtually made a scripture out of *that*.

The architecture of Baldwin's everyday existence was totally ramshackle—he borrowed and couldn't pay back, took commissions and didn't fulfill them, made appointments and failed to keep them—yet somehow quite elegant at the same time. He was generous with his money on the rare occasions when funds allowed him to be, and with his time and sympathy when they did not. He offered wise counsel to friends in need; with a drink in one hand and a cigarette in the other, he was a wit, a talker of brilliance, a writer of potential genius.

Except that he never seemed to find the time, or the space, or the warmth (cheap hotel rooms were cold) to get much writing done. People went to cafés to keep warm, and sometimes to write; but in the cafés they would meet other people, and the one thing Baldwin never could resist was conversation.

One of Baldwin's new friends from the Hôtel de Verneuil was an American, even younger than Baldwin himself but with equally intense ambitions to write, called Otto Friedrich. He soon began to make a record of his encounters with the youthful literati in St.-Germain. One evening in the summer of 1949, he had an argument with Herbert Gold, who also lived at the Hôtel de Verneuil, and one or two others, about Baldwin. A man called Newman was "denouncing Jimmy," saying that the twenty-five-year-old Baldwin had never fulfilled himself.

> Somehow this turned into an argument with Gold and his wife about Saul Bellow, now living on the rue de l'Université, and Edith Gold said Bellow is the most talented writer in America. . . . I said Jimmy had more talent than Saul Bellow would ever have, and they all glared at me. Edith said it was "presumptuous" of me to compare someone who had published two novels with someone who hadn't published a single one.[5]

A few nights later, Newman got into an argument with Baldwin himself, and Baldwin "raged at him about all kinds of past history from Greenwich Village. Newman got very defensive. 'Well, I may not know much about literature,' he began one round, and Jimmy said, 'Why, you know nothing *whatever* about literature.'"

The hangout for Baldwin and his crowd of writers, radicals, runaway youths, and assorted patrons who helped provide him with food and beer was La Reine Blanche, on the other side of the street—in every sense—from the Café de Flore. Cheap and seedy, it had a reputation of being a place for homosexuals, but it was popular with the Verneuil set, whatever their orientation happened to be. Otto himself was engaged to be married to a girl who had her own room at the Verneuil—in 1949, even when in Paris, respectable young Americans did not cohabit before marriage—and Baldwin was just as often seen in the company of one of his many "girlfriends" as with another male. Paris was a magnet for young people from all over Europe after the war, some of them illegal, and one night La Reine Blanche was raided by "two fat characters in raincoats" looking for foreign *rats-de-cave* without identity papers. Otto Friedrich (typically) had his papers in order, so there was no trouble for him, but Baldwin (typically) had forgotten to carry his with him.

> So, they said, "Ah-hah, and what do you do?" He said, "I'm a writer." They said, "Ah-hah, and what do you write?" He said, "Novels, stories, articles." They said, "Ah-hah, and who do you write for?" He said, "*Partisan Review* and *Commentary* and the *Nation*." They said, "Qu'est-ce que c'est ça?" They looked as if they were about to drag him away, but then he had an inspiration and said, "And also for *Les Temps Modernes*—for Jean-Paul Sartre." And then they said, "Ah," and there was no further trouble.[6]

He hadn't written anything for *Les Temps Modernes*, in fact, though Hoetis—"the social lion," as Otto called him—had taken him to lunch with Sartre, at which he tried to inveigle Sartre into writing a piece for *Zero*. Sartre promised to think about it, and at the same lunch expressed an interest in republishing an essay Baldwin had written for the American magazine *Commentary*, entitled "The Harlem Ghetto." Nothing came of either project.[7]

Baldwin was now cut off from the New York journals which had sustained him—just—and was deeply involved in café life and in his own mostly desperate love affairs. "Crying Holy" took on the aspect of a prison, from which he frequently attempted to escape through new projects, new titles, new first chapters. "The new novel is only on page 19," wrote Friedrich in his ongoing commentary on the Verneuil scene at the beginning of October 1949, "which doesn't look very promising";

I was in his room this afternoon, and read what was in the typewriter, and it sounds just like "Crying Holy" all over again—has a character called Gabriel who discovers the Lord, and whose mother was a slave. I said, "Is this new novel just a new version of 'Crying Holy'?" He said, "Well, yes and no."[8]

"Crying Holy" was constantly being smoothed and rechiseled—taking different titles at different stages. It would eventually turn into *Go Tell It on the Mountain*, but that would take another three years.

One thing Baldwin did manage to complete, however, was the essay he had promised to give Hoetis for the first issue of *Zero*, "Everybody's Protest Novel." He finished it eventually, that is—while the rest of the issue was being printed, Baldwin's piece was still stuck in his typewriter.[9] "Everybody's Protest Novel" was surrounded by confusion, in fact. It had been started while Baldwin was still in New York, and was expected by *Partisan Review*. To the slightly disgruntled *Partisan* editor, William Phillips, a slightly apologetic Baldwin explained, as his essay came off the presses, "*Zero* was here and you were there."[10] (*Partisan* reprinted it anyway.) This tangle of intentions was nothing compared to what followed the essay's publication in Paris.

The bulk of the four-thousand-word piece is taken up with a discussion of Harriet Beecher Stowe's pro-emancipation novel, *Uncle Tom's Cabin*, which Baldwin had read and reread obsessively as a child, but which he now pronounced "a very bad novel." For Baldwin, it was the function of the novel to reveal the human being in all his complexity; "only within this web of ambiguity, paradox, this hunger, danger, darkness, can we find at once ourselves and the power that will free us from ourselves. It is this power of revelation which is the business of the novelist."

Seven or eight years earlier, he would have said "the business of the minister" before going on to preach a sermon. Although he had stepped down from the pulpit, it was a theological energy that continued to activate his language, refined and redirected. "Everybody's Protest Novel" is full of this energy: the words *truth*, *freedom*, *revelation* resound throughout it with a sacred purpose, which is to affirm a devotion to the human being, "not to be confused with a devotion to humanity which is too easily equated with a devotion to a Cause."

When Baldwin said that Mrs. Stowe's novel was "very bad," he meant that while it may have succeeded as a pamphlet, it failed dismally as a novel. And it was precisely here, in his apprehension of the aesthetic merit of a piece of literature, and in his consideration of the supremacy of that aspect, that he differed most from Richard Wright. Wright was a social realist, and the fervor of the ex-Communist fired his pen as much as that of the ex-minister fueled Baldwin's. For Wright, it was important that a novel, story, or play have not so much a revelatory or spiritually improving function as a socially improving one.

"Everybody's Protest Novel" is a remarkable piece of writing. One of Baldwin's first publications, it is already the product of a mature style. It not only contains all of Baldwin's preoccupations but suggests the totality of his potential. All his themes as a writer—with the exception of homosexuality, into which he was opening his investigation in a companion piece for the second issue of *Zero*—are present here. Most pronounced is the theme which had exercised him, in a different realm, while he was still an adolescent—the choice between redemption and damnation:

> We find ourselves bound, first without, then within, by the nature of our [social] categorization. And escape is not effected through a bitter railing against this trap; it is as if this very striving were the only motion needed to spring the trap upon us. We take our shape, it is true, within and against that cage of reality bequeathed us at our birth; and yet it is precisely through our dependence on this reality that we are most endlessly betrayed. Society is held together with legend, myth, coercion, fear that without it we will be hurled into that void, within which, like the earth before the Word was spoken, the foundations of society are hidden. From this void—ourselves—it

> is the function of society to protect us; but it is only this void, our unknown selves, demanding, forever, a new act of creation, which can save us—"from the evil that is in the world."

For a twenty-four-year-old from a Harlem slum, with an education which had to be curtailed, for economic reasons, when he was seventeen, this is precocious. Toward the end of his discussion, Baldwin fulfills a promise he had made at the beginning, to show that "those novels of oppression written by Negroes . . . raging, near paranoiac . . . [reinforce] the principles which activate the oppression they decry." If Richard Wright did not recognize his own silhouette in that sentence, he had only to read to the end of the essay to find it fleshed out. Baldwin suggested that Bigger Thomas, the protagonist of *Native Son*, was nothing more than Uncle Tom's descendant, "flesh of his flesh." Beneath the subversive facade of Wright's protest novel lay a continuation, "a complement of that monstrous legend it was written to destroy." Baldwin portrayed the nineteenth-century crusader and the contemporary novelist "locked together in a deadly timeless battle, the one uttering merciless exhortations, the other shouting curses."

It was a subtle argument, but its conclusion left no room for doubt over Baldwin's feelings about the work of the man everyone had taken for his mentor. "The failure of the protest novel lies in its rejection of life, the human being, the denial of his beauty, dread, power, in its insistence that it is his categorization alone which is real."

The protest novel was a ghetto; Baldwin would like to sweep it away—and, by extension, its architects along with it.

* * *

On the spring day on which *Zero* was published, Baldwin made a foray into the Brasserie Lipp. Whomever he was looking for, it was not Wright, but there he was, sitting at a table, and he called Baldwin over.

> Richard accused me of having betrayed him, and not only him but all American Negroes, by attacking the idea of protest literature. . . . And Richard thought that I was trying to destroy his novel and his reputation; but it had not entered my mind that either of these could be destroyed, and certainly not by me.[11]

This is more than slightly disingenuous. The page and a half devoted to *Native Son* at the end of "Everybody's Protest Novel" may be small-arms fire, but the aim is deadly. Then, hardly had Baldwin stepped back out on to the Boulevard St.-Germain than he set to work on another essay, "Many Thousands Gone." It is a prolonged attack on *Native Son*.

> *Native Son* does not convey the altogether savage paradox of the American Negro's situation. . . . *Native Son* finds itself at length so trapped by the American image of Negro life . . . that it cannot pursue its own implications. . . . This is the significance of *Native Son* and also, unhappily, its overwhelming limitation.

By the time this essay was completed, in the following year ("Many Thousands Gone" was published in *Partisan Review*, November-December 1951),[12] the rift between Baldwin and Wright had widened and was more or less unbridgeable. Hoetis's congenial notion of having "the old black writer and the young black writer" at the same table, thrashing out ideas over café au lait and funneling the results into *Zero*, was misjudged. The novel which Wright had looked through in 1944 was nearing completion, and Baldwin was launching it with high hopes indeed. He knew he was, as he said, "smart." He even knew he was smarter than Wright. "All literature is protest!" Wright had snapped at him in the Brasserie Lipp, a copy of *Zero* lying on the table before them like the map of a disputed territory. All literature may be protest, replied the pupil who has learned so much he can outsmart the teacher, "but not all protest is literature."

* * *

> Unable to see it, I invented the biggest and loveliest prick in the world. I endowed it with qualities: heavy, strong and nervous, sober, with a tendency towards pride, and yet serene. Beneath my fingers, I felt, sculpted in oak, its full veins, its palpitations, its heat, its pinkness, and at times the racing pulsation of the sperm.
>
> —Jean Genet, *Journal du Voleur*, 1949

Before getting down to work on the essay in which he would take direct aim at Wright, Baldwin had a second commission to fulfill for *Zero*. "Preservation of Innocence" was published in *Zero* no. 2, Summer 1949. Its theme, like the theme of "Everybody's Protest Novel," is "know thyself," though this time the subject of the sermon was not race but homosexuality. And the young ex-minister was preaching the virtues of that tendency, not the vices. It exposes the repressions implicit in the approved image of American machismo, as exemplified in the novels of James M. Cain and Raymond Chandler. And it shows the young homosexual to have been a feminist:

> In the truly awesome attempt of the American to at once preserve his innocence and arrive at man's estate, that mindless monster, the tough guy, has been created and perfected, whose masculinity is found in the most infantile and elementary externals and whose attitude towards men and women is the wedding of the most abysmal romanticism and the most implacable distrust. It is impossible for a moment to believe that any Cain or Chandler hero loves his girl; we are given overwhelming evidence that he wants her, but that is not the same thing and moreover, what he seems to want is revenge. . . . The woman, in these energetic works, is the unknown quantity, the incarnation of sexual evil, the smiler with the knife. It is the man, who, for all his tommy-guns and rhetoric, is the innocent. . . . Men and women have all but disappeared from our popular culture, leaving only this disturbing series of effigies with a motive power which we are told is sex. . . .

Sexual difference was not something Richard Wright had ever had cause to deal with at close quarters. It existed outside his nature, outside nature itself. It was linked to perversity. A friend wrote to Wright about Baldwin's using the word *filthy*. Yes, Wright replied, that was the word. He felt uncomfortable in Baldwin's presence. "It's always the same with homos."[13] Another friend told him: "Behind all that Baldwin says is a kind of useless, quiet, shameful weeping." Wright agreed with that, too. Unbowed by the worst that American racism could aim at him, homosexuality still presented itself as a threat. "Yeah, he can write," a friend of Baldwin's recalled Wright saying at the time, "but he's a faggot."[14]

Faggot, with its overtones of camp cliquishness, was precisely the wrong term for Baldwin's still developing, still exploratory, relationship with his own sexuality. The investigation of the self was a mission he undertook with displaced religious zeal. The pure in spirit, in Baldwin's lay theology, were those prepared to accept, not resist, the foul rag-and-bone shop of the heart. "Preservation of Innocence" is not as subtle a piece of writing as "Everybody's Protest Novel." But although the two essays share a set of overlapping concerns, "Preservation of Innocence" is distinct in a particular way—there is nothing in it about race—and Baldwin surely would not have written it had he stayed at home. This was a subject which, as Hoetis says, *Partisan Review* (which had reprinted "Everybody's Protest Novel" without stating where it had been first published) would not touch "with a ten-foot pole." Paris was freeing his pen and nourishing his ambition; the subtitle he gave to this, the second chapter of his search for the American soul, was "Studies for a New Morality."

From *Exiled in Paris: Richard Wright, James Baldwin, Samuel Beckett, and Others on the Left Bank* (2003), pp. 23-33.

Notes

1. Baldwin to William Phillips, April 1949; *Partisan Review* collection.

2. Fern Marja Eckman, *The Furious Passage of James Baldwin*, New York, 1966.

3. Otto Friedrich to author.

4. "Equal in Paris," in *Notes of a Native Son*, Boston, 1955.

5. Otto Friedrich, "Jimmy," in *The Grave of Alice B. Toklas*, New York, 1989.

6. *Ibid.*

7. Sartre gave Hoetis a prose outline of his new play, *Nekrassov*, in 1955, which Hoetis, by then publishing books rather than magazines, included in translation in *The Zero Anthology*, together with an extract from *Le Diable et le Bon Dieu* (1951).

8. Friedrich, "Jimmy," *op. cit.*

9. Hoetis to author.

10. Baldwin to Phillips, *op. cit.*

11. "Alas, Poor Richard," in *Nobody Knows My Name*, New York, 1961.

12. "Many Thousands Gone" was first published in *Partisan Review*, Nov.-Dec. 1951, and reprinted in *Notes of a Native Son*.

13. RW to Margrit de Sablonière, 4/8/60; Schomburg Center for Research in Black Culture (SCRBC), New York Public Library.

14. Bernard Hassell to author.

"This Web of Lust and Fury": Harriet Beecher Stowe, James Baldwin's Nineteenth-Century White Mother

Horace A. Porter

> I had read *Uncle Tom's Cabin* compulsively, the book in one hand, the newest baby on my hipbone. I was trying to find out something, sensing something in the book of immense import for me: which, however, I knew I did not really understand.
>
> My mother got scared. She hid the book. The last time she hid it, she hid it on the highest shelf above the bathtub. I was somewhere around seven or eight. God knows how I did it, but I somehow climbed up and dragged the book down. Then, my mother, as she herself puts it, "didn't hide it anymore," and, indeed, from that moment, though in fear and trembling, began to let me go.
>
> —James Baldwin, *The Devil Finds Work*

In "Everybody's Protest Novel," the opening essay in *Notes of a Native Son*, written in 1949 when James Baldwin was twenty-four, we see what Irving Howe appropriately describes as "gestures of repudiation, glimmers of intention."[1] Critics have failed to discuss the essay beyond what is usually considered Baldwin's harsh and opportunistic assessment of Harriet Beecher Stowe and of Richard Wright.[2] But it should be noted and counted singularly to Baldwin's credit that he does choose to discuss Stowe's *Uncle Tom's Cabin*. His choice (in the context of recent criticism about the novel) reveals his critical precociousness. He perceives and acknowledges, at twenty-four, the novel's uncanny socioliterary power. Although he attacks it scathingly, he spells out his position nearly forty years before professional literary critics would make a concerted rediscovery of what is now considered its inestimable literary value. Nor is his critique of the novel a literary fluke. It provides extraordinary evidence that this then unknown young black writer, writing with Jamesian syntax, already had a special and engaging angle of vision on American literary culture and social life.

The essay reveals, if inadvertently, a paradigmatic instance, articulately and contradictorily rendered, of a black writer starting out in America. His subject, the ironic legacy and horrible consequences of slavery, has already been given to him—even as he willfully and ambivalently turns away from it. Eschewing the artistic limitations of the protest tradition, he states, "What is today parroted as his [the writer's] Responsibility—which seems to mean that he must make formal declaration that he is involved in, and affected by, the lives of other people and to say something improving about this somewhat self-evident fact—is, when he believes it, his corruption and our loss."[3] But other aspects of the essay take us considerably beyond its implicit characterization of Baldwin's genesis as a writer. He provides a capsule summary of what will become the central theme in his writings and life. While ostensibly considering the limitations of the protest novel in general and the specific artistic failure of *Uncle Tom's Cabin* in particular, Baldwin proffers his criticism of white America's guilt-ridden vision of black humanity.

Thus, a crucial aspect of Baldwin's essay concerns white America's denial of—in American literature no less than in American life—the complexity of black humanity. In that light, he discusses *Uncle Tom's Cabin* as characteristic documentation of the self-destructive American vision that is as much a part of the American present as of the American past. Speaking of Stowe's novel, he asks, ". . . why are we bound still within the same constriction? How is it that we are so loath to make a further journey than that made by Mrs. Stowe, to discover and reveal something a little closer to the truth?" "Everybody's Protest Novel" displays what will emerge as Baldwin's preoccupation with the mythic, categorical perception and portrayal of blacks. He views Stowe's depiction of blacks as stereotypical, perniciously sentimental, and also violent:

> *Uncle Tom's Cabin* is a very bad novel, having, in its self-righteous, virtuous sentimentality, much in common with *Little Women.* Sentimentality, the ostentatious parading of excessive and spurious emotion, is the mark of dishonesty, the inability to feel; the wet eyes of the sentimentalist betray his aversion to experience, his fear of life, his arid heart; and it is always, therefore, the signal of secret and violent inhumanity, the mask of cruelty. *Uncle Tom's Cabin*—like its multitudinous, hard-boiled descendants—is a catalogue of violence. ("Everybody's Protest Novel," p. 14)

Baldwin's tone is captious and polemical when he asserts that Stowe's sentimentality "is the mark of dishonesty, the inability to feel . . . the signal of secret and violent inhumanity." Baldwin maintains that protest novels, like *Uncle Tom's Cabin*, instead of advancing the cause of black Americans actually strengthen the common myths, stereotypes, and prejudices about them. He argues that Stowe places a higher premium on sensationalism than on revelation. Thus, hard truths about the experience of the slaves and their masters are cruelly and superficially masked by what Baldwin calls Stowe's "catalogue of violence," her descriptions of "unmotivated and senseless" brutality. He charges that she leaves the only important question "unanswered and unnoticed"—she fails to show "what moved her people to such deeds." It would appear as though Baldwin's primary criticism of *Uncle Tom's Cabin* concerns aesthetic matter. He accuses Stowe of a failure of artistic imagination and execution. But, given the novel's extraordinary popularity, he certainly had the social consequences of her artistic failure in mind. Despite the protest novel's "avowed aim . . . to bring greater freedom to the oppressed," Baldwin views it as "a mirror of our confusion, dishonesty, panic." He writes, "Whatever unsettling questions are raised are evanescent, titillating, remote, for this has nothing to do with us, it is safely ensconced in the social arena, where indeed, it has nothing to do with anyone, so that finally we receive a very definite thrill of virtue from the fact that we are reading such a book at all." Referring to *Gentleman's Agreement* and *The Postman Always Rings*

Twice as exemplary of the same myths and fallacies found in Stowe's novel, Baldwin concludes, "in *Uncle Tom's Cabin* we may find a foreshadowing of both: the formula created by the necessity to find a lie more palatable than the truth has been handed down and memorized and persists yet with a terrible power."

As Baldwin views it, Stowe's self-righteous, purposeful desire merely to "prove that slavery was wrong" leads to an artistic failure. Thus, he considers her portrayal of her black characters as stereotypical. He refers to her "lively procession" of field hands and house niggers as "stock lovable figures." He ridicules the three most important black characters in the novel—Uncle Tom and George and Eliza Harris. He describes Uncle Tom as a stereotype: "jet-black, wooly-haired, illiterate . . . and phenomenally forbearing." George, Eliza, and their son, Harry, represent another stereotype. Unlike the field hands, who are apparently beyond social redemption or acceptability, George and Eliza suggest the possibility that the only slaves who can effectively undergo a transition from barbarism to civilization are those who are figuratively and literally "unnegroid":

> Eliza is a beautiful, pious, hybrid, light enough to pass . . . differing from the genteel mistress who has overseered her education only in the respect that she is a servant. George is darker, but makes up for it by being a mechanical genius, and is, moreover, sufficiently unnegroid to pass through town, a fugitive from his master, disguised as a Spanish gentleman, attracting no attention whatever beyond admiration. ("Everybody's Protest Novel," pp. 16-17)

Stowe's relentless insistence upon categorization leads to, as Baldwin puts it, her "overlooking, denying, evading" the "complexity" of black humanity. She sees her black characters categorically as a problem to be solved. Baldwin attempts to explain why, in fiction as well as in fact, what was once called "the Negro problem" is so uneasily and so inadequately negotiated. He suggests that Americans tend to evade reality, like Stowe seeing only the categorical personifications they wish to see. He considers it a potentially destructive vision based on the fallacious assumption that America is a white country. Baldwin concludes that the spirit of Stowe's faulty vision still holds sway:

> . . . the spirit that breathes in this book, hot, self-righteous, fearful . . . is not different from that terror which activates a lynch mob. One need not, indeed, search for examples so historic or so gaudy; this is a warfare waged daily in the heart, a warfare so vast, so relentless and so powerful that the interracial handshake or the interracial marriage can be as crucifying as the public hanging or the secret rape. This panic motivates our cruelty. ("Everybody's Protest Novel," p. 18)

As this passage indicates and as our discussion so far has attempted to demonstrate, Baldwin views the protest novel, the climate out of which it arises, and the assumptions upon which it is based as interrelated phenomena. And in this complex light, he does not feel that good intentions, sincerity, or justifiable moral causes should force us to suspend willingly artistic judgment, especially in the face of "whatever violence they [protest novels] do to language, whatever excessive demands they make of credibility." He realizes that his assessment of the protest novel will be strenuously opposed: "One is told to put first things first, the good of society coming before niceties of style or characterization. Even if this were incontestable—for what exactly is the 'good' of society?—it argues an insuperable confusion, since literature and sociology are not one and the same."

Baldwin's criticism of *Uncle Tom's Cabin* displays his repudiation of everything for which it stands. But, even within the context of this early essay, let alone in later works like *The Fire Next Time*, Baldwin portrays a profound ambivalence toward Stowe and the tradition of the protest novel as a whole. Baldwin's blunt criticism of *Uncle Tom's Cabin* ought to be taken seriously. It is instructive to note how recent critics, who consider *Uncle Tom's Cabin* a positive contribution to

American literature and life, respond to Baldwin's own earlier scathing attack. In *Sensational Designs: The Cultural Work of American Fiction, 1790-1860* (1985), Jane Tompkins provides one of the more notable recent critical discussions of *Uncle Tom's Cabin*.[4] Her chapter devoted to the novel, "Sentimental Power: *Uncle Tom's Cabin* and the Politics of Literary History," claims that it "is probably the most influential book ever written by an American."[5] She takes to task Perry Miller, F. O. Matthiessen, Harry Levin, Richard Chase, R. W. B. Lewis, Yvor Winters, and Henry Nash Smith, those patriarchal custodians of the American literary canon, who, she believes, fail to understand the singular significance of Stowe's novel.[6] But Tompkins ignores Baldwin's comments on Stowe in "Everybody's Protest Novel." Yet Baldwin's criticism is more challenging, more polemical, than the relatively genteel critics she cites. The reason why his criticism is not considered lies in a striking parallel between Baldwin's objections to *Uncle Tom's Cabin* itself and a crucial limitation of Tompkins's brand of criticism.

Apart from the difficult and perhaps unanswerable question she raises about the most influential book ever written by an American, she commits, with remarkable extravagance, a critical error analogous to the creative fault that Baldwin discovers at the heart of *Uncle Tom's Cabin*. Baldwin maintains that *Uncle Tom's Cabin* "was not intended to do anything more than prove that slavery was wrong." Tompkins's argument apparently intends to prove that established white male critics have all been wrong about *Uncle Tom's Cabin*. Tompkins attempts to bring an end to the damnation and neglect of women writers. The urgency and the morally justifiable nature of their causes blind both Stowe and Tompkins to crucial aspects of their subjects. In her zeal to prove that slavery was wrong, Stowe fails to present the complex nature of slave humanity. Similarly, Tompkins's own noteworthy cause impels her to overlook or deny the complicated and contradictory nature of *Uncle Tom's Cabin*'s great popularity and artistic limitation. This does not mean that *Uncle Tom's Cabin* must necessarily be judged in the same critical terms as, say, Herman Melville's *Benito Cereno* or Mark Twain's *The Adventures of Huckleberry Finn*. But how each work succeeds and fails in its own specific depiction of slavery and its consequences is an important question.

Tompkins maintains that a critical comparison of the sort is essentially useless because *Uncle Tom's Cabin* generically distinguishes itself as a "typological narrative." She states, "Therefore, what seem from a modernist point of view to be gross stereotypes in characterization and a needless proliferation of incident, are essential properties of a narrative aimed at demonstrating that human history is a continual reenactment of the sacred drama of redemption."[7] She concludes that Stowe's characters "are not defined primarily by their mental and emotional characteristics—that is to say, psychologically—but soteriologically, according to whether they are saved or damned."[8]

Should "stereotypes" in characterization and "needless proliferation of incident" necessarily be ignored because a writer attempts to portray human history as "a continual reenactment of the sacred drama of redemption"? Tompkins's sense of ideological and canonical urgency leads her to her conclusion. She argues further that *Uncle Tom's Cabin* does not concern slavery as much as it does motherhood. And in this novel light, Stowe becomes something other than the abolitionist whose book was initially written for and serialized in the abolitionist journal *The National Era*; she becomes instead the most celebrated champion of "the new matriarchy."

> The novel's deepest political aspirations are expressed only secondarily in its devastating attack on the slave system; the true goal of Stowe's rhetorical undertaking is nothing less than the institution of the kingdom of heaven on earth. . . . In this vision, described in the chapter entitled "The Quaker Settlement," Christian love fulfills itself not in war, but in daily living, and the principle of sacrifice is revealed not in crucifixion, but in motherhood. . . . The home is the center of all meaningful activity; women perform the most important tasks; work is carried on in a spirit of mutual

> cooperation; and the whole is guided by a Christian woman who, through the influence of her "loving words," "gentle moralities," and "motherly loving kindness," rules the world from her rocking chair.[9]

To be sure, motherhood and the home are central themes in Stowe's attack on slavery. Nevertheless, the dream Stowe presents in "The Quaker Settlement" appears "utopian and arcadian"[10] primarily in the sense that it represents a Christian and antebellum version of the fulfillment of American democratic promise. Thus, Eliza's escape from slavery to freedom becomes as significant as the nature and dynamics of Rachel Halliday's home. Tompkins does not fully address the significance of Stowe's negative portrayal of some of her mothers, especially Marie St. Claire. Even Tompkins's fine reading of the dynamics of sentimentalism in Little Eva's death scene privileges her death in what seems an inappropriate way. Little Eva, after all, is robbed of moral choice. She does not choose to die; she dies of disease. Stowe entitled her novel *Uncle Tom's Cabin* rather than *Little Eva's Heaven* for good reason. But an extended discussion of Uncle Tom's death scene, on the other hand, would lead Tompkins to the heart of the novel, the monstrous evil of slavery, the fact that some white men and women bought and sold black men, women, and children. In "Everybody's Protest Novel," Baldwin realizes that Stowe's treatment of slavery gives the novel an extraordinary power even as he attempts to clarify what he sees as the novel's overwhelming limitation.

Tompkins's interpretation provides a contemporary example of how good intentions and justifiable causes sometimes lead to questionable literary and critical results. In her enthusiasm to correct the critical wrongs committed by established male critics against women writers, Tompkins commits her own critical sins of omission and neglect. Her negligence of Baldwin's sharp comments symbolizes her ideological and literary readiness to exclude and neglect blacks while simultaneously supporting women and women's rights. Tompkins's omission is particularly glaring in light of her expressed purpose to study novels and stories because "they offer powerful examples of a way a culture thinks about itself, articulating and proposing solutions for problems that shape a particular historical moment."[11]

This assessment of Tompkins's interpretation does not involve a charge of racism. It concerns rather the very issue she so eloquently articulates when she castigates white male critics. Specifically, in matters pertaining to race, just as in consideration of gender, blindness often emerges as the Siamese twin of extraordinary insight. Consequently, in her reappropriation and reimagining of the place and meaning of Stowe's novel in American culture, the lives of the enslaved blacks within the novel, and by extension all slaves who lived and died, come across as less important than the careers of those nineteenth-century white women writers who have been excluded from serious consideration by the prejudices of white male critics. Moreover, whatever the function of Stowe's stereotypical depictions in the novel, Tompkins ignores the fact that they have social as well as literary consequences. In the collective black mind, "Uncle Tom" now stands as the shuffling personification of obsequiousness and self-hatred, the embodiment of slavery and the legacy of white supremacy.

Leslie Fiedler's "new" ideas about *Uncle Tom's Cabin* are also highly problematic.[12] He also argues, though not with Tompkins's polemical zeal, that *Uncle Tom's Cabin* celebrates the redeeming virtues of motherhood. But Fiedler distinguishes himself on at least two significant counts. First, he maintains that works like Stowe's *Uncle Tom's Cabin*; Thomas Dixon, Jr.'s *The Leopard Spots* and *The Clansman*; the film *The Birth of a Nation* (D. W. Griffith's adaptation of the Dixon novels); Margaret Mitchell's *Gone With the Wind* (both as a novel and movie), and Alex Haley's phenomenal *Roots* (in all of its popular forms) constitute an American "inadvertent epic."[13] Fiedler states, "Rooted in demonic dreams of race, sex and violence, which have long haunted us Americans, they determine our views of the Civil War, Reconstruction, the rise and fall of the Ku Klux Klan, the enslavement and liberation of African blacks, thus constituting a myth of our history unequalled in scope or resonance by any work of High Literature."[14] Fiedler quotes a passage from Baldwin's "Everybody's Protest Novel" on the negative effect of Stowe's sentimentality, but he effectively dismisses Baldwin's objection by pointing out Baldwin's admission elsewhere that he read the novel over and over as a child. Then Fiedler provides his own interpretation of *Uncle Tom's Cabin*'s influence:

> . . . it was Mrs. Stowe who invented American Blacks for the imagination of the whole world. Before *Uncle Tom's Cabin*, they existed as historical, demographic, economic facts, their existence acknowledged but not felt with the passion and intensity we accord what moves through our dreams as well as our waking lives. Afterwards, things were different; Tom, Eliza, and Topsy at least were immediately translated from the pages of Mrs. Stowe's book to the deep psyches of us all, Europeans and Americans, whites and Blacks. . . . these three have survived the fiction in which they appear; becoming, for better or worse, models, archetypal grids through which we perceive the Negroes around us, and they perceive themselves.[15]

Perhaps Fiedler overstates his case. Why would real black people, even though enslaved, have to be "invented" for the "imagination of the whole world"? The popularity of *Uncle Tom's Cabin* was necessarily enhanced by actual historical accounts of the horrors of slavery. Europeans and Northerners frequently traveled throughout the slave states recording brief and extended eyewitness accounts of the slaves—their life and work, religion and superstition, manners and morals, crimes and punishment. One notable example, of course, had been de Tocqueville.[16] During the antebellum period, fugitive and manumitted slaves journeyed throughout New England, Canada, and England, speaking before antislavery societies and telling the story of their bondage and their inspired escapes to freedom; as recent historians have clearly established, slaves themselves were hardly a docile and silent minority. Although forbidden to learn how to read and write, many slaves defiantly refused to remain illiterate. So close, in fact, and so inextricably bound are the quests for freedom and literacy in Afro-American culture, particularly during the antebellum period, that Robert Stepto argues that the dual quest is the quintessential pregeneric myth that underpins all Afro-American literature.[17] Speeches, letters, interviews, and serialized narratives of ex-slaves were regularly published in abolitionist newspapers. Sixty-eight slave narratives were published before the Civil War, thirty-three of them written by blacks themselves. Sixty-seven narratives of former slaves were written after 1860.[18] Thus Stowe could hardly have "invented American Blacks for the imagination of the whole world." The evidence is pervasive. These slave narratives are considerably more than arid historical accounts of the facts and statistics of slavery. It is a well-known fact that Stowe based her portrayal of Uncle Tom on the life of one of them, Josiah Henson.[19] But what has scarcely been commented upon is the degree to which Stowe exploits, with notable literary success, the lives and narratives of other well-known slaves. George Harris's defiant intellectual nature is reminiscent of Frederick Douglass's narrative of 1845. George and Eliza's story parallels, in crucial details, the escape of William and Ellen Craft, who fled to freedom when fair-skinned Ellen cropped her hair and masqueraded as an ailing planter with her faithful and humble servant, William, at her side. Even Cassy's fascinating story appears derived from the complex romantic life of Harriet Jacobs reported in *Incidents in the Life of a Slave Girl.*[20] Stowe, indeed, is known to have read parts of Jacobs's story in manuscript.

When Fiedler refers to Stowe's creation of "archetypal grids through which we perceive the Negroes around us and they perceive themselves," he inadvertently supports and promotes the appropriation of black humanity in the same breath and essay in which he argues against categorical definitions of women's literary works by men.

In the context of our discussion of Baldwin's complex genesis as a writer, the accuracy of Tompkins's and Fiedler's interpretations of *Uncle Tom's Cabin* pales in significance beside their inadvertent or benign neglect of "Everybody's Protest Novel." Whether we agree or disagree with Baldwin's conclusions or claims, the essay remains singularly engaging among discussions of Stowe's novel in this century. Indeed, part of the power of the essay lies in Baldwin's clairvoyant anticipation of the American critics of his future work. This intuitiveness represents the unconscious subtext of his essay. Thus, we witness glimmers of his own fear of being typecast "as *merely* a Negro; or, even, merely a Negro writer." For, once typecast, he perceives that he will be fatally doomed to be interpreted, neglected, or damned by literary and sociological criteria wholly inappropriate to the particular nature of his talent.

This odd combination of intuition and apprehension charges the essay with its polemical vigor and its rhetorical authority. Arguing against the artless fiction of the protest novel, which he takes *Uncle Tom's Cabin* to represent, we observe young Baldwin here impersonating Henry James with an authoritative difference. He is already warring against the threatening possibility of his own vocational limitation—a limitation imposing itself from without and simultaneously corroborating or inscribing itself from deep within. Thus, he comes across rhetorically as the prince par excellence of the disarming assertion—deriving his rhetorical authority from his frequent absolute claims about the human condition. These claims are strung together by precious aperçus no less authoritative. He devotes himself to the revelation of the truth—something he feels Stowe fails to deliver:

> Let us say, then, that truth, as used here, is meant to imply a devotion to the human being, his freedom and fulfillment; freedom which cannot be legislated, fulfillment which cannot be charted. . . . He is not, after all, merely a member of a Society or a Group or a deplorable conundrum to be explained by Science. He is—and how old-fashioned the words sound!—something more than that, something resolutely indefinable, unpredictable. In overlooking, denying, evading his complexity—which is nothing more than the disquieting complexity of ourselves—we are diminished and we perish;

> only within this web of ambiguity, paradox, this hunger, danger, darkness, can we find at once ourselves and the power to free us from ourselves. It is this power of revelation which is the business of the novelist, this journey toward a more vast reality which must take precedence over all other claims. ("Everybody's Protest Novel," p. 15)

Dangling rather precariously in this "web of ambiguity, paradox, . . . hunger, danger, darkness," we witness the "disquieting complexity" of Baldwin, the young and unfulfilled artist. "He is not, after all, merely a member of a Society or Group." He is hardly Stowe's Uncle Tom. Yet he is threatened by Uncle Tom's legacy and the tradition of which he is so grandly representative. Baldwin yearns for the power to "find" his true artistic self, a self he ironically wishes to be "resolutely indefinable, unpredictable," in other words, a highly creative self. Consequently, he ends his definition of the human by discussing "this power of revelation." Revelation "is . . . the business of the novelist, this journey toward a more vast reality which must take precedence over all other claims." True artists then must not allow themselves to be defined by any form of categorization that will corrupt their individual views. The tradition of the protest novel corrupts the artistic view—so much so in Stowe's case that Baldwin maintains that Uncle Tom "has been robbed of his humanity and divested of his sex."

Baldwin's objections to Stowe's dehumanization and emasculation of Uncle Tom highlight a deeper concern. To be sure, he devotes his essay to a serious look at the tradition of the American protest novel, past and present, and considers *Uncle Tom's Cabin* the "cornerstone of American social protest fiction." But on another level, Baldwin objects to Stowe's appropriation or, indeed, exploitation of black humanity because he, fledgling novelist, must rescue the image of black America from those who have so profoundly distorted it. Tompkins's and Fiedler's critical readings and evaluations of the book are motivated by canonical ambition, their desire to translate or promote Stowe's novel out of the minority idiom and status of abolitionism and sentimentality to a singular position of its own. Baldwin's concerns reveal the nature of his own ambition. He takes Stowe to task partly because she dares to bother with "the business of the novelist." Such is, according to Baldwin, "beyond Mrs. Stowe's powers" because "she was not so much a novelist as an impassioned pamphleteer." Yet, despite his derogatory comments, Baldwin's attitude toward Stowe is profoundly ambivalent. And his ambivalence characterizes his anxiety about his own work. He stands at a crucial fork in the road. He yearns to become a novelist, but that wish will remain unfulfilled for several years. He takes what he considers a principled artistic stand; he repudiates the tradition of the protest novel.

The polemical tone and rhetorical intensity of Baldwin's remarks clearly suggest a concern more crucial to his immediate life than "a very bad novel" written over a century earlier. "Everybody's Protest Novel" represents the public beginning of his struggle for clarity as a writer. His theoretical perception in this essay supersedes his critical comments on *Uncle Tom's Cabin*. The essay displays his early perception of what happens to the black American when his humanity gets trapped in the web of good ideological intentions, moral self-righteousness, sentimental rhetoric, and misguided thinking—coming from those who are staunch supporters of the principles and promises of democratic life. He prophetically perceives this as his peculiar burden and fate as an American writer, and, therefore, he lashes out at Stowe.

However, even as Baldwin rejects the tradition of protest of which Stowe's *Uncle Tom's Cabin* is so singularly representative, he unconsciously reflects, in his essay, both in tone and in substance, the exhortative rhetoric and aggressive morality of an "impassioned pamphleteer." And despite his apparent indifference to the so-called social "Responsibility" of the novelist, he unconsciously accepts Stowe's own legacy and assumes the responsibility of speaking on behalf of the oppressed.

> It is the peculiar triumph of society—and its loss—that it is able to convince those people to whom it has given inferior status of the reality of this decree; it has the force and the weapons to translate its dictum into fact, so that the allegedly inferior are actually made so, insofar as the societal realities are concerned. This is a more hidden phenomenon now than it was in the days of serfdom, but it is no less implacable. Now, as then, we find ourselves bound, first without, then within, by the nature of our categorization. And escape is not effected through a bitter railing against this trap: it is as though this very striving were the only motion needed to spring the trap upon us. ("Everybody's Protest Novel," p. 20)

Baldwin's concern here clearly goes beyond the mere literary. By pointing out the implacable, though superficially various, phenomenon of societal control of those it considers inferior, he speaks as a representative of the oppressed black masses. But as quickly as he moves unconsciously in the direction of Stowe, even alluding to the plight of blacks during slavery, he consciously and polemically veers away. He objects to "categorization" and sees societal definition as a "trap." The tradition of protest fiction, what he calls "a bitter railing against," hardly affords escape. "A bitter railing against" the trap provides the "only motion needed to spring the trap upon us."

The force of Baldwin's attack on Stowe was in part, I believe, an unconscious acknowledgment of the temptations and the impact of her work on his own. *Uncle Tom's Cabin* was, in effect, the hidden mother text conspiring to work itself out in his life and in what would be Baldwin's most widely read and, arguably, his most influential book, *The Fire Next Time.*

There are several significant biographical parallels between Baldwin and Stowe that affected the work of both. Stowe's father, Lyman Beecher, like Baldwin's, was a preacher. And so were six of her brothers.[21] She, of course, was excluded by gender from the ministry, and Baldwin gave up his own child evangelism. But both had grown up in a household where Christianity and a belief in moral righteousness were their daily bread. A century and a decade after the publication of *Uncle Tom's Cabin* in an abolitionist journal, Baldwin published *The Fire Next Time* in two parts, "My Dungeon Shook: Letter to My Nephew on the One-Hundredth Anniversary of the Emancipation" and "Down at the Cross: Letter from a Region in My Mind," the first in *The Progressive* (December 1962) and the second in *The New Yorker* (November 17, 1962). Baldwin, like Stowe in *Uncle Tom's Cabin*, was speaking to the converted. For, if right-minded citizens could see their complex personal connection to the national sin of slavery and racial injustice, perhaps Americans could, in Baldwin's words, "end the racial nightmare, and achieve our country, and change the history of the world."[22]

However, a crucial difference to bear in mind is the tenor of the period during which each writer wrote. The sixties were characterized by democratic and idealistic fervor with a few momentary stays against moral confusion. Its currency of verbal exchange was blunt, direct, exhortative. In poetry, fiction, and certainly in autobiography, the collective temporal urge was to "tell it like it is" and "to let it all hang out." Thus, the excessive sentimentality of Stowe's era, which afforded her readers certain tender mercies of incident, phrasing, and scene, are nonexistent in Baldwin. This difference, however, pales in significance to the similar manner in which they engage their readers. In the end, both Stowe and Baldwin want their readers to *feel right*. After the fashion of preachers, both lecture and exhort their readers on the wages of sins, those sins directly committed and those that are the indirect result of cowardice and moral negligence. The writers connect their literary texts to events of their own era, becoming voices of public conscience—Stowe appealing to the abolitionists and Christians in her audience, Baldwin to liberals and intellectuals, Christians or not.

Stowe and Baldwin employ similar strategies condemning the evils of society, and even the innate depravity of humankind, yet both somehow, rhetorically, excuse the shortcomings of their potential readers even as they abstractly condemn them. In her preface to *Uncle Tom's Cabin*, Stowe writes that the goal of "the artist," is to use "the allurements of fiction" to "breathe a humanizing and subduing influence, favorable to the development of the great principles of Christian brotherhood."[23] "In doing this," Stowe believes, "the author can sincerely disclaim any invidious feeling towards those individuals who, often without any fault of their own, are involved in the trials and embarrassments of the legal relations of slavery. Experience has shown her that some of the noblest of minds and hearts are often thus involved; and no one knows better than they do, that what may be gathered of the evils of slavery from sketches like these is not the half that could be told, of the unspeakable whole" (*Uncle Tom's Cabin*, pp. v-vi). So Baldwin, in what is, in effect, his preface to *The Fire Next Time*, "My Dungeon Shook: Letter to My Nephew on the One Hundredth Anniversary of the Emancipation," also points to the responsibility of whites for cruelty to blacks, but finds them "innocent and well-meaning":

> Now, my dear namesake, these innocent and well-meaning people, your countrymen, have caused you to be born under conditions not very far removed from those described for us by Charles Dickens in London of more than a hundred years ago. (I hear the chorus of the innocents screaming, "No! This is not true! How *bitter* you are!")
>
> You were born where you were born and faced the future that you faced because you were black and *for no other reason*. . . . You were not expected to aspire to excellence: You were expected to make peace with mediocrity. Wherever you have turned, James, in your short time on this earth, you have been told where you could go and what you could do . . . and where you could live and whom you could marry. (*The Fire Next Time*, pp. 20-21)

The writers employ similar rhetorical strategies to persuade their readers. They vividly depict the overwhelming facts of racial injustice. Just as Stowe presents a virtual catalogue of the evils of slavery Baldwin's *The Fire Next Time* records a twentieth-century urban slavery. He describes what he witnessed during the summer of his fourteenth year in Harlem:

For the wages of sin were visible everywhere, in every wine-stained and urine-splashed hallway, in every clanging ambulance bell, in every scar on the faces of the pimps and their whores, in every helpless, newborn baby being brought into this danger, in every knife and pistol fight on the avenue, and in every disastrous bulletin: a cousin, mother of six, suddenly gone mad, the children parcelled out here and there; an indestructible aunt rewarded for years of hard labor by a slow, agonizing death in a terrible small room; someone's bright son blown into eternity by his own hand; another turned robber and carried off to jail. (*The Fire Next Time*, p. 34)

In "Everybody's Protest Novel," Baldwin refers critically to Stowe's "catalogue of violence," which he sees as designed to inspire abolitionism; her book "was not intended to do anything more than prove that slavery was wrong." But Baldwin provides his own colorful and violent collage—the "ambulance bell," the "knife," the "pistol," incarceration, madness, suicide, "children parcelled out here and there." He clearly wishes to prove that the black American dream of freedom has been perpetually deferred. As he says in a new introduction to *Notes of a Native Son*: "There have been superficial changes, with results at best ambiguous and, at worst, disastrous. Morally, there has been no change at all and a moral change is the only real one. '*Plus ça change, . . . plus c'est la même chose*'" (*Notes of a Native Son*, p. xiii).

Stowe and Baldwin raise the fundamental issue of the black American's and white American's relationship to God. They warn their readers that the cruel and racist nature of American society mocks God and Christ. Both question why blacks, so horribly victimized, should believe in God at all. When, in *Uncle Tom's Cabin*, George Harris, the escaped slave, is urged by a sympathetic white, to "trust in the Lord," George asks bitterly, "'Is there a God to trust in? . . . Oh, I've seen things all my life that have made me feel that there can't be a God. You Christians don't know how these things look to us. There's a God for you, but is there any for us?'" (*Uncle Tom's Cabin*, p. 130). And Baldwin, relating his personal experience of religious conversion in the summer of his fourteenth year, writes that:

> All I really remember is the pain, the unspeakable pain; it was as though I were yelling up to Heaven and Heaven would not hear me. And if Heaven would not hear me, if love could not descend from Heaven—to wash me, to make me clean—then utter disaster was my portion. . . . And if one despairs—as who has not?—of human love, God's love alone is left. But God—and I felt this even then, so long ago, on that tremendous floor, unwillingly—is white. And if His love was so great, and if He loved all His children, why were we, the blacks, cast down so far? Why? (*The Fire Next Time*, p. 18)

Stowe uses Augustine St. Claire, the son of a New England "aristocrat" who inherits his slaves, to dramatize most effectively her more sophisticated arguments against slavery. St. Claire is an intelligent and relatively compassionate gentleman trapped in a web of familial and historical circumstances. He is deeply skeptical, even cynical, in his condemnation of the horrors of slavery and of the negligence of well-meaning Christians. St. Claire gives Stowe the opportunity to push her novel beyond the boundary lines imposed by sheer sentimentality and the melodramatic deus ex machina she employs. It is St. Claire, after all, who keeps the self-righteous Christians and "patronizing northerners" honest. His cousin, Miss Ophelia, is the most obvious representative of the type. When he speaks, he addresses, in effect, the reservations and questions about the dilemma of slavery Stowe's readers may have had. His remarks force readers to examine morally where they stand. His method of pedagogy is characterized in turn and sometimes in combination by Socratic doubt and devil's advocacy. Using St. Claire, Stowe makes accessible a series of abstract arguments while simultaneously creating the illusion that such utterances were essentially in accordance with St. Claire's forthright nature.

Marie St. Claire, St. Claire's wife, who is pro-slavery, recounts the wonders of a Sunday sermon in which the text was "He hath made everything beautiful in its season":

> "He showed how all the orders and distinctions in society came from God; and that it was so appropriate . . . and beautiful, that some should be high and some low, and that some were born to rule and some to serve . . . and he applied it so well to all this ridiculous fuss that is made about slavery, and he proved distinctly that the Bible was on our side." (*Uncle Tom's Cabin*, p. 200)

St. Claire reminds his wife that the religious arguments in favor of slavery were but sound and fury:

> "Religion! Is what you hear at church religion? Is that which can bend and turn, and descend and ascend, to fit every crooked phase of selfish, worldly society, religion? Is that religion which is less scrupulous, less generous, less just, less considerate for man, than even my own ungodly, worldly, blinded nature? No! When I look for a religion, I must look for something above me and not something beneath." (*Uncle Tom's Cabin*, p. 201)

Turning the rhetorical screw even more deeply into her reader's conscience, Stowe continues the debate, this time between St. Claire and Miss Ophelia. After St. Claire's daughter, little Eva, dies, he questions his own irresponsibility: "'What shall be said of one whose own heart, whose education, and the wants of society have called in vain to some noble purpose; who has floated on, a dreamy, mental spectator of the struggles, agonies, and wrongs of man, when he should have been a worker?'" (*Uncle Tom's Cabin*, p. 336). After Miss Ophelia replies by urging him to "repent and begin now," he argues: "'My view of Christianity is such . . . that I think no man can consistently profess it without throwing the whole weight of his being against this monstrous system of injustice that lies at the foundation of all our society, and if need be sacrificing himself in the battle.'"

St. Claire is, in a sense, Stowe's eloquent agent of right-minded rhetoric, since he has never acted according to his avowed sense of Christian responsibility in a nation where slavery is legalized. When Miss Ophelia asks St. Claire, "Do you suppose it possible that a nation will ever voluntarily emancipate?", his response clarifies the ironies and contradictions reflected in the lives of both Northern Christians and Southern slaveholders. It also raises crucial questions about the future well-being, the fate, of the newly freed slaves:

> "But, suppose we should rise up tomorrow and emancipate, who would educate these millions and teach them how to use their freedom. . . . is there enough Christian philanthropy, among your northern states to bear with the process of their education and elevation? . . . If we emancipate, are you willing to educate? How many families in your town would take in a negro man and woman, teach them, bear with them, and seek to make them Christians?" (*Uncle Tom's Cabin*, p. 338)

Writing one hundred years after Emancipation, Baldwin found himself addressing similar issues in similar terms. *The Fire Next Time*, which includes an extended discussion of the Black Muslim movement, was, in effect, criticism of the failure of Christianity. The aim of Black Muslims, he wrote, was to free themselves from the political tyranny and the religious hypocrisy of white American Christians. The Nation of Islam's basic philosophy was characterized by a passionate belief in separation of the races in the United States. Baldwin described his visit to the Chicago mansion of the Honorable Elijah Muhammad, leader of the Black Muslim sect. In Baldwin's account of how he responded to Elijah Muhammad, he presents himself as a dispassionate and objective observer, weighing the pros and cons of Black Muslim mythology:

> For the horrors of the American Negro's life there has been almost no language. . . . And, in fact, the truth about the black man, as a historical entity

> and as a human being, *has* been hidden from him deliberately and cruelly; . . . Why, then, is it not possible that all things began with the black man and that he was perfect—especially since this is precisely the claim white people have put forward for themselves all these years? Furthermore, it is now absolutely clear that white people are a minority in the world—so severe a minority that they now look rather more like an invention—and they cannot possibly hope to rule it any longer. If this is so, why is it not also possible that they achieved their original dominance through stealth and cunning and bloodshed and in opposition to the will of Heaven, and not, as they claim, by Heaven's will? And if this is so, then the sword they have used so long against others can now, without mercy, be used against them. (*The Fire Next Time*, pp. 83-84)

By taking the reader through the logic of the Black Muslim theology, by explaining its mythology and then rejecting it with cogent arguments of his own, Baldwin sets the stage for his exhortative closing.

If Uncle Tom symbolizes the monumental dignity and incandescent integrity of a Christian life, so the symbolic Negro is Baldwin's "martyr" in *The Fire Next Time*. The intensity, tone, and indeed the substance of his rhetoric at the essay's end are reminiscent of Stowe's own. It is as though, one hundred years after Emancipation, Stowe returns through Baldwin from her grave to appropriate with extraordinary eloquence the idiom of contemporary America when Baldwin writes:

> This past, the Negro's past, of rope, fire, torture, castration, infanticide, rape; death and humiliation; fear by day and night, fear as deep as the marrow of the bone; doubt that he was worthy of life, since everyone around him denied it; sorrow for his women, for his kinfolk, for his children, who needed his protection, and whom he could not protect; rage, hatred, and murder, hatred for white men so deep that it often turned against him and his own, and made all love, all trust, all joy impossible—this past, this endless struggle to achieve and reveal and confirm a human identity, human authority, yet contains for all its horror, something very beautiful. . . .

> That man who is forced each day to snatch his manhood, his identity out of the fire of human cruelty that rages to destroy it knows, if he survives his effort, and even if he does not survive it, something about himself and human life that no school on earth—and no church—can teach. He achieves his own authority, and that is unshakable. (*The Fire Next Time*, pp. 112-13)

Baldwin concludes his essay with this passionate prophecy:

> If we—and now I mean the relatively conscious whites and the relatively conscious blacks, who must, like lovers, insist on, or create, the consciousness of the others—do not falter in our duty now, we may be able, handful that we are, to end the racial nightmare, and achieve our country and change the history of the world. If we do not now dare everything, the fulfillment of that prophecy, recreated from the Bible in a song by a slave, is upon us: God gave Noah the rainbow sign, no more water, the fire next time. (*The Fire Next Time*, pp. 119-20)

This passage seems to me to reveal the hidden mother text. It is more than a matter of Baldwin's explicit references to "prophecy," "a slave," to God and the Bible. It is his direct appeal to conscience. Here are the final sentences of *Uncle Tom's Cabin*, the hidden mother text:

> A day of grace is yet held out to us. Both North and South have been guilty before God; and the *Christian Church* has a heavy account to answer. Not by combining together, to protect injustice and cruelty and making a common capital of sin, is this union to be saved,—but by repentance, justice and mercy; for, not surer is the eternal law by which the millstone sinks in the ocean, than that stronger law by which injustice and cruelty shall bring on nations the wrath of Almighty God! (*Uncle Tom's Cabin*, pp. 476-77)

The tone and substance of Stowe's remarks are strikingly similar to Baldwin's. Baldwin predicts that "historical vengeance, cosmic vengeance" will be inevitable if no change occurs in America's mind and heart. He warns of "the fire next time." Stowe warns of "the wrath of Almighty God." Both works are exhortative pleas for the fulfillment of the extraordinary promises of democracy. Each writer views the black American as the test of America's achievement of its democratic dream.

In "Everybody's Protest Novel" Baldwin foresees his own ambivalent position as a polemicist and as a serious novelist. His early essays bear witness to those paradoxical revelations. Thus, in his ambitious effort to identify the aesthetic limitations of *Uncle Tom's Cabin*, he brings up Wright's *Native Son*:

> Below the surface of this novel there lies, as it seems to me, a continuation, a complement of that monstrous legend it was written to destroy. Bigger is Uncle Tom's descendant, flesh of his flesh, so exactly opposite a portrait that, when the books are placed together, it seems that the contemporary Negro novelist and the dead New England woman are locked together in a deadly, timeless battle; the one uttering merciless exhortations, the other shouting curses. And, indeed, within this web of lust and fury, black and white can only thrust and counter-thrust, long for each other's slow exquisite death. ("Everybody's Protest Novel," p. 22)

It is often stressed that these comments led to Wright's and Baldwin's famous quarrel. This may be partly true. Their personal relationship is somewhat beside the point in the present critical context. Here we look at literary connections. Baldwin views *Native Son* as counterproductive and limited because it is a novel of social protest. Wright, by presenting Bigger Thomas as a symbolic or representative black American, so Baldwin complained, fuels the sentimental love and subconscious hatred of those who viewed blacks as either objects of pity and sympathy or of contempt and scorn. The novel, Baldwin writes, is "a complement of that monstrous legend it was written to destroy." That sort of assessment may seem extreme to readers now, but *Native*

Son was published fourteen years before *Brown v. Board of Education of Topeka, Kansas*. There is abundant evidence that the black image in the collective white liberal mind then was reminiscent of the romantic racialism of Stowe's era. The manner in which Baldwin's essay connects Stowe and Wright is striking. In a resonant congruity of metaphorical rhetoric and aesthetic critique, Baldwin discusses the Stowe-Wright connection in terms of interracial intercourse or miscegenation, describing Wright and Stowe as "locked together" in "a web of lust and fury." "Black and white can only thrust and counter-thrust." Stowe, he says, is "uttering merciless exhortations"; Wright is "shouting curses." Bigger, then, is conceived in a century-old totemic bed of misguided racial assumptions and taboos. He is "Uncle Tom's descendant, flesh of his flesh." His fate is prenatally sealed. He will necessarily be a hybrid creature of mixed aesthetic blood and uncertain social direction. He will, having been brought so traumatically and stereotypically to life, necessarily hate and murder in his protest against the artistic circumstances of his novelistic debut and also against his dim perception of his own life and death.

It is perhaps an instance of unconscious intent that Baldwin would, in his first published statement on Stowe and Wright, employ a metaphor of miscegenation. Stowe, with her religion of judgment and salvation, is, in a crucial literary sense, Baldwin's dead, white, nineteenth-century mother, and Wright, with his spirit of existential and violent defiance, is Baldwin's contemporary father. Their visions compete to meet "the Negro problem" or "the American dilemma." They leave Baldwin their complex and troubling double legacy.

Notes

1. The American version of "Everybody's Protest Novel" appeared in *Partisan Review*, June 1949. But the essay first appeared in *Zero*, a small French magazine. Ironically, Wright asked the editor of *Zero* to publish Baldwin's article, although he was unaware at the time of the latter's critical comments on *Native Son*. For a fuller discussion of this issue, see Michel Fabre, *The Unfinished Quest of Richard Wright* (New York: William Morrow & Co., Inc., 1973), pp. 362-63; see Irving Howe, "James Baldwin: At Ease in Apocalypse," *James Baldwin: A Collection of Critical Essays*, ed. Keneth Kinnamon (Englewood Cliffs, N.J.: Prentice-Hall, Inc., 1974), p. 97.

2. The work of Macebuh and Pratt are representative examples.

3. James Baldwin, "Everybody's Protest Novel," *Notes of a Native Son* (Boston: Beacon Press, 1955, 1984), pp. 15-16.

4. Jane Tompkins, *Sensational Designs: The Cultural Work of American Fiction, 1790-1860* (New York: Oxford University Press, 1985).

5. Ibid., p. 122.

6. Ibid., p. 123.

7. Tompkins argues that *Uncle Tom's Cabin* "stands opposed to works like [George Eliot's] *Middlemarch* and [Henry James's] *The Portrait of a Lady* in which everything depends on human action unfolding in a temporal sequence that withholds revelation until the final moment." Tompkins, *Sensational Designs*, p. 134.

8. Ibid., p. 135

9. Ibid., pp. 141-42.

10. Ibid., p. 141.

11. Ibid., p. xi.

12. Leslie A. Fiedler, *The Inadvertent Epic: From* Uncle Tom's Cabin *to* Roots (New York: Simon and Schuster, 1979).

13. Ibid., p. 16.

14. Ibid., p. 17.

15. Ibid., p. 27.

16. Alexis de Tocqueville, *Democracy in America* (New York: Vintage Books, 1945), pp. 343-452.

17. Robert B. Stepto, *From Behind the Veil: A Study of Afro-American Narrative* (Urbana: University of Illinois Press, 1979).

18. *Slave Testimony: Two Centuries of Letters, Speeches, Interviews, and Autobiographies*, ed. John W. Blassingame (Baton Rouge: Louisiana State University Press, 1977), p. xli.

19. Thomas F. Gossett, *Uncle Tom's Cabin and American Culture* (Dallas: Southern Methodist University Press, 1985), pp. 107-8.

20. Frederick Douglass, *Narrative of Life of Frederick Douglass, An American Slave, Written by Himself* (New York: Doubleday, 1845, 1963); William Craft, *Running a Thousand Miles for Freedom: Or the Escape of William and Ellen Craft from Slavery* (New York: Arno, 1860, 1970); Harriet Brent Jacobs, *Incidents in the Life of a Slave Girl: Mrs. Harriet Brent Jacobs, Written by Herself* (New York: AMS Press, 1861, 1973). Although Craft's and Brent's narratives were published after *Uncle Tom's*

Cabin, we know that many of the slaves wrote their stories years after delivering lectures before various antislavery societies. Thus, their stories were a part of an abolitionist oral history. Moreover, in the specific case of Brent, she lived with a distinguished abolitionist family for over a decade before writing her narratives.

21. Thomas F. Gossett, *Uncle Tom's Cabin and American Culture* (Dallas: Southern Methodist University Press, 1985), p. 3.

22. James Baldwin, *The Fire Next Time* (New York: The Dial Press, 1963), p. 119.

23. Harriet Beecher Stowe, *Uncle Tom's Cabin* (New York: New American Library, 1966), p. v.

Faith in Verse and Fiction:
James Baldwin's, Phillis Wheatley's, Octavia E. Butler's, and Tananarive Due's Creation of a Peaceful Space

Mildred R. Mickle

There is no question that James Baldwin was a remarkable human being and a phenomenal literary artist. The best of his stories, novels, and essays are a testament to his unflinching quest for honesty and self-knowledge. He sought the truth in both his writings and his interviews, even though, as he acknowledged in a 1987 interview with Quincy Troupe, many Americans could not accept him or the truth he told them (*Conversations* 290). Yet despite the racism and homophobia he met with, Baldwin persevered. As Troupe notes:

> He hoped that I and other writers would continue to be witnesses of our time; that we must speak out against institutionalized and individual tyranny wherever we found it. Because if left unchecked, it threatens to engulf and subjugate us all—the fire this time. (290)

Baldwin knew that if one does not denounce dishonesty and immorality, then one breaks faith with oneself. By pursuing truth, by putting his faith in his work, he provides readers with a central lesson: in order to find and retain faith, one must be sincere. The literary tradition of engaging religious faith and faith in oneself through fiction and poetry is an excellent lens through which to examine how Baldwin's works fit within African American letters. This essay will compare and contrast how James Baldwin's *Go Tell It on the Mountain*, Phillis Wheatley's "On Being Brought from Africa to America," Tananarive Due's *My Soul to Keep*, and Octavia E. Butler's *Parable of the Sower* explore conceptions of faith in verse and fiction to create a peaceful space in which history, mind, and body can meld and thrive.

Baldwin is neither the first nor the last African American to grapple with faith and sincerity. African American literature's engagement with religious faith and faith in the self extends back to the eighteenth century, to the first narratives that enslaved Africans dictated to amanuenses. As Henry Louis Gates, Jr., explains in his introduction to *The Classic Slave Narratives*, these early slave narratives were largely focused not on the atrocities of slavery but on the Africans' conversion to Christianity from what was deemed their heathen religions (ix-xviii). It was not until the latter part of the eighteenth century that enslaved Africans attained the wherewithal to write and publish their own stories about their experiences of slavery. One author in particular, Phillis Wheatley, stands out because she demonstrated to future generations of African American writers the powers of education and sincerity. Her poem "On Being Brought from Africa to America," published in *Poems on Various Subjects, Religious and Moral* (1773), provides a model of revolution against tyranny and immorality. Wheatley writes:

> 'Twas mercy brought me from my *Pagan* land,
> Taught my benighted soul to understand
> That there's a God, that there's a *Saviour* too:
> Once I redemption neither sought nor knew.
> Some view our sable race with scornful eye,
> 'Their color is a diabolic die.'
> Remember, *Christians*, *Negros*, black as *Cain*,
> May be refin'd, and join th' angelic train.
>
> (98)

Certainly, this is one of Wheatley's most controversial poems because on the surface it sounds like a Christian conversion piece and an endorsement of slavery. Yet it is much more complex than that: Gates contends that it is a tribute to Wheatley's providential relationship with her mistress, Susannah Wheatley, who nurtured her mind instead of abusing her as many slave owners did their slaves (*Trials* 83). And it was because of Susannah Wheatley's care that Phillis Wheatley was able to win the patronage of the Countess of Huntingdon to expedite the publication of her poems. But "On Being Brought from Africa to America" also lends itself to other interpretations, particularly when one studies Wheatley's other poems and learns of her life. Because of she was a slave, American law did not recognize her as a full person entitled to the law's protection or of equal status to white people. To appeal to a colonial readership, her poems had to present a humble, innocent, moral, but erudite persona. She played off of the colonists' desire for freedom from Britain and sought to convince them that she, too, valued freedom above all else. By aligning her values so closely with those of her readership, Wheatley had an excellent platform upon which to project her belief that true Christians would strive to free both the colonists and the enslaved Africans.

"On Being Brought from Africa to America" is a poem about agency. It is shows its author coming of age and demonstrating that she has found a strong voice with which to tell her story of salvation from the evils of slavery and discrimination. It is the voice of a young woman acknowledging that she cannot control whether people see her as ugly or subhuman, and it is an affirmation of her faith in her own beauty and humanity in the compassionate eyes of her Christian God. It is her poignant call for a reconciliation of the barbarity of the Middle Passage with Christian love and compassion; for a serious consideration of the trials enslaved Africans were forced to endure during the Middle Passage; and for an effort to end the trafficking of humans. Some may argue against this interpretation because Wheatley's age, poor health, and good fortune kept her from ever knowing manual labor, sexual exploitation, much of the atrocities of the Middle Passage, or all of the horrors of the sugar cane plantations of the West Indies. However, she did live and interact with other enslaved Africans who worked for the Wheatleys, and she could have heard and certainly read about the suffering of other enslaved people.

"On Being Brought from Africa to America" is one of the primary texts that encode African American literary struggle to syncretize religious faith and faith in the self in a world that perceives people of color as less than fully human. Finally, the poem is one of the first in the tradition of moral protest against the white lies that fueled the transatlantic slave trade and compromised America's founding principles of freedom and tolerance for all. It paves the way for later African American writers, including James Baldwin, who would draw on their faith—both in religion and in themselves—to call for love, compassion, and the acceptance of difference.

Though Baldwin never had to face the horrors of slavery, he did, like Phillis Wheatley, have to combat those who dismissed him because of his dark skin. Further, like Wheatley, who traveled to England to oversee the publication of her book, he had to travel to Europe to be free to live and publish, although, unlike Wheatley, he spent most of his adult life abroad. And, like Wheatley, he used his art to express his faith in himself and to encourage others to strive for self-acceptance. He fictionalizes his struggle with faith in his masterpiece *Go Tell It on the Mountain* (1953), a three-part novel that chronicles how a teenage boy, John Grimes, weathers conflicts with his father, his dysfunctional family, his ambivalence about his sexuality and appearance, and his community's high expectations of him.

As the novel begins, John feels vaguely dissatisfied with, yet accepting of, the role his family and community have cast him in—the upright minister's son who someday will carry on his father's work. Yet John has lost his faith in God. At fourteen, he is too young to understand why his father has turned away from the world, and it is by questioning his father's anger that John begins his quest for self-determination. In the end, it is this very questioning and ultimate rejection of his father that brings John to find faith and love within himself. Early on, as one of John's teachers praises him, John has an epiphany about himself that frees him to differentiate himself from his father and community and better understand who he is and what he wants from life:

> He apprehended totally, without belief or understanding, that he had in himself a power that other people lacked; that he could use this to save himself, to raise himself; and that, perhaps, with this power he might one day win that love which he so longed for. This was not, in John, a faith subject to death or alteration, nor yet a hope subject to destruction; it was his identity, and part, therefore, of that wickedness for which his father beat him and to which he clung to withstand his father . . . yet his father could never be entirely the victor, for John cherished something that his father could not reach. It was his hatred and his intelligence that he cherished, the one feeding the other. . . . though he had been born in the faith . . . John's heart was hardened against the Lord. His father was God's minister, the ambassador of the King of Heaven, and John could not bow before the throne of grace without first kneeling to his father. On his refusal to do this had his life depended, and John's secret heart had flourished in its wickedness until the day his sin first overtook him. (20-21)

In addition to his father, Gabriel, John struggles with his dark skin and African facial features. He and his community have been told all of their lives that, as Wheatley put it, their "color is a diabolic die." Yet when John wipes away the dust from a mirror so that he can inspect his face:

> With a shock he saw that his face had not changed, that the hand of Satan was as yet invisible. . . . He tried to look at it as a stranger might, and tried to discover what other people saw. . . . two great eyes, and a broad, low forehead, and the triangle of his nose, and his enormous mouth, and the barely perceptible cleft in his chin, which was, his father said, the mark of the devil's little finger. These details did not help him, for the principle of their unity was undiscoverable, and he could not tell what he most passionately desired to know: whether his face was ugly or not. (27)

In this scene, Baldwin throws into question the widespread view that only whiteness is beautiful. John wipes away the grime of white perceptions of beauty and, failing to see himself as ugly or evil, he begins his progression toward realizing his own beauty. That he doubts whether he truly looks evil shows that he has not internalized negative stereotypes as his family has and marks another step in his journey to trust himself. He finds hope and faith in what his eyes see, not in what others tell him he should see.

In the second part of the novel, Baldwin shows the antithesis of John's burgeoning faith by revealing his family's history of abuse and torment at the hands of racism. Carol E. Henderson had compared the significance of this and the third part of Baldwin's novel with Toni Morrison's *Beloved* in her essay "Refiguring the Flesh: The Word, the Body, and the Rituals of Being in *Beloved* and *Go Tell It on the Mountain*," in which she focuses on the symbol of "the threshing floor." She states:

> Although John's transformation on the threshing floor frames the vantage point from which the reader comes to understand not only the process of redemption but also John's development from child to man, Baldwin also positions the ritual of testifying as the mechanism that makes plain the spiritual pain of the other characters in the narrative, detailing in excruciating fashion the injuries to their souls. Florence, Gabriel, and Elizabeth form a collective triune that reflects upon the racial and gendered subjugation of African American people and allegorizes the journey of self-realization in terms that articulate John's ambivalent relationship with this ancestral and familial past. (152)

In the second part of the novel Baldwin chronicles how Florence, Gabriel, and Deborah have relied too heavily on the external referents of faith and how they have become embittered as they have been betrayed by these false things. Florence's constant use of cosmetics in the vain hope of having lighter skin symbolizes her larger attempt to escape from the abuse her black skin has brought on her by racist whites in the South and the North. She does not realize that she is perpetuating the rejection of herself by trying to emulate the aesthetic standards of people who despise her. Unlike John, who wipes the white dust from the mirror to see himself, Florence tries to cover herself with whiteness and thereby makes her true beauty inaccessible. Gabriel, in turn, internalizes the stereotypes that cast blackness as evil and seeks to counter them with his preaching. Rather than facing the true roots of his anger—discrimination, his dissatisfaction with his life, and his infidelity to his wife—he represses them and then unleashes his anger on his family. He puts his faith in the trappings of religion and the appearance of morality by denouncing the sins of others, but he knows that he is a fraud and a coward for not facing his own failings. John's mother, Elizabeth, puts her faith in her marriage to Gabriel, whom she sees as a redeemer who will save her from the tragedy she experienced with John's father; however, she has yet to come to terms with her grief and loss. Rather than look inside herself for affirmation, she seeks affirmation from and centers her hopes on her marriage and family.

Witnessing the turmoil of his family, John knows that none of them is happy with their conceptions of faith. As he goes through his conversion, he decides that he cannot perpetuate their destructive paths of rejecting black beauty, preaching faith in a wrathful god, or and hanging on to a loveless marriage. In his moment of conviction, he finds his faith more within himself than in God:

> John struggled to speak the authoritative, the living word that would conquer the great division between his father and himself. But it did not come, the living word; in the silence something died in John, and something came alive. It came to him that he must testify . . . 'I'm saved,' he said, 'and I know I'm saved.' . . . 'I'm going to pray God,' said John—and his voice shook, whether with joy or grief he could not say—'to keep me, and make me strong . . . to stand . . . to stand against the enemy . . . and against everything and everybody . . . that wants to cut down my soul.' (207)

In the heat of his conversion, John faces the demons—his family's past that informs their current unhappiness. He respects their perseverance, but he sees that the external referents they put their faith in are flawed. In a bittersweet moment that marks his separation from them, he rejects their conceptions of faith and resolves to choose his own path. John's revolt from familial and societal expectations is liberating and terrifying, for he knows his path will not be easy. Yet, as he faces the fear and ecstasy of determining what faith means to him, he finds peace.

Baldwin's *Go Tell It on the Mountain* continues Phillis Wheatley's call to resist tyranny with hope and faith as well as her conviction of the power of the written word to argue for compassion. John's path demonstrates how one individual can face an oppressive history and society, and yet not be overcome by them. Though he may not be able to control racism, his father's anger or zealotry, or his homosexuality, he is not undone by them because he is honest with himself, because he keeps faith with himself. By the end of the novel, his desire for the truth enables him to confront these obstacles, and it is this desire that gives him the faith that he can overcome them.

Later in his career, Baldwin would also stress the importance of understanding history and using one's knowledge of it to overcome it, to make a better future. Years after *Go Tell It on the Mountain* was first published, he stated in a 1973 interview with *The Black Scholar*:

> History was someone you touched, you know, on Sunday mornings or in the barbershop. It's all around you. It's in the music, it's in the way you talk, it's in the way you cry, it's in the way you make love. Because you are denied your official history you are forced to excavate your real history even though you can never say that's what you are doing. That is what you are doing. That is one of the reasons for the lifestyle of Black Americans, which is a real life style as distinguished from the total anonymity of white Americans who have so much history, all of which they believe. They are absolutely choked with it. They can't move because all the lies that they

have told themselves, they actually think is their history. We were able to raise our children because we had a real sense of the past. . . . the present and to have a hell of a lot of apprehension for the future so that the kid had to be prepared. All you have is your history, and you had to translate that through everything that you did, so the kid would live. That is called love, too. You try to become in a sense a model. (150-51)

John's story in *Go Tell It on the Mountain* prompted generations of readers to view the things they put their faith in more closely and to question their viability. Baldwin's literary critique of faith in religion and in the self set the stage for two women who published in the 1990s, Tananarive Due and Octavia E. Butler, both of whom furthered the act of questioning conceptions of faith. In Due's supernatural thriller *My Soul to Keep* (1997), faith becomes a living embodiment of history; in Butler's *Parable of the Sower* (1993), faith is shown to be malleable, a creative foundation for hope.

In "Representing the Black Male Body," an essay appearing in *Art on My Mind*, bell hooks writes:

The black body had always received attention within the framework of white supremacy, as racist/sexist iconography had been deployed to perpetuate notions of innate biological inferiority. Against this cultural backdrop, every movement for black liberation in this society, whether reformist or radical, has had to formulate a counter hegemonic discourse of the body to effectively resist white supremacy. In reformist agendas, that discourse invariably took the form of repression and erasure. If black men were seen as beasts, as rapists, as *bodies out of control*, reformist movements for racial uplift countered these stereotypes by revering the refined, restrained, desexualized black male body. If black women were depicted as sexual savages, hot pussies on the lookout for ready prey, then these stereotypes were countered by images of virtuous, repressed black ladyhood. . . . combined with a critique of white racist stereotypes. (202-03; emphasis added)

Traditionally in America and throughout the global sites affected by the slave trade, the black body, both female and male, has been a text molded and shaped by slave traders, slaveholders, and those people who directly or indirectly participated in or benefited from the subjugation and oppression of peoples of African descent. As such, the black body as text represents a repository of historico-aesthetic and commodificatory misappropriation, and black scholars, critics, and artists have sought and continue to seek avenues for both *exploring* the history of the black body as a created text of stereotypes and *reappropriating* the black body as it should be conceived: an individuated, human, humane, and beautiful site that resists normation. Tananarive Due's *My Soul to Keep* follows in this avenue as it explores and reappropriates the black body as text, portraying the black body as the subject of a subjected and subjective history. Due's male protagonist, Dawit, and her male antagonist, Khaldun, both ingest an agent of their faith to become immortal, and, as representatives of the indestructible and regenerative faith of history, their black immortal bodies are a key structuring device of the novel.

Dawit and his immortal Brethren have been injected with the Living Blood—that is, blood taken from Christ after his crucifixion—which makes them immortal. *My Soul* centers on Dawit's struggles with his love for mortals and his charge to not reveal his immortality to them. Due dramatizes this conflict through Dawit's relationship with a slave woman, Adele, particularly in the scene in which they are lynched.

> Before he could fight it, the horrible image swallowed Dawit's memories: Adele's naked corpse swinging from a rope tied around the thick branch of a tree. Adele's face, which had kissed his, wrenched in painful death; her fingers, which had owned his private parts, bumping lifeless against her hipbones. He hadn't remembered, until his eyes had seen Adele's twirling carcass, what a mortal's death meant. An end. A silenced voice. A stolen laugh. An emptied brain. Forever gone.
>
> His own lynching had been sweet relief, for a precious moment. He

> swung beside Adele for a full day, moaning and sobbing, the rope slicing into his neck, always seeking to make him quiet. Three times, he gave the rope its victory; when his breath stopped, when he felt his cervical vertebra about to snap beneath his flesh, he did not fight. He let death come. And when he awakened, each time gasping to breathe, new tears waiting, he let death come again. And again. His last sight, always, was Adele. (40)

The tension between Dawit's immortality and his love for a woman—who, as a woman, is not allowed to become part of the Brethren because she may give birth to more immortals and jeopardize the Brethren's secrecy—is indicative of the larger struggles black men have both individually and as a collective mired in history. Due reveals white hegemonic voyeurism and interference in black sexual relations when the slaveholder Lowell Mason attempts to breed the enslaved Dawit and Adele as cattle, as well as when the white men who capture the couple as they are running away from Mason gang-rape and lynch Adele and then lynch Dawit. As Due makes clear, Dawit's and Adele's sexuality and capacity to create human life are not things to be manipulated. They resist the slaveholder's efforts to own their bodies, to define their sexuality as bestial or "out of control," and to increase his wealth by refusing to bring a child into the world and by running away. Yet their resistance results in the violation and death of Adele and Dawit's three unsuccessful attempts to die, which allude to the three days Christ was dead before he rose. However, though Dawit is immortal, his continuous resurrections are a sad mimicry of the crucifixion and resurrection of Christ. They bring him no joy, only eternal life and separation from his love. His continued existence, and his lack of any rope scars to mark the legacy of enslavement and the violation of his humanity into his flesh, marks the continuing violent legacy of lynching that, although hidden from the general public because it is not taught as a part of American history, still affects the mental and emotional psyche of black and white men and women. Dawit's skin is smooth and untouched, but his violation has been burned into his memory. Due suggests with this image that, although future generations of black and white Americans do not bear the physical marks of slavery or lynching and although the American educational system has sought to erase the violence of slavery and lynching from America's past, this violent legacy still lives on in our present-day psyches. Through the rest of the novel, Dawit's relationships with women are constantly severed by the constraints of time. Though he has no visible scars from the lynching, he bears the invisible, mental scars for eternity.

As immortals, Dawit and his Brethren are metaphors for the mysterious and alien African and African American past that has been obscured first by the upheaval of the Atlantic slave trade and then by apathy and the conscious efforts of some historians to write Africans and African Americans out of history. We see this obscuration in the ritual Khaldun, the first Brother, performs to prove his immortality to the men he seeks to initiate into immortality. Khaldun explains to the initiates:

> "The Ritual of Life awakened me from the dead, and I drank what little blood remained. Its saltiness coated my throat. The Blood of Life is inside me. I have lived much like a hermit for many years, asking God to forgive me. But He does not hear my prayers because I have stolen from one of his favored children. So, I no longer seek redemption. I seek knowledge instead, because knowledge is infinite. And I seek pupils." (62)

He stabs his own side with a knife, wounding himself in a way that would be fatal for anyone else. Yet when Dawit opens his closed eyes, he "find[s] Khaldun standing before him, wearing the smile of a father. His bloody scar is gone, his belly healed with barely a trace of the knife's treachery" (64).

In Khaldun's macabre ritual, the unknown African past reveals itself. Having lived for centuries, he, whose true self is hidden to all but those who undergo the ritual of death, is a repository of African knowledge and history. And though the African past may be buried, it, like his body, is indestructible and always lives on to shape others' lives. To know this past, then, to accumulate centuries of hidden knowledge, one must sacrifice one's mortality. Through Khaldun and the other brethren, Due asks why it is that one must die to receive life or to touch the African past and whether the sacrifice is worth it. As she shows with Dawit's conflicted feelings about immortality and other mortals, there are no easy answers to this question.

With Khaldun and Dawit, Due also questions the very notion of humanity. Khaldun, as immortal history and historian, lives outside the realm of humanity, and, as empowering as his eternal life and his freedom to seek knowledge are, his immortal nature confounds the very history he embodies. He is dead to the world of humans, yet he lives. He is human history, yet he cannot directly share his knowledge or himself with humans. Nor can he create history with humans, for to interact with them would be to compromise his freedom to seek knowledge and to remain an inviolable repository of the African past.

Like Khaldun, Dawit is a repository of history; however, he differs from Khaldun in that he consciously inserts himself into African and African American history. Unlike Khaldun—who paradoxically is an immortal repository of human history yet does not interact with mortals so that he can remain untouched by them and pure—Dawit does interact with mortals. Khaldun is inviolate; Dawit is violated through his enslavement and through the damage that arises from his general interactions with humans. He also interacts directly with humans and visibly creates history. During his enslavement in America, for instance, he attempts to escape and is given one hundred lashes. Yet his back heals completely overnight. The whipping is the slaveholder's attempt to make a slave of Dawit, yet Dawit's power to heal his whip-scarred back reveals the slaveholder's failure to enslave him. With Dawit and Khaldun, Due asks whether it better to live pure and inviolate and not share knowledge with others outside one's intimate group or to live and risk impurity and share knowledge with and learn from others outside one's intimate group. Again, there are no easy answers as regards the purity of history.

By giving her Brethren immortality, Due reinforces Baldwin's assertion that history lives on in people, whether they are aware of it or not—that tangible history surrounds us and lives on in us, seen and yet unseen, perceived and yet not truly understood. She urges us to make an effort to reexamine what is before our eyes and within our homes and discover how things unseen shape us. Only then can we create our own peaceful spaces.

While Due places her faith in the engagement with living embodiments of history, Octavia E. Butler's conception of faith in *Parable of the Sower* is much more flexible. She writes:

> *God is Power–*
> *Infinite,*
> *Irresistible,*
> *Inexorable,*
> *Indifferent.*
> *And yet, God is Pliable–*
> *Trickster,*
> *Teacher,*
> *Chaos,*
> *Clay.*
> *God exists to be shaped.*
> *God is Change.*
>
> (22)

God is something to which one can give form; his shape depends upon one's imagination and need. Yet, because it can be crafted, it can sometimes lull one into complacency, and its ability to evolve indeterminately may upset the unprepared. *Parable of the Sower* is a story about Lauren Olamina, an African American teenager coming of age in a dystopian America. Like Baldwin's John in *Go Tell It on the Mountain*, she struggles to reconcile her father's Christianity with what she needs to survive. Unlike John, Lauren is not a homosexual, nor does her father abuse her. He provides for his family, and for a while they survive in America in the 2020s while other families are homeless and enslaved. While John clings to the tenets of Christianity, Lauren looks within and designs a new religion, Earthseed, whose god is simultaneously static and mobile. Surrounded by drug addiction, murder, and rape, Lauren puts her faith in the paradox that the one constant we can rely on is "change." This frees her to adapt to the horrors she encounters once she loses her family and to gather a new family, a congregation that has no color, gender, or sexual restrictions. She decides to use her faith to help others face the changes they encounter in a dystopian American state.

Lauren's faith enables her and her followers to respond to aspects of human nature that are difficult to understand or control; to deal with ostracism; and to negotiate radical changes to their environment or worldview. As Lauren travels and spreads her religion, she discovers the depth of the courage her faith brings her. Her faith and her need to help others adapt it to their own lives are what bring her hope.

Lauren is true to herself and her goal to create a peaceful space amid the chaos of an apocalypse. But her quest does not end with spreading her religion. Butler writes:

> We are all Godseed, but no more or less
> So than any other aspect of the universe,
> Godseed is all there is—all that
> Changes. Earthseed is all that spreads
> Earthlife to new earths. The universe is
> Godseed. Only we are Earthseed. And the
> Destiny of Earthseed is to take root among
> the stars.
>
> (68)

A central part of Lauren's Earthseed faith is encouraging the faithful to travel to other planets to test the limits of humanity's ability to adapt and survive. It is daunting to dream of space travel when life on Earth is precarious, but Lauren realizes that what allows people to survive in the face of adversity is the hope of achieving something great. It is not enough to simply react to the challenges of life; humans need loftier challenges. The novel ends with Lauren and her Earthseed family settling into a property in Oregon and making plans to create a thriving community that will someday travel in space.

James Baldwin was untiring in his fight for honesty. His integrity continues to influence writers to have faith in the power of their imaginations. *Go Tell It on the Mountain* carries on a literary investigation of faith that Phillis Wheatley began in the eighteenth century and encourages contemporary writers such as Tananarive Due and Octavia E. Butler to take interrogations of faith to further heights. For Baldwin, to write his own truth in a world full of deception was a daunting enterprise, but not to do so would have been a living death. His own words attest to that conviction and are a fitting way to remember him. He writes in his poem "Amen":

> No, I don't feel death coming.
> I feel death going:
> having thrown up his hands,
> for the moment.
>
> I feel like I know him
> better than I did.
> Those arms held me,
> for a while,
> and, when we meet again,
> there will be that secret knowledge
> between us.
>
> (1-11)

Works Cited

Baldwin, James. "Amen." *Jimmy's Blues: Selected Poems*. New York: St. Martin's Press, 1983. 75.

___________. "*The Black Scholar* Interviews James Baldwin." 1973. *Conversations with James Baldwin*. Ed. Fred L. Standley and Louis H. Pratt. Jackson: UP of Mississippi, 1989. 142-58.

___________. *Collected Essays*. New York: Library of America, 1998.

___________. *Go Tell It on the Mountain*. 1953. New York: Dell, 1985.

___________. "James Baldwin, 1924-1987: A Tribute—The Last Interview." Interview by Quincy Troupe. 1988. *Conversations with James Baldwin*. Ed. Fred L. Standley and Louis H. Pratt. Jackson: UP of Mississippi, 1989. 287-92.

___________. "Last Testament: An Interview with James Baldwin." Interview by Quincy Troupe. 1988. *Conversations with James Baldwin*. Ed. Fred L. Standley and Louis H. Pratt. Jackson: UP of Mississippi, 1989. 281-86.

Butler, Octavia E. *Parable of the Sower*. New York: Warner Books, 1993.

Due, Tananarive. *My Soul to Keep*. New York: HarperPrism, 1997.

Gates, Henry Louis, Jr. *The Trials of Phillis Wheatley: America's First Black Poet and Encounters with the Founding Fathers*. New York: Basic Civitas Books, 2003.

___________, ed. *The Classic Slave Narratives*. New York: Mentor, 1987.

Henderson, Carol E. "Refiguring the Flesh: The Word, the Body, and the Rituals of Being in *Beloved* and *Go Tell It on the Mountain*." *James Baldwin and Toni Morrison: Comparative Critical and Theoretical Essays*. Ed. Lovalerie King and Lynn Orilla Scott. New York: Palgrave Macmillan, 2006. 149-65.

Hill, Patricia Liggins. "Phillis Wheatley (1753?-1784)." *Call and Response: The Riverside Anthology of the African American Literary Tradition*. Ed. Patricia Liggins Hill. Boston: Houghton Mifflin, 1998. 92-97.

hooks, bell. "Representing the Black Male Body." *Art on My Mind: Visual Politics*. New York: New Press, 1995. 202-12.

Lorde, Audre. *Sister Outsider: Essays and Speeches*. Freedom, CA: Crossing Press, 1996.

Wheatley, Phillis. "On Being Brought from Africa to America." *Call and Response: The Riverside Anthology of the African American Literary Tradition*. Ed. Patricia Liggins Hill. Boston: Houghton Mifflin, 1998. 98.

James Baldwin's Critical Reception

D. Quentin Miller

Although literary critics, anthology editors, college professors, and other canon-makers agree that James Baldwin is one of the major American writers of the twentieth century, Baldwin's literary legacy is slippery. As a writer who bore the burden of representing so many identities on the margins of American society—bisexual, African American, expatriate—Baldwin alternated between prominence and reclusiveness in his lifetime. He was fiercely opposed to labels of any kind, frustrating critics, professors, publishers, and students who have attempted to categorize him. Unquestionably the most prominent African American writer of the civil rights era—a celebrated public figure as well as an important author—Baldwin remains a writer whom nearly all critics consider essential. They just cannot agree on what makes him essential.

Part of the reason behind Baldwin's shifting legacy is that he was restless in his literary output and too complex a thinker to be contained by any single ideology or set of critical assumptions. The bulk of his writing, which was a steady and prolific outpouring from his early stories, reviews, and essays in the late 1940s until his death in 1987, is nearly evenly divided between fiction and nonfiction prose. Even this basic distinction in genre confounded critics, who tended to want to praise Baldwin's mastery of one genre while belittling his shortcomings in the other. (It is a critical commonplace, for instance, to say that Baldwin's novels have too much of the essayist in them or that his essays tend to repeat the stories that he tells better in fiction.) Caught up debating whether Baldwin should be remembered as an essayist or a novelist, his critics often overlook the other works that round out his oeuvre—three plays (the last unpublished), two collections of poetry, a book of film criticism, a photo-essay collaboration with Richard Avedon, a children's book, a screenplay about the life of Malcolm X . . . the list goes on. Critics have had a difficult time ascertaining whether

Baldwin was really a novelist or an essayist, not willing to acknowledge that he could be both and much more.

The history of Baldwin criticism can be seen in four distinct phases: (1) initial praise of the early works through *The Fire Next Time*, (2) denigration of the latter half of Baldwin's career during his lifetime, (3) appreciation and recovery in the years following Baldwin's death, and (4) reassessment in the late 1990s and in the first decade of the twenty-first century. Critical interest in Baldwin's works is higher now than it has been since the height of his fame in the early 1960s. Toni Morrison, the only living American who has won the Nobel Prize in Literature (and the only African American recipient of the award in history), recently edited two Library of America editions of Baldwin's work, one consisting of essays and one of novels. In a tribute following Baldwin's death Morrison wrote of him, "You gave me a language to dwell in, a gift so perfect it seems my own invention. I have been thinking your spoken and written thoughts for so long I believed they were mine" (in Troupe 76). Morrison's acknowledgment of Baldwin's deep influence on her work as well as the imprimatur of the venerable Library of America certainly testify to Baldwin's ongoing importance; yet, aside from the nearly ubiquitous short story "Sonny's Blues," it is possible that Baldwin may be overlooked by current students of literature.

It has not always been so. For previous generations of high school and college students, *Go Tell It on the Mountain* and *The Fire Next Time* were required reading. Future generations will undoubtedly be exposed to these works or others, for although Baldwin's reputation has waxed and waned, his ability to produce writings that remain relevant over time has never been in question. The only labels that have stuck to him are "witness" and "prophet," words that indicate his ability to see both his present and the future.

Baldwin clearly and concisely stated his life's goal in "Autobiographical Notes," the piece that opens his first essay collection, *Notes of a Native Son*; he wrote with marvelous understatement, "I want to be an honest man, and a good writer." For him, a "good writer" was a writer who was not content to pander to public taste or fame. Born in Harlem on August 2, 1924, Baldwin was not a likely candidate for literary stardom. The oldest of nine children, he and his siblings grew up in abject poverty. He never knew his biological father, and his stepfather, David Baldwin, was, according to Baldwin, a tyrant to his children. After David's death in 1943, Baldwin developed a guarded sympathy for him, as detailed in the 1955 essay "Notes of a Native Son," which suggests that David was mentally ill by the end of his life, a condition exacerbated by a life of poverty and racial persecution. David and Baldwin's mother, Berdis, had emigrated from the American south to Harlem during the Great Migration, and their experiences are rendered imaginatively in the middle section of *Go Tell It on the Mountain*.

Baldwin's burning ambition to leave Harlem is evident in his first novel, *Go Tell It on the Mountain*. Before fleeing, at the age of fifteen he underwent a violent religious conversion experience that, in the parlance of his church, changed him from a "sinner" to a "saint" and that rendered him a preacher for three years. His budding homosexuality and antagonistic relationship with his stepfather, who was also a preacher, led Baldwin to leave the church by the time he graduated from DeWitt Clinton High School. After spending time in Greenwich Village and after experiencing racism firsthand during a year in New Jersey, Baldwin fled the United States for Paris with little money, minimal knowledge of French, and no job or place to stay. He was following in the footsteps of Lost Generation writers such as Ernest Hemingway and F. Scott Fitzgerald and joining a new community of African American expatriates that included Richard Wright. This journey initiated his life as a self-described "transatlantic commuter." From that moment on he seemed unable to stay in any place for long, and he lived for varying periods in Turkey, San Francisco, New York (but not Harlem), and the south of France, where he died in 1987.

With the publication of his first novel, the bildungsroman *Go Tell It on the Mountain*, in 1953, Baldwin set up certain expectations among his readers. With its psychological depth and emotional honesty as well as its deep consideration of the centrality of Christian fundamentalism to the African American experience, the novel stood in contrast to Richard Wright's *Native Son* and Ralph Ellison's *Invisible Man*, the agreed-upon (if controversial) classics of African American fiction of the mid-twentieth century. But as Baldwin said in a 1963 interview, "After *Go Tell It on the Mountain*, everybody expected me to write another book just like it. I wasn't about to do that" (*Conversations* 33).

Baldwin's second novel, *Giovanni's Room*, is an excellent illustration of his resistance to rewriting his first novel over and over again and to speaking for any group. A novel set in Paris and lacking black characters, *Giovanni's Room* is an intense study of the way society enforces its values, particularly with regard to sexuality, at the peril of individuals as well as society as a whole. The novel is an existential classic in which the protagonist finds himself in what he considers to be an impossible ethical dilemma; whatever choice he makes he will suffer eternally for it. At the same time, it is a watershed moment in the history of gay literature and a novel of the end of American innocence in Europe in the tradition of Hemingway and Henry James (Baldwin's favorite American novelist). His readers, though, expected something else. Where was the young man who had given voice in fiction to the despair of the ghetto? Or the sharp-tongued essayist who was not afraid to declare, at the end of his 1953 essay "Stranger in the Village," "This world is white no longer, and it will never be white again"? *Giovanni's Room* is just the first of many examples of Baldwin baffling his critics and readers. His restlessness and boundless energy, coupled with the needs of a country in the midst of a profound cultural revolution, made for a dizzying career that remains a challenge to assess.

In addition to his commitment to experimentation and change, Baldwin's early reputation was established through a few battles he fought with the established literary giants of his time. In his essay "Many Thousands Gone," he offered a stiff critique of *Native Son* that faulted the novel for failing to humanize its antihero, Bigger Thomas. The essay was perceived as an all-out attack (by Wright as well as by his many devotees), and it served both to announce Baldwin as a gutsy new voice on the literary scene and to alienate some readers who clung to *Native Son* as *the* important breakthrough work in African American literary history. Baldwin's battle with Wright, which he believed was overblown and misconstrued, was followed by other battles with such luminaries as Langston Hughes and Norman Mailer, as well as curt dismissals of the Beat generation. He also ran afoul of certain radical Black Power activists through his friendship with William Styron, whose 1967 novel, *The Confessions of Nat Turner*, was vilified by a great number of African American writers and activists. Eldridge Cleaver, in his 1968 Black Power manifesto *Soul on Ice*, wrote a scathing, homophobic assessment of Baldwin titled "Notes on a Native Son." Cleaver clearly indicated that Baldwin was excluded from the most radical, hypermasculine version of late 1960s black activism because of his sexuality and also because of his friendships with white people, writing that Baldwin displayed "the most shameful, fanatical, fawning, sycophantic love of the whites that one can find in the writings of any black American writer of note in our time" (106). There were certainly other factors for Baldwin's rapid descent in the late 1960s from his position on top of the literary world in the early 1960s, but Cleaver's attack was prominent and indicated radical divisions in the African American community at the time. The times were undeniably turbulent, and Baldwin, who can safely be described as emotionally volatile, was very much affected by this turbulence.

Baldwin's periods of exile affected his literary reputation as much as anything else, for while he was in Europe completing his first two novels and his first two collections of essays, the civil rights movement was kicking into high gear in his home country. The American South was a hotbed of activism, protest, and violent suppression in the early 1960s, and Baldwin returned to America to visit the front lines of the racial struggle in order to witness, to report, and to speak. Baldwin was a tremendously effective public speaker, and he found himself articulating African American rage in the early 1960s in a variety of public forums. When he was featured on the cover of *Time* magazine on May 17, 1963, his reputation was solidified. The article stated, "In the U.S. today there is not another writer—white or black—who expresses with such poignancy and abrasiveness the dark realities of the racial ferment in North and South."

His third novel, *Another Country* (1962), was his most successful in terms of initial sales, though reviews of it were mixed. A sprawling tale of Greenwich Village bohemia, the novel took on taboo issues of interracial coupling and bisexual experimentation with characteristic frankness. Baldwin's 1962 essay "Down at the Cross," frequently referred to as *The Fire Next Time*, which is the title of the book in which it was published in 1963, is arguably his most influential piece and the work most identified with him in his lifetime. The essay was originally published in a thick issue of *The New Yorker*, and it served as a loud wake-up call to the largely white readership of the magazine that the times certainly were changing and more rapidly than anyone might have known. The subject of the essay vacillates between Baldwin's upbringing in Harlem, the religious fervor that he thought would save him, and the Nation of Islam, whose willingness to separate from white America, from Baldwin's point of view, indicated a failure of the American Dream. Baldwin wrote memorably of "the relatively conscious whites and the relatively conscious blacks, who must, like lovers, insist on, or create, the consciousness of the others" in order to "end the racial nightmare, and achieve our country, and change the history of the world." He spoke simultaneously of the alternative, the vengeance that would destroy the nation if left unchecked. These ideas were a virtual blueprint for the late 1960s, marked by assassinations, race riots, and the rise of radical militants such as the Black Panther Party as well as by the nonviolent protests led by Martin Luther King, Jr.

The first of five biographies of Baldwin appeared soon after *The Fire Next Time*. Fern Marja Eckman's *The Furious Passage of James Baldwin* (1966) seeks to tie Baldwin to the African American anger that was almost palpable during the mid-1960s. Eckman's book contains liberal doses of Baldwin's own words, taken from interviews with Eckman, replete with numerous italicizations meant to preserve the emphatic inflections of Baldwin's voice, which had become familiar by the mid-1960s. The book solidified Baldwin's burgeoning reputation as a spokesman as much as a writer. Its emphasis, in keeping with the racial storm of the mid-1960s, is on Baldwin's race much more than on his artistry or his sexuality. *Giovanni's Room*, for instance, is described initially in terms of race: "Not a single Negro enters its radically segregated pages," Eckman writes (134), and she quickly sidesteps its homosexual content. Around the same time, Robert Bone revised his influential study *The Negro Novel in America* (first published in 1958) to assess Baldwin's reputation in the context of African American literary history, only one of many potential contexts through which Baldwin's work has been viewed. Bone pronounces Baldwin "the most important Negro writer to emerge during the last decade" but immediately finds it difficult to separate "the artist from the celebrity" (215). Bone perhaps initiated the trend in Baldwin criticism that was to persist over the next two decades: namely, the assertion that Baldwin's early works were vastly better than his later works.

Bone also initiated the battle over Baldwin's best genre; he writes, "I find Baldwin strongest as an essayist, weakest as a playwright, and successful in the novel form on only one occasion," referring to *Go Tell It on the Mountain* (215). Bone admired this novel greatly, putting it in the pantheon of African American novels that includes Jean Toomer's *Cane*, Ellison's *Invisible Man*, and Wright's *Native Son*. He says that Baldwin's first novel "cuts through the walls of the store-front church to the essence of Negro experience in America" (218) but goes on to say, "One senses in Baldwin's first novel a confidence, control, and mastery of style that he has not attained again in the novel form" (219). Bone also felt that Baldwin did not achieve much in his 1964 play *Blues for Mister Charlie*, calling it "one unspeakably bad propaganda piece" (216).

Blues for Mister Charlie is a pivotal point in Baldwin's oeuvre. Coinciding as it does with the pinnacle of his fame, it reflects the urgency, rage, and pessimism that would develop in his writings over the next decade. Inspired partly by the 1955 murder of Emmett Till and written in the aftermath of the 1963 murder of Medgar Evers, whom Baldwin met during a trip to the South, the play was an allegory of a nation ("Plaguetown") in crisis. The production of *Blues for Mister Charlie* was fraught with problems. Baldwin took a heavy hand in the production and threw a number of public fits. It opened on Broadway on April 23, 1964, and closed four months later. Baldwin had insisted that ticket prices be kept low so that black people could afford to see the performance, causing the production to earn little, even though it was well attended. The reviews were mixed, but mostly negative. Robert Brustein in *The New Republic* and Howard Taubman in the *New York Times* both found Baldwin's characters stereotypical. The year after the play was produced, Baldwin, back in Turkey, wrote another vitriolic story about racism in the American South, "Going to Meet the Man" (which became the title of his only story collection). This work, too, proved too angry and provocative for some readers and critics. Joseph Featherstone in *The New Republic* praised Baldwin's early work but said that the title story from *Going to Meet the Man* read like "the Book of Job in the form of a comic" and described it as "inanely simple" (in Standley and Burt 154) compared to the early work.

Baldwin was clearly hurt by the treatment of his play even as he remained defiant and committed to his artistic vision. He returned to his exile in Turkey in the mid-1960s and worked on a novel that received even poorer critical treatment than his previous two. *Tell Me How Long the Train's Been Gone* (1968) is even more sprawling than *Another Country*, with a meandering plot narrated by a protagonist who, like Baldwin, is tired of fame and tired of being encouraged to speak for his race. By the late 1960s, Baldwin had become convinced that he would be assassinated as Malcolm X and Martin Luther King had been, and his suspicions that the Central Intelligence Agency was following him were well-founded. At the same time, he was feeling increasingly isolated from the new generation of black leaders, who were fighting literal battles that landed them in jail or in early graves. Baldwin renders one such character, Black Christopher, in nearly heroic terms toward the end of *Tell Me How Long the Train's Been Gone*, but the novel's protagonist, Leo Proudhammer—a clear Baldwin alter ego—does not quite know what to do with such a figure. Reviews were not kind. Mario Puzo, author of *The Godfather*, called Baldwin's book "a simpleminded, one-dimensional novel with mostly cardboard characters" while still holding on to the commonplace that the author's "reputation is justified by his essays rather than his fiction" (in Standley and Burt 155).

As Baldwin's career waned through the 1970s and 1980s, even that commonplace no longer held. His final two novels, *If Beale Street Could Talk* (1974) and *Just Above My Head* (1979), fared equally poorly as his final books of nonfiction, *No Name in the Street* (1971), *The Devil Finds Work* (1976), and *The Evidence of Things Not Seen* (1985). The reviews were not uniformly bad, but the general feeling was that a new, younger, hipper generation of African American writers—among them Alice Walker, Ishmael Reed, Amiri Baraka, Morrison, and Ntozake Shange—had nudged him out of the limelight. Baldwin's published dialogue with the poet Nikki Giovanni was one attempt to keep him on stage; his choice of a teenage female narrator for *If Beale Street Could Talk* was another. Neither of these works gained anything like the attention Baldwin received in his early career. Other works, such as his poetry collection, *Jimmy's Blues*, were barely noticed by readers or critics, and the belief that Baldwin had lost his creative powers around the time he published *Blues for Mister Charlie* was accepted as fact. When Baldwin published his collected essays in 1985 as *The Price of the Ticket*, it was clear that even his reputation as perhaps the greatest living American essayist was in jeopardy. Julius Lester wrote in his review of the collection, "What has happened to James Baldwin since *The Fire Next Time* is that a black vision of the world has slowly gained precedence over his humanistic one" (in Standley and Burt 247). This assessment makes it clear that Baldwin could not win in the eyes of his critics during his lifetime: he was trapped by the racial context for his writing and judged by expectations, vacillating between the strictly aesthetic and the strictly political, that were very much the products of a turbulent time. Baldwin found himself inhabiting neither place rather than both. His relatively obscure death in the south of France in 1987 was marked by a funeral at the Cathedral of St. John the Divine in New York that featured some of the most prominent African American intellectuals of the time (and included tributes by Amiri Baraka, Toni Morrison, and Maya Angelou), and it symbolizes a shift away from the negative reviews that riddled his later years.

Beginning in the 1970s and 1980s, new books on Baldwin began to shape his literary reputation. In most cases, they took their lead from the sense of division that marked his critical reception in his lifetime, but academic analysis gradually replaced the journalistic criticism that disposed of much of Baldwin's later work in his lifetime—though the shopworn take on Baldwin's rise and fall is still evident in overviews such as Hilton Als's 1998 review of the Library of America editions, in which he refers to Baldwin's plays as "ill-conceived and poorly written," expresses gratitude that the new editions exclude the late novels, and proclaims that Baldwin "never possessed a novelist's imagination or sense of structure" (80).

Keneth Kinnamon's 1974 collection *James Baldwin* is an anthology of the important Baldwin criticism up until that date. Though it is obviously incomplete in terms of assessing the sweep of Baldwin's career, it does serve to highlight some enduring themes that began to lift Baldwin out of the quicksand of his alleged aesthetic decline. The role of music in his fiction, for instance, is the subject of essays by John M. Reilly and Sherley Anne Williams. Therman B. O'Daniel's collection *James Baldwin: A Critical Evaluation* (1977) represents a distinct turn away from the negative reviews that had begun to determine Baldwin's reputation in favor of assessments of his work based on interpretation rather than evaluation. Here we see more academic analyses of Baldwin, including feminist readings of individual works as well as more comprehensive assessments of his life's work. The collection is, like Fred L. Standley and Nancy V. Burt's *Critical Essays on James Baldwin* (1988), organized according to genre. Standley and Burt's book is a sort of hybrid of O'Daniel's and Kinnamon's and mixes reviews with original essays. Carolyn Sylvander's *James Baldwin* (1980) is the first book-length overview of Baldwin's career.

Immediately following Baldwin's death, W. J. Weatherby provided a second biography, *James Baldwin: Artist on Fire* (1989), which is, as Weatherby describes it, more of a "portrait" than a comprehensive biography, and its focus is perhaps more on Baldwin's public persona than on his writing. James Campbell's *Talking at the Gates* (1991) would follow two years later and be the first full biography to attempt to link Baldwin's life and works. The year 1989 also marked the publication of Horace A. Porter's *Stealing the Fire: The Art and Protest of James Baldwin*, the second book-length critical evaluation of Baldwin, and *James Baldwin: The Legacy*, edited by Quincy Troupe, largely a collection of interviews and appreciations by prominent writers, as well as *Conversations with James Baldwin*, edited by Fred L. Standley and Louis H. Pratt.

This flurry of books in the immediate aftermath of Baldwin's death seemed a collective attempt at appreciation, but none of them was a real expansion upon what had already been said about Baldwin's life and work thus far, though most did mark a turn away from the tendency to disparage Baldwin's later works. The 1990 film *The Price of the Ticket*, a marvelous documentary overview of Baldwin's life, is, like these other works, slightly hagiographical, and it also rushes quickly over the second half of Baldwin's career. Porter's study, without really explaining why, stops at the publication of *The Fire Next Time*. Mary McCarthy, in Troupe's book, admits that she also stopped reading Baldwin after she read that book. In the decade following Baldwin's death, critics and writers tended to keep one eye shut when they looked back on his life. Trudier Harris's 1996 collection, *New Essays on "Go Tell It on the Mountain,"* contains some excellent essays, but its narrow scope demonstrates that the novel was still being taken as representative of the author, even though it is unlike everything he wrote afterward.

Harris's 1985 book *Black Women in the Fiction of James Baldwin* initiated the fourth phase of Baldwin criticism that continues today. Although Harris concentrates only on Baldwin's fiction and excludes white women (who were prominent in Baldwin's fiction from his first story, "Previous Condition," onward) from her analysis, her study shows a willingness to evaluate Baldwin thematically rather than strictly aesthetically and to identify a theme that may lead to a more comprehensive vision of Baldwin's work and life. We see glimmerings of this approach in Kinnamon's and O'Daniel's essay collections, but Harris's is the first monograph to engage with a significant arc of Baldwin's writing.

David Leeming's 1994 biography, *James Baldwin*, is another breakthrough publication. As Baldwin's longtime friend and secretary, Leeming is able to provide a personal portrait of his subject, and as a scholar of mythology he also has a consistent critical perspective through which to unify Baldwin's writings. Leeming sees Baldwin's life as a series of related journeys (key word "related"), and his comprehensive biography begins to overturn the tendency to see Baldwin as a few separate writers fused into one person. Rosa Bobia's 1997 study *The Critical Reception of James Baldwin in France* also demonstrates the beginning of a new willingness to see Baldwin in expansive contexts.

Two collections of original essays published at the turn of the millennium marked the beginning of a new flourishing of Baldwin studies in the academy. Dwight McBride's *James Baldwin Now* (1999) and my own *Re-Viewing James Baldwin: Things Not Seen* (2000) introduced a new generation of Baldwin scholars who employ critical approaches largely unavailable to the previous generations of Baldwin's critics. McBride's collection emphasizes theory, including queer theory, and seeks to reposition Baldwin not only as the most prominent African American writer of his time but also as someone who anticipated the new openness to the topic of gender that has become common in the twenty-first century. My own collection emphasizes works by Baldwin that have been critically neglected, including his poetry and his text/image collaboration with Richard Avedon, and it also includes fresh readings of Baldwin's more canonical works, such as *Giovanni's Room* and *Another Country*. This trend of revisiting Baldwin's lesser-known works continues in Lynn Orilla Scott's 2002 study *James Baldwin's Later Fiction: Witness to the Journey*, which is the most thoroughgoing assessment to date of the three critically neglected novels Baldwin published in the latter half of his career. Scott argues that Baldwin's career cannot be so neatly divided:

> The supposed failure of these novels is typically blamed on Baldwin's political activism, anger, and his supposed ideological investment in black power. What is missing from most analyses is an understanding of the extent to which his later work is consistent with his earlier work, building upon, revising, and refocusing it, but never abandoning the critique of American racial and sexual identity. (xiii-xiv)

In recent years, scholars have continued to expand the contexts for studying and recovering Baldwin. Lawrie Balfour's *The Evidence of Things Not Said* (2001) examines Baldwin's nonfiction from a political scientist's perspective. Douglas Field's *A Historical Guide to James Baldwin* (2009) provides a set of essays that situate Baldwin historically, with an emphasis on the variety of cultures that surrounded him. Lovalerie King and Lynn Orilla Scott's *James Baldwin and Toni Morrison: Comparative Critical and Theoretical Essays* (2006) places Baldwin alongside the most prominent African American writer of the current generation. Magdalena Zaborowska's *James Baldwin's Turk-*

ish Decade: Erotics of Exile (2009) mixes biography with gender studies theory and a drive to recover Baldwin's previously neglected works, resulting in a work that represents the culmination of these more recent trends in Baldwin studies. These works together indicate a willingness to read Baldwin thoroughly, to shed light on some of the works that had been critically dismissed, and to explore a plurality of contexts in order to recognize fully the accomplishments of this complex writer.

In recent years, too, major conferences have been devoted to Baldwin alone at Howard University in Washington, D.C. (2002), at Queen Mary College in London (2007), and at Suffolk University in Boston (2009). The momentum around Baldwin studies seems to be gathering, and special journal issues devoted to Baldwin will soon be appearing. Yet, despite the resurgence of interest in Baldwin's life and work, there is still plenty of critical work to be done. Once critics have fully discarded their willingness to divide and label Baldwin, the process of understanding him as a rich, complex, and undeniably important American literary figure will flourish anew.

Works Cited

Als, Hilton. "The Enemy Within." *The New Yorker* 16 Feb. 1998: 72-80.

Baldwin, James. *Conversations with James Baldwin*. Ed. Fred L. Standley and Louis H. Pratt. Jackson: UP of Mississippi, 1989.

____________. *Notes of a Native Son*. Boston: Beacon Press, 1955.

Balfour, Lawrie. *The Evidence of Things Not Said*. Ithaca, NY: Cornell UP, 2001.

Bobia, Rosa. *The Critical Reception of James Baldwin in France*. New York: Peter Lang, 1997.

Bone, Robert. *The Negro Novel in America*. 1958. New Haven, CT: Yale UP, 1965.

Boyd, Herb. *Baldwin's Harlem*. New York: Atria, 2008.

Campbell, James. *Talking at the Gates: A Life of James Baldwin*. New York: Viking Press, 1991.

Cleaver, Eldridge. *Soul on Ice*. 1968. New York: Dell, 1992.

Eckman, Fern Marja. *The Furious Passage of James Baldwin*. London: Michael Joseph, 1966.

Field, Douglas, ed. *A Historical Guide to James Baldwin*. New York: Oxford UP, 2009.

Harris, Trudier. *Black Women in the Fiction of James Baldwin*. Knoxville: U of Tennessee P, 1985.

___________. *New Essays on "Go Tell It on the Mountain."* New York: Cambridge University Press, 1996.

King, Lovalerie, and Lynn Orilla Scott, eds. *James Baldwin and Toni Morrison: Comparative Critical and Theoretical Essays*. New York: Palgrave Macmillan, 2006.

Kinnamon, Keneth, ed. *James Baldwin: A Collection of Critical Essays*. Englewood Cliffs, NJ: Prentice-Hall, 1974.

Leeming, David. *James Baldwin*. New York: Alfred A. Knopf, 1994.

McBride, Dwight, ed. *James Baldwin Now*. New York: New York UP, 1999.

Miller, D. Quentin, ed. *Re-Viewing James Baldwin: Things Not Seen*. Philadelphia: Temple UP, 2000.

O'Daniel, Therman B., ed. *James Baldwin: A Critical Evaluation*. Washington, DC: Howard UP, 1977.

Porter, Horace A. *Stealing the Fire: The Art and Protest of James Baldwin*. Middletown, CT: Wesleyan UP, 1989.

Reilly, John M. "'Sonny's Blues': James Baldwin's Image of Black Community." *James Baldwin: A Collection of Critical Essays*. Ed. Keneth Kinnamon. Englewood Cliffs, NJ: Prentice-Hall, 1974. 139-46.

Scott, Lynn Orilla. *James Baldwin's Later Fiction: Witness to the Journey*. East Lansing: Michigan State UP, 2002.

Standley, Fred L., and Nancy V. Burt, eds. *Critical Essays on James Baldwin*. Boston: G. K. Hall, 1988.

Sylvander, Carolyn. *James Baldwin*. New York: Frederick Ungar, 1980.

Troupe, Quincy, ed. *James Baldwin: The Legacy*. New York: Touchstone, 1989.

Weatherby, W. J. *James Baldwin: Artist on Fire*. New York: Donald I. Fine, 1989.

Williams, Sherley Anne. "The Black Musician: The Black Hero as Light Bearer." *James Baldwin: A Collection of Critical Essays*. Ed. Keneth Kinnamon. Englewood Cliffs, NJ: Prentice-Hall, 1974. 147-54.

Zaborowska, Magdalena J. *James Baldwin's Turkish Decade: Erotics of Exile*. Durham, NC: Duke UP, 2009.

CRITICAL READINGS

Looking for Jimmy Baldwin:
Sex, Privacy, and Black Nationalist Fervor

Douglas Field

In an interview conducted shortly after the release of his film, *Looking For Langston* (1989), Isaac Julien remarked that his project could easily have been titled "Looking For Jimmy."[1] Instead, Julien's film, which explores the relationship between the black gay artist and the community, is dedicated to Baldwin, whose photograph weaves in and out of Julien's meditation on Langston Hughes. Julien's use of Baldwin's image renders visible a gay black artistic lineage that has historically been obscured.[2] By juxtaposing the Harlem-born Baldwin with his literary forefathers of the Renaissance, Julien suggests the ways in which Baldwin—as a gay black artist—is a direct descendant of homosexual and bisexual writers such as Bruce Nugent, Wallace Thurman, and Claude McKay.[3]

Unlike Hughes's sexuality, which Julien acknowledges has always been clouded in uncertainty, Baldwin has arguably been the most visible gay African-American writer since the Harlem Renaissance. Implicit in Julien's iconographic invocation of Baldwin is that we do not need to look for Jimmy since his sexuality—in contrast to that of Hughes—has never been in question.[4] Often cited as an inspiration to many black gay writers, Baldwin's work, according to Joseph Beam, helped rip the hinges off the closet.[5] Until the publication of *Just Above My Head* (1979), Baldwin's last novel, Beam claims that African-American writers had been suffering "a kind of 'nationalistic heterosexism.'"[6]

Whilst his writing offered solace and recognition for many of his contemporary readers, it was not until the 1980s that criticism (notably the work of Andrea Lowenstein and Emmanuel Nelson) began to argue for Baldwin's central place, not only as an important African-American writer, but as a black *and* gay artist. Even a cursory glance at recent scholarship on Baldwin indicates the ways in which the field is dominated by articles on Baldwin's explorations and depictions of black masculinity and sexuality. To cite one of many recent examples, Yasmin DeGout, in a recent collection of Baldwin essays, makes the point that "any reading of Baldwin's fiction reveals him to be progenitor of many of the theoretical formulations currently associated with feminist, gay, and gender studies. . . ."[7]

But even as Baldwin's reputation as an important—perhaps the most important—gay black American writer of the twentieth century becomes increasingly secure, a closer examination of his work reveals myriad ambiguities, contradictions and uncertainties that sit uneasily with his increasingly iconic status. Although Baldwin—and in particular his fiction—is noted for his bold portrayal of homosexual relationships, it was not until 1968 with *Tell Me How Long the Train's Been Gone* that Baldwin depicted sexual relations between two black men in a novel, and not until his last novel, *Just Above My Head* (1979), that he explores sexual love between African-American men. In fact, as David Bergman has pointed out, Baldwin is careful to frame his "homosexual" relationships through bisexuality, whether past or present.[8] Still more surprising is Baldwin's insistence that his second novel, *Giovanni's Room* (1956), a work that has emerged as a key work of twentieth century gay fiction, "is not about homosexuality."[9]

Not only did he steer readers away from the homosexuality of *Giovanni's Room*, but Baldwin repeatedly rejected the adjectives "homosexual," "gay," and "bisexual." "The word gay," Baldwin told Richard Goldstein, "has always rubbed me the wrong way. I never understood exactly what is meant by it," a view that Baldwin also forcefully echoed in an interview with James Mossman:[10]

> Those terms, homosexual, bisexual, heterosexual, are 20th century terms which, for me, have very little meaning. I've never, myself, in watching myself and other people, watching life, been able to discern exactly where the barriers were.[11]

Asked by Goldstein whether he considered himself gay, Baldwin replied that he did not: "I didn't have a word for it. The only one I had was homosexual and that didn't quite cover whatever it was I was beginning to feel."[12]

Not only did Baldwin repeatedly disavow the terms "gay," "homosexual," and "bisexual," but also he was deeply suspicious of the gay movement. Although, in 1982, he spoke in New York on "race, racism, and the gay community," Baldwin harshly condemned public exhibitions of gay solidarity, claiming that "they're involved in some kind of exhibition of their disaster."[13] The very negative language here ("disaster") suggests more than a suspicion of labels; whilst I resist the adjective "homophobic," it illustrates the complexity of Baldwin's views, which I will return to.[14] Baldwin's at times unsettling rhetoric and depiction of gay subculture have led some critics, such as Donald Gibson, to conclude that "[t]he fact of the matter is that Baldwin's attitude toward homosexuality is decidedly critical."[15] Similarly, Emmanuel Nelson, a pioneer in the treatment of Baldwin's accounts of homosexuality, concluded that *Giovanni's Room* evinced a Baldwin who had "not freed himself from the internalization of homophobic beliefs regarding the origins of male homosexual impulses."[16] While some writers such as Joseph Beam may have been inspired by Baldwin's depictions of black gay lives, others, such as the African-American gay science-fiction writer Samuel Delany, found his portraits far from positive. Whilst Delany acknowledges that Baldwin "at least, *had* talked about it [homosexuality]," displaying "a certain personal honesty," he groups *Giovanni's Room* with negative portrayals of homosexuality, such as the writing of Havelock Ellis.[17]

By drawing attention to his mercurial views on sexuality, my aim is not to displace Baldwin's central place as a key writer of black gay fiction. However, given his often-surprising views on sexuality, I argue that Baldwin's views operate along complex circuits of desire that make his work more challenging—and therefore more interesting—than is often assumed. Beginning by exploring the disparity between

Baldwin's prodigious examinations of sexuality in his fiction and his surprising silence in his essays, this article focuses on the turbulent arena of black radical politics during the 1960s. Whilst there has been much useful and pioneering work on the ways in which Baldwin was sidelined by civil rights activists on account of his sexuality, little has been done to examine his more uncomfortable and unsettling comments on black masculinity and sexuality during this turbulent period. What happens, this article asks, when we go looking for Jimmy?

For a writer who so fearlessly and tirelessly addressed issues of homosexuality and bisexuality in his fiction, Baldwin's relative silence about homosexuality in his essays seems surprising. It was as late as 1985 in an essay titled "Here Be Dragons," the closing piece in Baldwin's collected non-fiction, *The Price of the Ticket*, that Baldwin wrote about his sexuality openly. Homosexuality—although not explicitly Baldwin's—was discussed in two earlier essays, "The Preservation of Innocence" (1949) and "The Male Prison" (1954), the latter originally published in the *New Leader* as "Gide as Husband and Homosexual," later collected in *Nobody Knows My Name* (1961). Although Baldwin wrote little about homosexuality in his essays, he was more forthcoming in conversation. In an interview with Richard Goldstein in 1985 (published as "Go The Way Your Blood Beats"), Baldwin delivered his most candid discussion of homosexuality. Three important points emerge from this intriguing interview. First, Baldwin's repeated rejection of the terms "homosexual," and "gay," a point that I have raised; second, his insistence that sexuality is a private matter; and finally, his repeated statement that race is a more important question than issues of sexuality.

Given that Baldwin used the very public forum of the novel to explore homosexuality and bisexuality, Baldwin's insistence that "one's sexual preference is a private matter" sits at odds with his reputation as a key figure in gay literary history.[18] And yet Baldwin's insistence on privacy punctuates his commentaries on sexuality. In his essay on Gide, for example, Baldwin reprimanded the French author, insisting that he ought to have kept his sexuality hidden.[19] Baldwin's sexuality, as he recounted to Goldstein, was "very personal, absolutely personal. It was really a matter between me and God."[20]

Jerome de Romanet reaches the reasonable conclusion that Baldwin, on the whole "reserved the more public voice of spokesman (of the black community as a whole, of writers and artists) for his essays and formal addresses, while he often let his fictional characters discuss the more private issues of sexual politics and preference. . . ."[21] The division that I addressed earlier in Baldwin's work supports de Romanet's argument: in contrast to the paucity of essays dealing with sexuality, Baldwin's fiction is replete with depictions of same-sex desire. Why Baldwin chose to circumscribe homosexuality in his essays is a different question. One answer may lie in Baldwin's awareness that readers and critics who were uncomfortable with his fictional depictions of homosexuality and bisexuality were less troubled by the emphasis on race in his essays. Whilst critics are divided in their appraisal of Baldwin's strength as foremost an essayist or novelist, Emmanuel Nelson is surely right to suggest that many heterosexist critics felt more comfortable with Baldwin's relative silence on sexuality in his essays.[22]

The glaring disparity between discussions of sexuality in his essays and fiction also highlights the ways in which Baldwin was preoccupied by his roles both as an artist and as a spokesman. In the mid-1960s in particular, Baldwin came under increasing attack by a new generation of radical black American writers, such as Ishmael Reed and Amiri Baraka, who criticized his writing—and in particular his fiction—for not being sufficiently politically engaged. Importantly, criticism of Baldwin's political ineffectiveness was directly bound to the public knowledge of his sexual orientation. Although Henry Louis Gates, Jr., is careful to point out that black nationalism did not have a unique claim on homophobia, he rightly discusses the ways in which "national identity became sexualized in the 1960s, in such a way to engender a curious connection between homophobia and nationalism."[23]

Whilst I acknowledge Cheryl Clarke's admonishment that the black community is too frequently pilloried for its homophobia, Baldwin's insistence on privacy in relation to discussions of homosexuality came directly out of increasing attacks on his authority as a (homosexual) racial spokesman.[24] And yet Baldwin's distinctions between the public and the private spheres are difficult to constitute. Although Baldwin largely leaves his depictions of homosexuality to his fiction, his widely available novels of the 1960s hardly constitute a private sphere.

1. Black Nationalism, Homophobia and the Role of the Artist

According to James Campbell, Baldwin's "value to the [civil rights] movement was mainly symbolic."[25] Commissioned by *Harper's* magazine in 1957, Baldwin wrote emotionally about his first visit to the South and his first meeting with Martin Luther King, Jr.[26] After a second visit to the South in 1960, Baldwin became more actively involved in the civil rights struggle through work with the Congress of Racial Equality (C.O.R.E.), an organization—along with the Student Non-violent Co-ordinating Committee (S.N.C.C.)—that he later became a member of.[27] Tired of sojourning in France, "polishing my fingernails," as he recalled, Baldwin's new involvement in the South ignited in him a new political commitment: "I realized what tremendous things were happening," Baldwin averred, "and that I did have a role to play."[28]

Baldwin's role as writer/reporter was indeed unique. Richard Wright, whose reputation in the United States had dwindled by the late 1950s, remained in France until his death in 1960, and neither Ralph Ellison nor Langston Hughes played a significant role in writing of the civil rights era. With the success of *The Fire Next Time* (1963), Baldwin commanded a large and receptive audience, which he used to arrange a meeting with the Attorney General, Robert Kennedy.[29] But even as Baldwin courted more involvement with the civil rights movement, there were whispers of his misinformed views, and aspersion was cast on his ability—and suitability—as a race leader. Martin Luther King, for example, in a conversation secretly recorded by the F.B.I., expressed his reluctance at attending a television program with Baldwin. According to the F.B.I. report, King was "not enthusiastic about the idea because he felt that Baldwin was uninformed regarding his movement," a view that he maintained by excluding an eager Baldwin from speaking at the March on Washington in August 1963.[30] Echoing King, Harold Cruse concluded that Baldwin's contribution to the meeting with Kennedy was ineffectual, evincing the writer's "intellectual inconsistencies," and his refusal or inability to engage with "sociology and economics jazz."[31]

Although Baldwin would later explore his problematic role as both writer and spokesman in *Tell Me How Long the Train's Been Gone* (1968), emphatically telling *Mademoiselle* magazine in 1969 that "I am *not* a public speaker. I *am* an artist," his sexuality played a crucial and significant role in the deliberate downplaying of his involvement with civil rights.[32] According to Morris Dickstein:

> The crucial charges against Baldwin had little to do with his politics, or his literary craftsmanship, or even, for that matter, his precise position on the race questions. The argument was that Baldwin's homosexuality, his unconfident masculinity, is the hidden root of all his writing and completely disqualifies him as a representative spokesman.[33]

Evidence of how his sexuality undermined his authority as a racial spokesman is clearly illustrated by an issue of *Time* magazine in May 1963. Whilst the photograph of Baldwin on the cover testifies to a politically engaged African-American writer at the height of his success, the article overtly undermines his authority as a racial spokesman. Not only does the article emphatically state that Baldwin is "not, by any stretch of the imagination, a Negro leader," but the article tacitly emphasizes Baldwin's effeminacy as a euphemism for homosexuality:

Baldwin is described as a "nervous, slight, almost fragile figure, filled with frets and fears. He is effeminate in manner."[34] By framing Baldwin as weak, and by implying his sexuality, the *Time* article implicitly suggests that Baldwin is not threatening to its white readership, a point explicitly made by Calvin Hernton and Stanley Crouch. Hernton's brief discussion of the *Time* article concludes that white Americans love Baldwin because of his "lack of 'masculine aggressiveness,'" adding that he is "a sweet, exotic black boy who cries for mother love."[35]

Time's derisive caption could only have exacerbated Baldwin's problematic position, where it was common knowledge that he was nicknamed "Martin Luther Queen," with the implication that a "queen" could not participate in the violent and manly battle for civil rights, which several members of King's camp expressed directly.[36] King's lawyer, for example, Clarence Jones, whose telephone was wiretapped by the F.B.I., stated in a conversation that the Southern Christian Leadership Conference (S.C.L.C.) had a respectable reputation and "could hardly afford to have candid homosexuals close to the seat of power."[37] Similarly, King's right-hand man, Stanley Levinson, expressed his view that Baldwin and Bayard Rustin (a King aide later dismissed for his homosexuality), were "better qualified to lead a homosexual movement than a civil rights movement."[38]

Although knowledge of Baldwin's sexuality directly hindered his involvement with the S.C.L.C., by 1964 King's own message of nonviolence and Christian love was increasingly viewed as weak and ineffective. As Erika Doss has cogently documented, after the Civil Rights Act of spring 1964, notions of "conciliation and meditation" were soon rejected as ineffectual.[39] Disillusioned with the lack of political gain, both white and black activists turned their attention to the North, vying, as Doss outlines, for "consciousness raising and cultural awareness."[40] King's Southern message of tolerance was quickly dismissed. There was a new arena in the North that fostered more radical and violent ideologies.

For younger black radicals such as Eldridge Cleaver, King's message of nonviolence had become "a stubborn and persistent stumbling block in the path of the methods that had to be implemented to bring about a revolution in the present situation."[41] In contrast to King's emphasis on the good book, Cleaver notes how Frantz Fanon's *The Wretched of the Earth* was now known as "the Bible."[42] The time for Christian love and tolerance had been exhausted. According to one member of the Berkeley campus C.O.R.E., "[a] new leadership is emerging which reflects the aspirations of the urban Negro. . . . Yesterday's militants—like King and Rustin—are the new Uncle Toms."[43]

Baldwin's alignment with the sinking radical ship of Martin Luther King—what Cleaver referred to as his "Martin Luther King-type self-effacing love of his oppressors"—is crucial to an understanding of Baldwin's subsequent development as a writer.[44] As Cheryl Clarke and other cultural critics have shown, the mid-1960s "marked a resurgence of radical black consciousness . . . [which included] rejecting the values of WASP America and embracing our African and Afro-American traditions and culture."[45] Importantly, a rejection of white values included a repudiation of homosexuality, a phenomenon that increasingly became viewed as a white aberration.[46] Not only that, but black political action became increasingly gendered and sexualized. King, as Michele Wallace has argued, "represented a glaring impossibility—a dream of masculine softness and beauty, an almost feminine man."[47]

This important political shift in the mid-1960s, which became the Black Power Movement, resulted in an attempt to homogenize both political views and identity categories.[48] As Cheryl Clarke has noted, "[i]n order to participate in the movement one had to be black [of course], be male-orientated, and embrace a spectrum of black nationalist, separatist, Pan Africanist sentiments, beliefs, and goals."[49] Crucially, you also had to be heterosexual, and it helped if you were young.[50] For the middle-aged and homosexual Baldwin, it was not easy to gain membership to this club. "Baldwin, who once defined the cutting edge," Gates has noted, "was now a favorite target for the *new* cutting edge."[51] "Like Martin Luther King," Michele Wallace notes, "Baldwin was an anachronism come the sixties; but unlike King he was not conveniently murdered, so they had to dispose of him some other way."[52] This "other way," as I argue, deeply affected both Baldwin's depictions of homosexuality and subsequent political shifts.

As the political arena shifted dramatically after 1965, Baldwin was faced with a new strand of black radicalism. The Black Panther Party for Self Defense was formed in 1966, proselytizing a well-crafted message of potent masculinity and patriarchy, acutely illustrated by the masculine symbols of the panther and the gun.[53] The Black Power Movement, as Michele Wallace has reiterated, increasingly became synonymous with "the pursuit for manhood," a point that Eldridge Cleaver made explicit in an interview with Nat Hentoff in 1968.[54] According to Cleaver, the Black Panther Party "supplies very badly needed standards of masculinity," adding that "all the young chicks in the black community nowadays relate to the young men who are Black Panthers."[55]

Cleaver's assumption about male and female heterosexuality, and his emphasis on masculinity are illustrative of the Black Power Movement's increasingly intolerant ideology. As Erika Doss has outlined:

> by aligning black masculinity with symbols and styles traditionally associated with potent white masculinity, the Panthers also reinscribed the most egregious forms of patriarchal privilege and domination, from machismo and misogyny to violence and aggression. Their heterosexist and homophobic brand of revolutionary black nationalism excluded black women and homosexuals, and limited the context of black liberation and black power to conflicts over the definition and manifestation of black masculinity.[56]

Doss's emphasis on the increasingly homogenous inscription of black masculinity points to the ways in which women and especially homosexuals were increasingly scapegoated during the 1960s. As Ron Simmons and other critics have convincingly argued, homophobia in the black community traditionally "reinforces a false sense of manhood."[57] By delineating what is acceptable in male black subjectivity—and what is not—homophobia, according to Robert Reid-Pharr, humanizes the aggressors: "[t]o strike the homosexual, the scapegoat, the sign of chaos and crisis, is to return the community to normality, to create boundaries around Blackness, rights that indeed white men are obliged to recognize."[58]

Reid-Pharr's view is illustrated by Eldridge Cleaver's description of "Punk Hunting," an urban ritual that involves seeking out and targeting homosexuals in the community. Cleaver describes "punk hunting" as the need to "satisfy some savage impulse to inflict pain on the specific target, the 'social outcast.' . . ." What is most revealing is Cleaver's choice of analogy. Punk hunting, Cleaver asserts, "seems to be not unrelated . . . to the ritualistic lynchings and castrations inflicted on Southern blacks by Southern whites" (*SOI* 106). By aligning himself with white lynchers—who historically sought to scapegoat alleged black sexual transgressors—Cleaver reproduces what bell hooks has referred to as black resistance's equation of "freedom with manhood." By sharing white patriarchy's belief in the "erect phallus," the Black Power Movement, hooks contends, "forged a bond between oppressed men and their white male oppressors."[59]

Evidence of Baldwin's scapegoating is highlighted by a 1967 edition of the *Black Panther Magazine*, which featured Emory Douglas's cartoon, titled "bootlickers gallery." In this cartoon, photographs of Baldwin, Bayard Rustin and Martin Luther King, Jr., are placed subjacent to a picture of a prostrate black man, who is licking the cowboy boots of President Lyndon Johnson.[60] The framing of Baldwin parallels *Time*'s undermining of his suitability as a racial spokesman. In this cartoon, the image of a prostrate "bootlicker" illustrates the ways in which the Black Power Movement increasingly came to view "passivity" (i.e. non-aggression) with Uncle Tom behavior, which in turn became synonymous with homosexuality.[61] In Amiri Baraka's poem "Black Art," for example, he describes one "negroleader/ on the steps of the white house one/kneeling between the sheriff's thigh/ negotiating coolly for his people."[62] Echoing Baraka's undisguised disgust at the negro leader's passivity and kowtowing, Eldridge Cleaver forcefully condemned Baldwin's third novel, *Another Country*, derogating Baldwin's depiction of Rufus Scott. For Cleaver, Rufus is "a pathetic wretch . . . who let a white bisexual fuck him in the ass . . . [and] was the epitome of a black eunuch who has completely submitted to a white man" (*SOI* 107).

By emphasizing Rufus's submission, Cleaver implicitly conflates black homosexuality with his dubious views on the powerlessness of African-American women. More specifically, as Wallace has noted, Cleaver reduces black homosexuals "to the status of our black grandmothers who, as everyone knows, were fucked by white men all the time."[63] But if Cleaver suggests that power is enacted through fucking, then, as Wallace mischievously points out, might we not consider the black homosexual who fucks the white man as the most revolutionary of all? "If whom you fuck indicates your power," Wallace argues, "then obviously the greatest power would be gained by fucking a white man first, a black man second, a white woman third and a black woman not at all. The most important rule is that *nobody* fucks you."[64]

In Baraka and Cleaver's framework, however, ultimate power is gained by raping white women. For Cleaver, rape is explicitly "an insurrectionary act." By raping white women, Cleaver maintains that he "was defying and trampling on the white man's law . . . because I was very resentful over the historical fact of how the white man had used the black woman. I felt I was getting revenge" (*SOI* 14). Cleaver's act of revenge is rooted in the African-American man's historical lack of authority during slavery. As Robert Staples has documented, "[m]asculinity, as defined in this culture, has always implied a certain autonomy over and mastery of one's environment."[65] During slavery, as Staples outlines, African-American men had no legal authority over their wives and children, which accentuated a sense of emasculation. According to Cleaver, the legacy of psycho-sexual damage can be redressed through the reclamation of a pre-historical era. In his essay, "The Primeval Mitosis," Cleaver draws on Plato's *Symposium* to evoke a pre-social era in which the essence, the Primeval Sphere, became divided; but unlike Plato, this division is between not three, but two parts, male and female. Each part, Cleaver continues, longs for the opposite sex in order to create a Unitary Sexual Image. Cleaver argues that homosexuality disrupts the timeless process of synthesis: it is "the product of the fissure of society into antagonistic classes and a dying culture and civilization alienated from biology" (*SOI* 177). This point is further illustrated by the necessary, healing union with African-American women ("Black Beauty"): "Across the naked abyss of negated masculinity, of four hundred years minus my Balls, we face each other today, my Queen" (*SOI* 206). Cleaver maintains that it is only through "*re*-love" of Black Beauty that his "manhood can be redeemed" (*SOI* 207).

Cleaver's emphasis on the redemption and healing of a wounded masculinity not only framed "the pursuit of manhood" in exclusively heterosexual terms, but highlighted the increasingly pervasive move to redress the psycho-sexual crimes of slavery. During the mid-1960s, black masculinity was further damaged by the controversial findings in 1965 of what became known as the Moynihan Report. Concluding that the black family suffered from an "abnormal family structure," the report suggested that African-Americans suffered less from racism, and more from the dominant presence of black women.[66]

The complicated and competing images of masculinity highlight the difficult position that Baldwin faced. On the one hand, as Lee Edelman has noted, "[o]ne need not, of course, view patriarchy as itself a desideratum in order to recognize the destructiveness of a system that enshrined the paternal privilege . . . while at the same time disavowing the meaningfulness of the paternal relation for the slave."[67] But on the other hand, Cleaver's dichotomizing of white and black as the (white) Omnipotent Administrator and the (black) Supermasculine Menial exacerbated psycho-sexual myths of the black male as primarily physical and libidinous, whilst at the same time replicating white patriarchal and homophobic values.

By deploying white patriarchy's dominant ideologies, Cleaver's account points towards the complex entanglement of race, sexism and homophobia.

As Isaac Julien and Kobena Mercer have argued, black men have historically internalized and incorporated dominant images of masculinity in order to contest the power of racism, echoed by Alvin Poussaint's discussion of the ways in which African-American men have tended "to adopt the attitudes of the dominant group toward black women."[68] What both cases reveal—and particularly with Cleaver's raping of white women—is the diaphanous line between the empowering act of reclamation, and the danger of perpetuating recalcitrant myths of black sexual appetite.

This complicated position is illustrated by the ways in which Baldwin's criticism of "black manhood" set him at odds with the Black Power Movement. Whereas Cleaver celebrates "the walking phallus of the Supermasculine Menial," Baldwin vociferously repudiates this image: "It is still true alas," Baldwin wrote in 1961, "that to be an American Negro male is also to be a kind of walking phallic symbol: which means one pays, in one's personality, for the sexual insecurity of others."[69] Echoing Frantz Fanon's observation that the white gaze transforms black men so that "[h]e is turned into a penis. He *is* a penis," Hall Montana, Baldwin's narrator in *Just Above My Head*, bemoans that "its color *was* its size."[70]

Despite his conflict with Cleaver and others on the depiction of the black male, Baldwin continued to challenge and demystify myths of black sexual prowess. And yet, Cleaver's scabrous homophobic attack of Baldwin in *Soul on Ice* had a devastating effect on the older writer. Whilst Cleaver is not alone in his homophobic derogation of Baldwin, the severity of his attack produced a profound effect on Baldwin's writing. As late as 1984 Baldwin still spoke of trying to "undo the damage" that Cleaver had caused.[71] Henry Louis Gates, Jr., recalls Baldwin's remark that "being attacked by white people only made him flare hotly into eloquence; being attacked by black people, he confessed, made him want to break down and cry."[72] According to W. J. Weatherby, Cleaver's attack was extremely "important to Baldwin's development," a key moment that "helped to shape [Baldwin's] racial attitudes in middle age . . . making him re-examine his own situation."[73] Echoing Weatherby, Gates also notes that, in the aftermath of Cleaver's attack, Baldwin's essays "came to represent his official voice, the carefully crafted expression of the public intellectual, James Baldwin."[74] Baldwin, as Dwight McBride convincingly argues, increasingly adopted the voice of "representative race man," which in turn led to a silencing—or at least dilution—of his depictions of homosexuality.[75]

2. The Question of Sex Comes After the Question of Color

According to Henry Louis Gates, Jr., by the late 1960s "Baldwin bashing was almost a rite of initiation."[76] Middle-aged, homosexual and with inconsistent political views, Baldwin stood little chance against the fiery and youthful vitality of writers such as Ishmael Reed, who famously dismissed the older writer as "a hustler who comes on like Job."[77] But even as the younger writers of the Black Power Movement increasingly scapegoated Baldwin, the older writer—at least publicly—refused to fire back. In fact, as I argue in this section, from the late 1960s until the late 1970s, Baldwin was not only taciturn about the subject of homosexuality, but his language increasingly adopted a new radical rhetoric, particularly in his long essay, *No Name in the Street*, published in 1972, but begun in 1967.[78] In this section I examine Baldwin's repeated assertions that "the sexual question comes after the question of color."[79] I argue that Baldwin's move away from the subject of homosexuality came directly out of the criticism that he received from African-American writers such as Eldridge Cleaver; this in turn, I show, led to Baldwin's increasing anxiety over his role as both an artist and a spokesman.

Despite the suggestion by Gates and Campbell that his involvement with the Black Power Movement was symbolic and derivative, it is clear from Baldwin's writing of the late 1960s and early 1970s that he was both committed to radical change and deeply disillusioned. "Since Martin's death, in Memphis," Baldwin wrote in *No Name in the Street*, "and that tremendous day in Atlanta, something has altered in me, something has gone away."[80] Gone were Baldwin's more optimistic statements about the need for love between black and white people. In an essay on the head of the S.N.C.C., Stokely Carmichael, Baldwin described the shift in the young leader's ideology in terms that are readily applicable to Baldwin himself: "Stokely did not begin his career with dreams of terror," Baldwin wrote, "but with dreams of love. Now he's saying, and he's not alone, and he's not the first, if I can't live here, well neither will you."[81] Having fervently supported King's March on Washington, Baldwin later agreed with Malcolm X that the March was in fact "a sell-out" (*NNIS* 523). Although Gates is a little harsh when he claims that "Baldwin's reverence for Malcolm was real, but posthumous," by 1972, seven years after Malcolm X's assassination, Baldwin's recollection of the Nation of Islam leader borders on hagiography: "Malcolm, finally, was a genuine revolutionary," Baldwin recalled in *No Name in the Street*, adding that "[i]n some church someday . . . he will be hailed as a saint" (*NNIS* 499).[82]

But if Baldwin's support of Malcolm was, to a certain extent, retrospective, then he was eager to lend his support to the Black Power Movement that had so readily dismissed him.[83] Baldwin, as James Campbell recalls, "embraced the Panthers."[84] Striking a close and lasting relationship with the chairman of the Black Panther Party, Bobby Seale, Baldwin went on to write an introduction to Seale's second book, and also hosted a birthday party for the incarcerated Panther leader Huey Newton (*NNIS* 532). Although the project was never completed, Baldwin also began work in Hollywood on a film script of the life of Malcolm X in 1968, which was eventually published in 1972 as *One Day When I Was Lost: A Scenario Based on the Autobiography of Malcolm X*.[85]

In sharp contrast to his earlier more poetic language, came a new radical rhetoric that sounded borrowed and unsure in Baldwin's florid pen. The writer who had once famously claimed that he had to appropriate white culture, invoking Chartres Cathedral, Descartes and Shakespeare, now vehemently argued that the "South African coal miner, or the African digging for roots . . . have no reason to bow down before Shakespeare, or Descartes . . . or the Cathedral at Chartres" (*NNIS* 473).[86] Not only did Baldwin openly support the Panthers, proclaiming, for example, that African-American prisoners had never received a fair trial, but he increasingly referred to himself as a black radical writer (*NNIS* 507).[87] After *The Fire Next Time*, Baldwin's writing, according to Stanley Crouch, "began to espouse the kinds of simplistic conceptions Malcolm X became famous for."[88]

Baldwin's claim that he had, upon his arrival in Paris, lived with "*les misérables*" [Algerians] was a blatant rewriting of his first years in Paris, a period that he spent largely with white writers.[89] If Baldwin rewrote his past to suggest more radical political engagement, then he was no less self-conscious about his present situation. In *No Name in the Street*, only four years after Cleaver's violent dismissal of his political ineffectiveness, Baldwin refers to a disagreement with a young black militant woman, concluding that the scene "rather checked the company, which had not imagined that I and a black militant could possibly disagree about anything" (*NNIS* 457). A few years earlier, Baldwin had been dismissed because few black militants thought he could possibly *agree* with them about anything. Again in *No Name*, Baldwin is anxious to inflate and maintain his new radical persona: recollecting that the British Immigration considered him to be a "*persona non grata*"—with the implication that he was too politically dangerous—Baldwin describes how the British authorities "had thrown Stokely

[Carmichael] out a week before," in a desperate attempt to authenticate his political daring (*NNIS* 496).

Importantly, Baldwin's language increasingly borrowed from the pervasive heterosexist and machismo language of the Black Power Movement. According to the new Baldwin, when Bobby Seale proclaimed Huey Newton as "the baddest motherfucker in history," he "restored to the men and women of the ghetto their honour," a statement that strongly mirrors Cleaver's declaration that "I cannot help but say that Huey P. Newton is the baddest motherfucker ever to set foot in history" (*NNIS* 536).[90] Although Baldwin stated that "I do not carry a gun and do not consider myself to be a violent man," he began to claim that his life had "more than once depended on the gun in a brother's holster." Dialogue, the master of words now proclaimed, was no longer possible: "it is not necessary for a black man to hate a white man, or to have any particular feelings about him at all, in order to realize that he must kill him" (*NNIS* 550).[91] This new Baldwinian rhetoric sounded less and less like the author of *Go Tell It on the Mountain*, and more and more like the borrowed rhetoric of black radical writers. Baldwin's comment in "Notes for *Blues*" that "I hate them [white people] and would be willing to kill them," echoes Calvin Hernton's conclusion that "only violence . . . will at once be the tool of liberation," or Cleaver, who stated that, "[i]n order to bring this situation about, black men know that they must pick up the gun. . . ."[92]

Baldwin's exhortation that it might be necessary to kill white people recollects Philip Brian Harper's discussion of the ways in which the Black Power Movement aligned liberation with an aggressive and heterosexual masculinity. Not surprisingly, Baldwin's new self-proclaimed radicalism also tempered his discussion of homosexuality as he entered the arena of black macho, a point insightfully made by Stanley Crouch. According to Crouch, Baldwin's fascination with militancy and "increasing virulence had perhaps more than a bit to do with his homosexuality."[93] Baldwin began to dismiss "most American intellectuals," on account of what he "observed of their manhood," an observation that is framed in a language not dissimilar from Cleaver's derogation of Baldwin (*NNIS* 464). Although Baldwin did not go as far as Ossie Davis, who proclaimed Malcolm X as "our living manhood," Baldwin began to commemorate the assassinated leader as "a genuine revolutionary, a *virile* impulse long since fled from the American way of life" (*NNIS* 499; emphasis mine; *SOI* 60). Baldwin peppered his essays with discussions of how slavery "emasculated them [slaves] of any human responsibility," arguing that "a man without balls is not a man" (*NNIS* 482).

By repeatedly emphasizing the African-American male's loss of manhood, Baldwin, as Michele Wallace wryly points out, "had finally seen the light." Baldwin's work, Wallace argued, in fact "laid the groundwork for the deification of the genitals that would later characterize the prose of the Black Movement."[94] In short, Wallace argued that Baldwin had imbibed the Black Power rhetoric that the "black man's sexuality and the physical fact of his penis were the major evidence of his manhood and the purpose of it."[95] Whilst Wallace's judgment of Baldwin may seem too pronounced, it illustrates the ways in which Baldwin was viewed as an anachronism by Black Power leaders who were nonetheless indebted to his rhetoric. Cleaver's book of essays, *Soul on Ice*, with its blend of autobiography, history and politics, was clearly inspired by the author he soon dismissed. According to Crouch, Baldwin was in fact "a seminal influence" on the likes of Carmichael, Rap Brown, LeRoi Jones [Amiri Baraka] and Cleaver.[96]

Nowhere was Baldwin's influence to and by the Black Power Movement more acute than in his play *Blues for Mister Charlie* (1965). According to Stanley Crouch, Baldwin's play, which was performed four months after the assassination of John F. Kennedy in 1964, opened up the question of nonviolence, whilst Amiri Baraka even claimed that *Blues* "announced the Black Arts Movement."[97] Whilst Baraka's eulogy of Baldwin may overstate the importance of Baldwin's play, contemporary reviewers were quick to point out the shift in register. In his review of *Blues*, Philip Roth criticizes what he terms Baldwin's "sentimentalizing of masculinity," arguing that the play "is a soap opera designed to illustrate the superiority of blacks over whites." Echoing Calvin Hernton's conclusion that *Blues* demonstrated "an aggressive, a masculine Baldwin," Roth argues that Baldwin suggests that African-Americans, "even studious ones, make love better. They dance better . . . And their penises are longer, or stiffer."[98]

Why Baldwin dramatically changed his rhetoric is in part explained by his public acceptance of Cleaver's virulent attack on him in *Soul on Ice*. Rather than defending his position, Baldwin surprisingly writes that he "admired" Cleaver's book, writing—in what Gates terms "an exercise in *willed* magnanimity"—that Cleaver was "both vulnerable and rare" (*NNIS* 539).[99] Baldwin, we learn, understood why Cleaver felt impelled to condemn him: "He seemed to feel that I was a dangerously odd, badly twisted, and fragile reed, of too much use to the Establishment to be trusted by blacks." Although Baldwin lamented that Cleaver used his "public reputation against me both naively and unjustly," his subsequent justification of Cleaver's homophobia not only exonerates Cleaver but also complicitly borrows from his former critic's vocabulary: "I also felt I was confused in his mind with the unutterable debasement of the male—with all those faggots, punks, and sissies, the sight and sound of whom, in prison, must have made him vomit more than once" (*NNIS* 539). By employing a rhetoric (faggots, punks, and sissies) that even the Black Panther Party had by then officially prohibited, Baldwin not only distinguishes his sexual preference from a more deviant and degenerate behavior but also comes dangerously close to mimicking Cleaver's own homophobic diatribe.

Whilst Baldwin's writing shifted dramatically during the 1960s, it is important to emphasize that he experienced deep anxieties about his roles as both writer and revolutionary from the mid-1960s. Writing in *No Name in the Street*, Baldwin is clearly aware of the price he has paid as a best-selling author. On the one hand, Baldwin acknowledges that his success had driven a wedge between himself and those he grew up with: the feeling was, Baldwin, averred, "that I had betrayed the people who had produced me" (*NNIS* 455). Although Baldwin is anxious to write himself in the history of the Black Power Movement ("I will always consider myself among the greatly privileged because, however inadequately, I was there"), he also realizes that many people will be skeptical about his role: "one marches in Montgomery, for example [in my own case] to sell one's books" (*NNIS* 488, 459). Whilst I have focused on Baldwin's attempts to picture himself as a radical *picaro*, Baldwin is only too aware that he is a writer, as he acknowledged to Cleaver, who is "of too much use to the Establishment to be trusted by blacks." As the most visible African-American writer of the 1960s, Baldwin was, as he admits, "the Great Black Hope of the Great White Father" (*NNIS* 539, 498).[100] "The conflict," Baldwin recalled, "was simply between my life as a writer and my life—not spokesman exactly, but as public witness to the situation of black people. I had to play both roles" (*NNIS* 513).

To conclude this section, I turn briefly to Baldwin's last novel of the 1960s, *Tell Me How Long the Train's Been Gone* (1968). Despite being arguably Baldwin's least successful novel, *Tell Me How Long* is an important work, both because the voice of the thespian narrator, Leo Proudhammer, is at times inseparable from Baldwin's, and because the novel illuminates and examines Baldwin's problematic roles during the 1960s.[101]

As a successful actor, Leo is increasingly torn—like Baldwin—between his artistic and his political obligations. Compare, for example, Baldwin's acknowledgement in *No Name*, "what in the world was I by now but an aging, lonely, sexually dubious, politically outrageous, unspeakably erratic freak?," with Leo Proudhammer's conclusion that "[s]ome people considered me a faggot, for some I was a hero, for some I was a whore, for some I was a devious cocks-man, for some I was an Uncle Tom" (*NNIS* 458).[102] In particular I focus briefly on the minor but important character, Black Christopher, who is Proudhammer's lover in later life. I argue that, by invoking a black radical character who is both homosexual and politically engaged, that Baldwin attempted, towards the end of the 1960s, to reconcile his sexuality with a more fervent political role.

Reviews for *Tell Me* were little short of disastrous.[103] Irving Howe, in a scathing review, saw it as "the collapse of a writer of some distinction." For Howe, *Tell Me* was replete with "speechmaker's prose," a novel written to demonstrate Baldwin's new militant rhetoric, but one that resulted in "literary suicide."[104] "They beating on black ass all the time," declares Leo's brother Caleb, "[d]on't nobody care what happens to a black man" (*TMHL* 61). White people in the novel, as Campbell points out, are described variously as "'snooty,' 'bored,' 'distrustful,' 'dangerous,' 'brutally cruel,' 'successful and vocal Fascists,'" in contrast to the more positive, but no less generalized adjectives for African Americans.[105]

Tell Me is an angry novel, full of despair and disillusionment. Religion, far from offering solace, has become a tool of the white establishment: "Fuck Jesus," rails Christopher to Leo, "[t]hey didn't want to change their hearts, they just used him to change the *map*" (*TMHL* 403). African Americans, like Leo's father, are now turning, not to religion, but to black nationalism (*TMHL* 368). In sharp contrast to criticism that Baldwin offered love as a social and political palliative in *Another Country*, love in *Tell Me* is explicitly "not enough" to deal with the racism between Leo and his white lover, Barbara (*TMHL* 298).[106]

But if *Tell Me* exemplifies a new Baldwinian rhetoric of radicalism and even protest, then there is also a self-reflexive and brutal honesty to the narrative. We find this most acutely in the infrequent episodes between Leo—the middle-aged and ailing successful black actor—and "Black Christopher," the young Panther-esque radical, whose friends dress "in their Castro berets," "heavy boots," clutching works by Camus, Fanon and Mao (*TMHL* 382). "I really would like," Leo implores Black Christopher, "to know more than I do about what's going on in the streets." Christopher's reply to Baldwin/Leo is that whilst "these cats are out here getting their ass whipped all the time. . . . You get *your* ass whipped, at least it gets into the papers" (*TMHL* 402, 403). *Tell Me* is indeed a novel that oozes pathos, neatly summarised by Stuart Hall, who concluded that the novel "was a meditation by a middle-aged black revolutionary on a revolution he has witnessed—but cannot, finally, share."[107]

Although *Tell Me* is more often than not dismissed and ignored by critics, the novel offers a useful insight into Baldwin's assertion that race is a more important issue than sexuality. Published in 1968, at the height of black nationalist fervor—and the same year as Cleaver's *Soul on Ice*—I want to suggest that *Tell Me* was Baldwin's attempt to reconcile his sexuality with black radical politics. Although critics such as James Giles have argued that Baldwin toned down the homosexuality in his fiction to appease black critics, I want to argue that Baldwin hinted at the ideal of an erotic and revolutionary black companionship that was most keenly articulated by the white homosexual writer Jean Genet.[108] By comparing Genet and Baldwin's involvement with the Panthers, I illustrate the extent that race, sexuality, and nationality figured in Baldwin's difficulty to immerse himself in black radical politics.

Although Black Christopher is only present in *Tell Me* for a dozen or so pages, he functions as a symbolic ideal for the ageing Leo. Whilst Christopher affectionately calls Leo his "dirty old man," there is never any explicit sexual interaction between the two men (*TMHL* 373). In fact Baldwin is careful to distinguish the love between Leo and Christopher from the "degeneracy" of other artists, such as the "broken down British faggot" actor and "the faggot painter and his lesbian wife" (*TMHL* 291, 316).[109] Like most Baldwin protagonists, Leo is bisexual, and Christopher offers his "dirty old man" both physical protection and emotional security, functioning as both bodyguard and mother/father-figure. Crucially, by naming Leo's lover *Black* Christopher, Baldwin offers an explicit rebuttal to the notion that homosexuality negates or dilutes blackness. Christopher, Leo ponders, "was black in many ways—black in colour, black in pride, black in rage"

(*TMHL* 68). Christopher, as his name suggests, is Leo's Black Christ, redolent with the homoeroticism of Countee Cullen's poem, "The Black Christ."[110] Christopher is Baldwin's ideal for the late 1960s: a young and beautiful radical black man who combines tenderness with aggressive political action.

Baldwin's minor but important characterization of Black Christopher is a quiet but subversive attack on black nationalism's homophobic and heterosexist ideology. By emphasizing the homosociality of organizations such as the Black Panthers, Baldwin suggests the thin line between companionship, eroticism and love:

> But my own instinct as to the male relation, is that men, who are far more helpless than women . . . need each other as comrades . . . need each other for tears and ribaldry, need each other as models, need each other indeed, in sum, in order to be able to love women. (*TMHL* 81)

Baldwin's emphasis on the need for male companionship and love is illustrated most acutely by the idealized relationship of Black Christopher and Baldwin/Leo. Importantly, this idea/ideal was not articulated by Baldwin's public voice, through his essays or his interviews during the late 1960s and early 1970s. The public voice on the relationship between eroticism and revolution came, not from an African-American writer, but from a white French homosexual writer, Jean Genet.

Given the vocal homophobia of the Black Panther Party, Genet's invitation to work with the Black Panthers in 1970 was little less than remarkable.[111] Although some African-American radicals, such as the playwright Ed Bullins, dismissed Genet's "faggoty ideas about Black Art, Revolution, and people," Genet's sexuality was largely accepted.[112] In contrast to Baldwin, Genet's presence with the Panthers was both highly publicized and visible. Although both Baldwin and Genet—who were friends from the early 1950s—spoke together at the American Center in Paris in 1970 to defend George Jackson and the Panthers, Genet's output was far more prodigious.[113] Whereas Genet was unprecedentedly soliciting interviews in well-known magazines and churning out publications, such as the collected essays *Here and Now for Bobby Seale* (1970), *May Day Speech* (1970), the introduction to the prison letters of George Jackson, *Soledad Brother* (1970), and then later *Prisoner of Love* (1986), Baldwin was licking his wounds after Cleaver's vicious attack.[114]

Still more surprising were Genet's repeated references to what he described as the irresistible eroticism of the Panthers.[115] Whilst Genet's declaration that he was "in love" with the Black Panthers curiously mirrors Cleaver's recollection that "I fell in love with the Black Panther Party," for Genet, as Jonathan Dollimore has argued, the Panthers' eroticism was "inseparable from their politics and the challenge they presented to white America."[116] For Genet, not only did the Panthers, like the Palestinians, exude "a very strong erotic charge," but he intimated that the former were sexually drawn to one another.[117] According to Genet, the Panthers "consisted of magnetized bodies magnetizing one another," what he elsewhere referred to as "their whole block and tackle, [which] was much in evidence through their trousers."[118]

Genet's emphasis on black manhood does little to shatter stereotypes of black sexual prowess, a point that the French writer is only too aware of: "[i]f sexual images keep cropping up it's because they're unavoidable, and because the sexual or erectile significance of the Party is self-evident."[119] But whilst Genet arguably pervades black sexual stereotypes, he also emphasized the tenderness beneath the black machismo. David Hilliard, Genet repeats, was a mother to him, recalling that the Panther's kindness was "an education in affection."[120] Genet's emphasis on the Panthers' gentleness bears a striking resemblance to Baldwin's insistence that Stokely Carimichael had set out with a message of love. Malcolm X, Baldwin noted in *No Name*, "was one of the gentlest people I have met" (*NNIS* 498). In *Tell Me How Long*, the militant Christopher cooks and shops for the ailing Leo, paralleling David Hilliard's role as "mother" with Genet. Genet's description of *Soledad*

Brother as "a book, tough and sure, both a weapon of liberation and a love poem" could equally have come from Baldwin's pen.[121]

Despite the similarities between Baldwin and Genet, the former, as I have illustrated, was largely circumscribed by the Black Power Movement. In contrast to Genet, Baldwin was seen less as a revolutionary, and more as a source of poetic inspiration: both Angela Davis and Bobby Seale borrowed from Baldwin to create titles for their books.[122] Whereas the involvement with the Panthers gave Genet a new momentum and impetus to publish, the late 1960s is generally considered as Baldwin's demise.[123] On the one hand, Baldwin was frequently criticized for being politically too vague, but I also want to emphasize that, unlike Genet, Baldwin's sexuality was a direct hindrance to his contribution to black politics.[124]

The fact that the Panthers embraced Genet, who was not only white but French, illustrates how Baldwin, by contrast, was hindered by his sexuality, race, and nationality. Whereas Genet not only claimed identification with African Americans, but also stated that he *was* black, his nationality and color enabled him to invoke this identity at will, just as he later identified with the plight of the Palestinians.[125] Although Genet precipitated direct political action, such as Huey Newton's open letter "The Women's Liberation and Gay Liberation Movements," in August 1970—which stated that "maybe a homosexual could be the most revolutionary"—Baldwin only solicited criticism of his sexuality.[126] The different responses to Baldwin and Genet are illustrated by the latter's account of how David Hilliard not only accepted Genet's sexuality, but stated "it would be great if all homosexuals would come twelve thousand kilometers to the defense of the Panthers."[127] Baldwin, too, had traveled twelve thousand kilometers from Paris to join the civil rights struggle, but Baldwin was also African American.

The impact of the late 1960s and early 1970s on Baldwin is clearly illustrated by his first novel of the new decade, *If Beale Street Could Talk* (1974). Not surprisingly, given the homophobia that Baldwin experienced, this is his first novel that deals exclusively with heterosexual relationships, and his first to use a female narrator. In rhetoric reminiscent of *Tell Me How Long*, the characters, according to Michele Wallace, "positively gush the dogma of the Black Movement."[128] In contrast to the period until circa 1962 (with the publication of *Another Country*), Baldwin was increasingly less vocal about the subject of sexuality, both in his fiction and his essays.

To look for what Baldwin himself called "all those strangers named Jimmy Baldwin" is to be faced with myriad contradictions and frustrations, but it is also to perceive a fervent and burning intensity that pierces Baldwin's more mercurial comments.[129] In his last novel, *Just Above My Head* (1979), Baldwin boldly prepared African-American gay writing for the 1980s, radically portraying the intense love between black characters such as Arthur and Crunch, and Arthur and Jimmy. Countering critics such as Stanley Crouch, who refused to align homosexuality with liberation, or the First National Plenary Conference on Self-Determination, which argued that "[r]evolutionary nationalists . . . cannot uphold homosexuality in the leadership of Black Liberation," Baldwin's radicalism came in his continued insistence that "all love was holy."[130] If, as Joseph Beam declared, "Black men loving Black men is the revolutionary act of the eighties," then it is in Baldwin's conceptions "of love and sex," as Lorelei Cederstrom pointed out in 1984, "that his ideas are the most revolutionary."[131] As Baldwin scholarship increasingly turns to confront the much-needed lacunae in the complicated nexus of race and sexuality, Baldwin's complexity should be celebrated, not ignored. If, as he bemoaned early in his writing, America is a "country devoted to the death of the paradox," then his legacy is a reminder to resist—and to not smooth out—life's inescapable complexity.[132]

Notes

1. Essex Hemphill, "Looking for Langston: An Interview with Isaac Julien," *Brother to Brother: New Writings By Black Gay Men*, ed. Essex Hemphill (Boston: Alyson Publications, Inc., 1991), 175.

2. For work on the Harlem Renaissance and sexuality, see Eric Garber, "A Spectacle in Color: The Lesbian and Gay Subculture of Jazz Age Harlem," *Hidden From History: Reclaiming the Gay and Lesbian Past*, ed. Martin Duberman, Martha Vicinus, and George Chauncey (London: Penguin, 1991), 318-32; Gregory Woods, "Gay Re-Readings of the Harlem Renaissance Poets," *Gay and Lesbian Writers of Color*, ed. Emmanuel Nelson (New York & London: Harrington Park Press, 1993), 318-332. For a cultural historical account, see George Chauncey, *Gay New York: The Making of the Gale Male Underworld, 1890-1940* (London: Flamingo, 1995), 227-310.

3. Apart from Baldwin's image, Julien uses a photograph of Countee Cullen, who was Baldwin's French teacher and literary advisor to the English dept. at Frederick Douglass Junior High, which further forges Julien's connection between Baldwin and the Harlem Renaissance; see James Campbell, *Talking at the Gates: A Life of James Baldwin* (London & Boston: Faber & Faber, 1991), 13.

4. See Arnold Rampersad, *The Life of Langston Hughes*, vol. 2 (New York: Oxford University Press, 1988), where Rampersad notes that "Hughes made almost a fetish of the secrecy about his sexual interests," adding that "the truth about his sexuality will probably never be discovered" (336).

5. Amongst numerous references to Baldwin as an inspiration to gay writers (both black and white), see Joseph Beam, ed., *In the Life: A Gay Black Anthology* (Boston: Alyson Publications, Inc., 1986), 90, 95, 231; Barbara Smith, "We Must Always Bury Our Dead Twice: A Tribute to James Baldwin," *The Truth That Never Hurts: Writings on Race, Gender, and Freedom* (New Brunswick, N.J. & London: Rutgers University Press, 1998), 75-80.

6. Joseph Beam, "Not a Bad Legacy, Brother," *Brother to Brother*, 185.

7. Yasmin DeGout, "'Masculinity' and (Im)maturity: 'The Man Child' and Other Stories in Baldwin's Gender Studies Enterprise," *Re-Viewing James Baldwin: Things Not Seen*, ed. D. Quentin Miller, foreword by David Leeming (Philadelphia: Temple University Press, 2000), 134.

8. David Bergman, "The Agony of Gay Black Literature," *Gaiety Transfigured: Gay Self-Representations in American Literature* (Wisconsin: University of Wisconsin Press, 1991), 165.

9. Richard Goldstein, "Go The Way Your Blood Beats: An Interview with James Baldwin," *Village Voice* 26 (June 1984): 13. A number of critical works have focused on *Giovanni's Room* as an important gay text: Claude J. Summers, "'Looking at the Naked Sun': James Baldwin's *Giovanni's Room*," *Gay Fictions: Wilde To Stonewall* (New York: Continuum, 1990), 172-194; Marlon B. Ross, "White Fantasies of Desire: Baldwin and the Racial Identities of Sexuality," *James Baldwin Now*, ed. Dwight McBride (New York & London: New York University Press, 1999), 13-55; Kemp Williams, "The Metaphorical Construction of Sexuality in *Giovanni's Room*," *Literature and Homosexuality*, ed. Michael Meyer (Amsterdam: Rodopi, 2000), 23-33.

10. Goldstein: 13.

11. James Mossman, "Race, Hate, Sex, and Colour: A Conversation with James Baldwin," *Conversations with James Baldwin*, ed. Fred L. Standley and Louis H. Pratt (Jackson & London: University of Mississippi Press, 1989), 54.

12. Goldstein: 13.

13. Cited by Eve Auchincloss and Nancy Lynch, "Disturber of the Peace: James Baldwin," *Conversations with Baldwin*, 80. Baldwin's negative statements are even more surprising given the prevalence of AIDS in the black community; see Phillip Brian Harper, "Eloquence and Epitaph: Black Nationalism and the Homophobic Impulse in Responses to the Death of Max Robinson," *The Lesbian and Gay Studies Reader*, ed. Henry Abelove, Michèle Aina Barale, and David M. Halperin (New York & London: Routledge, 1993), where Harper notes that, although African Americans account for less than 6% of the U.S. population, 23% of reported cases of AIDS were African American (159); Leeming, 359.

14. It should be noted that Baldwin was also against all forms of exhibition; see Fern Marja Eckman, *The Furious Passage of James Baldwin* (London: Michael Joseph, 1966), where Baldwin states, "I loathe parades. . . . The whole *parade* idea—there's something in me that profoundly disapproves of it" (215). For a further example, see James Mossman, "Race, Hate, Sex, and Colour: A Conversation with James Baldwin and Colin MacInnes," *Conversations with Baldwin*, where JB describes the public intimacy of interracial couples as "a kind of desperate advertising" (49).

15. Donald Gibson, "The Political Anatomy of Space," *James Baldwin: A Critical Evaluation*, ed. Therman B. O'Daniel (Washington, D.C.: Howard University Press, 1977), 9.

16. Emmanuel Nelson, "The Novels of James Baldwin," 13; see also Carolyn Sylvander, *James Baldwin* (New York: Frederick Ungar Publishing, Co, 1980), who notes that David is "a negative and confusing embodiment of the homosexual experience . . ." (51).

17. See Samuel R. Delany and Joseph Beam, "Samuel Delany: The Possibility of Possibilities," *In the Life*, 185-208, esp. 196.

18. Goldstein: 14.

19. Baldwin, "The Male Prison," *Nobody Knows*, 131.

20. Goldstein: 13.

21. Jerome de Romanet, "Revisiting *Madeleine* and 'The Outing': James Baldwin's Revisions of Gide's Sexual Politics," *MELUS* 22.1 (spring 1997): 8.

22. Emmanuel Nelson, "Critical Deviance: Homophobia and the Reception of James Baldwin's Fiction," *Journal of American Culture* 14 (1991): 91.

23. Henry Louis Gates, Jr., "The Black Man's Burden," *Fear of a Queer Planet: Queer Politics and Social Theory*, ed. Michael Warner (London & Minneapolis: University of Minneapolis Press, 1993), 234.

24. Cheryl Clarke, "The Failure to Transform: Homophobia in the Black Community," *Home Girls: A Black Feminist Anthology*, ed. Barbara Smith (1983; reprint, New Brunswick, N.J.: Rutgers University Press, 2000), 198; see also bell hooks, "Homophobia in Black Communities," *The Greatest Taboo: Homosexuality in Black Commu-*

nities, ed. Delroy Constantine-Simms (Los Angeles & New York: Alyson Books, 2001), 67-73.

25. Campbell, *Talking at the Gates*, 175.

26. This account was reprinted as "A Fly in Buttermilk," *Nobody Knows My Name: More Notes of a Native Son* [1964] (London: Penguin, 1991), 76-87; hereafter abbreviated in the notes as *Nobody Knows*.

27. Leeming, 175.

28. Campbell, *Talking at the Gates*, 125.

29. For a detailed account of this meeting, which included Lorraine Hansberry and the white actor Rip Torn, see Campbell, *Talking at the Gates*, 163-179. According to Campbell, the meeting failed "to achieve anything significant" (165).

30. James Campbell, "I Heard It Through the Grapevine," *Granta* 73 (spring 2001): 175.

31. Harold Cruse, *The Crisis of the Negro Intellectual: A Historical Analysis of the Failure of Black Leadership* (1967; reprint with a foreword by Bazel E. Allen and Ernest J. Wilson III. New York: Quill, 1984), 194; Cruse also notes Norman Podhoretz's attempts to get Baldwin "off that personal kick and make him talk about solutions and programs," which failed (194).

32. Eve Auchincloss and Nancy Lynch, "Disturber of the Peace: James Baldwin—an Interview," *Conversations with Baldwin*, 81.

33. Morris Dickstein, *Gates of Eden: American Culture in the Sixties* (New York: Basic Books, Inc., 1977), 168.

34. "Races: Freedom—Now," *Time* 81.20 (17 May 1963): 26; see also Jean François Gounard, *The Racial Problem in the Works of Richard Wright and James Baldwin*, trans. Joseph J. Rodgers, Jr., foreword by Jean F. Béranger (London & Connecticut: Greenwood Press, 1992), who notes that Baldwin's upbringing gave him "an unpredictable temperament. It made him a sensitive and nervous person. Thus the slightest event could have surprising effects on him" (149-50); see also Calvin C. Hernton, *White Papers For White Americans* (New York: Doubleday, 1966), who writes that it "is immensely revealing that the first Negro to get his face on a full page of the very feminine *Harper's Bazaar* (April 1963) is James Baldwin" (120).

35. See Stanley Crouch, "Chitlins at the Waldorf: the Work of Albert Murray," 113; Hernton, *White Papers*, 119.

36. For an insightful discussion of the term "queen," see Lee Edelman, "The Part for the (W)hole: Baldwin, Homophobia and the Fantasmatics of 'Race,'" *Homographies: Essays in Gay Literary and Cultural Theory* (New York & London: Routledge, 1994), esp. 42-4.

37. Campbell, "I Heard it Through the Grapevine," 171.

38. Campbell, "I Heard it Through the Grapevine," 171.

39. Erika Doss, "Imaging the Panthers: Representing Black Power and Masculinity, 1960s-1990s," *Prospects* 23 (1998): 486.

40. Doss, 488.

41. Eldridge Cleaver, "The Death of Martin Luther King," *Post-Prison Writings and Speeches*, ed. and introd. Robert Scheer (New York: Random House, 1969), 73.

42. Cleaver, "Psychology: The New Black Bible," *Post-Prison Writings*, 18; Cleaver argues that Fanon's book "legitimize[s] the revolutionary impulse to violence" (20).

43. Doss: 478.

44. Eldridge Cleaver, *Soul on Ice*, introd. Maxwell Geismar (New York, etc.: Ramparts, 1968), 106; hereafter abbreviated as *SOI.*

45. Clarke, 191.

46. King's chief-of-staff, Bayard Rustin, was dismissed under the guise of his left-wing commitments but mainly on account of his homosexuality. See W. J. Weatherby, *James Baldwin: Artist on Fire* (London: Michael Joseph, 1990), 143; see also Reginald Lockett, "Die Black Pervert," *Black Fire: An Anthology of Afro-American Writing*, ed. LeRoi Jones and Larry Neal (New York: William Morrow & Co., 1968), 354.

47. Michele Wallace, *Black Macho and the Myth of the Superwoman*, (1978; reprint with a new introduction by Wallace, New York: Dial Press, 1990), 37.

48. See Harper, esp. 165-6.

49. Clarke, 191.

50. See Cleaver, "Stanford Speech," *Post-Prison Writings*, 125, who notes that at 38, he was the oldest Panther; see also James Baldwin, "An Open Letter to My Sister, Miss Angela Davis," *New York Review of Books* 15.2 (7 January 1971) where he acknowledges George Jackson's dismissal of his generation (15).

51. Henry Louis Gates, Jr., "The Welcome Table," *Lure and Loathing: Essays on Race, Identity, and the Ambivalence of Assimilation*, ed. and introd. Gerald Early (London & New York: Allen Lane, 1993), 153.

52. Wallace, 59.

53. For a useful overview of how the Black Panthers took over from the ailing political impact of the Nation of Islam, see Cleaver, "The Decline of the Black Muslims," *Post-Prison Writings*, 13-17.

54. Wallace, 33.

55. Cleaver, "*Playboy* Interview with Nat Hentoff," *Post-Prison Writings*, 203.

56. Doss: 493.

57. Ron Simmons, "Some Thoughts on the Challenges Facing Black Intellectuals," *Brother to Brother*, 223; see also Marlon Riggs, "Black Macho Revisited: Reflections of a SNAP! Queen," *Brother to Brother*, esp. 254.

58. Robert Reid-Pharr, "'Tearing the Goat's Flesh': Homosexuality, Abjection and the Production of a Late Twentieth Century Masculinity," *Studies in the Novel* 28.3 (1996): 373-4.

59. bell hooks, "Reflections on Race and Sex," *Yearning: Race, Gender and Cultural Politics* (Boston: South End Press, 1990), 58.

60. Doss: 496.

61. See Cleaver, "Stanford Speech," *Post-Prison Writings*, where he states that black people "have turned away from the bootlicking leadership . . ." (116).

62. LeRoi Jones, "Black Art," *Black Fire*, 302.

63. Wallace, 68; see Clarke, who argues that Wallace does not debunk this view of homosexuality (197); see also Edelman, who notes the pervasiveness in African-American literature of the black man who is forced to submit to sex by a white male.

Rather portrayed "as 'being' homosexual," he notes that homosexuality is depicted as "the conflictual undoing of one man's authority by another" (54).

64. Wallace, 68.

65. Robert Staples, *Black Masculinity: The Black Man's Role in American Society* (San Francisco: Black Scholar, 1982), 2.

66. Wallace, 31; see Staples, who contested the report's findings on matriarchy; see also his article, "The Myth of the Black Matriarchy," *Black Scholar* (January 1970): 8-16.

67. Edelman, 48-9.

68. Kobena Mercer and Isaac Julien, "Racism and the Politics of Masculinity," *Male Order: Unwrapping Masculinity*, ed. Rowena Chapman and Jonathan Rutherford (1988; reprint, London: Lawrence & Wishart, 1996), 112; Staples, 64.

69. James Baldwin, "The Black Boy Looks at the White Boy," *Nobody Knows*, 178.

70. Frantz Fanon, *Black Skins, White Masks*, trans. Charles Lam Markamm, introd. Homi K. Bhabha [1952] (London: Pluto Press, 1986), 170; James Baldwin, *Just Above My Head* [1978] (London: Penguin, 1994), 105.

71. Jordan Elgrably and George Plimpton, "The Art of Fiction: James Baldwin," *Conversations with Baldwin*, 252.

72. Gates, "The Black Man's Burden," *Fear of a Queer Planet*, 233.

73. Weatherby, 293.

74. Gates, "The Welcome Table," *Lure and Loathing*, 159.

75. Dwight McBride, "Can the Queen Speak? Racial Essentialism, Sexuality and the Voice of Authority," *Callaloo* 21.2 (1998): 10.

76. Gates, "The Welcome Table," *Lure and Loathing*, 154.

77. Gates, "The Welcome Table," *Lure and Loathing*, 153.

78. See Campbell, *Talking at the Gates*, who notes that "it seems safe to quote Baldwin's remarks on certain events as if they were written at the time" (219).

79. Goldstein: 14.

80. James Baldwin, "No Name in the Street," *The Price of the Ticket: Collected Nonfiction, 1948-1985* (New York: St. Martin's/Marek, 1985), 453; hereafter abbreviated as *NNIS*.

81. James Baldwin, "From Dreams of Love to Dreams of Despair," *Natural Enemies? Youth and the Clash of Generations*, ed. Alexander Klein (New York & Philadelphia: J.B. Lippincott, 1967), 278.

82. Gates, "The Welcome Table," *Lure and Loathing*, 156.

83. See Campbell, *Talking at the Gates*, who notes that Baldwin "said little that was positive about Malcolm X . . . until Malcolm was killed" (219).

84. Campbell, *Talking at the Gates*, 219.

85. See Leeming, 284, 288, 299, 301-3, 306, 313.

86. Baldwin, "Autobiographical Notes," *Notes of a Native Son* [1955] (London: Penguin, 1995), 14; hereafter abbreviated in the notes as *Notes*.

87. See also James Baldwin and Margaret Mead, *A Rap on Race* (New York: Dell, 1971), 64.

88. Stanley Crouch, "The Rage of Race," *Notes of a Hanging Judge: Essays and Reviews, 1979-1989* (New York & Oxford: Oxford University Press, 1990), 234.

89. See Campbell, *Talking at the Gates*, who notes that Baldwin romanticises this period of his life (247-8).

90. Cleaver, "Introduction to the Biography of Huey P. Newton," *Post-Prison Writings*, 41.

91. See also, "Conversation: Ida Lewis and James Baldwin," [1970] *Conversations with Baldwin*, where JB states that with the deaths of Malcolm X and King, "dialogue is gone" (85); see also Cleaver, "Stanford Speech," *Post-Prison Writings*, where he states that "words are becoming more and more irrelevant" (114).

92. James Baldwin, "Notes for *Blues*," *Blues for Mister Charlie* [1964] (New York: Vintage Books, 1992), xiv; Calvin C. Hernton, "Dynamite Growing Out of Their Skulls," *Black Fire*, 101; Cleaver, "The Land Question and Black Liberation," *Post-Prison Writings*, 72.

93. Crouch, "Race Rage," *Notes of a Hanging Judge*, 234.

94. Wallace, 60, 62.

95. Wallace, 62; for examples of Baldwin's emphasis on black manhood and disagreements with black female radicals, see "Revolutionary Hope: A Conversation Between James Baldwin and Audre Lorde," *Essence* 15 (December 1984): 72-4, 129-33; see also James Baldwin and Nikki Giovanni, *A Dialogue*, foreword by Ida Lewis, afterword by Orde Coombs (London: Michael Joseph, 1975), esp. 7, 39-40, 41-2, 45, 49, 52-5.

96. Crouch, "The Rage of Race," *Notes of a Hanging Judge*, 231.

97. Crouch, "Meteor in a Black Hat," *Notes of a Hanging Judge*, 197; Amiri Baraka, "*Jimmy!*—James Arthur Baldwin," *Eulogies* (New York: Marsilio Publishers, 1996), 96.

98. Philip Roth, "Blues for Mister Charlie," *Modern Critical Views: James Baldwin*, ed. Harold Bloom (New York & Philadelphia: Chelsea House Publishers, 1986), 41; Hernton, *White Papers*, 131.

99. Gates, "The Welcome Table," *Lure and Loathing*, 158.

100. For an explanation of this term, which refers to the white search for a contender to beat the first black heavyweight champion, Jack Johnson, see Carlton Moss, "The Great White Hope," *A Freedomways Reader*, ed. Ernest Kaiser, foreword by James Baldwin (New York: International Publishers, 1977), 50-63.

101. For example, see James Baldwin, *Tell Me How Long the Train's Been Gone* [1968] (London: Penguin, 1994), where Leo recalls his relationship with a Harlem racketeer (210); compare this to his recollection in "Here Be Dragons," *The Price of the Ticket*, 681; hereafter abbreviated in the notes as *Price*; see also Leeming, 279-80.

102. James Baldwin, *Tell Me How Long the Train's Been Gone*, 382; hereafter abbreviated as *TMHL*.

103. Campbell, *Talking at the Gates*, 228.

104. Irving Howe, "James Baldwin: At Ease in Apocalypse," *Harper's* 237 (September 1968): 95, 96, 100.

105. Campbell, *Talking at the Gates*, 227.

106. See Campbell, *Talking at the Gates*, where Baldwin notes that Leo was Rufus Scott, but without the suicide (228).

107. Cited by Leeming, 281.

108. James Giles, "Religious Alienation and 'Homosexual Consciousness' in *City of Night* and *Go Tell It on the Mountain*," *College English* 36 (1974): 378; see also Emmanuel Nelson, "The Novels of James Baldwin: Struggles For Self-Acceptance," *Journal of American Culture* 8, no. 4 (winter 1985), who suggests that JB tried to appease black militants by his negative portrayals of white homosexuality (15).

109. See also where Baldwin refers to a "poor white faggot" and "another faggot" (325).

110. Countee Cullen, *The Black Christ and Other Poems* (New York and London: Harper & Brothers, 1929), 69-110.

111. See "Hubert Fichte Interviews Jean Genet," *Gay Sunshine Interviews*, vol. 1, ed. Winston Leyland (San Francisco: Gay Sunshine Press, 1978), 69.

112. Cited by White, 441. Occasionally Genet did provoke outrage: on one occasion, White notes that Genet "took too many Nembutals and danced in a pink negligée for Hilliard and three other Panthers" (529).

113. See White, who notes that Baldwin and Genet often dined alone and frequented the same gay bar in Paris in the early 1950s. Baldwin was also a great admirer of *The Blacks* (439). For details of their collaboration with the Panthers, see White, 544, 563; for details of Genet's input, see ch. 18, esp. 521-46; see also Jean Genet, *May Day Speech*, introd. Alan Ginsberg (San Francisco: City Lights, 1970); Jean Genet, *Prisoner of Love*, trans. Barbara Bray, introd. Edmund White (London: Picador, 1989), esp. 41-9, 83-6, 213-20, 258-61.

114. Jean Genet, *Here and Now For Bobby Seale* (New York, 1970). White notes that Genet contacted a journalist from the widely-read magazine *Le Nouvel Observateur* to discuss the plight of the Panther; the interview was soon translated into English, German and Italian (539).

115. See Fichte, esp. 93.

116. Fichte, 93; Cleaver, "The Courage to Kill: Meeting the Panthers," *Post-Prison Writings*, 23; Cleaver also describes his first meeting with the Panthers as "the most beautiful sight I had ever seen" (29); Dollimore, 353. For brief but useful overview of Genet's "revolutionary erotics," see Pascale Gaitet, "Jean Genet's American Dream: The Black Panthers," *Literature and History* 1.1 (spring 1992): 48-63.

117. Fichte, 80.

118. Genet, *Prisoner of Love*, 126, 260.

119. Genet, *Prisoner of Love*, 259.

120. Genet, *Prisoner of Love*, 260, 83.

121. George Jackson, *Soledad Brother: The Prison Letters of George Jackson*, foreword Jonathan Jackson, Jr., introd. Jean Genet [1970] (Chicago: Lawrence Hill Books, 1994), 332.

122. See Angela Davis, *An Autobiography* [1974] (London: The Women's Press, 1990). Davis notes that she used part of Baldwin's open letter to her in 1970 to name her anthology *If They Come in the Morning* (306).

123. See Edmund White's introduction to *Prisoner of Love*, where he notes that "political action filled the void left in his life when he was awakened from his reverie as an artist" (ix).

124. See Campbell, *Talking at the Gates*, who cites criticism that Baldwin held a

"vague position," in contrast to the Panthers (219); see also Gates, "The Welcome Table," where he states that "his [Baldwin's] arguments, richly nuanced and self-consciously ambivalent, were far too complex to serve straightforwardly political ends" (150).

125. See Fichte, where Genet says, "[p]erhaps I'm a black with white or pink skin, but I'm a black" (75).

126. Cited by White, 528. The open letter was published in the *Black Panther Magazine* (15 August, 1970). See Fichte, where Genet claims that he told Bobby Seale that if he attacked homosexuals, he would attack black Americans. According to Genet, Newton's letter was published one week later (93).

127. Fichte, 92.

128. Wallace, 61-2.

129. Eve Auchincloss and Nancy Lynch, "Disturber of the Peace: James Baldwin—an Interview," *Conversations with Baldwin*, ed. Fred L. Standley and Louis H. Pratt (Jackson & London: University Press of Mississippi, 1989), 79.

130. Stanley Crouch, "Clichés of Degradation," *Village Voice* (29 October 1979): 39; cited by Emmanuel Nelson, "Critical Deviance: Homophobia and the Reception of James Baldwin's Fiction," *Journal of American Culture* 14 (1991): 92; James Baldwin, *Just Above My Head* [1978] (London: Penguin, 1994), 471.

131. Joseph Beam, "James Baldwin: Not a Bad Legacy, Brother," *Brother to Brother*, 240; Lorelei Cederstrom, "Love, Race and Sex in the Novels of James Baldwin," *Mosaic* 17, no. 2 (1984): 176.

132. Baldwin, "Everybody's Protest Novel," *Notes*, 26.

Works Cited

Auchincloss, Eve and Nancy Lynch. "Disturber of the Peace: James Baldwin." *Conversations with James Baldwin*. Ed. Fred L. Standley and Louis H. Pratt. Jackson & London: University of Mississippi Press, 1989.

Baldwin, James. "The Black Boy Looks at the White Boy." *Nobody Knows My Name: More Notes of a Native Son*. 1961. London: Penguin, 1991.

___________. "Here Be Dragons." *The Price of the Ticket: Collected Nonfiction, 1948-1985*. New York: St. Martin's/Marek, 1985.

___________. *Just Above My Head*. 1978. London: Penguin, 1994.

___________. "No Name in the Street." *The Price of the Ticket: Collected Nonfiction, 1948-1985*. New York: St. Martin's/Marek, 1985.

___________. *Tell Me How Long the Train's Been Gone*. 1968. London: Penguin, 1994.

___________, and Margaret Mead. *A Rap on Race*. New York: Dell, 1971.

Baraka, Amiri. *Eulogies*. New York: Marsilio Publishers, 1996.

Beam, Joseph. "James Baldwin: Not a Bad Legacy, Brother." *Brother to Brother: New Writings By Black Gay Men*. Ed. Essex Hemphill. Boston: Alyson Publications, Inc., 1991. 184-186.

Bergman, David. *Gaiety Transfigured: Gay Self-Representation in American Literature*. Wisconsin: University of Wisconsin Press, 1991.

Campbell, James. *Talking at the Gates: a Life of James Baldwin*. London & Boston: Faber & Faber, 1991.

___________. "I Heard It Through the Grapevine." *Granta* 73 (spring 2001): 153-82.

Clarke, Cheryl. "The Failure to Transform: Homophobia in the Black Community." *Home Girls: A Black Feminist Anthology*. Ed. Barbara Smith. New Brunswick, N.J.: Rutgers University Press, 1983; reprint, 2000.

Cleaver, Eldridge. *Soul on Ice*. Introd. Maxwell Geismar. New York & Toronto: Ramparts, 1968.

Crouch, Stanley. "Chitlins at the Waldorf: the Work of Albert Murray." *Notes of a Hanging Judge: Essays and Reviews, 1979-1989*. New York: Oxford University Press, 1990.

Cullen, Countee. *The Black Christ and Other Poems*. New York and London: Harper and Brothers, 1929.

DeGout, Yasmin. "'Masculinity' and (Im)maturity: 'The Man Child' and Other Stories in Baldwin's Gender Studies Enterprise." *Re-Viewing James Baldwin: Things Not Seen*. Ed. D. Quentin Miller, foreword by David Leeming. Philadelphia: Temple University Press, 2000.

Delany, Samuel R. and Joseph Beam. "Samuel Delany: The Possibility of Possibilities." *In the Life: A Gay Black Anthology*. Ed. Joseph Beam. Boston: Alyson Publications, 1986. 185-208.

Dickstein, Morris. *Gates of Eden: American Culture in the Sixties*. New York: Basic Books. 1977.

Doss, Erika. "Imaging the Panthers: Representing Black Power and Masculinity, 1960s-1990s." *Prospects* 23 (1998): 483-516.

Edelman, Lee. *Homographies: Essays in Gay Literary and Cultural Theory*. New York & London: Routledge, 1994.

Fanon, Frantz. *Black Skins, White Masks*. Trans. Charles Lam Markmann. Foreword by Homi K. Bhabha. 1952. London: Pluto Press, 1986.

Fichte, Hubert. "Hubert Fichte Interviews Jean Genet." *Gay Sunshine Interviews*. Vol. 1. Ed. Winston Leyland. San Francisco: Gay Sunshine Press, 1978.

Gates, Henry Louis, Jr. "The Black Man's Burden." *Fear of a Queer Planet: Queer Politics and Social Theory*. Ed. Michael Warner. London & Minneapolis: University of Minnesota Press, 1993.

___________. "The Welcome Table." *Lure and Loathing: Essays on Race, Identity and the Ambivalence of Assimilation*. Ed. & introd. Gerald Early. London and New York: Allen Lane, 1993.

Genet, Jean. *May Day Speech*. Introd. Alan Ginsberg. San Francisco: City Lights, 1970.

___________. *Here and Now For Bobby Seale*. New York, 1970.

___________. *Prisoner of Love*. Trans. Barbara Bray. Introd. Edmund White. London: Picador, 1989.

Gibson, Donald. "James Baldwin: The Political Anatomy of Space." *James Bald-*

win: A Critical Evaluation. Ed. Therman B. O'Daniel. Washington, D.C.: Howard University Press, 1977. 3-19.

Goldstein, Richard. "Go The Way Your Blood Beats: An Interview with James Baldwin." *Village Voice* 26 (June 1984): 13, 14, 16.

Harper, Phillip Brian. "Eloquence and Epitaph: Black Nationalism and the Homophobic Impulse in Responses to the Death of Max Robinson." *The Lesbian and Gay Studies Reader*. Ed. Henry Abelove, Michèle Aina Barale, and David M. Halperin. New York & London: Routledge, 1993.

Hemphill, Essex. "Looking For Langston: An Interview with Isaac Julien." *Brother to Brother: New Writings By Black Gay Men*. Ed. Essex Hemphill. Boston: Alyson Publications, Inc., 1991. 174-80.

Hernton, Calvin C. "A Fiery Baptism." *James Baldwin: A Collection of Critical Essays*. Ed. Keneth Kinnamon. New Jersey: Prentice-Hall, Inc., 1974.

Jackson, George. *Soledad Brother: The Prison Letters of George Jackson*. Foreword by Jonathan Jackson, Jr. Introd. Jean Genet. Chicago: Lawrence Hill Books, 1994.

Leeming, David. *Baldwin: a Biography*. New York: Alfred A. Knopf, 1994.

Mossman, James. "Race, Hate, Sex, and Colour: A Conversation with James Baldwin." *Conversations with James Baldwin*. Ed. Fred L. Standley and Louis H. Pratt. Jackson & London: University of Mississippi Press, 1989.

Nelson, Emmanuel. "Critical Deviance: Homophobia and the Reception of James Baldwin's Fiction." *Journal of American Culture* 14 (1991): 91-6.

Reid-Pharr, Robert. "'Tearing the Goat's Flesh': Homosexuality, Abjection and the Production of a Late Twentieth Century Masculinity." *Studies in the Novel* 28.3 (1996): 373-4.

Romanet, Jerome de. "Revisiting *Madeleine* and 'The Outing': James Baldwin's Revision of Gide's Sexual Politics." *MELUS* 22, 1 (spring 1997): 3-14.

Roth, Phillip. "Blues for Mister Charlie." *Modern Critical Views: James Baldwin*. Ed. Harold Bloom. New York and Philadelphia: Chelsea House Publishers, 1986.

Simmons, Ron. "Some Thoughts on the Challenges Facing Gay Black Intellectuals." *Brother to Brother: New Writings by Black Gay Men*. Ed. Essex Hemphill. Boston: Alyson Publications, Inc., 1991. 211-228.

Wallace, Michele. *Black Macho and the Myth of the Superwoman*. Reprint, with introduction by Michele Wallace. 1978. New York: Dial Press, 1990.

Weatherby, W. J. *James Baldwin: Artist on Fire: a Portrait*. London: Michael Joseph, 1990.

White, Edmund. *Genet: a Biography*. New York: Alfred A. Knopf, 1993.

The Tale of Two Cities in James Baldwin's *Go Tell It on the Mountain*

Charles Scruggs

Generally regarded as one of the great Negro novels of twentieth-century America, *Go Tell It on the Mountain* has received a variety of critical responses since it was first published in 1953. Critics have seen Baldwin's novel as a psychological study of the clash between father and son, as a sociological examination of the role of the church in the black community, and as a black *Bildungsroman*.[1] What has been overlooked is that Baldwin's themes transcend the life of one black youth and the lives, past and present, of one black family. Baldwin places his characters in a recognizable intellectual tradition, and he uses this tradition to express their individual destinies.

Throughout intellectual history, the city as an *idea* has been haunted by double moral judgments, and Americans too have shared these ambiguities. Scripture, as Maynard Mack observes, "begins with a garden and ends with a city"; and yet the Bible sometimes exhibits extreme hostility to the city.[2] Greco-Roman culture manifests the same ambivalence. Classical antiquity celebrated the city as civilization and community—only to condemn it, as Juvenal did Rome, as that environment which dehumanizes.[3] Americans as well have had their own urban version of the earthly paradise at the same time that they have remained deeply skeptical of real cities.[4]

Although the setting of *Go Tell It on the Mountain* is the all too real city of New York, especially Harlem, Baldwin then has based his novel's meaning on one of the richest, most complex of configurations in the history of thought: the idea of the city. In *Go Tell It on the Mountain*, Baldwin juxtaposes two cities, the earthly and the heavenly, and together they help to focus the novel's various themes: father and son, individual and community, the sacred and the profane. Baldwin obviously depends upon Saint Augustine's two cities to give structure to these thematic oppositions, but he does not believe that Augustine tells the whole truth about the earthly city. At the end of *Go Tell It on the Mountain*, John Grimes, Baldwin's young protagonist, will have a transcendent experience reminiscent of John of Patmos's vision in the Book of Revelation. Nevertheless, his moment of truth will be fraught with ambiguity, for the New Jerusalem which he sees has its psychological roots in the very earthly city which he rejected.

The Negro spiritual, "Go Tell It on the Mountain," whose title Baldwin appropriated for his novel, presents an Augustinian view of man's lot in the world. For Augustine, the true Christian is only a pilgrim in this life but a citizen in the next.[5] A wayfarer and a "seeker," he would be lost without Christ's help, but Christ has graciously shown him "the way." Thus he is capable of achieving a heavenly city within himself, yet it is in constant peril from the evil forces outside "the city wall":

> Oh when I was a seeker,
> I sought both night and day,
> I asked the Lord to help me,
> And He showed me the way.
>
> And He made me a watchman
> Upon the city wall;
> And if I am a Christian
> I am the least of all.

In the novel, the "city wall" also refers to the Negro church, the community of true believers who do daily battle with the frightening reality of Harlem. "The Temple of the Fire Baptized" stands on a corner "facing the hospital to which criminal wounded and dying were carried almost every night."[6] The hospital is an apt symbol, for Harlem is the earthly city sickened unto death.

The earliest memories of John Grimes are of Harlem as a diseased city. On their way to Sunday morning service, he and his family had walked its streets and had seen the men and women who had "spent the night in bars, or in cat houses, or on the streets, or on rooftops, or under the stairs." These people had seemed to haunt the Sunday mornings like angry ghosts: "They talked, and laughed, and fought together, and the women fought like the men." One time, he and his brother Roy "had watched a man and woman in the basement of a condemned house. They did it standing up. The woman had wanted fifty cents, and the man had flashed a razor" (p. 12). These images of Harlem which John remembers are worthy of William Blake's "London," and their import is the same as the tenor of Blake's poem: in this world there exists only a terrible mockery of the human community.

Harlem is an urban nightmare. New York is Vanity Fair: its attractive surface is deceptive. Yet Baldwin, finally, is not content to reduce New York to the dimensions of the treacherous city of *Pilgrim's Progress*. Although garish Fifth Avenue is one symbol of New York in the novel, Baldwin reminds us that this earthly city also contains the New York Public Library, the Museum of Natural History, and the Metropolitan Museum of Art. Viewed from this angle, the earthly city casts an ironic light upon the themes of the Negro spiritual. The watchman on the Augustinian "city wall" has myopic vision; he can see the icons of the earthly city but not their meaning. Thus the tension in *Go Tell It on the Mountain* arises from the clash between two conceptions of the earthly city: New York versus Harlem and New York versus itself.

I

As John Grimes approaches manhood, his confused feelings about his stepfather, his home, and himself have become unbearable. On the one hand, he hates Gabriel (whom he believes to be his real father) and the shabby life Gabriel has created for his family. As a substitute preacher in a storefront church in Harlem, Gabriel professes contempt for the goods of this world, and John actively rebels against his austere religion. On the other hand, John is constantly seeking Gabriel's approval, because he does not understand why his "father" abuses him.

Also, although John finds Gabriel's view of man (naturally sinful) repugnant, he has unconsciously accepted his stepfather's grim, Calvinistic theology. On his fourteenth birthday, the day on which the action of the novel takes place, John has committed a sin of the flesh (masturbation), and a yellow stain on the ceiling of his room seems to call attention to his human depravity (p. 18). Thus coming of age, John is torn by a dilemma. He desperately wants to embrace the earthly city to escape Gabriel's circumscribed world, but he cannot free himself from seeing this city through Gabriel's eyes.

John believes that his intelligence will be his passport to "another life." His teacher at school had praised his work, and her esteem "rose in his mind like a great brass gate, opening outward for him on a world where people did not live in the darkness of his father's house, did not pray to Jesus in the darkness of his father's church, where he would eat good food, and wear fine clothes, and go to the movies as often as he wished" (p. 19). However, whenever John does try to enter the earthly city, Gabriel hovers over him like a persistent spirit. It soon becomes clear that John's ambivalent response to his stepfather is a reflection of another problem—his inability to accept either view of the earthly city: a place of liberation or a place of damnation.

This theme is made dramatically apparent in a scene which takes place in Central Park. On the Saturday afternoon of his birthday, John climbs his favorite hill which overlooks New York. Running to the top, he is overcome by feelings of wonder and power as he gazes upon the sublime vista of the city. Suddenly, he has an urge "to throw himself headlong into the city that glowed before him." This, he thinks, is the "shining city which his ancestors had seen with longing from far away." Now "it was his; the inhabitants of the city had told him it was his; he had but to run down, crying, and they would take him to their hearts and show him wonders his eyes had never seen" (p. 33). The situation, of course, is archetypal: the view from the mountain of the glorious earthly city. It is reminiscent of Anchises taking Aeneas to a mountain top and showing him Rome.[7]

Yet as John experiences these emotions, he simultaneously hears the voice of his stepfather: this city would bring his soul to "perdition" (p. 33). Broadway, the street whose name implied a world more expansive, now calls forth a biblical meaning: "the way that led to death was broad, and many could be found thereon; but narrow was the way that led to life eternal, and few there were who found it" (p. 34). Still, John tries to resist Gabriel:

> But he did not long for the narrow way, where all his people walked; where the houses did not rise, piercing, as it seemed, the unchanging clouds, but huddled, flat, ignoble, close to the filthy ground, where the streets and the hallways and the rooms were dark, and where the unconquerable odor was of dust, and sweat, and urine, and homemade gin. In the narrow way, the way of the cross, there awaited him only humiliation forever; there awaited him, one day, a house like his father's house, and a church like his father's, and a job like his father's, where he would grow old and black with hunger and toil. The way of the cross had given him a belly filled with wind and had bent his mother's back; they had never worn fine clothes, but here, where the buildings contested God's power and where the men and women did not fear God, here he might eat and drink to his heart's content and clothe his body with wondrous fabrics, rich to the eye and pleasing to the touch. (p. 34)

The glories of paradise were "unimaginable," he concludes, but "the city was real." Ironically, John cannot imagine a celestial city because in his mind Christianity cannot be separated from the hellishness of his father's house.

Convinced that New York is his true home, John leaves the hilltop and enters Fifth Avenue. The affluence and elegance of this street remind him of a movie set, and he imagines himself a member of a marvelous community. But again the spirit of Gabriel pursues him. These people have *no* church, John tells himself: "They were in the world, and of the world, and their feet laid hold on Hell" (p. 36). Besides,

"Niggers did not live on these streets," John thinks, now sounding like Gabriel. Nor were they allowed to enter the wonderful shops and apartments: "not today," and he hears his stepfather's laughter, "*No, nor tomorrow neither!*" (p. 36).

Fleeing Fifth Avenue, John walks over to 42nd street where, significantly, the spirit of his stepfather does not follow him. "He loved this street," Baldwin says of John, "not for the people or the shops but for the stone lions that guarded the great main building of the Public Library" (p. 37). The library is the heart of the earthly city, as the "temple" is the heart of the heavenly city.[8] In the novel, "The Temple of the Fire Baptized" not only stands in direct opposition to the hospital but also to the Public Library. Thus Baldwin shows us both the strength and weakness of the Negro church.[9]

What prevents John from entering the Public Library is not his fear of the lions, which to him are symbols of the intellectual treasures of the earthly city, but rather his fear of the "maze" within the enormous building in "which he would be lost and never find the book he wanted" (p. 37). In other words, it is his inexperience which keeps him out of the library, and not Gabriel's nay-saying voice. This scene, short as it is, serves to point to an important distinction between John and his stepfather. Gabriel's "lions," as we shall see, have never ceased to consume him. The suggestion that John is a black Daniel, who will live in the world without being destroyed by it, is made manifest in the nature of his subsequent religious experience. Furthermore, his love of the Public Library establishes a link between him and his real father, who also sought the wisdom which the city offered.

Seeing a movie climaxes his visit to the earthly city on his birthday. At first, the film's tuberculosis-ridden, wicked heroine (probably Bette Davis in *Of Human Bondage*) appealed to John because of her insolence and urban self-assuredness: "It was unimaginable that she would ever bend her knees and come crawling along a dusty floor to anybody's altar, weeping for forgiveness" (p. 39). But the film is soon to become a reflection of the two faces of New York which torment him.

Confronted by death, the woman with whom John identifies loses her worldliness and becomes a repentant sinner. It was almost as if God had sent him to this theater "to show him an example of the wages of sin" (p. 40). Yet sitting in the theater at the movie's end, made miserable by the thought of eternal damnation, John still seeks, Baldwin says, "to find a compromise between the way that led to life everlasting and the way that ended in the pit" (p. 40). His conversion to Christ in the last section of the novel springs from his desire to find a "middle way" between the broad and narrow roads to Hell or Heaven. The "compromise" he achieves humanizes the demands of one city and helps keep in abeyance the dangers of the other.

II

Baldwin once said that he agreed with the Old Testament view that the "sins of the fathers are visited upon their children."[10] In the middle section of the novel, there are four "fathers": Florence (John's aunt), Gabriel, Elizabeth (John's mother) and Richard (John's real father). Their histories cast a shadow upon John, for all have been "seekers" whose quests are ironically fulfilled. Each quest is circular; its end lies in its beginning.

The middle section of *Go Tell It on the Mountain* is a descent into Augustine's City of Man. As Florence, Gabriel, and Elizabeth pray in "The Temple of the Fire Baptized" on the evening of John's birthday, they are incapable of transcendence. Each is haunted by his or her own past, and each is trapped within his or her own ego. If they are incapable of hope, it is because they have no future. Unlike John, their portraits are already drawn; their memories provide the brush strokes of those deeds which have made them who they are. Also, the landscape of their memories is not factual but moral. In this part of the novel, Baldwin locates his theme of the two cities within a familiar Christian-pastoral tradition in which reflection upon past events supposedly leads to spiritual enlightenment. But here the irony is apparent, for each character's remembrances repeat the same refrain: none of them has escaped the earthly city.

Florence remembers the most significant event in her past, the day she walked out her mother's front gate to live in New York City. As the older female child in the family, Florence had been expected to sacrifice everything, including her education, for her spoiled brother Gabriel. Furthermore, her mother's pious resignation hung over their house like a dark cloud, so that New York became her private symbol of freedom and of a promise of earthly happiness commensurate with her intelligence. Thus when her white employer offered to make her his mistress, she decided that she had had enough. On that very day, even though her mother lay dying, she bought a train ticket for New York. As she closed the gate behind her, the insult she hurled at Gabriel is an indication of the great flaw in her dream: "If you ever see me again . . . I won't be wearing rags like yours" (p. 80).

For in fleeing the peasant vulgarity of the rural South, Florence soon became trapped by the vulgarity of her own worldly ambitions. Committed to the proposition of upward social mobility, she was incapable of compromise. Frank, her husband, lacked her ambition, for he believed that it was futile in a white man's city. His virtues are resiliency and humor, but Florence refused to recognize these. Worshipping the gods of frugality and industry, she became, paradoxically, as puritanical as Gabriel. Hence, she lost any possible happiness she might have had with her husband because she was constantly trying to change his life rather than trying to enlarge her dream.

Frank finally left her for another woman, and as we see her in the present, she is reduced to wearing "rags" as she works as a cleaning lady in a New York office building. Dying of cancer, she is haunted by guilt and revenge, guilt for her treatment of Frank and her mother and revenge against Gabriel for his cruel hypocrisy. Gabriel, however, is merely a target at which to vent her frustration and rage. It is the world which she feels has betrayed her, and even when death is near, she cannot transcend it; guilt and hatred are more real to her than God. In seeking her dreams of the earthly city, she has come to experience only its nightmares.

Gabriel thinks that he has escaped the earthly city, but in reality he dwells right at its center. As a young man, he had "feared and hated the lions of lust and longing that prowled the defenseless city of his mind" (p. 94). After a night of debauchery, however, he discovered God one spring morning on a hilltop, and thereafter he has traveled "the high road of holiness" (p. 88). "The lions of lust and longing," he felt, had been conquered.

Throughout the middle section of the novel, Gabriel is associated with the "mountain" of the novel's title, but this symbol reverberates with irony, for it also suggests the nature of Gabriel's pride and self-deception. Because of his transcendental experience on a hilltop, Gabriel has placed himself above others; he judges them without ever looking into the recesses of his own heart. Thus Gabriel's "mountain" provides him with the illusion of both his spiritual superiority over his fellow man and his control over his riotous ego, "the defenseless city of his mind." In the novel's middle section, there are two dramatic illustrations of Gabriel's misperception that he has risen above the earthly city.

One night, just before his marriage to Deborah, he had two dreams. In one, he found himself ensnared by the sexual lusts of his past, and in the other, he imagined himself arduously climbing a steep mountain toward God. In the second dream, after much travail, he reached the top which was suddenly blanketed in glorious sunshine. He then heard a voice telling him to look down the side of the mountain. He saw a file of saints following in his footsteps, and the voice said prophetically to Gabriel, "So shall thy seed be" (p. 112).

When he woke from the second dream, he interpreted it as a sign to marry Deborah and father a "royal line" of saints. His religious vision, however, is *not* religious; it is secular, a dream of power in this world. Gabriel has imagined himself as the founder of a mighty empire, and his marriage to the tainted Deborah[11] was to be visible proof of his spiritual purity. Thus in trying to escape "the defenseless city of his mind," Gabriel has climbed a mountain only to fall back into himself.

Gabriel's sexual affair with Esther is another manifestation of his self-deception. Thinking that he was bringing another sinner to God, he had invited this beautiful, brazen woman to attend church and hear his sermon. He preached so passionately that Esther was pleased "as though she were at a theater" (p. 121). Without realizing it, Gabriel had staged this event for Esther's benefit and had transformed the church, the fortress protecting Christians from the temptations of the earthly city, into Vanity Fair. Moreover, Gabriel's text was from "the second book of Samuel, the story of the young Ahimaaz who ran too soon to bring the tidings of battle to King David." Not knowing the outcome, Ahimaaz confusedly tells David "I saw a great tumult but I knew not what it was" (p. 119). Like Ahimaaz, Gabriel "ran too soon"; in his passion to travel the "high road" to the celestial city, he never stopped to examine his own life—he "knew not what it was." His treatment of Esther, whom he abandoned, of Royal, whom he refused to recognize as his son, of Elizabeth, whom he tries to make pay for his sins, of John, whom he hates as a sign of Elizabeth's sin—these acts stem from his inability to recognize that he too is a pilgrim in the earthly city.

In Elizabeth's "prayer," Baldwin again uses the images of city and mountain to reveal the pattern of his character's fate. John saw the glorious earthly city from a mountaintop; Gabriel, the celestial city. Elizabeth remembers the New York of her youth as a perilous city perched on a high cliff.

As young people, she and Richard had seen New York as an escape from an intolerable situation in the South. For Elizabeth, it meant release from a tyrannical aunt; for Richard, from a racist society. The city also had held out a promise. Elizabeth viewed New York as a refuge for her innocent love, and Richard imagined it as a crucible containing the intellectual and aesthetic heritage of Civilization.

They soon discovered that the city's freedom was a double-edged sword. If no one zealously watched over them, no one cared about them either:

> Here, in this great city . . . where people might live in the same building for years and never speak to one another, she [Elizabeth] found herself, when Richard took her in his arms, on the edge of a steep place: and down she rushed, on the descent uncaring, into the dreadful sea. (p. 162)

Richard had tried to go to school and work both, and so they had remained unmarried. But even before Elizabeth had discovered her pregnancy, she had begun to fear "the tigerish lights of the city" (p. 163).

To Elizabeth, New York's nervous energy became a reflection of Richard's personality (p. 163), for Richard was seeking his identity in this labyrinthine city, and he was desperately trying to find the thread that would lead him to it. On Saturday afternoons, Richard would take Elizabeth to the Museum of Natural History or the Metropolitan Museum of Art. In the latter, he gazed, "with such melancholy wonder," upon an "African statuette, or totem pole," that Elizabeth was bewildered by his adoration of "things that were so long dead." She sensed, however, that they gave Richard

> a kind of bitter nourishment, and that the secrets they held for him were a matter of his life and death. It frightened her because she felt that he was reaching for the moon and that he would, therefore, be dashed down against the rocks. . . . (p. 166)

Knowledge was to be Richard's key to unlocking the prison house of his cultural past and, thereby, the prison house of himself. In addition, Richard strove to achieve an intellectual equality with the white man. He was determined, as he told Elizabeth, "to get to know everything them white bastards knew" (p. 167).

All his dreams came to nothing. As he discovered later, there was a fundamental flaw in his plan. He had subscribed to the ideal of Western

Civilization, the life of the intellect, without ever ascertaining whether it would be recognized in a black man. One night, while waiting for a subway, he was unjustly arrested by the police for robbing a grocery store. Its white owner could not distinguish him from the others who did the robbing because, to him, Richard was just another "nigger." In a scene reminiscent of Ellison's *Invisible Man*, Richard insisted upon his "visibility":

> "But I wasn't there! Look at me, goddammit—I wasn't *there*!"
>
> "You black bastards," the man said, looking at him, "you're all the same." (p. 171)

It is this conversation, not the beatings in jail, which broke Richard's spirit and caused him to commit suicide. The very structure of his life had been called into question. He discovered, to his dismay, that lie had built his house upon a marsh. No matter how smart he is, he remains a "nigger."

Richard's death changed Elizabeth. New York now became in her mind the City of Destruction. Pregnant with an illegitimate child, she looked for sanctuary in the wilderness of New York. After giving birth to John, she married Gabriel who seemed to her to be a "hiding-place hewn in the side of the mountain" (p. 186).

The first meeting between Gabriel and Elizabeth underscores the symbolic issues of the novel. After Deborah's death, Gabriel had joined his sister in New York, and Elizabeth encountered him one Sunday afternoon at Florence's home. Next door a phonograph record was playing, and the music could be heard through the walls. Gabriel associated it with the "Devil's" work in the earthly city (p. 184); whereas John, a baby, instinctively responded to it "by wriggling, and moving his hands in the air, and making noises meant . . . to be taken as a song" (p. 182). The music reminds us of Richard—his importance in Elizabeth's life and his living influence in the life of their son.

Just as Gabriel and Elizabeth have become emotionally interested in one another, each for different reasons, the music heard through the walls of Florence's room was interrupted by a flaw in the record. The phonograph needle had stuck

> on a grinding, wailing, sardonic trumpet-note; this blind ugly crying swelled the moment and filled the room. . . . A hand somewhere struck the gramophone arm and sent the silver needle on its way through the whirling, black grooves, like something bobbing, anchorless, in the middle of the sea. (p. 185)

Richard had been a lost soul, "anchorless, in the middle of the sea," yet there had been something vital in him too, for he had tried to grasp the aesthetic richness of the world. The music Gabriel will make on his trumpet will be harsh and out of tune. In time Elizabeth will discover that the strong mountain is also stark and barren, but now, thinking of her future, she willingly chooses Gabriel over the intense, vibrant city which had symbolized Richard's life.

III

In the last section of the novel, John also makes a choice, one which cures his emotional paralysis. The basic paradox of John's religious experience is that John's "victory" is only the beginning of a new battle. Unlike the decisions of his elders, which were inexorable in their finality, John's choice represents a temporary solution to an unsolvable problem.

In the middle of Saturday night service at "The Temple of the Fire Baptized," John is possessed by the "spirit" and falls to the floor of the church. At first, an "ironic voice" in his mind tells him "to rise . . . and, at once, to leave this temple and go out into the world" (p. 193). Otherwise, he would "become like all the other niggers" (p. 194). This is the voice of the earthly city, urbane and cynical, the voice of Bette Davis in the movie he has seen that afternoon. Although the "ironic voice" is insistent, it is weak, because John is now convinced, albeit subconsciously, that the appeal of the earthly city is overshadowed by its uncertainties.

The death of the earthly city in the young boy's imagination is vividly portrayed in a dream sequence. John sees himself walking with Gabriel through the street of a mysterious city. The buildings are narrow, "rising like spears into the sky and they were made of beaten gold and silver" (p. 198). But this is not the heavenly city of the Bible, for "John knew that these buildings were not for him—not today–*no, nor tomorrow, either!*" The echo of his stepfather's voice in his mind reminds us of his earlier journey that day on Fifth Avenue. Continuing their walk through this street, Gabriel and John encounter an ugly, old hag. Gabriel points to her: "You see that? That's sin. That's what the Devil's son runs after" (p. 198). The allusion, of course, is to the whore of Babylon who dwells in the earthly city. Gabriel then threatens to beat sin out of John, and the young boy "looked about him for deliverance; but there was no deliverance in this street for him" (p. 199).

In his second dream, he observes the wretched of the earth in their pain and despair, and he realizes that their misery is his. Appalled by this spectacle, he cries out to Christ. Then as he hears the singing of the congregation, he recalls the words of John of Patmos:

> I, John, saw a city, way in the middle of the air,
> Waiting, waiting, waiting up there.

He now rejects the "ironic voice" which had urged him to rise above the herd. In his imagination, he joins the suffering multitude as they "moved on the bloody road forever, with no continuing city, but seeking one to come: a city out of time, not made by hands, but eternal in the heavens" (p. 204).

John's two dreams both explain and solve his troubled relationship with Gabriel. Finding God is an unconscious attempt to please his "father," but it is also a way of freeing himself from Gabriel if the latter continues to hate him. The sanctity of his stepson's revelation places Gabriel in a dilemma because his own righteousness is based upon an identical inner light. It is this irony which creates an important dramatic moment at the novel's end. When the family arrives home after the ordeal of the night, John asks Gabriel for the living word which would bind "father" and son in the name of Christ. Gabriel refuses to give it, and John warns him that he has found salvation on his own and that *his* God will protect him "against everything and everybody . . . that wants to cut down my soul" (p. 207). Christianity has given John a new "Father."

More important than his need to make a separate peace with Gabriel is John's desire to find a sense of community. It is significant that as John awakens from his religious trance, he hears Sister McCandless sing, "Lord, I ain't / No stranger now." Baldwin has shown us that both Harlem and New York have failed the black child in his search for community. John is denied the sustenance of the earthly city but is given its horrors; it either rejects him or tries to destroy him.

Whereas for Gabriel the Negro church was to be a vehicle for achieving political power, for John it symbolizes a humanized heavenly city. John's affection for Elisha, an older boy who has already "found" Christ, helps to explain his new attitude toward the church. On the Saturday night of John's birthday and his "birth" into Christianity, he has a friendly wrestling match with Elisha. In his mind, he now identifies Christianity with Elisha's kindness instead of Gabriel's oppressive severity. It is no longer a nay-saying religion but one which makes life tolerable by binding people together in a meaningful community. From Baldwin's point of view, the church allows the two boys to express their love for one another within an ordered framework; it metamorphoses a potentially illicit passion into something transcendental.[12]

Although John is elated by what has happened to him, his mother's reaction is one of disillusionment. She is persuaded that John has embraced Gabriel's gloomy religion and that Richard's presence in him has died. As members of the church congratulate her on John's triumph, she recalls her first conversation with Richard. Her memory focuses upon a small detail: Richard was reading a book when they met (p. 210). In trying to be like Gabriel, John, she feels, is cut off forever from the humanistic spirit of his real father.

Elizabeth's view is incomplete, but it serves to qualify the importance of John's religious experience. Finding Christ is less than a victory because John can no longer be an explorer of life's possibilities; but his conversion is much more than a defeat because, unlike Richard, he is given a haven until he has acquired the strength and patience to live in the world. Also, unlike Gabriel, he has envisioned Christianity as a joyful city, a community of men and women. He has not demeaned religion by making it a morbid reflection of "the defenseless city of his mind," nor will he use it as a means for self-aggrandizement.

Walking home from church in the early Sunday morning light, John believes that Harlem has been transformed by his inner illumination, that *this* street will never "return to the avenue it once had been" (p. 215). Nevertheless, Baldwin points out that Harlem has not changed even though John has:

> The water ran in the gutters with a small, discontented sound; on the water traveled paper, burnt matches, sodden cigarette-ends; gobs of spittle, green-yellow, brown, and pearly; the leavings of a dog, the vomit of a drunken man, the dead sperm, trapped in rubber, of one abandoned to his lust. (p. 216)

If the world's ugliness is still there, so is its beauty. The church protects the black child from the former but for a price. It demands that he repudiate "life, and love, and revelry, and . . . hope," and in so doing, the church asks too much from the human heart (p. 175). If John is to mature into a man, he must once again enter those streets which so delighted and terrified him. That is, he must not pretend that all the splendors of the earthly city are unreal because he has seen the glories of paradise.

That Baldwin intended us to see John's conversion as a rite of passage and not as a final answer[13] is apparent in the novel's last words. At the conclusion of *Go Tell It on the Mountain*, John does not say "It is finished," but rather "I'm ready . . . I'm coming. I'm on my way" (p. 221).[14] The Negro church is a halfway station for John, an end and a beginning. It is significant that John is linked with Daniel,[15] the biblical prophet who was both a man of God and an important government official in the courts of his enemies (Babylonia and Media). An analogue for Daniel, John will continue to draw strength from the Negro church even when he reenters the world of time and history.[16] In this respect, Daniel makes a striking contrast to another biblical figure associated with apocalyptic prophesy, the archangel Gabriel. Although Daniel predicted a future Kingdom of God, he did not live long enough to see the temporal liberation of his own people.[17] Gabriel, on the other hand, exists outside of time, and he brings an end to history. He not only announced Christ's birth to Mary,[18] but he will blow his trumpet at the world's conclusion. His namesake Gabriel Grimes is a grotesque parody of the archangel. Gabriel Grimes believes that he has escaped history by being chosen by God; he mistakenly thinks that he has transcended the petty world of men.

As we have seen, Gabriel cannot transcend himself, and herein lies the meaning of John's conversion. John began his birthday by taking a journey to the gate of the earthly city, but he was unable to enter. He ended his birthday by opening the gate of the celestial city, and along this way, he has already gained some of the confidence and courage needed to complete the journey which his real father never finished. Although it took place in the earthly city, that journey, too, was religious.

From *American Literature* 52, no. 1 (March 1980): 1-17.

Notes

1. See, e.g., Shirley S. Allen, "Religious Symbolism and Psychic Reality in Baldwin's *Go Tell It on the Mountain*," *CLA Journal*, 19 (1975), 173-99; Michel Fabre, "Pères et fils dans *Go Tell It on the Mountain* de James Baldwin," *Études Anglaises*, 23 (1970), 47-61; Albert Gerard, "The Sons of Ham," *Studies in the Novel*, 3 (1971), 148-64; Roger Rosenblatt, *Black Fiction* (Cambridge: Harvard Univ. Press, 1974), pp. 36-54; Nathan A. Scott, "Judgment Marked by a Cellar: The American Negro Writer and the Dialectic of Despair," in *The Shapeless God*, ed. Harry J. Mooney and Thomas F. Staley (Pittsburgh: Univ. of Pittsburgh Press, 1968), pp. 159-64; Marcus Klein, *After Alienation: American Novels in Mid-Century* (Cleveland: World Press, 1965), pp. 178-84.

2. Maynard Mack, *The Garden and the City: Retirement and Politics in the Later Poetry of Pope, 1731-1743* (Toronto: Univ. of Toronto Press, 1969), p. 3. Also, see Herbert N. Schneidau, *Sacred Discontent: The Bible and Western Tradition* (1976; rpt. Berkeley: Univ. of Calif. Press, 1977), pp. 5-6.

3. See Monroe K. Spears, *Dionysus and the City: Modernism in Twentieth-Century Poetry* (New York: Oxford Univ. Press, 1970), p. 70: "The word *city* derives from *civitas*, city-state, which is properly an aggregation of *cives*, citizens; *civilization* has the same derivation." Also see Werner Jaeger, *Paideia: The Ideals of Greek Culture*, 2nd ed. (New York: Oxford Univ. Press, 1945). I, Introduction, p. xxii.

4. See Michael H. Cowan, *City of the West: Emerson, America, and Urban Metaphor* (New Haven: Yale Univ. Press, 1967). Also, see Janis P. Stout, *Sodoms in Eden: The City in American Fiction Before 1860* (Westport, Conn.: Greenwood Press, 1976), pp. 5, 7.

5. Saint Augustine, *De Civitate Dei*, Book 15, Chapter 1.

6. James Baldwin, *Go Tell It on the Mountain* (1953; rpt. New York: Dell, 1975), p. 50. All references to Baldwin's novel are from this edition and appear in the text.

7. Shirley S. Allen sees this scene as a parody of John of Patmos's vision in the Book of Revelation (Allen, pp. 179-80), but her interpretation overlooks a well-established tradition concerning the idealized earthly city. If this scene is indeed a parody, it is probably a parody of Ezekiel 40:1-2: ". . . in the fourteenth year after the city [Jerusalem] was conquered, on that very clay, the hand of the Lord was upon me, and brought me in the visions of God into the land of Israel, and set me down upon a very high mountain, on which was a structure like a city opposite me." It is significant that Ezekiel's dream of the New Jerusalem occurs "fourteen years" after the fall of the actual Jerusalem and that this visionary city is both earthly and apocalyptic.

8. See Ezekiel 40-48.

9. Early in the novel, Baldwin illustrates the negative side of the Negro church. Because Elisha and Ella Mae have been "walking disorderly" (p. 16), Father James chastises them in front of the whole congregation. Although the church takes an extreme measure like this out of concern for its members, such puritanism stifles normal emotional and intellectual growth.

10. Margaret Mead and James Baldwin, *A Rap on Race* (Philadelphia: Lippincott, 1971), p. 176.

11. As a young girl, Deborah had been ravished by a gang of white men, and for this reason she had become a pariah within the black community. Both she and Esther bear the names of famous Old Testament heroines; in the Bible, Deborah was a bold warrior and Esther, a loyal and courageous wife. That the Esther and Deborah of the novel are both victimized by Gabriel is intended as yet another comment on the latter's moral blindness.

12. "The Outing" is a Baldwin short story which depicts adolescent love without the protection of this ordered framework. The characters are the same as those in *Go Tell It on the Mountain*, but in the short story John suffers because of his frustrated love for a boy named David.

13. Critics tend to see John's entrance into the Negro church as a permanent condition, but they cannot agree on whether it is a victory or a defeat. Roger Rosenblatt argues that the ending is a "dead one" for John since he has merely conformed to the expectations of those around him. See Rosenblatt, pp. 51, 54. Edward Margolies says of all the characters that "they are as utterly hopeless at the end of the novel as at the beginning." See *Native Sons* (Philadelphia: Lippincott, 1968), p. 114. Robert Bone believes that everything "which attends [John's] conversion makes it clear that Christ is an unsatisfactory solution to the real problem facing him: being black in America." See "The Novels of James Baldwin," *Tri-Quarterly*, No. 2 (1965), rpt. in *The Black Novelist*, ed. Robert Hemenway (Columbus: Merrill, 1970), p. 112. However, David E. Foster claims that at the novel's end John "accepts his blackness and the suffering it entails, and thus enables himself to know the redeeming love God eternally proffers." See "'Cause My House Fell Down': The Theme of the Fall in Baldwin's Novels," *Critique: Studies in Modern Fiction*, 13 (1971), No. 2, p. 55. Shirley S. Allen takes essentially the same view: "In accepting manhood he [John] is accepting the human condition, which is redeemed by the love of God." See Allen, p. 198.

14. For a slightly different interpretation of these words, see Colin MacInnes, "Dark Angel: The Writings of James Baldwin," *Encounter*, 21 (1963), rpt. in *Five Black Writers*, ed. Donald B. Gibson (New York: New York Univ. Press, 1970), p. 125.

15. John's name also connects him to John the Baptist; both their mothers are named Elizabeth. See Luke 1:13. If we are to see John's triumph as a qualified victory, then this biblical analogue is even more important than his identification with John of Patmos. As John the Baptist said of himself, "I am not the Christ . . . I am the voice of one crying in the wilderness."

16. Much of Baldwin's novel is autobiographical. In *The Fire Next Time*, Baldwin documents his own religious conversion at age fourteen. He recalls his need to come to terms with a hostile world, to find a "gimmick, to lift him out, to start him on his way." The "gimmick" turned out to be the church, an institution which he eventually outgrew but which he never forgot. See *The Fire Next Time* (1962; rpt. New York: Dell, 1969), pp. 37-59.

17. Daniel 9:24.

18. Luke 1:26-27. The archangel also tells Mary that her "kinswoman Elizabeth" will give birth to a child. See Luke 1:36. The irony in the novel is that Gabriel wants all or nothing. Disappointed that his own son, Roy, has turned away from Christ, he refuses to accept his stepson's conversion as a substitute.

The Treacherous Body: Isolation, Confession, and Community in James Baldwin

Peter Kerry Powers

> The great problem is how to be in the best sense of that kaleidoscopic word—a man.
>
> —James Baldwin, "The Male Prison"

Early in James Baldwin's *Go Tell It on the Mountain* (1953), young John Grimes sits by a window, "dusty and weary" from cleaning his family's living room in preparation for Sunday morning. Watching the boys in the street, he sees their rough, loose play as a kind of freedom denied him in the stringent morality of his Christian home:

> [H]e wanted to be one of them, playing in the streets, unfrightened, moving with such grace and power, but he knew this could not be. Yet, if he could not play their games, he could do something they could not do; he was able, as one of his teachers said, to think. But this brought him little consolation, for today he was terrified of his thoughts. He wanted to be with these boys in the street, heedless and thoughtless, wearing out his treacherous and bewildering body.[1]

As John imagines being worn out in the street instead of his home, "these boys" represent an escape from his Christian duties; however, their graceful bodies also bring forth his fearful, only half-acknowledged awakening to homoerotic desire. John's longing signifies his need to escape not only the church but also the isolating implications of an illicit desire he cannot control. This passage crystallizes a number of tensions in the novel and throughout Baldwin's work, especially the tension between the social demand that desire be controlled and the individual's need to express desire that comes unbidden, and is uncontrollable.

For John, as for Baldwin, a childhood in the Holiness tradition of the Christian church pits desire against duty. Perhaps more than most Christian movements, Holiness denominations believe that the body is the site within which the spirit is dramatically transformed. They therefore place strictures on dress and adornments and forbid what they consider the sins of the body—especially smoking, drinking, and illicit sex. Rooted in the Wesleyan doctrine that the critical Christian experience is a warming of the heart by the indwelling of the Holy Spirit, Holiness Christianity was transformed—and divided—through its contact with African traditions of spirit possession in the nineteenth century. Then, in the decades surrounding the turn of the century, it was transformed and divided again by the revivalist upheavals that gave birth to Pentecostal and charismatic movements. Holiness Christianity insists not only on the possibility of moral perfection but also on the individual human body as the dwelling space of the Spirit of God, the true Temple of the Holy Spirit.[2]

But treacherous sins of the flesh can prevent this transformation. Paradoxically, despite its attention to matters of the spirit, Holiness Christianity encourages a meticulous attention to and monitoring of the body. At any moment, the body can be invaded by temptation and so must be opened instead to God in order to serve as an instrument of the Holy Spirit. Because the body functions as a readable sign of a mysterious spiritual core, congregations use the body not only to display a hidden inner life that otherwise only God can see but also to reinforce the spiritual and social hierarchies of the community. Thus, we could say that the apparent spontaneity of ecstatic worship in many Holiness churches depends on an unacknowledged liturgy that members enact with varying degrees of intensity and devotion. This liturgy is less programmed than an Episcopal prayer book, but its performance is scripted nonetheless. According to Cheryl Sanders, even unplanned manifestations of the Spirit follow recognizable patterns:

> [The] quintessential ecstatic expression in sanctified worship is the shout, or holy dance, which usually occurs as a spontaneous eruption into coordinated, choreographed movement. There are characteristic steps, motions, rhythms, and syncopations associated with shouting. It is not a wild and random expression of kinetic energy. Rather, a culturally and aesthetically determined static structure sustains the expressions of ecstasy in a definite, recognizable form. . . .[3]

Sanders further suggests that some churches promote glossolalia (speaking in tongues) at specific points in a service and that intelligible forms of ecstatic speech tend to follow locally acceptable patterns.

These "spontaneous" expressions of the ecstatic body, then, signify more than an individual in communion with God. As a kind of discourse, ecstasy is predicated on the practices of a community and signifies one's membership in that community. Indeed, Sanders points out that Holiness churches that encourage more ecstatic forms of worship will shame members of the congregation into bodily manifestations of the spirit, such as raising one's hands in prayer or shouting, while congregations that prefer more quiet worship will censure members who begin to exhibit those forms of ecstatic behavior.[4] Thus, the body in worship speaks a theological and spiritual language that the community encourages, recognizes, and confirms. Experiences during worship that present themselves as mysterious and unique, even nonrational, are in fact so common that they can be articulated as ritual formulas. And private moments of individual mystical transport are so deeply scripted that individuals who reveal their divine experiences in inappropriate ways may be censured, excommunicated, or simply ignored. Baldwin himself eventually gave up his role as a child preacher because he came to feel that the high drama of the Holiness service was a dramatic trick that he could pull off at will. In the last months of his crisis of faith, Baldwin performed these rituals of the spirit in private for his incredulous and amused high school friends, a performance without power outside the church community.[5]

In this essay, I examine the complicated and often divided text that is the scripted body in Baldwin's work. I'm particularly interested in what it reveals about how Baldwin negotiates conflict between the unarticulated desires of the body and the community's demand for scripted confession, and how that negotiation further frames his response to the treacherous bodily intersection of masculinity and race. Rooted in his early experiences of confession, testimony, and conversion in the church, Baldwin regarded the confession of secrets hidden in the body—and the acceptance of our need for others that such confession implies—as the necessary precursor to authentic masculinity and life with others. This essay troubles the question of whether Baldwin's work bears the weight of hope he has for confession, asking what happens if confessing the hidden truth of the inward self is only possible through rituals of the body that a community not only recognizes but also demands.

* * *

Shortly after the publication of *Go Tell It on the Mountain*, Baldwin published his first essay devoted to questions of sexuality and gender, "The Male Prison" (1954). Here Baldwin explores André Gide's decision, confessed in his memoirs, to live as a domestic, heterosexual male while privately pursuing his homoerotic desire, in shame and secrecy, in the evening streets. Although Baldwin was living in France, his imaginative center rarely strayed far from the American scene; thus, he took Gide's confession as an opportunity to address the icon of the strong, silent man enclosed in personal armor that dominated the post-World War II American imagination. Baldwin reads Gide's silence as typifying not simply the life of a closeted gay man but also the prison of mid-century American masculinity, exemplified, in Baldwin's view, by the "heroes of Mickey Spillane" and other pop icons of stage and screen.[6] Gide's confession is testimony of a courageous, if last-minute, effort to break through the isolation that normative heterosexuality had imposed on him and, in different ways, imposes on all men. "Nothing is more dangerous," writes Baldwin,

> than this isolation, for men will commit any crimes whatever rather than endure it. We ought, for our own sakes, to be humbled by Gide's confession as he was humbled by his pain and make the generous effort to understand that his sorrow was not different from the sorrow of all men born. For, if we do not learn this humility, we may very well be strangled by a most petulant and unmasculine pride.[7]

Postwar masculinity in literature and popular culture often included suspicion of women and contempt for those that failed to meet criteria for integrity founded on inviolable isolation. Marlon Brando, in Elia Kazan's film version of *A Streetcar Named Desire*, is barely articulate. His animalistic shriek "Stella! Stella!" suggests the inhumanity of male isolation. James Dean parlayed the persona of a sullen, alienated, and potentially violent adolescent into a lucrative Hollywood career. In African American literature, isolated and, to varying degrees, inarticulate protagonists are at the center of the two most notable novels of the period: in Richard Wright's *Native Son*, Bigger can barely speak, and Ellison's *Invisible Man*, while endlessly eloquent within the text, lives underground, incommunicado.

Ironically, the pervasiveness of this masculinity based on isolation obscures the degree to which men in the postwar period felt themselves increasingly enveloped by economic and cultural networks that compromised their individuality. In his study of homosexuality during the Cold War, Robert Corber demonstrates that the tough-guy icons of film noir and the Western compensated for many men's actual domesticated masculinity, especially visible in public policy and economic life. While fascinated with the hard-nosed or seemingly primitive masculinity of such heroes as John Wayne in *Fort Apache* or Brando in *The Wild One*, most middle-class, white men had entered the era of the gray flannel suit. Government policies encouraged suburbanization and catered to white-collar employment, while dominant business models encouraged standardization in both labor and product. Men "were expected to define themselves through their identities as consumers—an expectation hitherto confined to women—and to take an active role in child rearing. . . . Moreover, men were discouraged from competing aggressively with one another and were expected to submit to corporate structures in exchange for obtaining a secure place in the organizational hierarchy."[8]

Corber's analysis suggests a fissure in postwar discourses of masculinity. Official culture encouraged masculine domestication while popular culture reinforced a masculine fantasy of primitive independence. Baldwin's analysis of Gide delves beneath this fissure and demonstrates the common texture of masculine silence and isolation that underlay the divide. Baldwin sees Gide's self-repression and the self-repression of men generally symbolized in the defiantly heterosexist private eyes in film noir, who were designed to compensate for the failings of masculine domestic life. This mode of masculinity relied on a rigorous self-containment that left a man isolated and often enraged. For Baldwin, the "dilemma" of Gide's masculinity was not exceptional but typical:

> Gide's dilemma, his wrestling, his peculiar, notable and extremely valuable failure testify—which should not seem odd—to a powerful masculinity and also to the fact that he found no way to escape the prison of that masculinity. And the fact that he endured this prison with such dignity is precisely what ought to humble us all, living as we do in a time and country where communion between the sexes has become so sorely threatened that we depend more and more on the strident exploitation of externals, as for example, the breasts of Hollywood glamour girls and the mindless grunting and swaggering of Hollywood he-men.[9]

Gide's "failure" resulted in a nearly debilitating isolation despite his having bent the knee to a publicly acceptable form of masculinity.

While early in his essay Baldwin expresses annoyance at Gide's expression of guilt, by the end, he regards Gide's torment and determined struggle as worthy of respect. In contrast, the inarticulate "he-men" of Hollywood typify American men who display a perverse form of cowardice that masquerades as courage. If in his confessions Gide is incapable of overcoming his guilt, he has at least taken the courageous step of self-exposure. For Baldwin, confession is not everything, but it is a necessary first step to personal and social transformation.

Baldwin's affirmation of Gide's confession is situated at a difficult moment in the history of masculine speech as a private or public phenomenon. On one hand, as the province of glossy confessional magazines and soap operas, confession has often signified a feminine or feminizing force in the American cultural imagination. On the other hand, Baldwin's focus on an individual ethic—Gide's courage or cowardice—partly obscures the critical role confession played in the political and juridical processes of the nation-state in the mid-twentieth century. Indeed, in *Giovanni's Room* (1956), Baldwin goes on to portray the ways in which private homoerotic desire is contained not just by its conflict with the dominant cultural imaginary but directly through the legal prohibitions of the French state. This is perhaps especially true of the United States during the Cold War, a period when the mechanisms of confession formed an ideological apparatus constructed on the assumption that there are threatening secrets that must be confessed.

Commenting on the influence of the Rosenberg case during the Cold War, Oliver Harris points out that "the early Cold War years were marked by an unprecedented politicization of culture and by the conscription of private life in the name of national security. The key to political containment abroad was, then, personal self-containment at home, and the Cold War penetration of the private by the public was as much a matter of patriotic self-policing and voluntary self-censorship as of panoptic state surveillance."[10] Making a similar point, Donald Pease suggests that "[t]he chief political consequence of this confusion of the realms of inner psychology and the national interest was a blurring of the line separating the powers of the state from the civil liberties of private citizens. The search for enemies of the state in the public world was internalized in private citizens' surveillance of their psyches for signs of the enemy within."[11] Both Pease and Harris point toward the Cold War idealization of a self-policing citizenry without secrets, either fully transparent in having made the inner self available to others for examination, or else fully opaque in imagining that there is no inner self, no hidden secret, beyond the surface manifestations of the body at work. The organization man lives for the company; the citizen for the state. The end point of the politics of the Red Scare is that every citizen becomes his or her own McCarthy.

Self-containment or policing, of course, is provoked by a threat the individual must counter or appease. As the McCarthy hearings investigated the private lives of citizens in the nation's battle against Communism, citizens were expected to expose or confess their secret political alliances but also to identify friends and acquaintances known or suspected of being in league with Communism. Citizens affirmed their belonging to the community of the state either through a purified transparency, allowing the gaze of others to confirm that they had no secret life, or through a kind of disavowal and repudiation that took the form of a confession. Langston Hughes, as only one example, downplayed or disavowed his links to radical politics in the 1930s; he reaffirmed this disavowal by suppressing much of his political poetry for his *Selected Poems* (1950), as if to say he was no longer the same person.[12]

In such a structure of surveillance, secrecy, and containment, the desire of the body comes in for particular scrutiny because it entails a potential betrayal of the law upon which the social order depends, *law* here indicating not only stated laws of the polis but also the regulatory norms through which a culture encourages self-policing. Like the spirits of temptation in a Holiness church, desire remains hidden, the surface of the body a sign but not a transparent one. Moreover, to the degree that desire signifies an absence or, rather, the presence of dissatisfaction, it threatens the social order by being both evidence of that order's insufficiency and a rationale for change. Desire is thus always potentially treasonous, and the body treacherous, as both Baldwin's John Grimes and the House Un-American Activities Committee well understood.

Judith Butler has suggested that the body represents a threat to the social order because it points to the limits of the law. Although the body assumes its performative role as a "forcible reiteration of [regulatory] norms," the very fact of this reiteration suggests that "bodies never quite comply with the norms by which their materialization is impelled."[13] In other words, the very force by which the law says "No" to desire silently implies the possibility of the body's "Yes," an insight delivered to different ends when the apostle Paul recognizes that the law provokes the very desire it is designed to contain.[14] Because the threat that desire poses depends on desire's being hidden away as a secret, confession—one form of what Foucault calls the "incitement to discourse"—can be a coercive means by which the state controls and ultimately displaces desire with behavior that conforms to socially approved constraints.[15] In the Cold War era, this coercion manifested itself forcefully in the link that powerful public figures drew between sexual deviance and Communist sympathy (or, more broadly, inadequate patriotism). Anti-Communists on the left, such as Arthur Schlesinger, and on the right, such as Billy Graham, descried an unholy trinity of pink, lavender, and red subversives, seeing American manliness and self-reliance undermined in a Communism that embraced diseased togetherness with frankly homoerotic possibilities.[16] Moreover, political culture imagined that homosexuals were not only more likely to be manipulated into being subversives out of fear but also that they were simply more likely to be subversive. Senator Kenneth Wherry described the link as follows: "[Y]ou can't hardly separate homosexuals from subversives. Mind you, I don't say every homosexual is a subversive, and I don't say every subversive is a homosexual. But a man of low morality is a menace in the government, whatever he is, and they are all tied up together."[17] Characteristically more blunt, Joseph Mc-

Carthy suggested to reporters that "[i]f you want to be against McCarthy, boys, you've got to be either a Communist or a cocksucker."[18] Of course, the fact that Roy Cohn could long give service to McCarthy and his committee while pursuing his own homoerotic life suggests the nearly impenetrable secrecy of desire, a hiddenness that generated the furious quest for confession in the first place.

The context into which Baldwin inserts the promise of confession is complicated further by the history of African American men. Like homosexuality, blackness has been construed in popular and political parlance as the embodiment of desire and, therefore, as a threat to the social order.[19] In the early years of the century, films such as *Birth of a Nation* (1915) justified Jim Crow segregation and Klan violence by representing black male desire as an uncontrollable force that would use the apparatus of the nation to achieve its true end, sex with white women. During the Cold War, African Americans were a particular focus of FBI harassment and were presumed, like homosexuals, to embody the possibility of subversion. This presumption played out quite literally in the case of Paul Robeson, whose artistic career was derailed on the suspicion that his political activism was subversive.[20]

Unlike gay men, however, African Americans were visibly marked as subversives through skin color. The split that Gide could maintain between a life of private desire and public approbation could not be so readily enacted by a black man. Nevertheless, African Americans have rarely responded to an invasive public (and white) gaze with the strategy of open and direct confession of desire, more often opting for what could be described as a strategic hiddenness.[21] The Invisible Man lives underground in preparation for an apocalyptic emergence. In Nella Larson's novel *Passing*, blackness is equated with a secret desire that longs to be revealed. Earlier, Paul Laurence Dunbar's poem "We Wear the Mask" describes presenting a false face to the master while acknowledging a sequestered self only to God and to others who wear the mask. In a world where the open expression of desire is only a small step from social exclusion, the jail cell, or the lyncher's rope, confession seems an unlikely route toward a transformative politics. It is not immediately clear, then, why Baldwin could see in Gide's confession the potential for heroic struggle against normative masculinity. Why would Gide's confession not simply be a final humiliation, a final yielding to the priorities of the state and the culture? Why not, in fact, refuse this incitement to discourse and retain a sense of one's own integrity over and against the oppressive power that demands speech?

Baldwin's hope for the efficacy of confession—and his broad reliance on the confessional mode generally in his work—springs from his understanding of the psychology of shame, the role of silence in domination, and an ambitious, if only partially successful, rereading of the practices of confession in Christianity. First, Baldwin understood that the power through which social norms induce self-containment depends on the fear of exposure. To confirm the suspicions of the social gaze, then, is to liberate oneself from fear, if from nothing else. One doesn't have to be afraid, that is, of others finding out what they already know. Baldwin asked of Gide, indeed of all sexual beings, the same kind of visibility that was unavoidable for black men. Although there may be other consequences to living with one's desires in the open, fear of being named as a gay or black man can generate self-policing only in those intent on hiding. Baldwin suggests that whatever he could or couldn't do about society, he could at least refuse to collaborate by refusing to interiorize the principles of McCarthyism.

Even when viewed as a mode of resistance to the invasive gaze of the state, the armored self-silencing typical of film noir detectives poses as a pugnacious individualism but replicates, in effect if not in full, the state's desire for a transparent citizenry. While appearing to be a renegade who opposes the corruption or fecklessness of the state, the film noir detective always ultimately reinforces the control of law and order. His apparently hard-edged masculine independence is little different from the frightened timidity of the self-policing organization man to the extent that both refuse to admit desire and the need that desire implies.

But merely expressing oneself holds little promise for overcoming the threat of isolation. Baldwin's "grunting . . . he-men" are perversely isolated in their attempts to guarantee their right to belong to a society that insists on extinguishing desire. Baldwin sees in confession the potential of an alternative community, a society without fear. He develops this vision out of his experience of the Holiness church, not so much in its actual practice but in its ideals.[22] In Holiness Christianity, confession is the means by which the body's desire may be expunged in preparation for the indwelling of the Holy Spirit. The secrets of the body must be repudiated and the inner self transformed by becoming one with Christ. For Baldwin, confession reveals the secrets of the body so that the self can be liberated rather than betrayed. In both instances, until confession, the public flesh hides the true nature of the individual. For the church, the body's sinful desire occupies the space properly occupied by the Holy Spirit, and so it must be displaced. For Baldwin, however, desire points to a hidden self that has been imprisoned by social convention. Rather than a source of evil, desire is a longing for some difference not available in the alienating social world. This hidden self must be revealed through confession, displacing the false social self imprinted on the body. Such a truth-telling self can then enter into genuine relationships with others in a community of mutual respect.

Both the popular Christian formulation and Baldwin's revision of it involve a kind of betrayal. As I have suggested, Butler argues that the regulation of the body suggests the possibility of its treachery. For the church, the body is treacherous because it is the prime instrument of the sinful self; it always raises the possibility that the law is insufficient. The Spirit of the Father, therefore, must possess the sinful body so that it is better able to fulfill the demands of the law. For Baldwin, however, the physical body and its desires are less threatening than the public gaze that induces self-policing and the possibility of self-betrayal. It is this self-betrayal and the denial of desire it entails that are the ultimate sins against the body. Ultimately, Baldwin is more concerned with this violence against the self than even the regulation of the body by the church or the state.

Baldwin feels called to come out because the refusal to acknowledge desire brings betrayal of the self and others. In Baldwin's terms, this opening of the self to others not only redeems the individual from an act of bad faith, it also delivers a more authentic social existence, because a society based on deception can exist only in an oppressive relationship to its members. Given the culture of isolation that normative masculinity encourages, Baldwin's analysis leads inevitably to the conclusion that a healthy and authentic masculinity can only be achieved by refusing to "be . . . a man."

Baldwin's confessional dynamic calls for a bold openness by which a kind of nonreligious salvation can be effected. But loosed from the traditional communities that might have received and reaffirmed that confession, it runs the risk of expression in a vacuum, or worse, of censure and exclusion by communities unable or unwilling to bear the burden of another's desire. Like the performances of religious ecstasy that Baldwin pulled off for his friends, confession may have no power in the absence of a community that can hear and validate it. While traditional confessions open pathways for belonging, Baldwin's confessions seek to create a community without shame that can only be imagined in a realm that borders on the apocalyptic; thus, confession bears a weight of responsibility it cannot always deliver. As a black man who faced censure both inside and outside his racial community because of his sexual desires, and as a gay man whose racial identity made no alliance with whites straightforward, Baldwin saw the problem of community as more than a theoretical problem of reception. Communities are social structures that threaten him with isolation or even destruction, regardless of the courage of his confession and the freedom from guilt the confession can afford.

* * *

"The Male Prison" and the difficult nexus it examines between desire, confession, and containment can be read as a discursive summation of the issues with which Baldwin had struggled in *Go Tell It on the Mountain*. In some ways a novel of the Great Migration, *Go Tell It on the Mountain* is predominantly a psychological history of secret desire. In his role as a preacher, first in the rural South, then later in Harlem, Gabriel Grimes represents a particular mode of black masculine responsibility and race leadership. Despite his aura of authority and self-possession, Gabriel is a man driven by terror, a terror provoked by his own desire and that of others. In different ways, the psychic and spiritual crises facing Gabriel and his stepson, John, announce a thematic of race, sexuality, and gender that occupied Baldwin throughout his career.

After a youthful period of debauchery and years of pleading from his dying mother, Gabriel gives his life over to God and the church. As if to purify his past, he moves to the opposite extreme in his adulthood, denying and even condemning the body's desires. Indeed, he pursues a stringent sexual purity, marrying Deborah, a woman whom he does not find desirable, in order to father a holy racial lineage that he fantasizes will be analogous to the line of David in the Hebrew Scriptures. However, Gabriel's strenuous pursuit of sexual purity fails to extinguish desire, as his adulterous affair with Esther demonstrates. His first sexual encounter with Esther suggests the degree to which his religious language silences the body, even while that same language gradually begins to express the body, becoming a way to confess desire he cannot countenance:

> He held onto her hands as though he were in the middle of the sea and her hands were the lifeline that would drag him in to shore. "Jesus Jesus Jesus," he prayed, "oh, Jesus Jesus. Help me to stand." He thought that he was pulling back against her hands—but he was pulling her to him. And he saw in her eyes now a look that he had not seen for many a long day and night, a look that was never in Deborah's eyes.

> "*Yes*, you know," he said, "why I'm all the time worrying about you—why I'm all the time miserable when I look at you."
>
> "But you ain't never told me none of this," she said. (126)

In this passage, Gabriel speaks as clearly to sexual desire as to spiritual desire for Jesus. Following the outline Baldwin suggests in "The Male Prison" for a more vital masculinity, we can see in Gabriel a man who needs to confess that he is not a savior upon whom others should depend but simply a man with desires that do not readily conform to public expectations. He chooses, however, the role of savior. And upon discovering that Esther is pregnant, he begins immediately to isolate himself:

> "You want me," he asked at last, "to leave my wife—and come with you?"
>
> "*I* thought," she answered, "that you had done thought of that yourself, already, many and many a time."
>
> "You know," he said, with a halting anger, "I ain't never said nothing like that. I ain't never told you I wanted to leave my wife."
>
> "I ain't talking," she shouted, at the end of patience, "about nothing you done *said*!" . . .
>
> "Girl," he said, "does you reckon I'm going to run off and lead a life of sin with you somewhere, just because you tell me you got my baby kicking in your belly? How many kinds of fool you think I am? I got God's work to do—my life don't belong to you. Nor to that baby, neither—if it *is* my baby." (131)

Like the "grunting . . . he-men" of "The Male Prison," Gabriel fails to wrestle manfully with his desire or its consequences. Exercising a single-minded will to independence, he refuses to acknowledge his love and need for Esther and hers for him. His dishonesty, predicated on his belief that his moral and religious purity will redeem the world, contributes more clearly to the violence of the world than to its redemption, because his unwillingness to declare the child his own eventually leads to the death of both mother and son.

Gabriel's fear of exposure is rooted in multiple aspects of his life, including his negotiation of the American racial divide. As I suggested earlier, racial politics and sexual politics were deeply entwined during the Cold War. Whether envisioning black men as "priapic black studs" or sexual criminals, or even desexualized Uncle Toms, the white social gaze, driven by its own sexual fears, has been an emphatic and often literal prison for black men.[23] Indeed, Baldwin's career is best described as an effort to parse the complicated intersections of race, racism, and sexuality and to describe the various strategies, failed and successful, that African American men have employed to survive that crossroads.

In his essay "The Fire Next Time" (1963), Baldwin describes the need of every African American boy to have what Baldwin calls a "gimmick" for surviving a racist culture. Baldwin interprets his conversion and his years as a young preacher in the church as his personal gimmick.[24] For Gabriel, the desires of his body threaten to undermine his gimmick. Indeed, race plays a role in nearly every major sexual event of Gabriel's life. Race influences his initial decision to marry Deborah, if only because Deborah's social degradation had accompanied the violation of her body by white men. Gabriel's desire to rescue her and to establish a royal line through her reflects an effort to garner and sustain social power over and against the threats from white society.

Gabriel's sense of racial threat exacerbates his frantic need to hold what little social power he has been able to hoard. Later in his marriage, he succumbs to his desire for a liaison with Esther, a woman with whom he works in a white household. As their desire is consummated in the master's kitchen, Gabriel's terror of being discovered is *racial* terror. He remains as aware of his location in the house and the open kitchen door as he is of Esther's body. Later, when Esther confronts him with her pregnancy, Gabriel shushes her and looks frantically around the white folks' yard to make sure they are not overheard.

Gabriel's fearful attention to the master's white space suggests that his holiness is at least as much a negotiation with the white as with the African American community. His tenuous position is reinforced when he walks the streets to get medicine for Deborah during a period of white rioting in the black community, which results in the lynching and ritual emasculation of a black soldier returning from the war:

> Night had not yet fallen and the streets were gray and empty—save that here and there, polished in the light that spilled outward from a poolroom or a tavern, white men stood in groups of half a dozen. As he passed each group, silence fell, and they watched him insolently, itching to kill; but he said nothing, bowing his head, and they knew, anyway, that he was a preacher. There were no black men on the street at all, save him. . . . Now, someone spat on the sidewalk at Gabriel's feet, and he walked on, his face not changing, and he heard it reprovingly whispered behind him that he was a good nigger, surely up to no trouble. He hoped that he would not have to smile into any of these so well-known white faces. While he walked, held by his caution more rigid than an arrow, he prayed, as his mother had taught him to pray, for loving kindness; yet he dreamed of the feel of a white man's forehead against his shoe; again and again, until the head wobbled on the broken neck and his foot encountered nothing but the rushing blood. (141-42)

As this passage implies, Gabriel's will to power is driven by a deep-seated fear that he will lose his self. The caution by which he holds himself "more rigid than an arrow" while negotiating the dangerous streets fathers the moral rigidity by which he represses his sexual desire in order to claim a position of power in the black community. The suppressed desire to lash out violently against those who force him to contain even the movements of his own body is directly related to the power he can exercise among the relatively powerless as a minister in the church. Gabriel's lack of power in society at large translates into an obsessive mythology of his control of the present (in the community of the church) and of the future (in his fantasy of a royal line). A confession of his desire for Esther would threaten the source of his power because such a revelation would fracture his reputation as a preacher. But even beyond this, such a confession would threaten the fantasies upon which Gabriel has built his identity. It would reveal the cracks in the mask of his moral purity, and the uncontrollable quality of desire would give the lie to the myth of self-control upon which the fantasy of a royal and blessed line depends.

John appears as a counterpoint to Gabriel. Both contend with the nexus of secret desire and racial oppression that defines their masculinity. John's perception of his hazily defined homoerotic desire as a threat and his body as treacherous replicates his father's terrors.[25] As the child of his mother's love affair prior to meeting Gabriel, John seems to embody a desire that Gabriel cannot control. Thus, John's body is not only the site of his own unexpressed longing but also the screen upon which the fantasies and fears of others are projected, especially those of his father in the face of his wife's unspoken memories of an erotic life.

Unlike Gabriel, John's fear is generated not through a threatened loss of power or control but through the threat of not belonging, of being cast into an abyss of isolation without even the comfort of love and family. Early in the novel, John imagines his sexual awakening as the source of such separation:

> John wondered at his panic, then wondered about the time; and then (while the yellow stain on the ceiling slowly transformed itself into a woman's nakedness) he remembered that it was his fourteenth birthday and that he had sinned. . . .
>
> He had sinned. In spite of the saints, his mother and his father, the warnings he had heard from his earliest beginnings, he had sinned with his hands a sin that was hard to forgive. In the school lavatory, alone, thinking of the boys, older, bigger, braver, who made bets with each other as to whose urine could arch higher, he had watched in himself a transformation of which he would never dare to speak. (18-19)

The yellow-stained ceiling beneath which John masturbates resolves itself into the figure of "a woman's nakedness," the only shape he can give to the desire to which the stain speaks and which it displaces. John's inability to visualize his homoerotic desire in terms other than those sanctioned by dominant social norms mirrors Gabriel's inability to speak of his desire for a life with Esther. In both cases, desire is silenced by the fear generated in community.

Indeed, John's religious community takes the repression of desire as the necessary precondition for participation, a requirement that Gabriel recognizes and embraces, with brutal consequence. John experiences this call to repression in many different ways but most vividly in the church's public exposure and rebuke of the young preacher Elisha for his sin with his girlfriend Ella Mae. Father James, the lead minister of John's church, calls Ella Mae and Elisha to the front of the church for public chastisement. Public humiliation transforms their relationship into one that meets the acceptable code of relationships for men and women in the church: "If they came together again it would be in wedlock. They would have children and raise them in church. . . . This was what was meant by a holy life, this was what the way of the cross demanded" (17-18).

Commenting on this section of the novel, Trudier Harris notes the panoptic quality of fundamentalist African American churches:

> The idea that such churches regulated private lives led to such practices as young girls who became pregnant out of wedlock having to go before entire congregations, beg pardon for their sin, and ask formally to be reinstated into the church. If the church is viewed as having ever-present eyes on the lives of its members, how much more strongly must the members believe that God, whose "eye is on the sparrow," is watching and judging them.[26]

The community's knowledge of its members may be a means of uniting them, but it can also be a means of controlling them. This knowledge and power enable the community to expel those whose sins of the flesh are seen as contrary to the community's iteration of itself through marriage, childbearing, and church attendance. Elisha, the primary object of John's desire in the novel, erases his desire for Ella Mae in order to follow the way of the cross, the sacrifice of the body that community demands. Similarly, John never tells anyone about his desire for other boys, and for Elisha specifically, because it would consign him to social death. Confession, then, both reveals and erases, both expresses and refuses to speak the self. Confessing the self proceeds only in ways preordained by the community of hearers awaiting such confession.

Despite this problem, it would be too easy to reduce confession to a Foucauldian method of social control. The problem of John's sexuality, like his stepfather's, is entangled with the question of race. Unlike Gabriel, John responds to his desire not with rigid self-containment or the will to domination but through a fantasy of flight into whiteness. In the opening sections of the novel, John quite literally runs away from his blackness toward the white part of town. Secreted in a movie theater, he projects his desire for self-expression onto the white heroine who aggressively displays her sexuality and dies a romantically tragic death, scorning those who have spurned her. Faced with the possibility of being rejected for being gay, John imagines himself as the screen's white heroine—remote, distant, heedless of others' opinions. Momentarily a white woman, John imagines an escape from the possibility of rejection by rejecting others. Like the film noir detective who appears to rebel against social convention while ultimately interiorizing its imperatives, John mitigates the possibility of rejection by idealizing a romantic fantasy of social ostracism.

John's conversion at the end of the novel attempts to imagine yet another route toward an authentic masculinity as he opens himself to others and the possibility of community. Far from the hidden desire for power operating in Gabriel's faith, John's conversion is public and abject:

And something moved in John's body which was not John. He was invaded, set at naught, possessed. This power had struck John in the head or in the heart; and, in a moment, wholly, filling him with an anguish that he could never in his life have imagined, that he surely could not endure, that even now he could not believe, had opened him up; had cracked him open, as wood beneath the axe cracks down the middle, as rocks break up; had ripped him and felled him in a moment, so that John had not felt the wound, but only the agony, had not felt the fall, but only the fear; and lay here, now, helpless, screaming at the very bottom of darkness. (193)

The emotional violence of this moment marks an absolute negation of the armored self that Baldwin saw at the root of a potentially "petulant and unmasculine pride" in American men. Perhaps equally important in this scene is the public, communal character of John's experience. Authentic community depends on an unguarded self, and the penetration of the guarded self depends upon the presence of a beloved community. Whereas Gabriel's conversion occurs in an isolated field, John's need to rise and join is accomplished through an embrace of the blackness of the church community. But first he must resist the malicious voice of racism that "insisted yet once more that he rise from that filthy floor if he did not want to become like all the other niggers" (194). Unlike Gabriel, John resists the temptation to seek the powers associated with whiteness and instead chooses empathetic identification with his fellow African Americans as he rises up to join the saints:

"Rise up, rise up, Brother Johnny, and talk about the Lord's deliverance." . . .

"Amen!" cried Sister McCandless, "rise up, and praise the Lord!" . . . "Rise up, Johnny," said Elisha, again. "Are you saved, boy?"

"Yes," said John, "oh, yes!" and the words came upward, it seemed, of themselves, in the new voice God had given him. Elisha stretched out his hand, and John took the hand, and stood—so suddenly, and so strangely, and with such wonder!—once more on his feet. (205-6)

Standing on his feet suggests the achievement of manhood. But John has become a man by taking the hand of another man, Elisha. And he is immediately embraced by the other men and women of the community—by everyone but his stepfather, Gabriel, who stands apart in bitter self-righteousness, unwilling to rejoice.

This vision of love and community that enfolds John contrasts markedly with Gabriel's isolation. According to Joseph Brown, the conversion places John on an equal social footing with his father while not reducing him to his father's brutality. Fred Standley, however, has suggested that the conclusion of the novel speaks more to John's confusion than to his emergence as a man. Other critics fall at various points along this spectrum.[27] I suggest, however, that the ambiguities at the end of the novel are rooted in Baldwin's understanding of confession as a transforming experience, a conception that only partially overcomes the tension between community and desire.

The end of the novel raises the question of whether confession alone can produce community, or whether every confession of the self requires a hiding of the self. Like the Holiness churches that both encourage and delimit ecstatic experience, John's confession, along with others throughout Baldwin's work, is enabled and restricted by the kinds of community to which it is made. While John's embrace of others marks a significant departure from Gabriel's will to power, solidarity comes at the expense of the explicit manifestation of homoerotic desire that has shadowed the surface of the text, especially in John's relationship to Elisha. Of course, the language of the conversion, focused on images of penetration, opening, and possession, and its culmination in an expression of masculine affection can be read as implicitly homoerotic; nevertheless, desire remains implicit, unspoken. Ironically, communal solidarity in this novel is ultimately achieved at the expense of unorthodox desires of the body whose admission Baldwin cites elsewhere as the source of any courageous confession and true community.

Thus, while Patrick Johnson argues that John's love for Elisha in the novel means that "the Christian body may also be a queer body," Gabriel, Elisha, and even John suppress their sexual desires, suggesting that gayness and holiness, and gayness and blackness, cannot be spoken of together; or, at least, that those simultaneous confessions remain a dream of a world unavailable in 1953 except in Baldwin's imagination and the portions of his manuscript that were not ultimately published.[28] But John's embrace of community is meant to be celebrated, especially in comparison to Gabriel's will to power. Such freedom and such confessions are no doubt a precondition for the kind of human solidarity that Baldwin imagined. They do not, however, create the human community of which he dreamed. Indeed, it remains worth asking what price communities exact for communion. The ending of the novel suggests that John's arrival as a man through confession and conversion depends as much on the self's substantial enclosure as on its disclosure. While John's conversion bridges the gulf of separation between self and others in the formation of community, it does so only by maintaining a gulf inside John himself between public role and private desire. Baldwin's men remain caught poignantly in the excruciating contradictions of confession and isolation. While community is only possible if the self is revealed, communities enable or privilege certain revelations and not others. A person confesses what a community can hear, and what a community can hear is what can count as a genuine confession. John's desire, finally, is still a love that dare not speak its name.

This silence at the end of *Go Tell It on the Mountain* resounds more definitively given the novel's publishing history, a history that suggests that Baldwin's problems with confession and solidarity went far beyond the confines of the Holiness church. Baldwin's editors urged him to get rid of most of the religious aspects of the novel—an editorial misprision that provoked in Baldwin a panic-induced nausea—and they may have urged him to rewrite the conclusion to mute its homoerotic theme.[29] In at least one late draft of the novel, Elisha's embrace of John after his conversion is frankly homoerotic—a public confession of faith that is also a confession of same-sex desire—making explicit what remains only implicit in the published version. Emile

Capouya, Baldwin's friend since childhood, reported that the ending of the draft was indeed an open revelation of John's homosexuality and that Baldwin had removed it at the insistence of his editors. Whether he did so for this reason or for more obscure personal or aesthetic reasons, Baldwin's decision to alter the ending is significant.[30] The homoeroticism of the unpublished ending suggests a vision of a self and a community whose members are fully transparent to one another: that is, a community that enables but does not constrain. By this time in his life, Baldwin made no secret of his unconventional sexuality. And he had left the church—in body if not in spirit. His experience with the community of writers and publishers was not substantially different from his experience with his church, at least with regard to self-revelation. The expectations of the publishing community—driven by the logic of the niche market reserved for "The Negro Writer"—were different in detail but not in kind from the constraints John experiences in church. That is, communities listen only with reluctance to confessions they do not want to hear. This is true of all communities—whether of publishers, readers, or saints.

This does not make Baldwin's vision a failure, as if absolute freedom from constraint were the only success that counts. In her reading of the biblical story of Esther as an analogy of coming out, Eve Sedgwick contends that the belief in explicit revelation as a means to systematic cultural change verges on sentimentality:

> First, we have too much cause to know how limited a leverage any individual revelation can exercise over collectively scaled and institutionally embodied oppressions. Acknowledgment of this disproportion does not mean that the consequences of such acts as coming out can be circumscribed within *predetermined* boundaries, as if between "personal" and "political" realms, nor does it require us to deny how disproportionately powerful and disruptive such acts can be. But the brute incommensurability has nonetheless to be acknowledged. In the theatrical display of an *already institutionalized* ignorance no transformative potential is to be looked for.[31]

Sedgwick, drawing on Foucault, emphasizes that there is no easy binary to be drawn between speech and silence, that there are many forms of silence and many modes of deployment.[32] John's silence at the end of the novel can't be equated simply with the silent and disapproving gaze of his stepfather. The implicit homoeroticism of his conversion and the novel's culmination at least point toward and symbolize a mode of masculinity at odds with his father's even while he uses his father's language and lives in his father's house. What seems finally to frustrate Baldwin's design is that confession is a ritual enabled by communities, while communities cannot be created by confessions alone.

* * *

These conflicts involving confession, desire, and community—announced first in *Go Tell It on the Mountain* and explored explicitly in "The Male Prison"—suggest a thematic that informs most of Baldwin's work as he returns repeatedly not only to the confessional form but also to the unfulfilled possibilities of community and confession. Baldwin's first explicit fictional investigation of homosexuality, *Giovanni's Room*—a novel that one editor suggested he burn and which much of the African American press excoriated—deals explicitly with the way in which unconfessed homoerotic desire does violence to the self and to others. It also mutes the racial element of Baldwin's desire for solidarity, figuring it only obscurely in the olive-skinned Giovanni. *Another Country* explores similar themes but can only imagine community through a collection of bohemian, would-be artists who, ultimately, are little better at hearing and receiving one another openly than Gabriel's church. Not until well into mid-career did Baldwin begin to bring these elements together in his fiction; it could be argued that he did not integrate them fully with his religious imagination and experience until his final novel, *Just above My Head* (1979). It may be instructive that the politics of confession in *Just above My Head* achieves this integration through the microcosm of family life, whose relationship to broader social or political institutions remains untranslated and perhaps untranslatable.

Very late in his career, in his last published essay, Baldwin again meditated on the debilitating qualities of the isolation that accompanies unspoken and unheard desire, though figured now through the imagery of the seen and unseen:

> I hazard that the physically androgynous state must create an all-but-intolerable loneliness, since we all exist, after all, and crucially, in the eye of the beholder. We all react to and, to whatever extent, become what that eye sees. This judgment begins in the eyes of one's parents (the crucial, the definitive, the all-but-everlasting judgment), and so we move, in the vast and claustrophobic gallery of Others, on up or down the line, to the eye of one's friend or one's lover.
>
> It is virtually impossible to trust one's human value without the collaboration or corroboration of that eye—which is to say that no one can live without it. One can, of course, instruct that eye as to what to see, but this effort, which is nothing less than ruthless intimidation, is wounding and exhausting: While it can keep humiliation at bay, it confirms the fact that humiliation is the central danger of one's life. And since one cannot risk love without risking humiliation, love becomes impossible.[33]

Here again is the theme Baldwin first sounded in *Go Tell It on the Mountain* and then made explicit in "The Male Prison." The young Baldwin had judged Gide's confession a "failure" because he could not embrace the desire he spoke of in his fiction and revealed finally in his journals and late memoirs. The Baldwin of "Here Be Dragons" might have tempered this judgment by noting that the success or failure of any confession depends not only on the will and courage of those who speak but also on the courage and loving regard of those who listen. Baldwin's excision of John's declaration of love for Elisha from *Go Tell It on the Mountain* can be read as an unfortunate repression and, therefore, his judgment on Gide as a judgment on himself. It can also be read more sympathetically as Baldwin's acknowledgment that communities that hear such confessions are as rare as those who are willing to make a confession to be heard. While the community of *Go Tell It on the Mountain* could not be imagined without John's religious conversion, it could perhaps only be imagined without explicit manifestation of Elisha's and John's forbidden desire. The church, and Baldwin's editors—and perhaps even Baldwin, in the end—remained unable to imagine a community in which an embrace like that of John and Elisha could be recognized as a confession not only of faith but also of desire. In this respect, both community and confession remained idealizations throughout Baldwin's career, realized as a sign, imagined as a hope.

From *American Literature* 77, no. 4 (December 2005): 787-813.

Notes

1. James Baldwin, *Go Tell It on the Mountain* (New York: Dell, 1985), 30; further references are to this edition and will be cited parenthetically in the text.

2. For overviews of the Holiness and Pentecostal movements in the United States, see Melvin Dieters, *The Holiness Revival of the Nineteenth Century* (Metuchen, N.J.: Scarecrow, 1980); and John Peters, *Christian Perfection and American Methodism* (New York: Abingdon, 1985); see also Zora Neale Hurston, *The Sanctified Church: The Folklore Writings of Zora Neale Hurston* (Berkeley, Calif.: Turtle Island Foundation, 1981), 79-107. The best contemporary examination of this tradition can be found in Cheryl Sanders, *Saints in Exile: The Holiness-Pentecostal Experience in African American Religion and Culture* (New York: Oxford Univ. Press, 1996). My analysis of Baldwin is inevitably shaped by my having been raised in one of the Holiness traditions. While my own intellectual journey has taken me nearly as far afield from those beginnings as Baldwin's own, I hope my reflections suggest a respect for Holiness Christianity born of intimacy.

3. Sanders, *Saints in Exile*, 61. Judith Butler's analysis of the interplay between bodies and discursive systems, especially her understanding of the body's performance as an iterated style, has been helpful to my thinking. Butler speaks against the notion that the body exists as a fundamental and undiscursive ground: "'[S]ex' is an ideal construct which is forcibly materialized through time. It is not a simple fact or static condition of a body, but a process whereby regulatory norms materialize 'sex' and achieve

this materialization through a forcible reiteration of those norms" (*Bodies That Matter: On the Discursive Limits of Sex* [New York: Routledge, 1993], 1-2). Building on Butler's insight, I am suggesting that the body as it performs in a particular social space is a system of recognizable signs even when it is apparently spontaneous or uncontrolled.

4. Sanders, *Saints in Exile*, 61-62. Sanders notes that some churches will enforce quiet in worship not only by controlling the order of worship but also by allowing public rebuke by church leaders. More ecstatic churches are known for "exhorting persons to speak aloud, stand, raise their hands, or shout and subjecting them to verbal ridicule if they refuse, as in 'You think you're too cute and too sophisticated to shout'" (62).

5. See W. J. Weatherby, *James Baldwin: Artist on Fire* (London: Michael Joseph, 1989), 27.

6. James Baldwin, "The Male Prison," in *The Price of the Ticket: Collected Nonfiction, 1948-1985* (New York: St. Martin's, 1985), 105.

7. Ibid.

8. Robert Corber, *Homosexuality in Cold War America: Resistance and the Crisis of Masculinity* (Durham, N.C.: Duke Univ. Press, 1997), 6; see also 1-9.

9. Baldwin, "Male Prison," 105.

10. Oliver Harris, "Cold War Correspondents: Ginsberg, Kerouac, Cassady, and the Political Economy of Beat Letters," *Twentieth-Century Literature 46* (summer 2000): 172.

11. Donald Pease, "Leslie Fiedler, the Rosenberg Trial, and the Formulation of an American Canon," *boundary 2* 17 (summer 1990): 162.

12. For a full description of Hughes's response to the McCarthy hearings and his revision of his association with Communism, see Arnold Rampersad, *The Life of Langston Hughes, Volume II, 1941-1967: I Dream a World*, 2nd ed. (New York: Oxford Univ. Press, 1988), 208-22.

13. Butler, *Bodies That Matter*, 2.

14. Paul is at some pains in Romans to declare that the law is good, whatever the complications; nevertheless, he clearly recognizes the peculiar double role that prohibition plays, giving birth to desire even while it imposes restraints: "Yet, if it had not been for the law, I would not have known sin. I would not have known what it is to covet if the law had not said, 'You shall not covet.' But sin, seizing an opportunity in the commandment, produced in me all kinds of covetousness. Apart from the law sin lies dead. I was once alive apart from the law, but when the commandment came, sin revived, and I died, and the very commandment that promised life proved to be death to me" (Romans 7:7-10, New Revised Standard Version).

15. Michel Foucault, "Introduction," *The History of Sexuality*, vol. 1, trans. Robert Hurley (New York: Random House: Vintage, 1990), 17.

16. See K. A. Courdileone, "'Politics in an Age of Anxiety': Cold War Political Culture and the Crisis in American Masculinity, 1949-1960," *Journal of American History* 87 (September 2000): 515-45.

17. Senator Kenneth Wherry, quoted in Max Lerner, *The Unfinished Country: A Book of American Symbols* (New York: Simon and Schuster, 1959), 313; see also Courdileone, "'Politics in an Age of Anxiety,'" 532.

18. Joseph McCarthy, quoted in David Halberstam, *The Fifties* (New York: Villard,

1993), 54; see also Edwin R. Bayley, *Joe McCarthy and the Press* (Madison: Univ. of Wisconsin Press, 1981), 73; and Courdileone, "'Politics in an Age of Anxiety,'" 521.

19. This attitude toward black male sexuality is perhaps epitomized by Malcolm Cowley's remark in the 1920s: "One heard it said that the Negroes had retained a direct virility that the whites had lost through being overeducated" (quoted in David Levering Lewis, *When Harlem Was in Vogue* [New York: Penguin, 1997], 91). Perhaps the most important general theoretical argument concerning this attitude comes from Frantz Fanon: "The civilized white man retains an irrational longing for unusual eras of sexual license, or orgiastic scenes, or unpunished rapes, or unrepressed instinct. . . . Projecting his own desires onto the Negro, the white man behaves 'as if' the Negro really had them" (*Black Skin, White Masks* [New York: Grove, 1952], 165). See also Harry Stecopoulos and Michael Uebel, eds., *Race and the Subject of Masculinities* (Durham, N.C.: Duke Univ. Press, 1997), especially the essay by Robyn Wiegman, "Fiedler and Sons," 45-70. On the stereotyping of African Americans generally, including the stereotyping of sexuality, see Marlon Riggs's documentary film *Ethnic Notions: Black People in White Minds* (San Francisco: California Newsreel, 1986).

20. See John Vernon, "Paul Robeson, the Cold War, and the Question of African-American Loyalties," *Black History Bulletin* 62 (April-September 1999): 47-51. For more general work on the relationship between racial politics and the Cold War, see Thomas Borstelmann, *The Cold War and the Color Line: American Race Relations in the Global Arena* (Cambridge: Harvard Univ. Press, 2001); and Mary L. Dudziak, *Cold War Civil Rights: Race and the Image of American Democracy* (Princeton, N.J.: Princeton Univ. Press, 2000).

21. See Henry Louis Gates, Jr.'s discussion of signifying as a rhetorical strategy of indirection (*The Signifying Monkey: A Theory of African American Literary Criticism* [New York: Oxford Univ. Press, 1988], 53-54).

22. While Marlon Ross is not concerned with the dynamics of confession and community or its relationship to Baldwin's religious background, his essay "White Fantasies of Desire: Baldwin and the Racial Identities of Sexuality" clarifies the degree to which Baldwin understood that the exposure of secret desires to the light was a necessary process for personal and political healing: "The uncloseting of desire—sexual desire—would be a necessary step if Americans hoped to unwarp their imaginations from the destructive bent of racism" (in *James Baldwin Now*, ed. Dwight A. McBride [New York: New York Univ. Press, 1999], 34). To date, Michael F. Lynch has written the most extensively on the question of Baldwin's experience of Christianity and its consequences for his fiction; see, for example, "The Everlasting Father: Mythic Quest and Rebellion in Baldwin's *Go Tell It on the Mountain*," *College Language Association Journal* 37 (December 1993): 156-75. Lynch sees Baldwin's work as embodying a form of dialectical embrace and rejection of the church and its doctrine because the practice of the church is contrary to its highest ideals. I think there is more at stake, however, which the conflict between desire and Christian duty in Baldwin's work makes clear. If I am correct that despite his theory of community and confession, Baldwin's fiction suggests that the price of belonging is the deferral of desire, then the problem for Baldwin is the ideals of the church, not simply its practice. See also Michael F. Lynch, "A Glimpse of the Hidden God: Dialectical Vision in Baldwin's *Go Tell*

It on the Mountain," in *New Essays on "Go Tell It on the Mountain,"* ed. Trudier Harris (New York: Cambridge Univ. Press, 1996), 29-57; "*Just above My Head*: James Baldwin's Quest for Belief," *Literature and Theology: An International Journal of Theory, Criticism, and Culture* 11 (September 1997): 284-98; and "Staying Out of the Temple: Baldwin, the African American Church, and *The Amen Corner*," in *Re-Viewing James Baldwin: Things Not Seen*, ed. D. Quentin Miller (Philadelphia: Temple Univ. Press, 2000), 33-71.

23. The reference to "priapic black studs" is from "The Fire Next Time," in *The Price of the Ticket*, 350. Baldwin's well-known critique of Harriet Beecher Stowe's Uncle Tom is contained within his critique of Richard Wright's Bigger Thomas, whom he describes as another white fantasy of black masculinity ("Everybody's Protest Novel," in *The Price of the Ticket*, 27-33).

24. Baldwin, "The Fire Next Time," *The Price of the Ticket*, 341.

25. Houston A. Baker Jr. sees all the features of the bildungsroman in John's anxiety about his awakening sexuality and his efforts to escape the claustrophobic religion of his family (*Black Literature in America* [New York: McGraw, 1971], 16).

26. Trudier Harris, "Introduction," *New Essays on "Go Tell It on the Mountain,"* ed. Harris, 20-21.

27. See Joseph A. Brown, "I, John, Saw the Holy Number: Apocalyptic Visions in *Go Tell It on the Mountain* and *Native Son*," *Religion and Literature* 27 (spring 1995): 53-70; and Fred Standley, "*Go Tell It on the Mountain*: Religion as the Indirect Method of Indictment," in *Critical Essays on James Baldwin*, ed. Fred Standley (Boston: Prentice Hall, 1988), 188-94. For an overview of criticism on *Go Tell It on the Mountain*, see Trudier Harris's introduction to *New Essays*, 1-28.

28. E. Patrick Johnson, "Feeling the Spirit in the Dark: Expanding Notions of the Sacred in the African-American Gay Community," *Callaloo* 21 (spring 1998): 404.

29. See James Baldwin, introduction to *The Amen Corner* (New York: Dell, 1968), xiv.

30. See Weatherby, *James Baldwin*, 96.

31. Eve Kosofsky Sedgwick, *Epistemology of the Closet* (Berkeley and Los Angeles: Univ. of California Press, 1990), 78.

32 Ibid., 3.

33. James Baldwin, "Here Be Dragons," in *The Price of the Ticket*, 679-80.

Subversive Anti-Stalinism:
Race and Sexuality in the Early Essays of James Baldwin

Geraldine Murphy

The value of James Baldwin's stock in the literary critical market, like Ralph Ellison's, rose with the political fortunes of racial integration in the postwar period. "Everybody's Protest Novel," Baldwin's well-known attack on Harriet Beecher Stowe and Richard Wright, represents an African American contribution to the larger postwar effort to repress the cultural and political legacy of the Red Decade. Baldwin's rejection of the protest tradition of American literature is consistent with the discourse of Cold War liberalism associated with the anti-Stalinist intellectuals of *Partisan Review*, yet as a gay African American—or, in postwar parlance, a Negro and a homosexual—Baldwin had little stake in the domestic arrangements of *pax Americana*. He thus employed end-of-ideology rhetoric to other ends besides the cultural erasure of Communism, namely, the extension of liberal subjectivity to blacks and gays. Through what seems today like a withdrawal from political engagement, Baldwin carried on the struggle for equal rights, not "by any means necessary" but by means that seemed most promising to him and other black writers during the early years of the Cold War.

* * *

In a recent reassessment of Wright, Houston Baker cites Baldwin's essays on *Native Son* as "paradigm instances" of traditional bourgeois aesthetics in their dismissal of the "merely" social in favor of individuality and their celebration of a transcendent sphere of Art.[1] Baker is right about the liberal-humanist inscriptions of "Everybody's Protest Novel" and "Many Thousands Gone," but bourgeois aesthetics covers a wide territory; the specific Cold War context of Baldwin's critique of

Wright must be taken into account in order fully to understand Baldwin's liberal aesthetics. In the wake of World War II and the Holocaust as well as a series of betrayals by the Communist Party culminating in the "iron curtain" across Eastern Europe, liberal intellectuals "abandoned many traditional liberal tenets . . . replacing them with a chastened and, in their view, 'realistic' philosophy which stressed man's sinfulness, the seeming inevitability of conflict among nations, and the dangers of democratic rule."[2] The old left's faith in progress was equated with a dangerous utopian innocence, and solidarity shaded into a dark surrender of individual consciousness to the totalitarian state.

Among those redefining liberalism in the postwar era were the disillusioned former leftists later known as the New York Intellectuals. Arthur Schlesinger, Jr.'s *The Vital Center* (1949) and Lionel Trilling's *The Liberal Imagination* (1950) provide valuable guides to their rapprochement with the welfare state and their hostility to the political and cultural left. Published the same year as "Everybody's Protest Novel," *The Vital Center* describes a politics of consensus in which moderate liberals and conservatives join forces against the extremes of Communism on the left and fascism on the right. Schlesinger and company traded a Marxian model of society, where the bourgeoisie and proletariat were locked in decisive struggle, for a pluralist model, in which a complex web of tensions were continually being negotiated—pragmatically, non-ideologically—by responsible leaders in government, business, unions, and so forth. Although it bred "contradiction" and "strife," conflict must be entertained rather than suppressed because it was "the guarantee of freedom."[3] In effect, the one big dialectic was dropped in favor of a multitude of little dialectics. The New York Intellectuals never really conceded the vocabulary of the left, its embattled stance, or its moral high ground; throughout *The Vital Center*, in fact, Schlesinger keeps referring to the "new radicalism," not the new liberalism. The pluralist model, however, with its intricate network of conflicts dispersing power and providing a "natural" system of checks and balances, ultimately insured stability rather than revolution. It permitted former leftists, in an age of nuclear stalemate, to fetishize struggle and agonize over the burdens of "freedom" without any messy social consequences.

Trilling's contribution to the discourse of anti-Stalinist liberalism was to shift the pluralist drama of multiple dialectics to the individual psyche. Throughout the forties and fifties, Trilling would refer to Keats's "negative capability" and Montaigne's approbative "*ondoyant et divers*" to describe the ideal posture of a complex mind confronting a complex reality. One of the best known explications of his view is found in "Reality in America," a critique of V. L. Parrington that targets the Progressive and Popular Front traditions of American letters. "A culture," says Trilling, disputing the title of Parrington's *Main Currents in American Thought*,

> is not a flow, nor even a confluence; the form of its existence is struggle, or at least debate—it is nothing if not a dialectic. And in any culture there are likely to be certain artists who contain a large part of the dialectic within themselves, their meaning and power lying in their contradictions; they contain within themselves, it may be said, the very essence of the culture, and the sign of this is that they do not submit to serve the ends of any one ideological group or tendency.[4]

The classic American authors whom Parrington slighted—Poe, Melville, Hawthorne, James—were "repositories" of that cultural dialectic; according to Trilling, "they contained both the yes and no of their culture" (RA, 9). Eschewing the security of ideology, the liberal imagination hosted the dynamic contradictions that a "free" society and a "free" mind were heir to.

Trilling defended nineteenth-century American romancers in "Reality in America" as adjuncts to the tradition of high modernism from Flaubert and Dostoyevsky to Kafka, Joyce, and Lawrence. Symbolistic, self-referential, formally innovative, and intellectually demanding, the modernist text best represented the heroic, critical subjectivity the New York Intellectuals valued in reaction to the realist aesthetics of the left. Through their strategic conflation of modernism and the avant-garde, these critics maintained the illusion of an adversarial cultural politics; their construction of modernism, however, was entirely compatible with their consensus liberalism, as the tropes of irony, complexity, ambiguity, and maturity, common to both discourses, suggest. The realism/modernism debate thus provided a literary parallel to the global opposition of totalitarianism/freedom. The gender inscriptions of these cultural and political divisions are clear from Schlesinger's depiction of "totalitarian liberals" as soft and sentimental and freedom as a "fighting faith": the annihilating threat of a feminized left fostered a kind of anti-Stalinist machismo that made modernism and liberalism strenuous, manly propositions.[5]

Baldwin began his literary career in the bosom of anti-Stalinism. In his early twenties, having been passed over by black editors, Baldwin earned money writing book reviews and essays for Sol Levitas of the *New Leader*, Elliott Cohen and Robert Warshow of *Commentary*, and Philip Rahv of *Partisan Review* as well as Randall Jarrell of the *Nation*. Despite his youth, he managed in these first published pieces to catch the irony and authority of the New York Intellectuals' style. "He had what is called taste," Mary McCarthy recalled, "—quick, Olympian recognitions that were free of prejudice."[6] Baldwin's engagement with the official left, moreover, enacted a light version of the anti-Stalinists' political narrative: he joined the Young People's Socialist League in 1943 and shortly thereafter became a Trotskyite. Baldwin remembered these first editors, especially Levitas, with a good deal of affection and gratitude. Although later in life he would claim that his left-wing experience was negligible, his coming of age in a period of disillusionment with the left inevitably shaped his political and aesthetic convictions.[7]

Baldwin's essays in the forties and early fifties reflect his anti-Stalinist origins. As he remembers it, he gave up reviewing after a year or so because he grew weary of books on the "Negro problem" and re-sented the assumption that his race made him an authority on the subject.[8] Yet his primary theme was not race but rather the political and literary shortcomings of proletarian and Popular Front literature. Characterizing Maxim Gorki's novel *Mother* as typically childish and simplistic, Baldwin further maligns it by calling it a "best seller" and associating it with mass cultural melodrama. "With some ideological concessions and the proper make up," says Baldwin, "*Mother* would make an impressive vehicle for, say, Bette Davis." Gorki's novel demonstrates the "invalidity" of the doctrine that art is a weapon in the class struggle. Art, he intones, with the youthful solemnity of Arthur Schlesinger, Jr., "belongs to us all, including our foes; who are as desperate and as virtuous and as blind as we are and who can only be as evil as we are ourselves."[9] Like the anti-Stalinists, he is even more contemptuous of the progressive, celebratory literature associated with the Popular Front. Comparing Ross Lockridge, Jr.'s *Raintree County* to "The Battle Hymn of the Republic," Baldwin remarks that unfortunately the novel "is not nearly so concise [and] it is a good deal more difficult to get through without gagging." Lockridge's Whitmanesque celebration of the people "define[s] the individual out of existence."[10] The first sentence of his review of Hodding Carter's *Flood Crest* describes the novel as "yet another addition to the overburdened files of progressive fiction concerning the unhappy South." Ridiculing the clichés of this genre, Baldwin observes that Carter is for "Change" and "Progress" brought about by "the Common People" acting together in "The American Way."[11] He criticizes black novelist Chester Himes's *Lonely Crusade* along the same lines and attributes its undistinguished prose and its shapelessness to Himes's ambition to treat exhaustively the subject of Negroes and the left. "The resolution—the holding aloft of the union banner—," observes Baldwin, "leaves one with that same embarrassed rage produced by a reading of *Invictus*."[12] Baldwin's attitude toward Erskine Caldwell's novel, *The Sure Hand of God*, is obvious from the title of his review: "Dead Hand of Caldwell." In "Journey to Atlanta," he describes the ill-fated encounter of "The Melodeers," a

Harlem vocal group to which two of his brothers belonged, with Henry Wallace's Progressive Party and characterizes the Wallacites as the anti-Stalinists would: as aristocratic do-gooders abstractly committed to racial brotherhood and insensitive to individual blacks.

This synopsis of Baldwin's early reviews doesn't mean that he was unconcerned with race; he did review books by and about African Americans and the "Negro problem," and his first stories profoundly explore race and racism in the United States. Nevertheless, the debt to anti-Stalinist liberal discourse is obvious in his disdain for left-wing faith in a committed art, for abstractions like "the common man" and "the people," for sentimentalism and mass culture as well as in his corresponding respect for individuality and psychological complexity, for social contradiction over false unity, for political and aesthetic maturity and the *succes d'estime*.

Baldwin develops these themes in "Everybody's Protest Novel" and "Many Thousands Gone," essays that were published in 1949 and 1951 respectively in *Partisan Review*—that is, at the beginning of the Cold War in the most influential organ of cultural anti-Stalinism. One of Baldwin's best known essays, "Everybody's Protest Novel" has been widely admired as a manifesto of artistic independence in which Baldwin repudiates second-class citizenship in the republic of letters by refusing to write the kind of "Negro problem" novel a white readership expected of him. *Uncle Tom's Cabin* is the protest novel in question, the paradigmatic literary treatment of the Negro problem. "Many Thousands Gone" works out the critique of Richard Wright's *Native Son* that Baldwin touched upon in the concluding paragraphs of the earlier essay.[13] For Baldwin, these novels represented two ends of the spectrum of American protest literature: nineteenth-century evangelical reform and twentieth-century proletarian aesthetics. In the gendered terms implicit in Baldwin's evaluation, they are the feminine and masculine traditions of literary realism. The tensions between "sentimental" and "sociological" realism, however, are subordinated to the broader oppositions of anti-Stalinist liberal discourse which shape

Baldwin's thinking in these essays: propaganda versus art (Stowe "was not so much a novelist," he says, "as an impassioned pamphleteer" [EPN, 14]); realism versus modernism; and mass culture versus the avant-garde. These polarities are ideologically charged and magnetized in their alignment by the Cold War agon of east and west, totalitarianism and freedom.

If, for her well-known recuperation of *Uncle Tom's Cabin*, Jane Tompkins had wanted to find the *locus classicus* of modernist contempt for sentimentality, she need have looked no further than "Everybody's Protest Novel."[14] "Sentimentality," says Baldwin,

> the ostentatious parading of excessive and spurious emotion, is the mark of dishonesty, the inability to feel; the wet eyes of the sentimentalist betray his aversion to experience, his fear of life, his arid heart; and it is always, therefore, the signal of secret and violent inhumanity, the mask of cruelty. (EPN, 14)

Baldwin wrests moral authority from the left by probing for the unconscious motives of political altruism as Trilling had in his short stories and his novel, *The Middle of the Journey* (1947). It's not goodness that motivates do-gooders like Stowe's or Trilling's fellow travelers, but rather fear, guilt, and hatred. Uncle Tom—feminized, Christ-like victim though he is—is really a displacement of white terror, for Stowe's "virtuous rage," says Baldwin, stems from "a panic of being hurled into the flames, of being caught in traffic with the devil" (EPN, 17). Conflating Stowe's evangelical novel with the kind of middlebrow "problem" fiction that the anti-Stalinist intellectuals associated with the Popular Front and held in utter contempt, Baldwin argues that novels like Laura Z. Hobson's *Gentleman's Agreement* (1947) reveal a "terror of the human being, the determination to cut him down to size" (EPN, 16). Their objective, he continues, invoking simultaneously the nightmare of totalitarian conformity and the benign populism of the Popular Front, is "to reduce all Americans to the compulsive, bloodless dimensions of a guy named Joe" (EPN, 19). Although Baldwin doesn't explicitly draw on the contemporary critique of mass culture, his indictment of the sentimental, the feminine, the popular, and the left in "Everybody's Protest Novel" is ideologically compatible with the views of the Frankfurt school and of Clement Greenberg and Dwight Macdonald.

Following Baldwin's own psychoanalytical example, we might conclude that his energetic repudiation of Stowe is motivated by an equally powerful attraction and susceptibility to *Uncle Tom's Cabin*. Indeed, in the "Autobiographical Notes" that precede "Everybody's Protest Novel" in *Notes of a Native Son*, Baldwin describes the novel's formative importance. The eldest child of a large family, he helped raise his younger brothers and sisters: "As they were born," he recalls, "I took them over with one hand and held a book with the other . . . and in this way I read *Uncle Tom's Cabin* and *A Tale of Two Cities* over and over and over again" (AN, 7). In a later memoir, *The Devil Finds Work*, Baldwin returns to this primal literary scene and reveals that he read Stowe's novel "compulsively, the book in one hand, the newest baby on my hipbone. I was trying to find out something, sensing something in the book of immense import for me." His mother was concerned enough to keep hiding the book, and Baldwin obsessed enough to keep finding it.[15] In one sense, Baldwin's rejection of his favorite childhood novel marks an intellectual development that resonates with what Thomas Hill Schaub has called "the liberal narrative": the odyssey from innocence to maturity, from moral simplicity to ambiguity, from sentimental idealism to modernist irony. Baldwin, moreover, had been a teenaged preacher in a pentecostal Harlem church, and Stowe's evangelical Christianity was a powerful reminder of the "provincial" Harlem roots he had severed in his bid for the "cosmopolitan" life of the artist. This putting away of the things of childhood, politically or otherwise, is not the only significance Stowe has for Baldwin in the context of Cold War liberalism, however. There are issues of gender and sexuality to be explored as well, but they must be deferred to a consideration of Baldwin's larger argument regarding Stowe and Richard Wright.

According to Baldwin, *Native Son* doesn't represent an advance over *Uncle Tom's Cabin* but is instead its mirror image; if Uncle Tom, the emasculated black saint, is ultimately the embodiment of white terror, so too is Bigger Thomas, the rapist-murderer. Although Baldwin never utters the word "ideology," contaminated as it is in anti-Stalinist discourse, it is precisely what he means by "the cage of reality bequeathed us at our birth." The oppressed internalize the oppressor's view and thus are "bound, first without, then within, by the nature of our categorization" (EPN, 20). Bigger, a character created by a black author, is nonetheless a projection of white racial hostility, the "native son" as "nigger." The concrete, inescapable experience of racial oppression in everyday life inevitably provokes black rage, yet every African American must resist the temptation to live up—or down—to the worst expectations of the normative (white) culture. He is obliged, says Baldwin, "to make his own precarious adjustment to the 'nigger' who surrounds him and to the 'nigger' in himself." This "tension" must be "perpetually sustained—for without this he has surrendered his birthright as a man no less than his birthright as a black man" (MTG, 36). In terms of character and characterology, Bigger does not sustain the tension; he is objectified, a cipher, a one-dimensional construct of white racism.

Ironically, Bigger is also the projection of white revolutionary desire. Published in 1940, *Native Son* is a product of the thirties, when, "swallowing Marx whole," black intellectuals like Wright elided "the Negro" and "the Worker" and committed themselves to "class struggle" (MTG, 31). Baldwin, on the other hand, calls the final courtroom speech of Max, Bigger's lawyer, "one of the most desperate performances in American fiction" (MTG, 38). To entertain the notion that Bigger is a harbinger of black revolution is "to exploit the national innocence," for the African American has neither "the means of wreaking vengeance upon the state" nor "any desire to do so." The "savage paradox" of his condition is that it is not defined solely by oppression and hatred but also by "the force and anguish and terror of love" (MTG, 39). Baldwin's affirmation of black ambivalence over black militancy, of integration over revolution, might reasonably leave *him* open to charges of Uncle Tomism, but he legitimates his position as black spokesman by associating the white heat of Bigger's anger with white racism, and by identifying revolutionary aspiration with conventional American optimism and innocence. "Red," in other words, is more white than black.

In the symbolic order of Cold War liberalism, red is also more feminine than masculine. As many critics have noted, Baldwin's struggle with Wright is Oedipal; one of his boldest tactics, as a gay man whose masculinity is open to question, is pre-emptively to feminize Wright in the masculinist terms of anti-Stalinist discourse. Baldwin kills the literary father, that is, by smearing him as the literary mother. Just as Bigger *is* Uncle Tom (since he is merely the flip side of the same ideology of white fear and hatred), so Wright *is* Harriet Beecher Stowe. "Everybody's Protest Novel" ends with a gothic image of the two writers' interracial coupling:

> the contemporary Negro novelist and the dead New England woman are locked together in a deadly, timeless battle; the one uttering merciless exhortations, the other shouting curses. And, indeed, within this web of lust and fury, black and white can only thrust and counter-thrust, long for each other's slow, exquisite death. (EPN, 21-22)

This *danse macabre* of eros and sadomasochism, a parody of genuine integration, reconstructs Wright, the virile black revolutionary, as a schoolmarm in bustle and whiteface. Baldwin thus exorcises the threatening feminine and maternal tendencies associated with Stowe and *Uncle Tom's Cabin*—"the book in one hand, the newest baby on my hipbone"—and, indeed, with his role within "his father's house."[16] The young Baldwin provides a textbook case of gender anxiety: he was illegitimate, the child of his mother and not David Baldwin, his stepfather; he was cast in the role of surrogate mother as eldest daughters often are; he was effeminate and tormented about his sexual identity. Vulnerable to the neo-traditionalist gender and sexual prescriptions of the Cold War period, he shores up his own masculinity at the expense of Wright. There is, finally, no difference between the feminine and masculine traditions of literary realism. The crucial distinction is not between Stowe and Wright, but between Stowe and Wright on the one hand and Baldwin on the other.

Baldwin's second major point in these two essays concerns the limitations of Marxism's conception of reality, its exclusive focus on the economic and social facts of life. In "Many Thousands Gone" he rejects Wright's materialist analysis of the race problem and takes a therapeutic approach that presumably owes its inspiration to Freud, the intellectual hero of anti-Stalinist intellectuals. Referring to "the Negro" in the third person, Baldwin brackets his own racial identity and adopts a persona that is implicitly white insofar as it represents the authoritative voice of consensus. Racism has created a kind of national neurosis, and the psychic cost of repressing the Negro is too high; "in our estrangement from him," says Baldwin, "is the depth of our estrangement from ourselves" (MTG, 23). Denying "the Negro" his human complexity, "we"—white Americans—reduce him to a one-dimensional social problem and thereby displace and manage our own guilt; "if he breaks our sociological and sentimental image of him," says Baldwin, "we are panic-stricken and we feel ourselves betrayed" (MTG, 24). The health of the national psyche thus depends on our confronting and owning what we've repressed.

"Problem" literature by white or black writers perpetuates this neurotic denial and displacement. Far from liberating its object of concern, Baldwin argues, the protest novel actually ratifies the status quo by staying safely on the plane of the social and thereby allowing us to evade the universal heart of darkness within. The existential self, however, the "void" of the unconscious, is the true source of freedom and salvation. It is also the source of art: "the reality of man as a social being is not his only reality," says Baldwin, "and that artist is strangled who is forced to deal with human beings solely in social terms" (MTG, 31). Stereotypes of black goodness (Uncle Tom) or evil (Bigger Thomas) are both denials of black subjectivity and the complexities of black community. If Wright had explored Bigger's inner contradictions, his character's fate would have been "human" and "tragic." If he had explored the rhythms of black social life instead of accumulating socioeconomic detail, we would better understand "the relationship that Negroes bear to one another, that depth of involvement and unspoken recognition of shared experience which creates a way of life" (MTG, 33). Protest novels give us the mistaken impression "that in Negro life there exists no tradition, no field of manners, no possibility of ritual or intercourse." African Americans do have a rich cultural heritage, Baldwin asserts, only "there has as yet arrived no sensibility sufficiently profound and tough to make this tradition articulate" (MTG, 34). As David Leeming points out, Baldwin had, hopefully, that sensibility, and he was struggling to articulate that tradition in his first novel, *Go Tell It on the Mountain* (1953), published two years after "Many Thousands Gone."[17]

Others have noted that Baldwin's complaint about the perceived absences in African American culture—"no tradition, no field of manners, no possibility of ritual or intercourse"—alludes to Henry James's famous catalogue, in his study of Hawthorne, of "absent things in American life": "No sovereign, no court, no personal loyalty, no aristocracy, no church, no clergy, no army, no diplomatic service, no country gentlemen, no palaces, no castles . . ." (Lacking these furnishings of the novel in nineteenth-century America, Hawthorne, according to James, was obliged to exploit the resources of romance.) Another plausible source for Baldwin, however, is Lionel Trilling's "Manners, Morals, and the Novel." This essay, which cites James's list, addresses concerns that are closer to Baldwin's own, namely the liberal left's ideological conception of reality and its vitiating effect on culture.

Trilling describes manners as the nuanced social consequences of brute economic facts of money and class, the "hum and buzz of implication" within a particular cultural setting.[18] Manners are the lifeblood of the classic novel, but according to Trilling they make right-thinking, educated Americans uncomfortable. Although these readers can't get enough of society in their fiction, their "abstract" and "doctrinaire" notions of reality explain their preference for problem novels like *The Grapes of Wrath*, *Gentlemen's Agreement*, and *Native Son* over the great novelistic tradition of "tragic reality" that Faulkner alone is keeping alive.[19] "In proportion as we have committed ourselves to our particular idea of reality we have lost our interest in manners," he says (MMN, 203-4). Our "moral righteousness," however, needs a stiff dose of "moral realism":

> We have the books that point out the bad conditions, that praise us for taking progressive attitudes. We have no books that raise questions in our minds not only about conditions but about ourselves, that lead us to refine our motives and ask what might lie behind our good impulses. (MMN, 207)

The similarity to the sentiments expressed in "Everybody's Protest Novel" and "Many Thousands Gone" is striking, yet even if "Manners, Morals, and the Novel" was not specifically on Baldwin's mind, Trilling apparently influenced the style and substance of his work. The Baldwin persona, for example—ironic, modulated, and assured, even in his fledgling reviews—closely resembles the voice of Trilling, whose essays, later collected in *The Liberal Imagination*, were appearing in the same journals. Trilling had democratized the royal "we" which Baldwin as a black writer used to unexpected effect in "Many Thousands Gone." (Baldwin also shares Trilling's bad habit of sometimes coasting on rhetorical skill, strewing prose bouquets over lapses in linear development.) More to the point, the two writers were engaged in the same task of redefining political and aesthetic "reality" for the anti-Communist moment; they helped license an epistemological shift in intellectual discourse from the social to the individual, from objective to subjective. The "savage paradox" of African American ambivalence toward the United States, the "tension" between "the nigger without" and "the nigger within" that blacks must perpetually manage—both situations correspond to Trilling's "yes and no of culture," the multiple dialectics that heroic white liberals must contemplate and sustain. What Baldwin demonstrates in his protest against the protest novel is that blacks are equal to the demands of the liberal imagination.

In making this assertion, I'm not implying that Baldwin was a dupe of anti-Stalinism or that he played Rochester to Trilling's Jack Benny. On the contrary, there was a critical dimension to his position that was largely absent from the anti-Stalinist discourse of white liberals like Trilling. Before turning to the element of resistance in Baldwin's early work, though, I want to consider its significance within the contemporary context of Cold War cultural politics.

* * *

Baldwin and Wright were both living in Paris when "Everybody's Protest Novel" and "Many Thousands Gone" appeared. After the second attack on him, by a young writer who'd been his protégé, Wright began to suspect that Baldwin had been recruited by the United States government to harass him. This was hardly pure paranoia on Wright's part, for he had been under FBI surveillance in the States, and the CIA cooperated in that effort once he moved abroad. Baldwin wasn't an informer, and he smiled at Wright's efforts to keep meetings of the French-American Fellowship Club that Wright had organized a secret.[20] Wright's FBI file reveals, however, that in Paris, in 1951, "one James Baldwin," incorrectly identified as a student, "attacked the hatred themes of the Wright writings" and opposed the Club's efforts to "perpetuate 'Uncle Tom Literature methods.'" Somebody had been taking notes. By the end of the sixties, ironically, Baldwin's own FBI dossier, over 1,400 pages long, would dwarf Wright's. In the eyes of the government the mature James Baldwin was a "pervert," a "Communist," "an advocate of Black Power," and a writer "likely to furnish aid or other assistance to revolutionary elements."[21] In the forties and fifties, however, Wright, the former Party member, was the black writer under suspicion for subversive tendencies—which included a too-fervent commitment to civil rights. "His interest in the problem of the Negro," according to one 1944 FBI report, "has become almost an obsession."[22]

How Wright's George Harris sentiments could be squared with "Uncle Tom Literature methods" was not the sort of question FBI agents pondered. Conservative racists like J. Edgar Hoover regarded all black intellectuals with suspicion and were not likely to appreciate or even recognize divergent opinions within this community on politics or literature. For Hoover, the "Negro problem" simply meant trouble.[23] Anti-Stalinist liberals, however, were still liberals. Their commitment to civil rights was genuine, even though it was complicated by the exigencies of the Cold War.

For most Americans, *Brown v. Board of Education of Topeka* (1954) marks the beginning of the modern civil rights movement, yet in order to understand the attitude of anti-Communist liberals toward race in the first phase of the Cold War, it's important to recognize the efforts to end segregation—outside of the south, at least—that were underway in the 1940s. The Brotherhood of Sleeping Car Porters, for example, prompted Roosevelt to issue an executive order in 1941 to end employment discrimination. The Congress of Racial Equality (CORE), established in 1942, led several successful campaigns to desegregate movie theatres, restaurants, and playgrounds. And while the Brown case was its crowning achievement, the NAACP won a series of legal victories starting in 1946 with the desegregation of interstate buses. Jackie Robinson, who joined the Brooklyn Dodgers in 1947, opened doors for other athletes and also made black Americans more visible to the national consciousness. During the Second World War, racial discrimination and segregation within the armed forces provided a particularly compelling example of the contradiction between American ideals and

American social realities.[24] Truman's Executive Order of 1948 led to the desegregation of the military and set an important precedent for the federal government's intervention on behalf of racial equality.[25] These are the social advances Baldwin had in mind when he made the following observation in "Many Thousands Gone":

> Aunt Jemima and Uncle Tom are dead, their places taken by a group of amazingly well-adjusted young men and women, almost as dark, but ferociously literate, well-dressed and scrubbed, who are never laughed at, who are not likely ever to set foot in a cotton or tobacco field or in any but the most modern of kitchens. (MTG, 26)

On the other hand, he was under no illusion about the persistence of racism in American society and the barriers these "well-adjusted young men and women" would encounter. "In a land where, it is said, any citizen can grow up and become president," he had dryly observed in an earlier essay, "Negroes can be pardoned for desiring to enter Congress."[26]

Anti-Stalinist intellectuals supported civil rights legislation. As pluralists they believed in negotiation among various interest groups, or at least the responsible leaders of interest groups; the NAACP could be a player as well as, say, the United Auto Workers or the New York Stock Exchange. Theoretically, as one film historian put it, "People who came in from the cold, regardless of race, color, or creed, found a warm welcome, a job with an equal-opportunity employer, and shelter from the stormy weather that made life outside the vital center very difficult indeed."27 The anti-Communist liberals of the Americans for Democratic Action pressed successfully for inclusion of a civil rights plank in the Democratic Party Platform of 1948, even though it antagonized southern Democrats.[28] Since "freedom" was the trump card of the United States, the Cold War provided opportunities for civil rights advocates, just as the Second World War and the "four freedoms" it was fought for had. But the commitment of anti-Stalinist liberals to desegregation was subordinated to the fight against Communism. "We Put Freedom First," a pamphlet of the American Committee for Cultural Freedom, asserted that Soviet propaganda exaggerated racial tensions "to divert attention from the totalitarian threat and to spread confusion in the progressive camp." The authors were confident that the condition of blacks in the United States had been steadily improving since the Emancipation Proclamation, and although the struggle for racial equality was not yet won, it would be "madness" to risk "the total enslavement of Europe because in the Southern states of America Negroes still have to travel in separate railway compartments."[29] Cold War liberals had, so to speak, reassigned slavery to the overseas bureau and thus relegated the central fact of African American experience and the most potent symbol in a continuing struggle for equality to a historical footnote. Whatever racial problems persisted in American society could be resolved by what Karl Popper had called "piecemeal social engineering."[30]

In the polarizing atmosphere of the Cold War, the Oedipal struggle between Wright and Baldwin assumed a larger political significance than most literary feuds. That two prominent African American literary intellectuals had chosen exile in Paris, at a time when the United States was struggling for the hearts and minds of Europe, was a fact not lost on either the American Embassy or dissident French intellectuals. Wright, who'd had some difficulty getting abroad in the first place due to his outspoken criticism of the United States, was buttonholed at an Embassy function by a white compatriot; "Listen, for God's sake," he begged, "don't let these foreigners make you into a brick to hurl at our windows!"[31] Wright nevertheless continued to denounce American racial discrimination and supported the non-aligned leftist groups who made up the *Rassemblement Démocratique Révolutionnaire.*

The anti-Stalinists, on the other hand, enlisted Baldwin in the cultural Cold War by reprinting "Everybody's Protest Novel" in *Perspectives USA*, one of the journals founded in the early fifties to woo European intellectuals to the side of freedom.[32] Trilling was the guest editor of the issue in which Baldwin's essay appeared, and he both acknowledged and deflated this agenda when he distinguished between his ostensible role as American "Cultural Ambassador" and his more modest, "true" identity as a writer. The former, he says, is a propagandist who would celebrate "the *energy* and *reality*" of American literature "—quite as if energy and reality were new criteria of literature invented by the simple, passionate people who swept over the middle part of the great North American continent." The writer, on the other hand, is "a lover of discord" for whom "it is impossible to stand in a simple relation to a whole national literature."[33] He is, in short, the familiar Trillingesque figure who says yes and no. In a typical rhetorical maneuver of Cold War liberal rhetoric, Trilling establishes his authority by disavowing it (updating the time-honored American strategy of "Ben Franklin, printer"). He pairs Baldwin's essay with black novelist Richard Gibson's "A No to Nothing" under the rubric of "Two Protests against Protest." Gibson's imaginary dialogue between a publisher and a black novelist reiterates many of the same themes as "Everybody's Protest Novel." According to Gibson, the black writer has two choices: he can either succumb to the demands of totalitarian liberal publishers and become one of the legion of "puerile imitators of Richard Wright" or struggle for the freedom of claiming his modernist heritage as a contemporary of "Joyce, Proust, Mann, Gide, Kafka and not merely . . . Chester B. Himes . . . of Eliot, Valery, Pound, Rilke, Auden and not merely of Langston Hughes." In a striking mixed metaphor, Gibson chooses the west for the African American writer: "His black skin is no iron curtain about his brain; he is not cut off from the main stream."[34] The "Notes on Contributors" cite Baldwin's critiques of the protest novel in which "he has condemned the generalized story of social criticism, and has insisted that fiction be motivated by the truly individual concern."[35] In one sense, then, Richard Wright was wrong about Baldwin; the younger writer didn't spy on him for the United States. But in another, of course, he was right, for Baldwin's attack on *Native Son* became propaganda in the war against Communism.

* * *

There is more than one way to read Baldwin's "protest against protest," however. Although he opposed the politics and aesthetics of the Communist Party, he was not willing to sacrifice the struggle for civil rights to Cold War objectives. Freedom, as I mentioned above, had a historical resonance for African Americans long before the Cold War; its binary opposite was not Soviet totalitarianism but American slavery.[36] The tragic past and the burdens of history which consensus historians counterposed to Progressive optimism had a specific referent for Baldwin in his stepgrandmother; Barbara Baldwin, who spent her last years living in the Baldwin's Harlem apartment, had been born a slave in the south. As Leeming observes, this mother of fourteen children, "white" as well as black, would represent to her impressionable grandchild "the prototype of that ancient forced motherhood that makes black and white Americans 'brothers' and 'sisters' whether they like it or not."[37] If Baldwin would not defer the black/white conflict to the east/west conflict, he might adapt the ideology of the latter to his own uses.

In his analysis of *Invisible Man*, Schaub asserts that Ralph Ellison was redefining reality in subjective, universalist terms in order "to wrest reality not only from the Stalinists . . . but from the misperceptions of all white Americans."[38] Baldwin, who admired Ellison as the first African American novelist to represent "the ambiguity and irony of Negro life," was engaged in a similar project (AN, 12). The perceptual limitations of "Stalinist" reality that he outlined in "Everybody's Protest Novel" and "Many Thousands Gone"—a tendency toward simplification and stereotyping—were the perceptual limitations of white Americans toward black Americans. For the former to objectify the latter as a "sociological or sentimental image" was to behave like—a Communist. If "reds" are "white" and "whites" are "red," then perhaps the only true blue Americans are black. Baldwin, of course, never advances an argument so fancifully tendentious, yet his concluding remarks in "Many Thousands Gone" depict the black struggle for subjectivity as a particularly American endeavor. If the African American capitulates to white definitions of black identity, he says, he "can only acquiesce in the obliteration of his own personality, the distortion and debasement of his own experience, surrendering to those forces which reduce the person to anonymity and which make themselves manifest daily all over the darkening world" (MTG, 42). Baldwin invokes the specter of totalitarianism—the extinction of the individual under Communism—to mark the urgency of the race problem in America. Unlike white anti-Stalinists who subordinated race to the arms race, Baldwin appropriated Cold War rhetoric to denounce domestic oppression.

Baldwin's perception that the greater threat to American society was racism rather than Communism was shared by black leaders. Testifying before the House Committee on Un-American Activities, Lester B. Granger of the National Urban League cited the Ku Klux Klan as an appropriate target for HUAC investigation.[39] Clarence Mitchell of the NAACP declared that southern blacks "could not believe that the threat of Communism was as much a menace to their freedom as the actual and present danger of mob violence." A young former Party member named Foster Williams testified that the Party was more interested in exploiting black struggle for propaganda purposes than supporting it. "In looking at the achievements and contributions of the American Negro," he said, "we see at once that they have been made within the framework of our American political system."[40] Although it is possible that Williams was simply telling HUAC what it wanted to hear, there is no question that Party policy in the forties and fifties was out of step with black organizations and the aspirations of most African Americans. With the revival of the Popular Front in 1941, the Party's commitment to civil rights took a back seat to the war effort. According to Irving Howe and Lewis Coser, "the Communists were the main force within the Negro community in favor of muting—and often preventing—the campaign for equal rights."[41] When Earl Browder was removed from office in 1945, the Party reinstated the "Black Belt" thesis of the militant Third Period, which envisioned a separate black state south of the Mason-Dixon line federated with the United States according to the Soviet model.[42] During the great integrationist phase of modern black protest, then, the Party espoused a separatist policy, only to abandon it in 1959 when self-determination and Black Power were on the horizon.

The question that remains to be asked is what the critical potential of subjectivity and freedom was for blacks in the postwar period. In light of poststructuralist postmortems on the bourgeois subject, we might be inclined to write off Baldwin's bid for this piece of the democratic-capitalist pie as either historically quaint or politically benighted or both. The ideological crimes of bourgeois liberalism—its spurious claims to objectivity and equality—have been well documented. There's no question that for most anti-Stalinist intellectuals, Cold War liberalism marked a retreat from the left yet provided an illusory iconoclasm in the figure of the heroic, tragic individual at odds with society. In short, the anguished dialectics of saying yes and no inside and out masked accommodation to the warfare-welfare state. But as Elizabeth Fox-Genovese points out, those groups to whom subjecthood has historically been denied are not so eager to attend the funeral of the bourgeois subject. "Surely it is no coincidence," she continues, "that the Western white male elite proclaimed the death of the subject at precisely the moment at which it might have had to share that status with the women and peoples of other races and classes who were beginning to challenge its supremacy."[43] Neither the affirmation of the liberal self (Trilling) nor the "de-facement" of it (de Man) comes naturally to marginalized Others who cannot take their subjectivity for granted. Thus, Baldwin's embrace of Cold War liberalism should not be regarded as mere capitulation; it is in itself a political act necessarily different from Trilling's, and it opens up unanticipated possibilities for claims upon the social order. His subsequent involvement in the civil rights movement—so different from the New York Intellectuals' distance from the grassroots political movements of the fifties and sixties—demonstrates as much.[44] Baldwin's efforts to secure the full rights of a complex, contradictory consciousness for the black artist in the early fifties complement the efforts of black leaders like Martin Luther King, Jr., and Thurgood Marshall to secure the full civil rights of black citizens. In this sense they represent a continuation of the left's struggle more than a repudiation of it.[45]

* * *

Baldwin, it should be remembered, was a member of a sexual minority as well as a racial minority. My reading of "Everybody's Protest Novel" and "Many Thousands Gone" earlier in this essay addressed the gender and sexual implications of Baldwin's repudiation of Wright; by way of conclusion, I'd like to return to this subject and consider Baldwin's explicit comments on sexuality, for here, too, he managed to adapt Cold War liberalism to his own purposes.

"The contemporary sexual attitudes," he observed somewhat wistfully in an early review of an obscure novel called *The Sling and the Arrow*, "constitute a rock against which many of us founder all our lives long; no one escapes entirely the prevailing psychology of the times."[46] Since the "prevailing psychology" of the early Cold War conceived of homosexuality as a form of deviance and traced its roots to arrested Oedipal development, the classic shift of allegiance among Cold War liberals from Marx to Freud was complicated in Baldwin's case by sexual identity, if not race. Baldwin didn't write as extensively about homosexuality in this period as he did about the "Negro problem"; historically, the concept of gay civil rights had yet to take its cue from the earlier movement for racial equality. Moreover, in the postwar imaginary, homosexuality was politically contaminated by Communism and thus engaged the messy issue of civil liberties rather than civil rights. In his few discussions of it, however, Baldwin staked the male homosexual's claim for the same kind of complex subjectivity he had demanded for the African American.

The title of his most explicit postwar statement, "Preservation of Innocence" (1949), suggests his strategy for reconciling homosexuality and Cold War liberalism. Published in the second issue of a new Parisian journal, *Zero*, the essay establishes the axes which construct postwar homosexuality—good/evil, natural/unnatural—and then cannily dismantles them. The current "hysteria" over homosexuality, Baldwin argues, is related to rigidly defined gender roles: the "present debasement [of the homosexual] and our obsession with him corresponds to the debasement of the relationship between the sexes."[47] Popular culture, specifically the *roman* and *film noir*, provides an index to the debasement of masculinity and femininity in the cartoonish stereotypes of the tough guy and the treacherous *femme fatale*. Baldwin's primary concern is the tough guy, "who, for all his tommy-guns and rhetoric is the innocent" (PI, 19). The hard-boiled genre ultimately endorses an adolescent sentimentalism of boy meets girl typical of "The Rover Boys and their golden ideal of chastity" (PI, 21). Baldwin reveals a particular animus against James M. Cain; in fact, his review of *The Moth* (1948) a year earlier in the *New Leader* was called "Modern Rover Boys."[48] In that novel, set in the Depression, the protagonist's love for a twelve-year-old girl revealed how "preposterous and tasteless" his ideal of feminine purity was. Cain's homophobia is explicit in an earlier novel, *Serenade* (1939), in which "the hero's mistress, a lusty and unlikely señorita," stabs to death a predatory "invert," thereby preserving the protagonist's "immaculate manliness" and destroying any threat to "the union of the Boy and Girl." This gesture, however, is futile; killing the homosexual doesn't restore sexual order, "for the boy cannot know a woman since he has never become a man" (PI, 20).

Baldwin's argument in "Preservation of Innocence" turns postwar Freudianism on its head. It's not the homosexual male who fails to resolve the Oedipus complex but rather the hypermasculine, heterosexual male. Furthermore, the psycho-sexual innocence and immaturity of the tough guy implicates him in the political innocence of Communists and fellow travelers. According to Baldwin, gender and sexuality are paradoxical, complex phenomena which cannot be reduced to the simple binarisms of popular culture and Christian morality. "The recognition of this complexity," he says, "is the signal of maturity; it marks the death of the child and the birth of the man" (PI, 18). Only by embracing every aspect of human experience are we able to "free" ourselves. For all his talk about gender complexity and the "communion" of the sexes, however, both in "Preservation of Innocence" and a 1954 essay on Gide's homosexuality, Baldwin shows no interest in deconstructing the Freudian female, straight or lesbian. Several critics have remarked on the misogyny of such protagonists as David and Giovanni in *Giovanni's Room* (1956) and Rufus in *Another Country* (1962). Many of his female characters, moreover, are models of essentialist feminine masochism and passivity. In his interpretation of *Another Country*, William A. Cohen argues that for Baldwin gender is "a rigidly fixed, virtually incontestable axis of difference" while sexuality, on the other hand, is remarkably fluid, "to the extent that 'gay' and 'straight' barely constitute identities."[49] Baldwin was essentially a critic of heterosexism rather than sexism. Although he was sensitive to the excesses of Cold War machismo, his feminization of Wright and the left which I described earlier shows that he wasn't above deploying gender categories to his own advantage. Suspect as a gay man, politically and psychologically, Baldwin was more eager to appropriate masculinity than revise it.

Baldwin's insight about the relationship between homophobia and neo-traditionalist gender roles in the postwar period anticipates the work of later historians. According to Elaine Tyler May, Cold War anxieties were expressed in a domestic ideology which made the "nuclear" family the vehicle for personal fulfillment and social stability: "if presumably subversive individuals could be contained and prevented from spreading their poisonous influence through the body politic, then the society could feel secure."[50] Feminism posed one threat to the nuclear family and, by extension, to the global balance of power; the male homosexual represented another. McCarthy and other right-wing forces railed with equal vehemence against Communists and queers in the government and subjected both groups to purges. The "striped pants set" in the State Department which "lost" China to the Reds was coded as homosexual by its critics; these cookie-pushing diplomats lacked the masculine wit and will essential to the fight against Communism.[51] Baldwin's FBI file also illustrates the conflation of political and sexual deviance in anti-Communist discourse; agents kept track of Baldwin's sexual preferences and the interracial and homosexual themes of his novels as well as his political activity. One of the reports prompted Hoover's handwritten question, "Isn't Baldwin a well known pervert?"[52] On the heels of wartime heroism, the Cold War ushered anti-Communist machismo into fashion among liberals as well as conservatives. Endless debates in liberal journals over the "hards" and the "softs" on the Communist question provide one example of its rhetoric.[53] The "soft" Stalinist/homosexual was the fifth columnist who allowed—invited—penetration and infiltration by a foreign power.

Baldwin's recuperation of the homosexual, however, like his recuperation of the African American in the early Cold War, was essentially literary rather than political. There was hardly a flourishing subgenre of progressive homosexual "problem" novels; nevertheless, Baldwin equated Gore Vidal's *The City and the Pillar* (1948), William Maxwell's *The Folded Leaf* (1945), and Charles Jackson's *The Fall of Valor* (1946)—contemporary novels that addressed the subject of homosexuality—with the likes of *Gentleman's Agreement*:

> It is quite impossible to write a worthwhile novel about a Jew or a Gentile or a Homosexual, for people refuse, unhappily, to function in so neat and one-dimensional a fashion. If the novelist considers that they are no more complex than their labels he must, of necessity, produce a catalogue, in which we will find, neatly listed, all those attributes with which the label is associated; and this can only operate to reinforce the brutal and dangerous anonymity of our culture. (PI, 21-22)

The indirect allusion to totalitarianism at the end of the passage, the aversion to ideological simplification and innocence, the privileging of complexity, maturity, and masculinity—these are the same strategies Baldwin used to negotiate a modernist African American literature in Cold War terms. His own treatment of male homoeroticism in *Giovanni's Room* and *Another Country* would be a far cry from either the sentimental problem novel or the "case history" of "abnormal psychology" he described in his review of *The Sling and the Arrow.*

* * *

In the late forties, the New York Intellectuals gave Baldwin his start and his subject as a writer. Following their example, he rejected the Communist left along with the realist literary traditions associated with it, and he embraced the cultural tropes of irony, ambivalence, complexity, and maturity that defined Cold War liberalism and modernism. How admirable "Everybody's Protest Novel" is as "a call for the integrity and freedom of art from the shackles of ideology" must be determined in light of its historical context, for its compatibility with the hegemonic discourse of Cold War liberalism made it a missile in the international propaganda war between east and west.[54] Baldwin's own objectives, however, were not entirely congruent with those of the New York Intellectuals, and they would become ever more divergent as the civil rights struggle gained momentum in the late fifties and early sixties. Ultimately, the Cold War construct of the dynamic liberal subject lent itself to different agendas for white and black anti-Stalinists, and perhaps straight and gay anti-Stalinists. To the former, it provided a retreat not only from vulgar Marxism's *homo economus* but from the left altogether; to Baldwin, it offered equal status under the imagination. Existential selfhood (ironically, like the Christian soul in nineteenth-century abolitionist discourse) was a radically egalitarian concept that transcended race and sexual orientation. Baldwin's liberal faith in a shared, complex humanity as the basis of social change may seem naive or simply conservative to a contemporary audience versed in postmodernist concepts of difference, the decentered self, identity politics, and queer theory, but liberalism is as liberalism does, even Cold War liberalism. "Freedom," said Schlesinger in *The Vital Center*, "must become, in Holmes's phrase, a 'fighting faith,'"[55] to which Baldwin on the home front replied, "Amen."

Notes

1. Houston A. Baker, Jr., *Blues, Ideology, and Afro-American Literature: A Vernacular Theory* (Chicago: Univ. of Chicago Press, 1984), 140-43.

2. Mary Sperling McAuliffe, *Crisis on the Left: Cold War Politics and American Liberals, 1947-1954* (Amherst: Univ. of Massachusetts Press, 1978), 63.

3. Arthur M. Schlesinger, Jr., *The Vital Center: The Politics of Freedom* (Boston: Houghton Mifflin, 1949), 255.

4. Lionel Trilling, "Reality in America," in *The Liberal Imagination: Essays on Literature and Society* (1950; New York: Harcourt Brace Jovanovich, 1979), 9; hereafter cited parenthetically in the text as RA.

5. For more detailed descriptions of Cold War liberalism, see McAuliffe, 63-74, and Thomas Hill Schaub, *American Fiction in the Cold War* (Madison: Univ. of Wisconsin Press, 1991), 3-24.

6. Quoted in James Campbell, *Talking at the Gates: A Life of James Baldwin* (New York: Viking, 1991), 40.

7. James Baldwin, "Introduction: The Price of the Ticket," in *The Price of the Ticket: Collected Nonfiction 1948-1985* (New York: St. Martin's, 1985), xii-xiii.

8. James Baldwin, "Autobiographical Notes," in *Notes of a Native Son* (1955; New York: Dial, 1963), 8; hereafter cited parenthetically in the text as AN. See also Campbell, 38.

9. James Baldwin, "Battle Hymn," *New Leader* 30 (29 November 1947), 10.

10. James Baldwin, "Lockridge: 'The American Myth,'" *New Leader* 31 (10 April 1948), 10.

11. James Baldwin, "Change within a Channel," *New Leader* 31 (24 April 1948), 11.

12. James Baldwin, "History as Nightmare," *New Leader* 30 (25 October 1947), 11.

13. "Everybody's Protest Novel" was published for the first time in *Zero*, a short-lived European journal, a few months before it appeared in *Partisan Review*. Both this

essay and "Many Thousands Gone" are collected in *Notes of a Native Son*; hereafter they are cited parenthetically in the text from this volume as EPN and MTG.

14. Jane Tompkins, *Sensational Designs: The Cultural Work of American Fiction, 1790-1860* (New York: Oxford Univ. Press, 1985), 122-46. See Horace A. Porter, *Stealing the Fire: The Art and Protest of James Baldwin* (Middletown: Wesleyan Univ. Press, 1989), 46-49.

15. James Baldwin, *The Devil Finds Work* (New York: Laurel-Dell, 1976), 16-17.

16. "In My Father's House" was for years the working title of Baldwin's autobiographical first novel, *Go Tell It on the Mountain*. Although the biblical and Oedipal allusions of the original title are obvious, the similarity to *Uncle Tom's Cabin* and the traditions of literary domesticity should not be overlooked.

17. David Leeming, *James Baldwin: A Biography* (New York: Knopf, 1994), 84.

18. Lionel Trilling, "Manners, Morals, and the Novel," in *Liberal Imagination*, 194; hereafter cited parenthetically in the text as MMN.

19. Trilling doesn't mention these titles, but they may be assumed from the following passage, along with *A Bell for Adano*, *The Man in the Gray Flannel Suit*, and *The Snake Pit*: "What is the situation of the dispossessed Oklahoma farmer and whose fault it is, what situation the Jew finds himself in, what it means to be a Negro, how one gets a bell for Adano, what is the advertising business really like, what it means to be insane and how society takes care of you or fails to do so—these are the matters which are believed to be most fertile for the novelist, and certainly they are the subjects favored by our reading class" (MMN, 202).

20. James Baldwin, "Alas, Poor Richard," in *Nobody Knows My Name: More Notes of a Native Son* (New York: Laurel-Dell, 1961), 165.

21. Quoted in Natalie Robbins, *Alien Ink: The FBI's War on Freedom of Expression* (New York: William Morrow, 1992), 345, 348-49.

22. Quoted in Robbins, 285.

23. See Richard Gid Powers, *Secrecy and Power: The Life of J. Edgar Hoover* (New York: Macmillan, 1987), 127-28, 323-24.

24. As the sole support of his large family, Baldwin was not drafted. He remembered, however, the heightened racial tensions in Harlem during the war: "everybody felt a directionless, hopeless bitterness, as well as that panic which can scarcely be suppressed when one knows that a human being one loves is beyond one's reach, and in danger." The danger he referred to was military training in the south; families in Harlem experienced "a peculiar kind of relief" when black soldiers were shipped to overseas theaters of war.

The funeral of David Baldwin, Sr. took place on 2 August 1943, the same day a major riot broke out in Harlem over the shooting of a black serviceman by a white policeman. The next day, Baldwin recalled, he and the family "drove my father to the graveyard through a wilderness of smashed glass" ("Notes of a Native Son," in *Notes*, 90-91, 98-100, 76; hereafter cited parenthetically in the text as NNS).

25. My brief sketch of integrationist efforts in the forties draws on Marty Jezer, *The Dark Ages: Life in the United States 1945-1960* (Boston: South End Press, 1982), 296-98; and Richard M. Dalfiume, *Desegregation of the U.S. Armed Forces: Fighting on Two Fronts, 1939-1953* (Columbia: Univ. of Missouri Press, 1969), 2-4.

26. James Baldwin, "The Harlem Ghetto," in *Notes*, 53.

27. Peter Biskind, *Seeing Is Believing: How Hollywood Taught Us to Stop Worrying and Love the Fifties* (New York: Pantheon-Random House, 1983), 228.

28. McAuliffe, 37.

29. *We Put Freedom First* (New York: American Committee for Cultural Freedom, 1950; Reprint, with Preface by Sidney Hook, Congress for Cultural Freedom, n.p., n.d.), 11, 12.

30. Karl R. Popper, *The Poverty of Historicism* (Boston: Beacon Press, 1957), 64-70.

31. Quoted in Michel Fabre, *The World of Richard Wright* (Jackson: Univ. Press of Mississippi, 1985), 179.

32. *Encounter*, published by the Congress for Cultural Freedom, is a better-known example because of the discovery in the sixties that it had accepted funding from the CIA. In the eyes of the New Left at least, anti-Stalinist claims of independence and iconoclasm were thus compromised. See Christopher Lasch, *The Agony of the American Left* (New York: Knopf, 1969), 101-10. *Perspectives USA* was funded by the Ford Foundation.

33. Lionel Trilling, "Editor's Commentary," *Perspectives USA* 2 (Winter 1953), 7.

34. Richard Gibson, "A No to Nothing," in "Two Protests against Protest," *Perspectives*, 91.

35. "Notes on Contributors," *Perspectives*, 179.

36. The testimony of Paul Robeson before the House Committee on Un-American Activities in 1956 neatly dramatizes the clash of black and white discourse on slavery during the Cold War. When asked about Stalin, Robeson replied that it was up to the Soviet Union to pass judgment and reminded the committee members of their own national disgrace. "You are responsible, and your forebears," he charged, "for sixty million to one hundred million black people dying in the slave ships and on the plantations, and don't you ask me about anybody, please."

"I am glad you called our attention to that slave problem," a staff member of HUAC responded. "While you were in Soviet Russia, did you ask them there to show you the slave labor camps?"

"You have been so greatly interested in slaves," added the Chair of the Committee, "I should think that you would want to see that." Robeson, however, refused to concede slavery to the anti-Communist camp. "The slaves I see are still in a kind of semiserfdom," he replied. "I am interested in the place I am, and in the country that can do something about it." See *Thirty Years of Treason: Excerpts from Hearings before the House Committee on Un-American Activities, 1938-1968*, ed. Eric Bentley (New York: Viking, 1971), 785-86.

37. Leeming, 4.

38. Schaub, 99.

39. Delacy Wendell Sanford, "Congressional Investigation of Black Communism, 1919-1967" (Ph.D. diss., SUNY Stony Brook, 1973), 117.

40. Quoted in Sanford, 126, 153.

41. Irving Howe and Lewis Coser, *The American Communist Party: A Critical History (1919-1957)* (Boston: Beacon Press, 1957), 415-16.

42. "On balance," says Gerald Horne, "the Black Belt thesis was probably not an

asset for the party, particularly during the postwar period when blacks moved en masse to the North and West" ("The Red and the Black: The Communist Party and African-Americans in Historical Perspective," in *New Studies in the Politics and Culture of U.S. Communism*, ed. Michael E. Brown, Randy Martin, Frank Rosengarten and George Snedeker [New York: Monthly Review Press, 1993], 205).

43. Elizabeth Fox-Genovese, "The Claims of a Common Culture: Gender, Race, Class, and the Canon," *Salmagundi* 72 (Fall 1986), 134. For a fuller consideration of this subject, see Betsy Erkkila, "Ethnicity, Literary Theory, and the Grounds of Resistance," *American Quarterly* 47 (1995): 563-94.

44. Relations between Baldwin and the New York Intellectuals became increasingly strained through the fifties as black and white intellectuals developed different analyses of the race question. Although Baldwin soon revised the view expressed in his 1947 review of Chester Himes's *Lonely Crusade* that "no real group identification is possible" among blacks and that there is no "Negro tradition to cling to in the sense that Jews may be said to have a tradition" ("History as Nightmare," 11), his respect for Jewish culture is still apparent in "Many Thousands Gone." A decade later, however, *The Fire Next Time* (1963) provoked Norman Podhoretz to pen "My Negro Problem—and Ours," an essay which marked the neo-conservative turn of *Commentary.* On black-Jewish tensions in the sixties, see Alexander Bloom, *Prodigal Sons: The New York Intellectuals and Their World* (New York: Oxford Univ. Press, 1986), 331-37.

45. Porter makes a similar point when he observes that in "Many Thousands Gone," Baldwin "projects a social message that is closely akin to Wright's." In his view, the essay owes its "striking rhetorical power" to the tension between Baldwin's "conscious repudiation and unconscious affirmation" of Wright (79).

Robert J. Corber considers Baldwin's critique of Wright in light of Trilling's "subjectivization of experience" and argues that Baldwin did *not* renounce the social sphere: "Although Baldwin seemed to share Trilling's assumptions about the nature of reality in that he criticized Wright for ignoring the construction of Bigger's subjectivity in relation to racist constructions of African-American male identity, he was not interested in shifting attention away from the historical specificity of the individual's identity as a social being. Rather, he wanted to show that the individual's subjective experience of the material world was complexly related to her/his identity as a social being" (*In the Name of National Security: Hitchcock, Homophobia, and the Political Construction of Gender in Postwar America* [Durham: Duke Univ. Press, 1993], 34). At the risk of sounding Jesuitical, I am arguing that Baldwin carries on the social struggle by exploring the resources of subjectivity. Corber's formulation underestimates Baldwin's debt to anti-Stalinist discourse.

46. James Baldwin, "Without Grisly Gaiety," *New Leader* 30 (20 September 1947), 12.

47. James Baldwin, "Preservation of Innocence," *Zero* 2 (Summer 1949), 16; hereafter cited parenthetically in the text as PI.

48. Although the hard-boiled genre developed by Cain, Hammett, and Chandler owes something to the proletarian novel, Baldwin's consistent association of Cain with the middlebrow problem novel is puzzling, particularly since Cain was never involved

with the Popular Front and in fact was staunchly anti-Communist in the late forties and fifties. See Roy Hoopes, *Cain* (New York: Holt, Rinehart, Winston, 1982), 389-90.

49. William A. Cohen, "Liberalism, Libido, Liberation: Baldwin's *Another Country*," *Genders* 12 (1991), 2.

50. Elaine Tyler May, *Homeward Bound: American Families in the Cold War Era* (New York: Basic Books, 1988), 14.

51. See John D'Emilio and Estelle B. Freedman, *Intimate Matters: A History of Sexuality in America* (New York: Harper and Row, 1988), 292-94; May, 95; Corber, 8-9.

52. Robbins, 347-48. Hoover's own sexual orientation was the subject of speculation and rumor because of his unorthodox companionate "marriage" to Clyde Tolson. See Powers, 171-73, 185. In his sensational biography, Anthony Summers attributes Hoover's animus toward gays to the Director's closet homosexuality (*Official and Confidential: The Secret Life of J. Edgar Hoover* [New York: Putnams & Sons, 1993], 91-95), a position Athan Theoharis refutes in *J. Edgar Hoover, Sex, and Crime: An Historical Antidote* (Chicago: Ivan R. Dee, 1995), 11-55.

53. See McAuliffe, 109-10.

54. Quotation from Leeming, 64.

55. Schlesinger, 245.

"Sonny's Blues":
James Baldwin's Image of Black Community

John M. Reilly

A critical commonplace holds that James Baldwin writes better essays than he does fiction or drama; nevertheless, his leading theme—the discovery of identity—is nowhere presented more successfully than in the short story "Sonny's Blues." Originally published in *Partisan Review* in 1957 and reprinted in the collection of stories *Going to Meet the Man* in 1965, "Sonny's Blues" not only states dramatically the motive for Baldwin's famous polemics in the cause of Black freedom, but it also provides an aesthetic linking his work, in all literary genres, with the cultures of the Black ghetto.[1]

The fundamental movement of "Sonny's Blues" represents the slow accommodation of a first-person narrator's consciousness to the meaning of his younger brother's way of life. The process leads Baldwin's readers to a sympathetic engagement with the young man by providing a knowledge of the human motives of the youths whose lives normally are reported to others only by their inclusion in statistics of school dropout rates, drug usage, and unemployment.

The basis of the story, however, and its relationship to the purpose of Baldwin's writing generally, lies in his use of the Blues as a key metaphor. The unique quality of the Blues is its combination of personal and social significance in a lyric encounter with history. "The Blues-singer describes first-person experiences, but only such as are typical of the community and such as each individual in the community might have. The singer never sets himself against the community or raises himself above it."[2] Thus, in the story of Sonny and his brother an intuition of the meaning of the Blues repairs the relationship between the two men who have chosen different ways to cope with the menacing ghetto environment, and their reconciliation through the medium of this Afro-American musical form extends the meaning of the individual's Blues until it becomes a metaphor of Black community.

Sonny's life explodes into his older brother's awareness when the story of his arrest for peddling and using heroin is reported in the newspaper. Significantly the mass medium of the newspaper with the impersonal story in it of a police bust is the only way the brothers have of communicating at the opening of the story. While the narrator says that because of the newspaper report Sonny "became real to me again," their relationship is only vestigially personal, for he "couldn't find any room" for the news "anywhere inside . . ." (103).

While he had had his suspicions about how Sonny was spending his life, the narrator had put them aside with rationalizations about how Sonny was, after all, a good kid. Nothing to worry about. In short, the storyteller reveals that along with his respectable job as an algebra teacher he had assumed a conventional way of thinking as a defense against recognizing that his own brother ran the risk of "coming to nothing." Provoked by the facts of Sonny's arrest to observe his students, since they are the same age as Sonny must have been when he first had heroin, he notices for the first time that their laughter is disenchanted rather than good-humored. In it he hears his brother, and perhaps himself. At this point in the story his opinion is evidently that Sonny and many of the young students are beaten and he, fortunately, is not.

The conventionality of the narrator's attitude becomes clearer when he encounters a nameless friend of Sonny's, a boy from the block who fears he may have touted Sonny onto heroin by telling him, truthfully, how great it made him feel to be high. This man who "still spent hours on the street corner . . . high and raggy" explains what will happen to Sonny because of his arrest. After they send him someplace and try to cure him, they'll let Sonny loose, that's all. Trying to grasp the implication the narrator asks: "You mean he'll never kick the habit. Is that what you mean?" He feels there should be some kind of renewal, some hope. A man should be able to bring himself up by his will, convention says. Convention also says that behavior like Sonny's is deliberately self-destructive. "Tell me," he asks the friend, "why does he want to die?" Wrong again. "Don't nobody want to die," says the friend, "ever" (108).

Agitated though he is about Sonny's fate the narrator doesn't want to feel himself involved. His own position on the middle-class ladder of success is not secure, and the supporting patterns of thought in his mind are actually rather weak. Listening to the nameless friend explain about Sonny while they stand together in front of a bar blasting "black and bouncy" music from its door, he senses something that frightens him. "All this was carrying me some place I didn't want to go. I certainly didn't want to know how it felt. It filled everything, the people, the houses, the music, the dark, quicksilver barmaid, with menace; and this menace was their reality" (107).

Eventually a great personal pain—the loss of a young daughter—breaks through the narrator's defenses and makes him seek out his brother, more for his own comfort than for Sonny's. "My trouble made his real," he says. In that remark is a prefiguring of the meaning the Blues will develop.

It is only a prefiguring, however, for by the time Sonny is released from the state institution where he had been confined, the narrator's immediate need for comfort has passed. When he meets Sonny he is in control of himself, but very shortly he is flooded with complex feelings that make him feel again the menace of the 110th Street bar where he had stood with Sonny's friend. There is no escaping a feeling of icy dread, so he must try to understand.

As the narrator casts his mind back over his and Sonny's past, he gradually identifies sources of his feelings. First he recalls their parents, especially concentrating on an image of his family on a typical Sunday. The scene is one of security amidst portentousness. The adults sit without talking, "but every face looks darkening, like the sky outside." The children sit about, maybe one half asleep and another being stroked on the head by an adult. The darkness frightens a child and he hopes "that the hand which strokes his forehead will never stop." The child knows, however, that it will end, and now grown-up he recalls one of the meanings of the darkness is in the story his mother told him of the death of his uncle, run over on a dark country road by a car full of drunken white men. Never had his companion, the boy's father, "seen anything as dark as that road after the lights of the car had gone away." The narrator's mother had attempted to apply her tale of his father's grief at the death of his own brother to the needs of their sons. They can't protect each other, she knows, "but," she says to the narrator about Sonny, "you got to let him know you's *there*" (119).

Thus, guilt for not fulfilling their mother's request and a sense of shared loneliness partially explain the older brother's feeling toward Sonny. Once again, however, Baldwin stresses the place of the conventional set of the narrator's mind in the complex of feelings as he has him recall scenes from the time when Sonny had started to become a jazz musician. The possibility of Sonny's being a jazz rather than a classical musician had "seemed—beneath him, somehow." Trying to understand the ambition, the narrator had asked if Sonny meant to play like Louis Armstrong, only to be told that Charlie Parker was the model. Hard as it is to believe, he had never heard of Bird until Sonny mentioned him. This ignorance reveals more than a gap between fraternal generations. It represents a cultural chasm. The narrator's inability to understand Sonny's choice of a musical leader shows his alienation from the mood of the post-war bebop subculture. In its hip style of dress, its repudiation of middle-brow norms, and its celebration of esoteric manner the bebop subculture made overtly evident its underlying significance as an assertion of Black identity. Building upon a restatement of Afro-American music, bebop became an expression of a new self-awareness in the ghettos by a strategy of elaborate nonconformity. In committing himself to the bebop subculture Sonny attempted to make a virtue of the necessity of the isolation imposed upon him by his color. In contrast, the narrator's failure to understand what Sonny was doing indicates that his response to the conditions imposed upon him by racial status was to try to assimilate himself as well as he could into the mainstream American culture. For the one, heroin addiction sealed his membership in the exclusive group; for the other, adoption of individualistic attitudes marked his allegiance to the historically familiar ideal of transcending caste distinctions by entering into the middle class.

Following his way, Sonny became wrapped in the vision that rose from his piano, stopped attending school, and hung around with a group of musicians in Greenwich Village. His musical friends became Sonny's family, replacing the brother who had felt that Sonny's choice of his style of life was the same thing as dying, and for all practical purposes the brothers were dead to each other in the extended separation before Sonny's arrest on narcotics charges.

The thoughts revealing the brothers' family history and locating the sources of the narrator's complex feelings about Sonny all occur in the period after Sonny is released from the state institution. Though he has ceased to evade thoughts of their relationship, as he had done in the years when they were separated and had partially continued to do after Sonny's arrest, the narrator has a way to go before he can become reconciled to Sonny. His recollections of the past only provide his consciousness with raw feeling.

The next development—perception—begins with a scene of a revival meeting conducted on the sidewalk of Seventh Avenue, beneath the narrator's window. Everyone on the street has been watching such meetings all his life, but the narrator from his window, passersby on the street, and Sonny from the edge of the crowd all watch again. It isn't because they expect something different this time. Rather it is a familiar moment of communion for them. In basic humanity one of the sanctified sisters resembles the down-and-outer watching her, "a cigarette between her heavy, chapped lips, her hair a cuckoo's nest, her face scarred and swollen from many beatings. . . . Perhaps," the narrator thinks, "they both knew this, which was why, when, as rarely, they addressed each other, they addressed each other as Sister" (129). The point impresses both the narrator and Sonny, men who should call one another "Brother," for the music of the revivalists seems to "soothe a poison" out of them.

The perception of this moment extends nearly to conception in the conversation between the narrator and Sonny that follows it. It isn't a comfortable discussion. The narrator still is inclined to voice moral judgments of the experiences and people Sonny tries to talk about, but he is making an honest effort to relate to his brother now and reminds himself to be quiet and listen. What he hears is that Sonny equates the feeling of hearing the revivalist sister sing with the sensation of heroin in the veins. "It makes you feel—in control. Sometimes you got to have that feeling" (131). It isn't primarily drugs that Sonny is talking about, though, and when the narrator curbs his tongue to let him go on, Sonny explains the real subject of his thoughts.

Again, the facts of Sonny's experience contradict the opinion of "respectable" people. He did not use drugs to escape from suffering, he says. He knows as well as anyone that there's no way to avoid suffering, but what you can do is "try all kinds of ways to keep from drowning in it, to keep on top of it, and to make it seem . . . like *you*." That is, Sonny explains, you can earn your suffering, make it seem "like you did something . . . and now you're suffering for it" (132).

The idea of meriting your suffering is a staggering one. In the face of it the narrator's inclination to talk about "will power and how life could be—well, beautiful," is blunted, because he senses that by directly confronting degradation Sonny has asserted what degree of will was possible to him, and perhaps that kept him alive.

At this point in the story it is clear that there are two themes emerging. The first is the theme of the individualistic narrator's gradual discovery of the significance of his brother's life. This theme moves to a climax in the final scene of the story when Sonny's music impresses the narrator with a sense of the profound feeling it contains. From the perspective of that final scene, however, the significance of the Blues itself becomes a powerful theme.

The insight into suffering that Sonny displays establishes his priority in knowledge. Thus, he reverses the original relationship between the brothers, assumes the role of the elder, and proceeds to lead his brother, by means of the Blues, to a discovery of self in community.

As the brothers enter the jazz club where Sonny is to play, he becomes special. Everyone has been waiting for him, and each greets him familiarly. Equally special is the setting—dark except for a spotlight which the musicians approach as if it were a circle of flame. This is a sanctified spot where Sonny is to testify to the power of souls to commune in the Blues.

Baldwin explicates the formula of the Blues by tracing the narrator's thoughts while Sonny plays. Many people, he thinks, don't really hear music being played except so far as they invest it with "personal, private, vanishing evocations." He might be thinking of himself, referring to his having come to think of Sonny through the suffering of his own personal loss. The man who makes the music engages in a spiritual creation, and when he succeeds, the creation belongs to all present, "his triumph, when he triumphs, is ours" (137).

In the first set Sonny doesn't triumph, but in the second, appropriately begun by "Am I Blue," he takes the lead and begins to form a musical creation. He becomes, in the narrator's words, "part of the family again" (139). What family? First of all that of his fellow musicians. Then, of course, the narrator means to say that their fraternal relationship is at last fulfilled as their mother hoped it to be. But there is yet a broader meaning too. Like the sisters at the Seventh Avenue revival meeting Sonny and the band are not saying anything new. Still they are keeping the Blues alive by expanding it beyond the personal lyric into a statement of the glorious capacity of human beings to take the worst and give it a form of their own choosing.

At this point the narrator synthesizes feelings and perception into a conception of the Blues. He realizes Sonny's Blues can help everyone who listens be free, in his own case free of the conventions that had alienated him from Sonny and that dimension of Black culture represented in Sonny's style of living. Yet at the same time he knows the world outside of the Blues moment remains hostile.

The implicit statement of the esthetics of the Blues in this story throws light upon much of Baldwin's writing. The first proposition of the esthetics that we can infer from "Sonny's Blues" is that suffering is the prior necessity. Integrity of expression comes from "paying your dues." This is a point Baldwin previously made in *Giovanni's Room* (1956) and which he elaborated in the novel *Another Country* (1962). The second implicit proposition of the Blues esthetics is that while the form is what it's all about, the form is transitory. The Blues is an art in process and in that respect alien from any conception of fixed and ideal forms. This will not justify weaknesses in an artist's work, but insofar as Baldwin identifies his writing with the art of the singers of Blues it suggests why he is devoted to representation, in whatever genre, of successive moments of expressive feeling and comparatively less concerned with achieving a consistent overall structure.

The final proposition of the esthetics in the story "Sonny's Blues" is that the Blues functions as an art of communion. It is popular rather than elite, worldly rather than otherwise. The Blues is expression in which one uses the skill he has achieved by practice and experience in order to reach toward others. It is this proposition that gives the Blues its metaphoric significance. The fraternal reconciliation brought about through Sonny's music is emblematic of a group's coming together, because the narrator learns to love his brother freely while he discovers the value of a characteristically Afro-American assertion of life-force. Taking Sonny on his own terms he must also abandon the ways of thought identified with middle-class position which historically has signified for Black people the adoption of "white" ways.

An outstanding quality of the Black literary tradition in America is its attention to the interdependence of personal and social experience. Obviously necessity has fostered this virtue. Black authors cannot luxuriate in the assumption that there is such a thing as a purely private life. James Baldwin significantly adds to this aspect of the tradition in

"Sonny's Blues" by showing that artful expression of personal yet typical experience is one way to freedom.

Notes

1. *Partisan Review,* XXIV (Summer, 1957), 327-58. *Going to Meet the Man* (New York, 1965), pp. 103-41. Citations in the text are from the latter publication of the story.

2. Janheinz Jahn, *Neo-African Literature: A History of Black Writing* (New York, 1968), p. 166.

The Queering of Memory: Nostalgia and Desire in Baldwin's "Going to Meet the Man"

Tiffany Gilbert

While pondering the "necessity of looking forward" in his seminal collection of autobiographical essays *Notes of a Native Son*, James Baldwin, in considering "the Negro problem," allows "that the past is all that makes the present coherent . . . [and] will remain horrible for exactly as long as we refuse to assess it honestly" (*CE* 7).[1] Later, in *The Fire Next Time*, he acknowledges "fearful paradox" of the future:

> The American Negro can have no future anywhere, on any continent, as long as he is unwilling to accept his past. To accept one's past—one's history—is not the same thing as drowning in it; it is learning how to use it. An invented past can never be used. (*CE* 333)

The Negro past, Baldwin argues here, records an "endless struggle to achieve and reveal and confirm a human identity" (*CE* 343). By turns horrific and beautiful, this past cannot be escaped; like a burning fire in the next room, it cannot be ignored. How this past is to be used, of course, presents other cultural and existential challenges.

Elsewhere in his extensive body of work, Baldwin takes a retrospective glance at his own life "to confirm" his own identity and humanity. In his essay "Freaks and the American Ideal of Manhood," Baldwin recollects his teenage flirtation with a "Harlem racketeer" more than twice his age and confides, "And though I loved him, too—in my way, a boy's way—I was mightily tormented, for I was still a child evangelist, which everybody knew, Lord. My soul looks back and wonders" (*ENS* 819). Yet Baldwin does not dwell too much on his past; instead, he extracts this valuable lesson:

> For what this really means is that all of the American categories of male and female, straight or not, black or white, were shattered, thank heaven, very early in my life. Not without anguish, certainly; but once you have discerned the meaning of a label, it may seem to define you to others, but it does not have the power to define you to yourself. (*CE* 819)

As Baldwin envisions in the essay "Many Thousands Gone," confronting and transforming the past makes a "dazzling future" possible. For him, the implications of understanding the past are simultaneously vexed and liberating: categories, labels, and classifications no longer carry weight and define the individual in narrow terms and instead become malleable, bending under the influence of individual will or desire.

Yet despite Baldwin's measured optimism about the past's rehabilitative power in his essays and social criticism, for many of Baldwin's fictional characters, the past is enemy territory. For members of the Grimes family in Baldwin's semiautobiographical novel *Go Tell It on the Mountain* (1953), for example, prayer plunges them into an abyss of remembrance, into the minefields of memory: Florence, the protagonist John's spinster aunt, nurses old regrets and resentments stemming from a disastrous marriage; Elizabeth, his mother, revisits the suicide of a former lover, who slashed his wrists out of utter existential despair; and Gabriel, domineering patriarch and minister, suffers "blood-guilt" over an adulterous affair and the loss of the favored child it produced (*ENS* 85). In Baldin's subsequent novel, the absorbing and controversial *Giovanni's Room* (1956), the past penetrates the suffocating confines of the titular space. On the eve of Giovanni's execution, David, Baldwin's sexually conflicted narrator, remembers his first encounter with a man:

> To remember it so clearly, so painfully tonight tells me that I have never for an instant truly forgotten it. I feel in myself now a faint, a dreadful stirring of what so overwhelmingly stirred in me then, great thirsty heat, and trem-

bling, and tenderness so painful I thought I would burst. But out of this astounding, intolerable pain came joy, we gave each other joy that night. It seemed, then, that a lifetime would not be long enough for me to act with Joey the act of love. (*ENS* 225)

Rather helping David realize a "dazzling" future, the memory of this encounter acts merely as a temporary buffer against the present, as the specter of Giovanni's pending execution forces David to return to the surface, to reality itself.

Thus, in the opening sequences of *Giovanni's Room*, Baldwin swiftly unites recollections of past desires with anxieties over the present. This same provocative nexus between nostalgia and desire finds stunning, graphic expression in Baldwin's 1965 short story "Going to Meet the Man." Here, nostalgia operates etymologically and literally as "longing," a longing for a sexual contact that is at once pathological and illicit.

To explicate how Baldwin obscures the objects of desire in "Going to Meet the Man," this essay utilizes queer theory, which pivots on the notion that gender or sexuality is a performance that coheres over time through repetition, hardening into behaviors that appear natural or naturalized. Leading queer theorist Judith Butler, in *Gender Trouble: Feminism and the Subversion of Identity*, conceptualizes gender

> as a relation among socially constituted subjects in specifiable contexts. This relational or contextual point of view suggests that what the person "is," and, indeed, what gender "is," is always relative to the constructed relations in which it is determined. As a shifting and contextual phenomenon, gender does not denote a substantive being, but a relative point of convergence among culturally and historically specific sets of relations. (10)[2]

Memory similarly rests on shifting sand, and by "queering" the memory of a lynching, Baldwin deconstructs a complex trifecta of whiteness, masculinity, and heterosexuality. For when viewed through a queer lens, the lynching of a black man, even as it consolidates a collective white identity, permits a kind of transgressive, homoerotic spectatorship. Baldwin's story, even as it describes the barbarism of vigilante justice, explores these "contextual" phenomena in relation to time, not only to discern the meanings of labels but to shatter them as well.

"Going to Meet the Man" exhumes the memories of Jesse, a virulently racist and sexually impotent police officer. Tired and overworked from arresting "niggers," Jesse seeks comfort in his wife, but is unable to achieve an erection. Frustrated, he distracts himself with recounting the day's events, which include his shocking of the ringleader of a group of black protesters with a cattle prod: "The boy rolled around in his own dirt and water and blood and tried to scream again as the prod hit his testicles, but the scream did not come out, only a kind of rattle and a moan" (*ENS* 936). The image of the boy's writhing body thrills Jesse and excites a long-suppressed memory out of his consciousness: "And now he [Jesse] was shaking worse than the boy had been shaking. He was glad no one could see him. At the same time, he felt very close to a very peculiar, particular joy; something deep in him and deep in his memory was stirred, but whatever was in his memory eluded him" (936-37).

However, Jesse's "peculiar, particular joy" does not solely arise from his expression of the power he holds as a white man and as a police officer. Baldwin implies strongly that this joy is not only homoerotic in nature but also grounded in prohibited interracial desires. He is impotent in the presence of his wife and even in the imaginary presence of a black girl, to whom he could appeal "to help him out": "The image of a black girl caused a distant excitement in him, like a faraway light; but, again, the excitement was more like pain; instead of forcing him to act, it made action impossible" (933). In contrast, he is aroused in the presence of the black boy lying prone on the floor of the cell, and it is here that, "*for some reason*," Jesse fondles himself (937; emphasis added). In short, Jesse desires the black man's body but masks this desire by abusing his professional authority.

The invocation of memory, however, suggests that there is a precedent or, at least, a reason for Jesse's attraction. His nostalgic reflex responds to the racial chaos in which he is immersed, as blacks in the community agitate for their civil rights: "They hated him, and this hatred was blacker than their hearts, blacker than their skins, redder than their blood, and harder, by far, than his club. Each day, each night, he felt worn out, aching, with their smell in his nostrils and filling his lungs, as though he were drowning—drowning in niggers; and it was all to be done again when he awoke. It would never end. It would never end" (939). Contemplating this present dilemma, Jesse considers the legacy of his father's generation, the men "who had been responsible for law and order" and for whom the past "could yet so stubbornly refuse to be remembered" (939; 941). This refusal conceals a horrific truth, "a secret which he could not articulate to himself, and which, however directly related to the war [against the civil rights movement], related yet more surely to his privacy and his past" (941). Even though, in reality, Jesse's and his ancestors' past is a sanctuary of ghosts, of black people terrorized and murdered to preserve white power and the illusion of cultural and racial stability, Jesse's memory of it is a refuge for him.

Nostalgia, as Linda Hutcheon avers,

> is less about the past than about the present. . . ." Simultaneously distancing and proximating, nostalgia exiles us from the present as it brings the imagined past near. The simple, pure, ordered, easy, beautiful, or harmonious past is constructed (and then experienced emotionally) in conjunction with the present—which, in turn, is constructed as complicated, contaminated, anarchic, difficult, ugly, and confrontational. (4)

Indeed, in analyzing the role of nostalgia in *Giovanni's Room*, Valerie Rohy asserts that the nostalgic desire to bring the past nearer "in racist or homophobic discourse . . . is the desire for the coherence of whiteness or heterosexuality, an impossible ideal that nevertheless must be sustained if dominant culture is to 'reproduce' itself" (230). Apropos Jane Gallop, who maintains in *Reading Lacan* that subjectivity is a product of time, "a succession of future perfects, pasts of a future, moments twice removed from 'present reality' by the combined action of an anticipation and a retroaction" (qtd. in Rohy 229), Rohy proposes, "If nostalgia, like passing, gestures toward an absent 'something else,' it does so not to displace but to locate and confirm individual or institutional 'identity'" (229). Accordingly, the lynching in "Going to Meet the Man," both in reality and in memory, operates to ratify Jesse's status as a straight white man.

The lyrics of a spiritual—"*I stepped in the river at Jordan*"—limn the distance between Jesse's present and his past, triggering a reverie into terror. The song, fragments of which come to Jesse as he struggles to sleep, intensifies his anxiety, producing a fear tinged with both "a curious and dreadful pleasure" (*ENS* 942). The spiritual connects Jesse not only to his childhood but also to his father. As a child, Jesse once overheard black farmhands singing the spiritual as he and his parents drove by the fields in the night. His father had dismissed the spiritual as something lascivious, not as a lamentation. "Even when they're sad, they like they just about to go and tear off a piece," he shares with his wife; despite his son's presence in the back seat of the car, he promises her "that's what we going to do" (942). Indeed, when they return home, Jesse agonizes over the sounds of his parents' lovemaking.

> The darkness pressed on his eyelids like a scratchy blanket. He turned, he turned again. He wanted to call his mother, but he knew his father would not like this. He was terribly afraid. Then he heard his father's voice in the other room, low, with a joke in it; but this did not help him, it frightened him more, he knew what was going to happen. He put his head under the blanket, then pushed his head out again, for fear, staring at the dark window. He heard his mother's moan, his father's sigh; he gritted his teeth. Then their bed began to rock. His father's breathing seemed to fill the void. (*ENS* 943)

Jesse's anxieties are founded not only in the uncomfortable realization of "what was going to happen" but also in the domineering figure of his father (943). When he contemplates calling out to his mother, he decides against it, fearing his father's anger. That Jesse needs his mother at the moment his father is making love to her suggests a kind of panic over sexuality and a fearful acknowledgment that his mother has needs and desires that exclude him.

Jesse's sexual impotence in the story's present is mocked by the memory of his father's virility. The sequence exposes not only Jesse's "generational" inadequacies but also his latent fear of what being a "man" means. Similar fears are expressed in the relationship between David and his father—and his sexuality—in *Giovanni's Room*. "I did not want to be his buddy, I wanted to be his son," David tells us.

> What passed between us as masculine candor exhausted and appalled me. Fathers ought to avoid utter nakedness before their sons. I did not want to know—not, anyway, from his mouth—that his flesh was as unregenerate as my own. The knowledge did not make me feel more like his son—or buddy—it only made me feel like an interloper, and a frightened one at that. (*ENS* 232-33)

In both episodes, Baldwin questions the genealogies of masculinity, the lessons of gender and sexuality passed down from father to son. Both fathers reduce manhood to the sexual act, denying their sons any different or nuanced view of themselves; both sons—tellingly—are "frightened." These fathers exhibit, in contrast to their progeny, what Baldwin facetiously calls "the American ideal of masculinity" (*CE* 815). This ideal, constructed along a strict binary,

> has created cowboys and Indians, good guys and bad guys, punks and studs, tough guys and softies, butch and faggot, black and white. It is an ideal so paralytically infantile that it is virtually forbidden—as an unpatriotic act—that the American boy evolve into the complexity of manhood. (*CE* 815)

In *Giovanni's Room* and in "Going to Meet the Man," Baldwin collapses the cultural scaffolding that props up such bifurcations and narrow views of identity. The American heterosexual ideal that both fathers embody is seen as something corrupt and limiting. In Baldwin's world, this overdetermined heterosexual image of the American male is itself the "freak."

The lynching spectacle, Baldwin later shows, also fills another void for this American boy: it provides the occasion for Jesse's introduction to unrestrained white power and homoerotic desire. Climbing the hill to the lynching tree, his parents seem different, transformed by their own bloodlust:

> He looked at his mother and father. They looked straight ahead, seeming to be listening to the singing which echoed and echoed in this graveyard silence. They were looking at something he could not see. His father's lips had a strange, cruel curve, he wet his lips from time to time, and swallowed. He was terribly aware of his father's tongue, it was as though he had never seen it before. And his father's body suddenly seemed immense, bigger than a mountain. His eyes, which were grey-green, looked yellow in the sunlight; or at least there was a light in them which he had never seen before. (*ENS* 946)

To young Jesse, his father appears monstrous, inhuman. His mother, viewing the smoldering, naked body suspended from the tree, is equally changed, looking "more beautiful than he had ever seen her, and more strange" (*ENS* 948). The crush of white onlookers becomes an amorphous mob of "millions" of voices, laughing and sneering at the awful spectacle. Observing the black man's body hovering above the fire, he experiences "a joy he had never felt before. He watched the hanging, gleaming body, the most beautiful and terrible object he had ever seen till then" (949). Indeed, even in the midst of the hellish scene brewing around him, Jesse feels more than a pang of penis envy, both literally and figuratively. Baldwin writes:

> In the cradle of the one white hand, the nigger's privates seemed as remote as meat being weighed in the scales; but seemed heavier, too, much heavier, and Jesse felt his scrotum tighten; and huge, huge, bigger than his father's, flaccid, hairless, the largest thing he had ever seen till then, and the blackest. The white hand stretched them, cradled them, caressed them. The man with the knife took the nigger's privates in his hand, one hand, still smiling, as though he were weighing them. (*ENS* 949)

Castrating the black man contains the threat his sexuality poses and validates the cultural authority of the white people participating in the spectacle. However, the salacious nature of Baldwin's descriptions suggests that the preponderance of attention paid to the victim's genitals is not merely theatrical. While analyzing Baldwin's lesser-known children's story *Little Man, Little Man: A Story of Childhood* (1976), Nicholas Boggs agrees that "Going to Meet the Man" enacts Eric Lott's provocative thesis about blackface mistrelsy. In his landmark study of this race-centered entertainment, *Love and Theft: Blackface Minstrelsy and the American Working Class*, Lott argues that blackface enabled antebellum whites to appropriate and embody blackness even as they denigrated it as inferior and repugnant. He maintains that

> this homosexual-homosocial pattern persisted all through minstrelsy's antebellum tenure, structuring in white men's "imaginary" relation to black men a dialectic of romance and repulsion. . . . [and] concerned itself with matters of the body—gender anxieties, unconventional sexuality, orality—which mediated, and regulated, the formation of white working-class masculinity. (86)

Moreover, Lott suggests that blackface minstrelsy's appeal in the antebellum South was in part based on its ability to nostalgically evoke the plantation system, which was increasingly coming under fire in the decades leading up to the Civil War. "What interests me here," he writes,

> is the allusive elasticity of nostalgia as a mode, its ability to join, through what [Alexander] Saxton calls "psychological identity," the facts of metropolitanization, the frontier, immigration, and urban weightlessness—to bring these together and to suggest by way of the black mask their relationship to racial matters. . . . Minstrel nostalgia intimated by emotional antidote all the forces in American life that seemed to be pulling the country apart. (191)

Indeed, minstrelsy provided a sexual antidote as well. Recalling famed minstrel star T. D. Rice's 1830s blackface performance in Pittsburgh, Lott illustrates that minstrelsy is as much about humiliation as it is about sexual titillation. In Rice's performance, a black man, Cuff, who earned his living carrying the luggage of passengers disembarking from steamboats, was tricked into accompanying Rice to the theater instead of the docks. Once they arrive, Rice ordered Cuff to give him his clothes and took the stage wearing them. During the performance, Cuff heard the sounds of an approaching steamboat and, needing to leave to attend to its passengers, appealed unsuccessfully to Rice for his clothes from the wings until, desperate to catch the boat, he joined Rice on stage. His nakedness usurped attention away from Rice and becomes the primary spectacle. Indeed, as Lott reasons:

> The fascination with Cuff's nakedness, moreover, highlights the affair as one of male bodies, in which racial conflict and cultural exchange are negotiated between men. Cuff's stripping, a theft that silences him and embarrasses him onstage but which nevertheless entails both his bodily presence in the show and the titillating threat that he may return to demand his stolen capital, is a neat allegory for the most prominent commercial collision of black and white cultures in the nineteenth century. (19)

Taken together, the dual image of Cuff's nakedness and Rice's masquerade consummates safely and publicly an illicit attraction to the black man's body.

A similar collision occurs in "Going to Meet the Man," as Baldwin's narration conveys the grotesque eroticism of the lynching. Once overwhelmed by and afraid of his father's virility, Jesse is aroused by the sight of the man's genitals; "bigger" and "blackest," they represents both sexual threat and desire. And, though the black man and his body are subject to the voyeuristic gaze of the white mob, he also, Baldwin reminds us, is watching the crowd: "Then the dying man's eyes looked straight into Jesse's eyes—it could not have been as long as a second, but it seemed longer than a year" (*ENS* 949). This moment at once implicates Jesse in the crime and signals the possibility of his homosexual attraction. For the lynching, in all its public horror, engenders and conceals desire otherwise forbidden or discouraged. It allows the male participants, in particular Jesse and the man with the knife, to gaze at and fondle the black man's penis with impunity, without eroding their own claims to heterosexual masculinity.

But the lynching is memory, shrouded in the vestments of a past that no longer exists, and serves only to succor the present. Jesse's contemporary reality confronts us with a different intellectual and narrative challenge. At the end of his reverie, Jesse, flush with "something that bubbled up in him," turns to his wife:

> His nature returned to him. He thought of the boy in the cell; he thought of the man in the fire; he thought of the knife and grabbed himself and stroked himself and a terrible sound, something between a high laugh and a howl, came out of him and dragged his sleeping wife up on one elbow. She stared at him in a moonlight which had now grown cold as ice. He thought of the morning and grabbed her, laughing and crying, crying and laughing, and he whispered, as he stroked her, as he took her, "Come on, sugar, I'm going to do you like a nigger, just like a nigger, come on, sugar, and love me just like you'd love a nigger." (*ENS* 950)

A surprising reversal takes place, as Jesse, with both the present and his erection restored, assumes the role of the "nigger," the archetypal black man about whom he fantasizes. In adopting this persona, Jesse appropriates and quells the threat the black man's sexuality may pose. Again, Nicholas Boggs: "The black victim is deprived of his masculinity by virtue of a castration that is enacted through the white man's myth of black sexuality" (145). At the same time, any residual homoerotic desire is sublimated into this hypersexual performance that is ostensibly meant to amplify Jesse's straight masculinity. Further, playing the part of a black man calls into question the idea of identity as a naturally occurring phenomenon, and yet, by creating an "other," it supports the illusion that identity is, indeed, stable, "natural." Baldwin himself commented on this cultural charade in a conversation with poet Nikki Giovanni: "People invent categories in order to feel safe: White people invented black people to give white people identity. . . . Straight cats invented faggots so they could sleep with them without becoming faggots themselves" (*Dialogue* 88-89). Memories of the lynching, therefore, allow Jesse to "queer" his illicit desire into a "safe" and vigorous heterosexuality that he performs with his complicit wife.

Returning to Valerie Rohy's reading of *Giovanni's Room*, we can appreciate how nostalgia similarly functions to reaffirm whiteness and normalize "errant" masculinity in "Going to Meet the Man." About Baldwin's novel, she argues compellingly:

> The nostalgia of the social works to vivify, and is in turn represented by, the particular desires of individuals: in *Giovanni's Room*, David's longed-for home in American heterosexual ideology is, like identity itself, revealed to be deeply nostalgic, retroactively produced as an origin from a position of belatedness and lack. . . . David's desire to return to America is insistent and deeply felt, but as the novel's brutal conclusion suggests, nostalgia and violence go hand in hand as inseparable aspects of the positing and policing of identity. That is, nostalgia's inevitability in no way means its effects are symmetrical, for it is precisely the nonidentity of the white, bourgeois, heterosexual culture that David represents in *Giovanni's Room*

> that must be phobically projected onto an other who, like Giovanni, will bear the burden of that nostalgia even to his death. (230-31)

So it is in "Going to Meet the Man." While violence may stimulate Jesse's desire for the black inmate and for the lynching victim, it also reaffirms his whiteness and authority over them. In both instances, he is in the position of either meting out or witnessing justice. But, in reality, nostalgic memories of the lynching—and collective white power in action—do not quite translate into individual power. Jesse's sexual impotence is merely symptomatic of a gradual erosion of white culture's racial superiority and social dominance.

Indeed, to satisfy his sexual urges as well as curtail this dissolution of power, he emerges from his nostalgic reflections and engages in a kind of bedroom minstrelsy. But, if minstrelsy is, according to Lott, primarily a theatrical negotiation of white, male homoerotic interracial desire, then Jesse's request that Grace "love me just like you'd love a nigger" does not quite square with assumptions about white heterosexual power. In Jesse's remembrance, white women are either coconspirators in mob justice, such as his mother, or victims of alleged affronts, such as old Mrs. Standish, the white woman whom the lynched man inadvertently knocked down in the street. Conscripted into Jesse's fantasy, Grace becomes invested with a kind of power and assertiveness that otherwise seem out of line with her character—and the myth of inviolate white womanhood. Nevertheless, this power is wielded to support Jesse's quasi-minstrel performance and to bolster his otherwise failing masculinity. In this exchange, Grace acts merely as a proxy, a cover to obscure the real object of Jesse's desire.

The conclusion of "Going to Meet the Man" is striking for many reasons, not the least of which is the attention Baldwin calls to the relationship between identity and performance. At bottom, for Baldwin, "nigger" is just another label, just as the "man" of the title is less about an individual than a concept, a construction. Jesse's impersonation evokes Judith Butler's arguments about drag as a "presentation" of gender:

> What is 'performed' in drag, of course, is *the sign* of gender, a sign which is not the same as the body it figures, but which cannot be read without it. . . . Insofar as heterosexual gender norms produce inapproximable ideals, heterosexuality can be said to operate through the regulated production of hyperbolic versions of "man" and "woman." These are for the most part compulsory performances, one which none of us choose but which each of us is forced to negotiate. (*BTM* 26)

Jesse's nostalgic reverie occasions an end run around these forced negotiations. In the story's present, Jesse's masculinity registers itself either through compensatory acts of violence, such as torturing the black inmate with a cattle prod, or through impersonating an idea of black masculinity that has been circulated in myth and stereotype. The outrageous nature of Jesse's request confirms, for Baldwin, the absurdity of labels in general. That Jesse can become or, at least pass as what he thinks is "nigger," reveals the seams of what Elaine K. Ginsberg has identified as "the contingencies of the categories 'white' and 'black'" (13). In other words, "white" and "black" are social and cultural designations deployed not only to "create" identity but to police it as well. Baldwin amplifies these racial contingencies to thwart an ostensibly rigid and secure sexual politics that privileges heterosexual desire.

In "Going to Meet the Man," there is no forgetting "*this* picnic," as Jesse's father promises him at the lynching tree (*ENS* 949). Yet, despite his recollections of a time in which racial boundaries were violently maintained to protect white supremacy, Jesse ultimately cannot return—the segregated world of his past no longer exists. But this does not mean that nostalgia itself has failed. Nostalgia operates in this story to reinforce white authority, but under the cover of this collectively—and savagely—articulated identity, interracial homoerotic desire goes undetected. When it manifests itself in Jesse's bedroom, this attraction is sublimated in an ersatz minstrel performance that simultaneously expresses power over and a desire for blackness as a sexual object and as an identity. Returning home after the lynching, Jesse "loved his father more than he had ever loved him. He felt that his father had carried him through a mighty test, had revealed to him a great secret which would be the key to his life forever" (*ENS* 949). The secret, of course, as Baldwin discloses in this disturbing narrative, lies in the fallibility of labels, of identity, of memory itself.

Notes

1. Baldwin's fiction and social criticism is extensive. Library of America's separate volumes on Baldwin, *Collected Essays* and *Early Novels and Stories*, contain the various works referenced in this article. They are hereafter cited in the text as *CE* and *ENS*.

2. Judith Butler's provocative investigations of gender and sexuality, which contend that gender is performative and the body is a malleable site on which these performances are enacted, have been enormously influential. Subsequent references to *Bodies That Matter* are cited in the text as *BTM*.

Works Cited

Baldwin, James. *Collected Essays*. Ed. Toni Morrison. New York: Library of America, 1998.

____________. *Early Novels and Stories*. Ed. Toni Morrison. New York: Library of America, 1998.

Baldwin, James, and Nikki Giovanni. *A Dialogue*. 1973. Philadelphia: Lippincott, 1975.

Boggs, Nicholas. "Of Mimicry and (*Little Man Little*) Man: Toward a Queer-sighted Theory of Black Childhood." *James Baldwin Now*. Ed. Dwight A. McBride. New York: New York UP, 1999. 122-60.

Butler, Judith. *Bodies That Matter: On the Discursive Limits of "Sex."* New York: Routledge, 1993.

____________. *Gender Trouble: Feminism and the Subversion of Identity*. New York: Routledge, 1990.

Gallop, Jane. *Reading Lacan*. Ithaca, NY: Cornell UP, 1985.

Ginsberg, Elaine K., ed. *Passing and the Fictions of Identity*. Durham, NC: Duke UP, 1996.

Hutcheon, Linda. "Irony, Nostalgia, and the Postmodern." University of Toronto English Library. 4 May 2010. http://www.library.utoronto.ca/utel/criticism/hutchinp.html.

Lott, Eric. *Love and Theft: Blackface Minstrelsy and the American Working Class*. New York: Oxford UP, 1992.

Rohy, Valerie. "Displacing Desire: Passing, Nostalgia, and *Giovanni's Room*." *Passing and the Fictions of Identity*. Ed. Elaine K. Ginsberg. Durham, NC: Duke UP, 1996. 218-33.

On James Baldwin's *Another Country*

Lionel Trilling

There is probably no literary career in America today that matches James Baldwin's in the degree of interest it commands. The reason for this is as deplorable as it is obvious. For it is not alone his talents, although these are indeed notable, but his talents in conjunction with his social circumstances that have put Mr. Baldwin into the unique position he holds in our cultural life. He is at the moment the only American Negro with a considerable body of respected work to his credit. And with the exception of Ralph Ellison, who has been silent for too long, he is the only Negro who has taken his place in the literary and intellectual *avant garde*—when he speaks to the general public about the life of his ethnic group, he is not confined to the wholesome simplicities of American libertarian thought, but ranges over the subtleties, complexities, and perversities of the modern ideology, and includes in his purview not only the particular anomaly of the Negroes in their disadvantaged situation, but the whole moral life of the nation.

Mr. Baldwin would surely be the first of us to wish that his uniqueness were not an element of his literary existence, that there might be standing with him other Negroes as articulate as he, and as fully heard. But things are as they are—Mr. Baldwin does stand in a striking isolation, and, as a consequence, what he writes must sound with an especial significance, and there will inevitably be a more than usual concern with the way he conducts his literary and intellectual life, with his powers of growth, with the changes and developments of his attitudes and opinions.

The position, it need scarcely be said, is an almost insupportably difficult one. How, in the extravagant publicness in which Mr. Baldwin lives, is he to find the inwardness which we take to be the condition of truth in the writer? How is he to make sure that he remains a person and a writer and does not become merely a figure and a representative?

Some such question would seem to have been present to Mr. Baldwin's mind from the very beginning of his career. His first novel, *Go Tell It on the Mountain*, was autobiographical, and this story of a family emigrated from the South to Harlem certainly had its due sense of a public issue in its due awareness of the bitterness of Negro life. Yet what made the book notable in its time was its bold assertion that it existed as a literary entity, as something more than a "social document." No reader could fail to be aware that Mr. Baldwin was determined not to fall into the stereotype of the Negro novelist which then prevailed. It was as if, by his concern with style, by his commitment to delicacy of perception, he insisted that his novel was not validated by its subject—to which every ordinarily moral reader was required to respond because it adumbrated a great national injustice—but by the writer's particular treatment of his subject. In making this insistence Mr. Baldwin laid claim not merely to some decent minimum of social rationality, but to all the possible fullness of life, to whatever in art and culture was vivacious, beautiful, and interesting. He was explicit about that claim in his well-known essay, "Everybody's Protest Novel," in which he declared his independence of the settled expectations which readers and critics had of the Negro writer. It was a remarkable statement, made the more dramatic by its comparison of Richard Wright with Harriet Beecher Stowe, for Bigger Thomas, Mr. Baldwin said, was really only the other side of Uncle Tom, falling as far short of human actuality in his raping, murdering rage as Uncle Tom fell short in his pious humility. Mr. Baldwin's point was that to see man under the aspect of "protest" was to see him in a merely institutional way, in a way that did not represent him in his variety and complexity and thus not in his full humanity: in effect, the protest novel affirmed the very qualities of society that it undertook to denounce. Only a mode of art which was subtle and complex and untrammelled by social theory could truly propose the idea of freedom by exhibiting the true nature of man.

This belief was implemented by Mr. Baldwin's second novel. *Giovanni's Room* abjured the advantage that any novel about Negroes almost inevitably has, that of bringing the news about a condition of human existence which is certain to involve the reader in the powerful emotions of guilt and indignation, and perhaps also in a covert and complicated envy. Set in Paris, and telling a story of homosexual love, *Giovanni's Room* dealt only with white people. It was manifestly the work of a very good and very serious writer, but it was not a really interesting novel. I am loath to believe what some people said and what perhaps Mr. Baldwin himself came to believe, that it was relatively a failure because its author had "denied" his "essential experience." The extent or nature of its failure was no different from that of any gifted novel which is primarily committed to observation and sensibility, which is not written out of some strong, even if hidden, intention of the will. But perhaps the failure in Mr. Baldwin's particular case seemed the more salient because there was so readily available to him a subject which required to be dealt with by many human faculties, but most especially by that of the will.

It was, I feel sure, all to the good that Mr. Baldwin took for a time the stand he did take. It was all to the good that he insisted upon his right and his duty to be first of all an artist, that, like Henry James's Hyacinth Robinson, he laid his claim to the full heritage of the culture into which he was born and gloried in its possibilities. It should be said at once that, unlike James's young proletarian revolutionary, Mr. Baldwin never did come to feel that his claim to full artistic freedom lessened his attachment to the social cause to which circumstance almost inevitably committed him—he was never led by his sense of a personal fate to become indifferent to the actualities of the Negro situation. Yet the emphasis did fall on the personal fate, and this, as I say, was all to the good. It was of the greatest value to his development that he withdrew for some years from the American scene to Europe, and that he should have written a novel which made no reference to Negroes. His new novel, *Another Country*, may be read as a very large modification of the earlier position, but there can be no doubt that it derives much of its force from Mr. Baldwin's refusal to be limited by the special exigencies of the Negro writer's life, by his having moved out into the larger and more various world.

Yet there also can be no doubt that the power of *Another Country* derives equally, and perhaps more than that, from another source. In recent years, Mr. Baldwin, who never, as I have said, was anything but committed to the Negro cause, has become responsive to the growing Negro intransigence and considerably more willing than formerly to conceive of himself as a Negro writer, or, at any rate, as a writer who speaks out of his identification with his ethnic group, which is, of course, also a social and cultural group. As such, he has become an increasingly public figure. I have heard it said in criticism of him that he has become an all too public figure; indeed, in the pages of this magazine, the reviewer of *Nobody Knows My Name*, Mr. Baldwin's latest collection of essays, chided him for an excessively ready acceptance of "his new role as 'a famous Negro writer'," which presumably would be deleterious to his creative gifts. This is not my sense of the matter. In the face of all our pieties about the artist's privacy, I think that the new public role has done Mr. Baldwin great good as a novelist.

I do not take *Another Country* to be a *fine* novel. It is not a novel controlled by delicacy of perception. But I do take it to be a powerful novel, a *telling* novel. If I compare it with another novel of equally intense contemporaneity and of similar theme, Philip Roth's *Letting Go*, it seems to me that, although Mr. Roth's novel is the more virtuoso and accomplished of the two, *Another Country* has an actuality of existence which *Letting Go* does not approach. Both novels deal with the difficulty, or the impossibility, in this country and at this time, of people having satisfying and significant relations with each other. And if I try to say why Mr. Roth's novel, for all its fullness of detail and frequent brilliance of representation, is merely depressing in its extended exposition of its sad subject and, for all its bulk, eventually not *there*, while Mr. Baldwin's novel, despite its faults, is invigorating and substantial, I should make the explanation in terms of Mr. Roth's having written chiefly out of sensibility and observation, and with some almost programmatic negation of will, while Mr. Baldwin has in this instance affirmed the primacy of the will, his affirmation arising out of his angry awareness of the Negro situation. *Another Country* is not a "protest novel"—it differs from that genre of the Thirties and Forties in the respect that anger at social injustice is but one element of the lives of certain of the characters. But it is an element that is definitive of their being, and Mr. Baldwin not only condones it, but celebrates it and makes it the presiding passion of his story.

I would not wish to palliate the faults of *Another Country*. No one of his natural delicacy of mind and ear should write as badly as Mr. Baldwin sometimes does in this book. ". . . The wind nibbled delightedly at him through his summer slacks." No, the wind did not, and nothing is gained by saying it did. "Newsstands, like small black blocks on a board, hold down corners of the pavements and policemen and taxi drivers and others, harder to place, stomped their feet before them and exchanged such words as they knew with the muffled vendor inside." This is as factitious as it is awkward. The time has long gone by when it was possible to say that "a hotel's enormous neon name challenged the starless sky," or that a subway train rushed "into the blackness with a phallic abandon," and what impulse of literary regression could have led a writer, in any year after 1910, to say of a woman that she wore "all her beauty as a great queen wears her robes"? It does not show respect for either love or language to say that the memory of the beloved's eyes "afford" the lover "his only frame of reference." Mr. Baldwin does indeed sometimes achieve a prose manner that is unexceptionable and even admirable, but it is always being threatened either by violent cliché or such flatness as marks the narrative of some of the social scenes: "Cass appeared in a high-necked, old-fashioned burgundy-colored dress, and with her hair up. Richard put on a sport shirt and a more respectable-looking sweater, and Ida vanished to put on her face. The people began to arrive."

Yet it does not matter, just as it does not matter in Balzac, just as it usually does not matter in Dreiser. The novel as a genre does not depend on fineness and delicacy of art, and there are even occasions when it is the better for doing without fineness and delicacy of art. I take *Another Country* to be such an occasion.

Another Country is about love, which is to say that it is about hate, rage, violence, and despair. The crucial figure of the story is Rufus Scott, a brilliant jazz drummer. He is loved by a perfect Griselda of a Southern poor-white girl, to whom he is bound and upon whom he inflicts extreme physical and emotional abuse, eventually driving her past distraction to insanity. Rufus is not, as we say, a naturally cruel person. It is in large part out of remorse for his treatment of Leona that he commits suicide. So far is he from being evil that he is celebrated throughout the novel as an especially beautiful and precious person. His parents cherish him, his sister adores him, and almost all the characters in the book direct toward him a sweetness and affectionateness of regard which they speak of as love. And Rufus is represented as being preeminently worthy of love because he is so capable of joy.

Why has Rufus become inaccessible to love, why has his own power of love turned to hatred, so that every erotic act must be violent and destructive, so that his very seed presents itself to his mind as "venom"? The formulated answer comes quickly; we all know it quite as well as Mr. Baldwin does. Rufus is a Negro, and American white society has robbed him of his self-respect. That is why his joy has turned to gall, why his love has turned to cruelty.

The fate of Rufus Scott is to be understood in terms that are no different from those in which we were asked to understand the fate of Bigger Thomas. Not much has changed since *Native Son* appeared in 1940. Where Bigger vented his rage in a single act of sexual violence, Rufus destroys his victim slowly and, as it were, with her consent, but the symbolic meaning of the behavior of each is the same. And yet there is a difference to be noted, for where Richard Wright conceived of Bigger as standing wholly outside white society, Mr. Baldwin represents Rufus as being sufficiently related to white society to serve as the limiting case of *Another Country*. His is the extreme fate, but almost all the other characters, black or white, suffer some corruption, perversion, or frustration of their erotic lives. Ida, Rufus's beautiful and talented sister, checks and bridles her own power of love in the interest of mastering the social order that had destroyed her brother—hating the white world, she moves toward a denial of herself on the tide of her contempt and revulsion. Her white lover, Vivaldo Moore, an undistinguished but warm-hearted young man, is unable to achieve the sense of identity which will permit him to be a novelist (or anything) and lives in a perpetual torture of sexual jealousy. His friend and former teacher, Richard Silenski, having at last achieved success with a mediocre book, becomes, or is discovered always to have been, a mediocre person, unable to maintain his once happy relation with his admirable wife Cass, who, having lived for love, is almost destroyed by the deprivation.

When the ruin is represented as being so widespread, we are ready to hear that a bad society has brought it about. The burden of *Another Country* is that our society corrupts and distorts the human spirit, poisons the roots of life and the wellsprings of love. And although Mr. Baldwin is too intelligent to believe that American society is unique in this respect, he yet represents it as mitigating the spiritual devastation by far fewer creature comforts than another society might give—the New York by which Mr. Baldwin exemplifies American life is wholly without grace or charm, is nothing but sordid and ugly, a veritable City of Dreadful Night.

From its doom only one person would seem to be saved. Eric Jones, an actor of considerable talent, is a young Southerner of good family. His homosexual tendencies, manifested in his boyhood, had made life in a Southern town impossible; in the freer atmosphere of New York and Paris, he has been able to "accept" his homosexuality. He alone exists with a degree of dignity and direction—he is in possession of himself, of *a* self, as none of his friends is. How he achieved this fortunate condition is not made clear; presumably it has a connection both with his homosexuality itself and the moral straightforwardness and balance with which he confronted it. One aspect of his selfhood is that he does not permit himself to fall prey to what Freud called "the overvaluation of love." It may be said that for Eric love is an emotion, but not, in the sense in which Spinoza used the word, a *passion*. His relation to Yves, the French youth he loves, is as constant and orderly, as controlled by the intelligence as if it had been imagined by Jane Austen. And by reason of his clearly defined selfhood, he has the power, when he engages in an affair with the deserted Cass and in a single erotic encounter with the confused and troubled Vivaldo, of giving these people some sense of the actuality of their own beings.

But Eric is an exception in the general ruin of lives. It is an old tale now, the story of generous aspirations baffled and perverted by society. It might be said that Mr. Baldwin tells us nothing that we did not know from Dos Passos's *USA*, and before that from Flaubert's *Sentimental Education* and Balzac's *Père Goriot*. But we cannot doubt that we will hear it again, and often, for it is the classic and typical story of the modern world, and it cannot possibly fail to be of moment if it is told, as Mr. Baldwin does tell it, with passion.

—September 1962

James Baldwin and the "Man"

F. W. Dupee

As a writer of polemical essays on the Negro question James Baldwin has no equals. He probably has, in fact, no real competitors. The literary role he has taken on so deliberately and played with so agile an intelligence is one that no white writer could possibly imitate and that few Negroes, I imagine, would wish to embrace *in toto*. Baldwin impresses me as being the Negro *in extremis,* a virtuoso of ethnic suffering, defiance, and aspiration. His role is that of the man whose complexion constitutes his fate, and not only in a society poisoned by prejudice but, it sometimes seems, in general. For he appears to have received a heavy dose of existentialism; he is at least half-inclined to see the Negro question in the light of the Human Condition. So he wears his color as Hester Prynne did her scarlet letter, proudly. And like her he converts this thing, in itself so absurdly material, into a form of consciousness, a condition of spirit. Believing himself to have been branded as different from and inferior to the white majority, he will make a virtue of his situation. He will *be* different and in his own way be better.

His major essays—for example, those collected in *Notes of a Native Son*—show the extent to which he is able to be different and in his own way better. Most of them were written, as other such pieces generally are, for the magazines, some obviously on assignment. And their subjects—a book, a person, a locale, an encounter—are the inevitable subjects of magazine essays. But Baldwin's way with them is far from inevitable. To apply criticism "in depth" to *Uncle Tom's Cabin* is, for him, to illuminate not only a book, an author, an age, but a whole strain in a country's culture. Similarly with those routine themes, the Paris expatriate and Life With Father, which he treats in "Equal in Paris" and the title piece of *Notes of a Native Son,* and which he wholly transfigures. Of course the transfiguring process in Baldwin's essays owes something to the fact that the point of view is a Negro's, an outsider's, just as the satire of American manners in *Lolita* and *Morte d'Urban* depends on their being written from the angle of, respectively, a foreign-born creep and a Catholic priest. But Baldwin's point of view in his essays is not merely that of the generic Negro. It is, as I have said, that of a highly stylized Negro, a role which he plays with an artful and zestful consistency and which he expresses in a language distinguished by clarity, brevity, and a certain formal elegance. He is in love, for example, with syntax, with sentences that mount through clearly articulated stages to a resounding and clarifying climax and then gracefully subside. For instance this one, from *The Fire Next Time*:

> Girls, only slightly older than I was, who sang in the choir or taught Sunday school, the children of holy parents, underwent, before my eyes, their incredible metamorphosis, of which the most bewildering aspect was not their budding breasts or their rounding behinds but something deeper and more subtle, in their eyes, their heat, their odor, and the inflection of their voices.

Nobody else in democratic America writes sentences like this anymore. It suggests the ideal prose of an ideal literary community, some aristocratic France of one's dreams. This former Harlem boy has undergone his own incredible metamorphosis.

His latest book, *The Fire Next Time,* differs in important ways from his earlier work in the essay. Its subjects are less concrete, less clearly defined; to a considerable extent he has exchanged prophecy for criticism, exhortation for analysis, and the results for his mind and style are in part disturbing. *The Fire Next Time* gets its title from a slave song: "God gave Noah the rainbow sign,/No more water the fire next time." But this small book with the incendiary title consists of two independent essays, both in the form of letters. One is a brief affair entitled "My Dungeon Shook" and addressed to "My Nephew on the One Hundredth Anniversary of the Emancipation." The ominous promise of this title is fulfilled in the text. Between the hundred-year-old anniversary and the fifteen-year-old nephew the disparity is too great even for a writer of Baldwin's rhetorical powers. The essay reads like some specimen of "public speech" as practiced by MacLeish or Norman Corwin. It is not good Baldwin.

The other, much longer, much more significant essay appeared first in a pre-Christmas number of *The New Yorker,* where it made, understandably, a sensation. It is called "Down At the Cross: Letter From a Region of My Mind." The subtitle should be noted. Evidently the essay is to be taken as only a partial or provisional declaration on Baldwin's part, a single piece of his mind. Much of it, however, requires no such appeal for caution on the reader's part. Much of it is unexceptionably first-rate. For example, the reminiscences of the writer's boyhood, which form the lengthy introduction. Other of Baldwin's writings have made us familiar with certain aspects of his Harlem past. Here he concentrates on quite different things: the boy's increasing awareness of the abysmally narrow world of choice he inhabits as a Negro, his attempt to escape a criminal existence by undergoing a religious conversion and becoming at fifteen a revivalist preacher, his discovery that he must learn to "inspire fear" if he hopes to survive the fear inspired in him by "the man"—the white man.

In these pages we come close to understanding why he eventually assumed his rather specialized literary role. It seems to have grown naturally out of his experience of New York City. As distinct from a rural or small-town Negro boy, who is early and firmly taught his place, young Baldwin knew the treacherous fluidity and anonymity of the metropolis, where hidden taboos and unpredictable animosities lay in wait for him and a trip to the 42nd Street Library could be a grim adventure. All this part of the book is perfect; and when Baldwin finally gets to what is his ostensible subject, the Black Muslims or Nation of Islam movement, he is very good too. As good, that is, as possible considering that his relations with the movement seem to have been slight. He once shared a television program with Malcolm X, "the movement's second-in-command," and he paid a brief and inconclusive visit to the first-in-command, the Honorable Elijah Muhammad, and his entourage at the party's headquarters in Chicago. (Muhammad ranks as a prophet; to him the Black Muslim doctrines were "revealed by Allah Himself.") Baldwin reports the Chicago encounter in charming detail and with what looks like complete honesty. On his leaving the party's rather grand quarters, the leader insisted on providing him with a car and driver to protect him "from the white devils until he gets wherever it is he is going." Baldwin accepted, he tells us, adding wryly: "I was, in fact, going to have a drink with several white devils on the other side of town."

He offers some data on the Black Muslim movement, its aims and finances. But he did a minimum of homework here. Had he done more he might at least have provided a solid base for the speculative fireworks the book abounds in. To cope thoroughly with the fireworks in short space, or perhaps any space, seems impossible. Ideas shoot from the book's pages as the sparks fly upward, in bewildering quantity and at random. I don't mean that it is all dazzle. On the cruel paradoxes of the Negro's life, the failures of Christianity, the relations of Negro and Jew, Baldwin is often superb. But a lot of damage is done to his argument by his indiscriminate raids on Freud, Lawrence, Sartre, Genet, and other psychologists, metaphysicians and melodramatists. Still more damage is done by his refusal to draw on anyone so humble as Martin Luther King and his fellow-practitioners of non-violent struggle.

For example: "White Americans do not believe in death, and this is why the darkness of my skin so intimidates them." But suppose one or two white Americans are *not* intimidated. Suppose someone coolly asks what it means to "believe in death." Again: "Do I really *want* to be integrated into a burning house?" Since you have no other, yes; and the better-disposed firemen will welcome your assistance. Again: "A vast amount of the energy that goes into what we call the Negro problem is produced by the white man's profound desire not to be judged by those who are not white." You exaggerate the white man's consciousness of the Negro. Again: "The real reason that non-violence is considered to be a virtue in Negroes . . . is that white men do not want their lives, their self-image, or their property threatened." Of course they don't, especially their lives. Moreover, this imputing of "real reasons" for the behavior of entire populations is self-defeating, to put it mildly. One last quotation, this time a regular apocalypse:

> In order to survive as a human, moving, moral weight in the world, America and all the Western nations will be forced to reexamine themselves and release themselves from many things that are now taken to be sacred, and to discard nearly all the assumptions that have been used to justify their lives and their anguish and their crimes so long.

Since whole cultures have never been known to "discard nearly all their assumptions" and yet remain intact, this amounts to saying that any essential improvement in Negro-white relations, and thus in the quality of American life, is unlikely.

So much for the fireworks. What damage, as I called it, do they do to the writer and his cause—which is also the concern of plenty of others? When Baldwin replaces criticism with prophecy, he manifestly weakens his grasp of his role, his style, and his great theme itself. And to what end? Who is likely to be moved by such arguments, unless it is the more literate Black Muslims, whose program Baldwin specifically rejects as both vindictive and unworkable. And with the situation as it is in Mississippi and elsewhere—dangerous, that is, to the Negro struggle and the whole social order—is not a writer of Baldwin's standing obliged to submit his assertions to some kind of pragmatic test, some process whereby their truth or untruth will be gauged according to their social utility? He writes: "The Negroes of this country may never be able to rise to power, but they are very well placed indeed to precipitate chaos and ring down the curtain on the American dream." I should think that the anti-Negro extremists were even better placed than the Negroes to precipitate chaos, or at least to cause a lot of trouble; and it is unclear to me how *The Fire Next Time,* in its madder moments, can do nothing except inflame the former and confuse the latter. Assuming that a *book* can do anything to either.

The Committed Writer:
James Baldwin as Dramatist

C. W. E. Bigsby

James Baldwin's dilemma is essentially that which has always faced that artist who is also, consciously or not, committed to a specific social problem. As an artist he has constantly expressed the need to see humanity as a whole—to escape the narrow vision which can be an aspect of involvement. Born in Harlem in 1924 he left the United States in 1948, hoping to escape the social and artistic limitations of the racial situation. "I doubted my ability to survive the fury of the color problem here. . . . I wanted to prevent myself from becoming merely a Negro, or even, merely a Negro writer!"[1] In rebellion against the degrading classifications of American society which left the Negro on the fringe of prosperity and dignity as it left him on the fringe of its cities, he adopted, as had so many before him, the immediate expediency of disaffiliation. In art he attacked the "unrewarding rage" of *Native Son* (1940) which, to his mind, had destroyed itself in the violence of its own commitment, just as he had attacked the sentimentalising of *Uncle Tom's Cabin*. Yet the nine years which he spent in Paris served to convince him of the virtual impossibility of transcending his own experience. Indeed he came to accept that this experience constituted the core of his creative ability. In a review of the *Selected Poems* of Langston Hughes, in March 1959, he expressed an opinion which would have shocked the twenty-four-year-old Baldwin who had sought artistic integrity and personal refuge in France. "Hughes" he said "is an American Negro poet and has no choice but to be acutely aware of it. He is not the first American Negro to find the war between his social and artistic responsibilities all but irreconcilable."[2]

The continuing battle which Baldwin has waged with the spirit of Richard Wright, a battle which started in 1949 with the publication of his essay, "Everybody's Protest Novel", is symptomatic of that tension which he was later to see, more sympathetically, in Hughes's poetry.

As evidence of this tension within his own work on the one hand he admits to a determinism not essentially different from Wright's and admits that "we cannot escape our origins, however hard we try"[3] while on the other he generalises from this and seeks to find in the Negro's experience an archetype for the human condition. "Which of us has overcome his past? And the past of a Negro is blood dripping down through leaves, gouged-out eyeballs, the sex torn from its socket and severed with a knife. But this past is not special to the Negro. This horror is also the past, and the everlasting potential, or temptation of the human race. If we do not know this, it seems to me, we know nothing about ourselves, nothing about each other."[4] He has to date written five essays on his relationship with Wright and this shows not merely the debt which he personally owed to the older writer but, more relevantly, his consciousness of the stance into which he, as a Negro, could so easily fall. In one such essay, "Many Thousands Gone", he identifies that tendency towards dehumanisation which he had seen as operating in Wright's work, "that artist is strangled who is forced to deal with human beings solely in social terms."[5] Here, of course, he is on the verve of coming to grips with the central problem of commitment. For didacticism is transformed into art precisely in the moment that the artist appreciates that, as Baldwin says, "literature and sociology are not one and the same".[6] It is Baldwin's ability to maintain this distinction in his novels which raises his work above the naive absolutism of Wright's. This does not imply that as a novelist he abandons faith in the validity of his own experience but that this experience is seen in the broader context of the human condition. *Another Country* (1961) confronts the fact of miscegenation but in doing so subordinates it to the more fundamental problem of isolation and the desperate failure of human communication. Superficially there are lines of force connecting this, the best of Baldwin's novels, with *Native Son*. Indeed Rufus, the protagonist, is driven to acts of violence and eventual self-destruction by the same sense of suffocating rage which had seized Bigger Thomas. Yet the injustice which sends him plummeting into the Hudson River goes deeper than the pigment of his skin. The poor Southern girl whom he brutally beats and who finally retreats into insanity is a victim not only of the tormented dementia of a Negro driven wild by prejudice but of the elemental failure of love and the instinct for masochism which is the sign of self-hatred. This is not to say that colour is peripheral to the novel, however, for Baldwin repeatedly insists on the gulf which it opens between those already terrifyingly alone. The studied cynicism with which Ida, Rufus's sister, sells out to the white world is certainly a sign of the corrupting power of that world but more significantly it is proof of the ease with which the genuine is sacrificed to the expedient and the arid relationship substituted for real communion. As Vivaldo, Ida's white lover, says, "suffering doesn't have a colour".[7] While the inferior position of the Negro emphasises his suffering it is equally true that white and coloured alike betray themselves in their willingness to sacrifice the real to the dream. In *The Fire Next Time* (1963) Baldwin identifies the principle which in essence is the theme of *Another Country*. Urging the need for renewal he points out the impossibility of such so long as one "supposes things to be constant that are not—safety, for example, or money, or power. One clings then to chimeras, by which one can only be betrayed".[8] The solution which he advances, like that suggested by Ida in his novel, is the need to confront "with passion the conundrum of life."[9] It is this ability to penetrate beyond the immediacies of injustice and prejudice, then, which marks his work off from that of those writers for whom the novel is an extension of the pamphlet. Like Arthur Miller he is concerned with man rather than men, and the savage perception which characterises his essays survives now with the added depth and perspective of the artist.

The writer who had lived for nine years in Paris, remote from the immediate dangers of a problem which was rapidly gathering to a head, came eventually, however, to feel guilty for his disaffiliation. The man who was later to point out the reason for white inactivity and indifference—"To act is to be committed, and to be committed is to be in danger"[10]—himself became increasingly certain of his need to return to America. As he explains in one of his essays, the time comes when "someone asks him to explain Little Rock and he begins to feel that it would be simpler—and, corny as the words may sound, more honorable—to go to Little Rock than sit in Europe, on an American passport, trying to explain it. . . ."[11] *Another Country* is the result of this return to the immediate pressures of the American experience while in 1957, for the first time, Baldwin visited the Southern states. It was out of this experience and at the urging of Elia Kazan, that he came to consider writing a play. *Blues for Mr. Charlie*, first produced in 1964, has for its protagonist a man who has returned to the South partly as a result of failure in the North and partly, one feels, because here the fury which he feels can provoke an open response. It would hardly be too fanciful to see Richard Henry as an expression of Baldwin's sense of guilt for his remoteness from the front line of the battle to which he is committed. For the play is dedicated to the memory of Medgar Evers who was murdered while working in the South and is based "very distantly indeed" on the murder of another Civil Rights worker, Emmett Till, who had been killed in Mississippi in 1955. The murderer, as in the play, had been acquitted and the frightening facts which surround the case are relevant in so far as they represent the challenge facing Baldwin. For he confesses to the fear that he would be unable to draw a valid picture of a murderer who would kill a man and then proudly recount the facts, after his trial, to a journalist. The fact that his brother, who Baldwin alleges had participated in the crime, is now a deputy sheriff in Rulesville, Mississippi, while not relevant to the play as such, does demonstrate the enormity of the crime and the extent of the injustice which he, as an artist, was concerned with transmuting not into social polemic but into valid drama. Indeed in choosing a murder as the central action of his play Baldwin was in danger of succumbing to that kind of sentimentality which Yeats has defined as unearned emotion. Certainly the *Actors' Studio*'s production of the play in London, in 1965, failed in large part because of its persistent efforts to sentimentalise. The parading of a coffin, while it has for long been a legitimate weapon of the revolutionary, can too easily degenerate into a substitute for the insight and perspective required of drama.

The play, then, is concerned with the murder of Richard Henry, the son of the reverend Meridian Henry—a Negro minister. Having been overwhelmed by the suffocating oppression of Harlem and having found in drugs a refuge from his own solitude he returns to the South bringing with him a fury which expresses itself in the contempt with which he confronts the white community. He refuses to accept the terms on which the precarious racial truce is based, boasts of the white women he has known in New York, and, in effect, forces the confrontation in which he is killed by Lyle Britten—a white storekeeper. Yet the play is concerned not only with the fate of an individual Negro who finds himself the victim of a Southern 'peckerwood'. For Baldwin the play "takes place in Plaguetown, U.S.A., now. The plague is race, the plague is our concept of Christianity: and this raging plague has the power to destroy every human relationship."[12] And here we might be forgiven for detecting echoes of Camus. For the grotesque code of honour which brings Richard and Lyle into direct confrontation is as arbitrary and irrational as that implacable plague which settled on Camus' Oran, while the two responses to this irrational suffering are typified in Baldwin's play by Meridian and Richard as they are in Camus' novel by Father Paneloux and Rieux. The one places faith in resignation or the positive power of love; the other in revolt. The parallel serves to emphasize too the crisis of faith which is the background not only to this play but also to most Negro novels and drama. As Camus' characters reject a God who can permit or even will purposeless suffering, so Baldwin's characters rebel against a religion which preaches passivity and yet which can be made to endorse violence. In Camus' Oran or Baldwin's 'plaguetown U.S.A.' the white God is alien to a people subjected to irrational suffering. When Camus says, "What I reproach Christianity with is being a doctrine of injustice"[13] he is identifying that same certainty which is felt by Lorenzo, a Negro student, when, standing in Meridian Henry's church, he says, " . . . you sit—in this—this—the house of this damn almighty God who don't care what happens to nobody, unless, of course, they're white. . . . It's that damn white God that's been lynching us and burning us and castrating us and raping our women and robbing us of everything that makes a man a man . . ." (B.C. p. 15). It is in this absolute necessity for revolt that the parallel between *The Plague* (1947) and *Blues for Mr. Charlie* can be most usefully urged. Faced with the reality of the plague "the only watchword for a man" Camus insists "is revolt".[14] So, too, Richard dies still expressing contempt for the white world as Rufus, in jumping from the George Washington Bridge, had cried out against the force which destroyed him, ". . . *all right, you motherfucking Godalmighty bastard, I'm coming to you.*"[15] Richard is killed essentially because of his refusal to conform. He steps, apparently with all the deliberateness of the conscious rebel, outside of the pattern imposed on him. Yet the dialogue which Baldwin wages with himself, through the person of Richard, remains finally unresolved. For where Rieux had contained his revolt within a determination to heal, Richard's death is a gesture of rebellion not essentially different from the "unrewarding rage" which had led Bigger Thomas to strike out against the white world in Richard Wright's novel. Baldwin has always been supremely conscious of the rage with which the Negro confronts the white world and has insisted that "the first problem is how to control that rage so that it won't destroy you."[16] The dilemma in which he finds himself in *Blues for Mr. Charlie* is that Richard's rage is the substance of his rebellion and if it destroys him it also constitutes his strength. For while the white world can afford to ignore and persecute the non-violent demonstrators organized by Meridian it cannot avoid the direct challenge represented by Richard and if that challenge leads inevitably to his death then there is a logic to that progression as disturbing but as direct as that which governed Bigger Thomas's career.

Richard returns to the South harbouring a bitter hatred for the whites which derives in part from his own experience and in part from his awareness of Negro impotence, manifested here by his father's inability to revenge his wife's murder. He sees the white man as responsible for "all the crimes that ever happened in the history of the world" (B.C. p. 31), and proposes the same radical cure which Bigger Thomas and a thousand street-corner messiahs had proclaimed before him, "the only way the black man's going to *get* any power is to drive all the white men into the sea" (B.C. p. 31). The same words which Milton had applied to Lucifer and Baldwin to Wright's most famous protagonist seem equally applicable to Richard Henry for he prefers, like Lucifer, "rather to rule in hell than serve in heaven".[17] Yet his rage is not unrelenting. He surrenders the gun which he has carried with him for "a long, long time" (B.C. p. 32) to his father. He establishes a genuine relationship with Juanita, a Negro student, and the complexion of his immediate world changes. "I been in pain and darkness all my life. All my life. And this is the first time in my life I've ever felt—maybe it isn't all like that. Maybe there's more to it than that" (B.C. p. 93). Baldwin casts doubt on the validity of this new vision, however. For Juanita is made to recall that Richard had seen their escape as desertion, insisting that "he wasn't going to run no more from white folks . . . but was going to stay and be a man—a *man*!—right here" (B.C. p. 103). Thus his death is charged with an ambiguity on which the play's moral emphasis depends. Is he killed because of his rebellious contempt or because of his growing magnanimity?

Camus has said, "We are in a world where we have to choose between being a victim or a hangman—and nothing else."[18] This is essentially the dilemma with which Baldwin wrestles in *Blues for Mr. Charlie* and the ambiguity with which Richard's character is drawn is a sign of the truth of Camus' further comment, "It is not an easy choice." For Richard's single-minded intensity seems to be purely destructive and if he stands as a warning that self-effacement has given way to self-assertion he also demonstrates the victory of hatred over compassion. Yet, more significantly his death would seem to demonstrate the truth of that choice identified by Camus. For in surrendering his gun he apparently declines the role of hangman and condemns himself to the role of victim. The tension thus created between Richard as contemptuous rebel and Richard as victim accounts for something of the play's moral confusion. For while there is never any doubt of the destructive power of the "plague of race", the play's conclusion, in which the Negroes retire for a prayer meeting and Meridian talks darkly of a solution lying with "the Bible and the gun" (B.C. p. 123), remains evenly balanced between the two extremes.

The pressures which had torn at the son also threaten the father and Baldwin continues the debate between passivity and active revolt in the tortured self-examination of Meridian. For the man who had himself borne his wife's murder without striking back and who had watched the young demonstrators beaten and reviled comes, after his son's death, to question both the virtues of non-violence and the value of Christianity. Yet Baldwin has said of this play that it is "one man's attempt to bear witness to the reality and the power of light" (B.C. p. 11), and one must presume that for him this light consists of the refusal of the Negro to retaliate and destroy. In a sermon which Meridian delivers over the dead body of his son he confesses to his fears and doubts but re-dedicates himself to a continued faith in the power of love: "What hope is there for a people who deny their deeds and disown their kinsmen and who do so in the name of purity and love, in the name of Jesus Christ? What a light, my Lord, is needed to conquer so mighty a darkness! This darkness rules in us, and grows, in black and white alike. I have set my face against the darkness, I will not let it conquer me . . ." (B.C. p. 83). This declaration of faith is tempered, however, by a demand for a sign which can give him some hope. In *Blues for Mr. Charlie* this sign can only lie in the self-examination which leads Parnell, the white liberal, to commit himself completely to the cause of Negro rights. For if Richard's death accomplishes nothing in itself it does precipitate the crisis in which those involved are forced to examine the nature and validity of their stance.

As in both Lorraine Hansberry's and LeRoi Jones' work the white liberals are the special targets for criticism. This is true also of Baldwin's *The Fire Next Time* in which he attacks them on the grounds that "they could deal with the Negro as a symbol or a victim but had no sense of him as a man" for their attitudes, he claims, have little connexion "with their perceptions of their lives, or even their knowledge."[19] Parnell James, in *Blues for Mr. Charlie*, is the editor of the liberal local paper. In contrast to the rest of the white community he refuses to accept the values on which that society has come to rest. When Richard is killed he forces the arrest of Lyle Britten in spite of the fact that he is a close friend. Yet beneath this exterior Parnell is guilty, not of racism but of the crime which Baldwin had identified in his essay. He sees the crime in terms of abstract values. He is committed to justice and equality but not to involvement in the details of inhumanity. Meridian attacks him for his clinical approach when dealing with the Police Chief, "for both of you . . . it was just a black boy that was dead, and that was a problem. He saw the problem one way, you saw it another way. But it wasn't a *man* that was dead, not my son—you held yourselves away from *that*!" (B.C. p. 48). Yet more fundamentally Parnell's stance is undermined by Baldwin's insistence on its sexual origin. For his liberalism appears to have stemmed from a youthful love affair with a Negro girl, an affair which has left in its wake an obsessive concern with Negroes which in reality owes little to a humanistic impulse. In an essay called "The Black Boy Looks at the White Boy" Baldwin has attacked that fascination with the Negro revealed by writers such as Mailer and Kerouac. For they had seen in the black world merely a confirmation of the stereotype—a sense of liberating sensuality. This, in essence, is the basis too of Parnell's fascination—a fascination which if it rationalises his support of 'blacktown' detracts from the force of his moral integrity. Indeed he admits to himself that "you don't love them" (B.C. p. 110) and recognises the self-hatred which stems from his obsession: "All your life you've been made sick, stunned, dizzy, oh, Lord! driven half mad by blackness. Blackness in front of your eyes. Boys and girls, men and women—you've bowed down in front of them all! And then hated yourself. Hated yourself for debasing yourself? Out with it, Parnell. . . . Black boys and girls! I've wanted my hands full of them, wanted to drown them, laughing and dancing and making love—making love—wow!—and be transformed, formed, liberated out of this grey-white envelope" (B.C. pp. 109-110). At the trial, which dominates the third act, Parnell betrays the Negro cause and the justice to which he had been committed by covering up a lie told by Lyle's wife. While he regrets this immediately after the trial his positive espousal of the Negro side, which climaxes the play, can hardly be taken as a sign that there is any justification for Meridian's faith. If Baldwin genuinely wishes to "bear witness to the reality and the power of light" he would have done better to allow Parnell the integrity which alone could grant a validity to his final decision. One is left finally, then, with a contradiction which, while it may accurately reflect the contemporary dilemma of Negro and white liberal, subverts Baldwin's declared faith. For if the logic of the final scene is seemingly dedicated to the validity of passive resistance, gathering to itself the genuinely committed, the force of Richard's death and the sad reality of liberal 'commitment' would seem to deny this logic. In a genuine attempt to avoid facile resolution Baldwin allows conscious ambiguity to degenerate into moral and dramatic confusion.

Neither is the play's climax made any more acceptable by the specious nature of the language which substitutes the cliché for genuine communication. On learning that the Negroes are to stage a march Parnell asks Juanita, to whom he has confessed a sexual attraction, "Can I join you on the march, Juanita? Can I walk with you?" Her reply would have done little credit to the poorest Broadway drama, "Well, we can walk in the same direction, Parnell. Come . . . let's go on" (B.C. pp. 123-124). Indeed where Baldwin had confessed to a fear that he would prove unable to "draw a valid picture of the murderer" (B.C. p. 10), it is rather his inability to draw a valid picture of the victim and his immediate society which ironically proves the source of the play's failure. For if some of the white characters tend to the stereotype they are at least drawn with a panache and a conscious irony which compensates for a lack of insight, while the precision of his satire is for the most part balanced with a perceptive humanity which grants to Lyle and his wife a reality denied to Richard and Juanita whose relationship is never convincingly established. For his inability to distinguish between rhetoric and genuine language has the effect of undermining the credibility of those Negro characters to whom he attributes a pretentious eloquence. Even a minor figure such as Pete Spivey, one of Juanita's suitors, is given the following speech which serves merely to destroy that empathy which he is clearly anxious to establish, "You take all my attention. My deepest attention . . . I think there's a lot of love in you, Juanita. If you'll let me help you, we can give it to the world. You can't give it to the world until you find a person who can help you—love the world" (B.C. p. 42).

Baldwin's chief fault lies, therefore, not so much in his dehumanisation of the whites as in his sentimentalising of the Negroes. Indeed from the heroic endurance of Mother Henry, whose faith in God rests in a certainty that "It's up to the life in you. . . . *That* knows where it comes from, *that* believes in God" (B.C. p. 30), to the sad posturing of Juanita and Meridian he demonstrates his failure to abide by his own strictures. For in his own early essay, "Everybody's Protest Novel", he had catalogued the faults of a literature which could more truly be seen as sociology. He had attacked its sentimentality and deplored the violence which such literature tended to do to language—an ironical comment on the pretentious dialogue of much of *Blues for Mr. Charlie*. He had then accused the protest novel of "overlooking, denying, evading"[20] man's complexity, again an accusation which could be justly applied to his own treatment not only of the white townspeople but also of Juanita and indeed Richard himself. Baldwin's essay closes with his attack on the fruitless rage of Wright's *Native Son* which provoked the breach between them which was to persist until Wright's death. Yet as we have seen Richard's life is as much "defined by his hatred"[21] as was Bigger Thomas's and if he becomes conscious of a more meaningful existence this awareness is never clearly motivated neither does it destroy the determinism which leads him to his death. So that Baldwin's play matches with disturbing precision his own definition of sterile protest literature. In the words of a *Times Literary Supplement* review *Blues for Mr. Charlie* "is a 1930s sociological play which contains the 'right' information and the 'right' accusatory attitudes towards poor whites and Southern justice but lacks insights into prejudice and ability to create character beyond stereotypes."[22]

In an earlier play, *Amen Corner*, written ten years before *Blues for Mr. Charlie* and yet to be published, Baldwin had attained to that same sense of objectivity and universality which he evidences in *Another Country*. Less squarely centred on the racial conflict it evidences something of that vital compassion which is to be found in Lorraine Hansberry's work. Margaret, the pastor of a storefront church in Harlem, like Miller's Quentin in *After the Fall*, propounds the need for a love which can encompass every aspect of the human condition and still endure. "I'm just now finding out what it means to love the Lord. It aint all in the singing and shouting. It aint all in the reading of the Bible. It aint even in runnin' all over everybody trying to get to heaven. To love the Lord is to love all His children—all of them?—And suffer and rejoice with them and never count the cost."[23] Between this play and *Blues for Mr. Charlie*, however, came the increasing violence of the Civil Rights movement and above all the death of Medgar Evers. For as Baldwin has admitted, "When he died, something entered into me which I cannot describe, but it was then that I resolved that nothing under heaven would prevent me from getting this play done" (B.C. p. 11). It is clear, then, that the war between his social and artistic responsibilities has become more intense. It is equally clear that the rage which he had felt at the death of his friend has betrayed him into the oversimplifications of a sociological literature which he had always consciously avoided.

Nevertheless something of Baldwin's failure in this play stems from his inability to master the dramatic form. Like Dos Passos in the thirties he was drawn to the theatre because it offered a platform for his views and a direct rapport between writer and audience not available to the novelist. Here he could publicly work out a compromise between the contradictory responsibilities of the Negro writer. The crude monologues of the third act of *Blues for Mr. Charlie* highlight, however, the difficulty of the novelist turned playwright. Denied the opportunity to develop character and motive at length he is easily tempted into radical simplification. Certainly Baldwin, failing to master the necessity for a revelation derived out of action, reverts to the embarrassing expedient of 'freezing' the action while the truth of a character's inner struggle is made apparent through the capsule comments against which Gelber had rebelled in *The Connection*.

Herbert Hill, in his anthology of Negro writers, *Black Voices* (1964), sees contemporary American Negro writing as characterised by an attempt to break out of racial parochialism and engage itself with those preoccupations which have seized the attention of modern writers. Certainly both Ralph Ellison's and James Baldwin's strength lies in the fact that they have fought against the simplicities of protest fiction and that they have succeeded in establishing the Negro experience as of immediate relevance to a society concerned with the problems of identity and alienation, for Ellison shares with Baldwin a belief that "people who want to write sociology shouldn't write novels."[24] Baldwin's failure to approach this same level of artistic responsibility in his drama, however, is an indication both of the greater discipline demanded by drama and of his own increasing personal commitment to the Civil Rights struggle. As with Lawson, Gold and Dos Passos in the thirties his commitment to one section of humanity tends to betray his sense of the universal. Arthur Miller has pointed out that drama "rises in stature and intensity in proportion to the weight of its application to all manner of men. It gains its weight as it deals with more and more of the whole man, not either his subjective or his social life alone."[25] For all the ambiguous fury of *Blues for Mr. Charlie*, however, we still have Baldwin's own assurance that he recognises the need for the artist to keep a "heart free of hatred". Indeed Baldwin has stated very succinctly the peculiar dilemma of the Negro writer influenced by dual and largely contradictory responsibilities. For, as he points out, on the one hand writing "demands a great deal of stepping out of a social situation in order to deal with it" while on the other hand "all the time you're out of it you can't help feeling a little guilty that you are not, as it were, on the firing line, tearing down the slums."[26] The danger which persists for the Negro writer is thus that the isolating prejudice of society will lead him to convert this social guilt into a literature of revenge. The reality of this danger, when placed beside the failings of the 'proletarian' protest plays of the thirties, lends something of the air of a fundamental law to Camus' comments on the imprisoned De Sade, "Intelligence in chains loses in lucidity what it gains in intensity. . . . He did not create a philosophy, he pursued a monstrous dream of revenge."[27]

From *Twentieth Century Literature* 13, no. 1 (April 1967): 39-48.

Notes

1. *Black Voices*, ed. Herbert Hill (London, 1964), p. 402.
2. Quoted in Maurice Charney, "James Baldwin's Quarrel with Richard Wright," *American Quarterly*, XV (Spring, 1963), 65.
3. James Baldwin, *Notes of a Native Son* (London, 1964), p. 31.
4. James Baldwin. *Nobody Knows My Name* (London, 1964), p. 174.
5. *Notes of a Native Son*, p. 36.
6. *Ibid.*, p. 24
7. James Baldwin, *Another Country* (London, 1965), p. 399.
8. James Baldwin, *The Fire Next Time* (London, 1963), p. 100.
9. *Ibid.*, p. 99.
10. *Ibid.*, p 20.
11. *Black Voices*, p. 402.
12. James Baldwin, *Blues for Mr. Charlie* (London, 1965), p. 10. All future references to this play will be abbreviated to B.C. and incorporated in the text.
13. Albert Camus, *Carnets 1942-1951*, trans. Philip Thody (London, 1966), p. 56.
14. *Ibid.*, p. 33.
15. *Another Country*, p. 91.
16. Charney, p. 65.
17. *Notes of a Native Son*, p. 48.

18. *Carnets 1942-1951*, p. 71.

19. *The Fire Next Time*, p. 67.

20. *Notes of a Native Son*, p. 21.

21. *Ibid.*, p. 27.

22. Anon., "New Light on the Invisible," *The Times Literary Supplement*, November 25, 1965, p. 1049.

23. Thomas Thompson, "A Burst of Negro Drama," *Life*, May 29, 1964, p. 62B.

24. *Black Voices*, p. 4.

25. Arthur Miller, "On Social Plays," Preface to *A View from the Bridge* (London, 1957), p. 4.

26. James Baldwin, Emile Capouya, Lorraine Hansberry, Nat Hentoff, Langston Hughes, Alfred Kazin, "The Negro in American Culture," *Cross Currents*, XI (Summer, 1961), 205-6.

27. Albert Camus, *The Rebel*, trans. Anthony Bower (London, 1953), p. 32-3.

If the Street Could Talk: James Baldwin's Search for Love and Understanding

Yoshinobu Hakutani

No Name in the Street, a book of essays Baldwin wrote immediately before *If Beale Street Could Talk*, is about the life of black people in the city just as the story of Beale Street takes place in the city. While *No Name in the Street* is a departure from Baldwin's earlier book of essays in expressing his theory of love, *If Beale Street Could Talk* goes a step further in showing how black people can deliver that love. In *No Name in the Street*, Baldwin does not talk like an integrationist; he sounds as if he is advocating the ideas of a militant separatist who has no qualm about killing a white enemy. Although the book turns out to be a far more sustained examination of the falsehood to which Americans try to cling than his previous works, it still falls short of a vision in which love can be seized and recreated as it is in *If Beale Street Could Talk.*

Whenever Baldwin wrote about American society, he became the center of controversy, for his career coincided with one of the most turbulent eras in American history, marked by the civil rights movement at home and the Vietnam War abroad. A realist as he was, he was forced to take a stance in dealing with the current issues of society and of race in particular. He has been both extolled and denounced for his unique vision of racial harmony in America. Praising him for his ideas is not difficult to understand, because he is not only an eloquent writer but an acute historian. Modern American society is predominantly urban; black and white people live and work together in the city. Those who look forward to the future embraced him as a prophet; those who want to place politics over history and impose the past on the future dismissed him as a dreamer.

Some black readers also disparaged Baldwin's work. "The black writer," Joyce Carol Oates observed in her review of *If Beale Street Could Talk*, "if he is not being patronized simply for being black, is in danger of being attacked for not being black enough. Or he is forced to represent a mass of people, his unique vision assumed to be symbolic of a collective vision."[1] A black writer like Richard Wright is seldom assailed because he not only asserts being black but openly shows his anger as a black man. To Baldwin, Wright's portrayal of the life of black people seems to be directed toward the fictional but realistic presentation of a black man's anger. Although sympathetic to this rage, Baldwin sees a basic flaw in Wright's technique, contending that the artist must analyze raw emotion and transform it into an identifiable form and experience.[2] Baldwin cannot approve of Wright's use of violence, which he regards as "gratuitous and compulsive because the root of the violence is never examined. The root is rage."[3]

This basic difference in vision and technique between Wright and Baldwin has a corollary in the difference between the two types of novels exemplified by *Native Son* and *If Beale Street Could Talk*. Both stories take place in the city, Chicago of the thirties in Wright's novel and New York of the sixties in Baldwin's. Bigger Thomas is accused of murder in the first degree for the accidental death of a white girl, and Fonny Hunt is imprisoned for the rape of a Puerto Rican woman, which he did not commit. Behind similar scenes of racial prejudice lie fundamentally different ideas about the existence of black people in American society. During his act of liberation, Bigger becomes aware of his own undoing and creation, but he achieves his manhood through murdering his girl friend. Fonny, an artist and an intellectual, consciously aware of the primacy of love, is able to revive that relationship and achieve his deliverance. Wright's novel, whether it is *Native Son* or *The Outsider*, ends tragically with the death of its hero, and neither of the victims can lead others to the discovery of love. Fonny's search for love and liberation, on the other hand, is accomplished through his sense of love, which others can emulate and acquire. Not only does he survive his ordeal, but his child is to be born.

Baldwin's technique of elucidating this idea of love and deliverance differs with that of a protest novel. *Native Son* was intended to awaken the conscience of white society, and Wright's strategy was necessarily belligerent. To survive in his existence, Bigger is forced to rebel, unlike Fonny who defends himself in the interior of his heart. Bigger learns how to escape the confines of his environment and gain an identity. Even before he acts, he knows exactly how Mary, and Bessie later, have forced him into a vulnerable position. No wonder he convinces himself not only that he has killed to protect himself but also that he has attacked the entire civilization. In contrast to *If Beale Street Could Talk*, *Native Son* departs from the principles of love and sympathy which people, black or white, have for their fellow human beings. In "How 'Bigger' Was Born," Wright admits that his earlier *Uncle Tom's Children* was "a book which even bankers' daughters could read and weep over and feel good about."[4] In *Native Son*, however, Wright could not allow for such complacency. He warns that the book "would be so hard and deep that they would have to face it without the consolation of tears" (xxvii).

The salient device in *If Beale Street Could Talk* is the narrative voice of a nineteen-year-old black girl named Tish. She is Fonny's fiancée and is pregnant with his child. Not only is she a compassionate and lovable woman, but the reality of her pregnancy inspires others to generate love and hope. Baldwin's concept of love and liberation is conveyed realistically by many of those involved in the story, her husband-to-be, their relatives, the lawyer, the landlord, the restaurant owner, and others regardless of their race. But what makes Baldwin's concept vibrant is Tish's voice through which it grows enriched and spiritualized. Her manner of speech is warm but calm and completely natural. Only through her vision can the reader learn to know the meaning of love and humanity.

By contrast, Wright's authorial voice, as Baldwin noted, succeeds in recording black anger as no black writer before him has ever done, but it also is the overwhelming limitation of *Native Son*. For Baldwin, what is sacrificed is a necessary dimension to the novel: "the relationship that Negroes bear to one another, that depth of involvement and unspoken recognition of shared experience which creates a way of life . . . it is this climate, common to most Negro protest novels, which has led us all to believe that in Negro life there exists no tradition, no field of manners, no possibility of ritual or intercourse, such as may, for example, sustain the Jew even after he has left his father's house."[5]

What Baldwin calls "ritual or intercourse" in black life is precisely the catalyst for the attainment of love and deliverance in *If Beale Street Could Talk*. To see the relationship of Tish and Fonny as spiritual rather than sexual, genuine rather than materialistic, is commonplace, but to make it thrive on the strength of the communal bond in black life is Baldwin's achievement. Baldwin seizes upon this kinship in family members, relatives, friends, and associates. Tommy in Saul Bellow's *Seize the Day*, like Fonny, falls a victim of circumstance, and changes his family name to Wilhelm but retains his Jewish heritage in his battle of life. "In middle age," Bellow writes about Tommy, "you no longer thought such thoughts about free choice. Then it came over you that from one grandfather you had inherited such and such a head of hair . . . from another, broad thick shoulders; an oddity of speech from one uncle, and small teeth from another, and the gray eyes . . . a wide-lipped mouth like a statue from Peru. . . . From his mother he had gotten sensitive feelings, a soft heart, a brooding nature."[6]

The antithesis to Baldwin's idea of bondage is the focus of an existentialist novel of Richard Wright's. Cross Damon in *The Outsider*, rejecting his heritage, wishes to be renamed. His mother, the product of the traditional Christianity in the South that taught black children subservient ethics, tries to mold her son's character accordingly. He thus rebels against his mother, who moans, "To think I named you Cross after the Cross of Jesus."[7] As he rejects his mother because she reminds him of southern black piety and racial and sexual repression, he, in so doing, discards genuine motherly love altogether. He resembles Meursault in Albert Camus's *The Stranger*, who stands his trial for the murder of an Arab.[8] Meursault is not only accused of murder, but condemned as immoral because he did not weep at his mother's funeral.

Damon's action, like Meursault's, derives from his nihilistic belief that "man is nothing in particular" (135). At the end of the story, however, Wright expresses a sense of irony about Damon's character. Tasting his agonizing defeat and dying, Damon utters:

> "I wish I had some way to give the meaning of my life to others. . . . To make a bridge from man to man. . . . Starting from scratch every time is . . . no good. Tell them not to come down this road. . . . Men hate themselves and it makes them hate others. . . . Man is all we've got. . . . I wish I could ask men to meet themselves. . . . We're different from what we seem. . . . Maybe worse, maybe better. . . . But certainly different . . . We're strangers to ourselves." (439)

As if to heed Damon's message, Baldwin challenged the climate of alienation and estrangement that pervaded black life. Not only did he inspire black people to attain their true identity, but, with the tenacity and patience seldom seen among radical writers, he sought to build bridges between black and white people. In contrast to African-American writers like Richard Wright and John A. Williams, who fled the deep South to seek freedom and independence in the northern cities, Baldwin always felt that he was a step ahead in his career. "I am a city boy," he declared. "My life began in the Big City, and had to be slugged out, toe to toe, on the city pavements."[9] For him the city was a place where meaningful human relationships could evolve through battle and dialogue. As in any confrontation of minds, there would be casualties but eventually a resolution and a harmony would emerge. In *Another Country*, a novel of black life in the city, Rufus Scott, once a black drummer in a jazz band but now lonely and desperate, meets with a poor white girl from Georgia. They are initially attracted to each other, but eventually she becomes insane and he commits suicide. Even though hate overrules love in their relationship, it is the traditional southern culture in which she was ingrained rather than the estranged environment of New York City that ruins their relationship.

Because *Another Country* is not a polemical tract but a powerful novel, as Granville Hicks recognized,[10] it seems to express a subtle but authentic dilemma a black man faces in America. The novel suggests not only that the South is not a place where black people can have their peace of mind and happiness, but also that the city in the North is not a place where they can achieve their identity and freedom. And yet the novel is endowed with an ambivalent notion that America is their destined home. It is well known that Baldwin loved to live in another country. Paris was his favorite city, where he felt one was treated without reference to the color of skin. "This means," he wrote, "that one must accept one's nakedness. And nakedness has no color" (*No Name* 23). But Baldwin returned home, as did American expatriates in the twenties, and trusted his fortune in America.[11] In "Many Thousands Gone," he stated, "We cannot escape our origins, however hard we try, those origins which contain the key—could we but find it—to all that we later become" (*Notes* 20).

In search of home, black writers quite naturally turn to the city in the North, where black and white citizens live side by side and talk to one another. In *No Name in the Street*, Baldwin intimated his sentiments: "Whoever is part of whatever civilization helplessly loves some aspects of it, and some of the people in it. A person does not lightly elect to oppose his society. One would much rather be at home among one's compatriots than be mocked and detested by them" (194-95). The black citizen would be drawn to city living only because the interracial relationship in a melting pot could thrive on mutual respect and understanding, the lack of which has historically caused black people's exodus from the South. Such a relationship, as Baldwin quickly warns, is possible only if white people are capable of being fair and having goodwill and if black people themselves are able to achieve their true identity.

The burden that falls upon the shoulders of both white and black citizens is poignantly expressed with a pair of episodes in *No Name in the Street*. For the white people's responsibility, Baldwin recounts a white juror's attitude toward the American system of justice. The juror spoke in court:

> "As I said before, that I feel, and it is my opinion that racism, bigotry, and segregation is something that we have to wipe out of our hearts and minds, and not on the street. I have had an opinion that—and been taught never to resist a police officer, that we have courts of law in which to settle . . . that I could get justice in the courts"—And, in response to Garry's [the defense attorney's] question, "Assuming the police officer pulled a gun and shot you, what would you do about it?" the prospective juror, at length, replied, "Let me say this. I do not believe a police officer will do that." (159-60)

The juror's reply not only provides a "vivid and accurate example of the American piety at work," as Baldwin observes, but also demonstrates the very honesty in Baldwin that makes his feeling credible to the reader.[12]

Baldwin calls for responsibility on the part of black people as well. In the middle of the chapter "Take Me to the Water," he now plunges himself into the dreary waters of urban society. This part of the narrative, in contrast to the personal and family episodes preceding it, abounds with experiences that suggest impersonality and superficiality in human relationships. After a long sojourn in France, Baldwin saw his school chum, now a U.S. post office worker, whom he had not seen since graduation. At once Baldwin felt a sense of alienation that separated the one who was tormented by America's involvement in Vietnam and the one who blindly supported it. Baldwin felt no conceivable kinship to his once friend, for "that shy, pop-eyed thirteen year old my friend's mother had scolded and loved was no more." His friend's impression of the famous writer, described in Baldwin's own words, is equally poignant: "I was a stranger now . . . and what in the world was I by now but an aging, lonely, sexually dubious, politically outrageous, unspeakably erratic freak?" What impressed Baldwin the most about this encounter was the fact that despite the changes that had occurred in both men, nothing had touched this black man. To Baldwin, his old friend was an emblem of the "white-washed" black who "had been trapped, preserved, in that moment of time" (*No Name* 15-18).

No Name in the Street is an eloquent discourse intended for all Americans to attain their identity and understanding. It takes its title from the speech by Bildad and Shuhite in the Book of Job that denounces the wicked of his generation:

> Yea, the light of the wicked shall be put out,
> And the spark of his fire shall not shine.
> His remembrance shall perish from the earth,
> And he shall have no name in the street.
> He shall be driven from light into darkness,
> And chased out of the world.[13]

Baldwin sees in Bildad's curse a warning for Americans: without a name worthy of its constitution, America will perish as a nation. "A civilized country," he ironically observes, "is, by definition, a country dominated by whites, in which the blacks clearly know their place" (177). He warns that American people must remake their country into what the Declaration of Independence says they wanted it to be. America without equality and freedom will not survive; a country without a morality is not a viable civilization and hence it is doomed. Unless such a warning is heeded now, he foresees that a future generation of mankind, "running through the catacombs: and digging the grave . . . of the mighty Roman empire" (178) will also discover the ruins of American cities.

The responsibility for American people to rebuild their nation, Baldwin hastens to point out, falls upon black people as heavily as upon white people. This point echoes what he has said before, but it is stated here with a more somber and deliberate tone. It sounds comfortable to hear Baldwin speak in *Notes of a Native Son* that "blackness and whiteness did not matter" (95). He thought then that only through love and understanding could white and black people transcend the differences in color to achieve their identity as human beings and as a nation. In *No Name in the Street*, such euphoria has largely dissipated; the book instead alludes to the reality that black Americans are descendants of white Americans. "The blacks," Baldwin stresses, "are the despised and slaughtered children of the great Western house—*nameless* and *unnameable* bastards" (185, my italics). A black man in this country has no true name. Calling himself a black and a citizen of the United States is merely giving himself a label unworthy of his history and existence. To Baldwin, the race problem is not a race problem as such; it is fundamentally a problem of how black Americans perceive their own identity.[14]

No Name in the Street also addresses their cultural heritage. Baldwin admonishes the reader that the term *Afro-American* does not simply mean the liberation of black people in this country. The word, as it says, means the heritage of Africa and America. Black Americans, he argues, should be proud of this heritage. He demands they discard at once the misguided notion that they are descendants of slaves brought from Africa, the inferiority complex deeply rooted in the American psyche. An Afro-American, in Baldwin's metaphysics, is defined as a descendant of the two civilizations, Africa and America, both of which were "discovered" not by Americans but by European settlers.

Baldwin's prophecy, moreover, is rendered in epic proportion. "On both continents," Baldwin says, "the white and the dark gods met in combat, and it is on the outcome of this combat that the future of both continents depends" (194). The true identity of an Afro-American, the very term that he finds the most elusive of all names, is thus given a historical light. To be granted this name, as he stresses, "is to be in the situation, intolerably exaggerated, of all those who have ever found themselves part of a civilization which they could in no wise honorably defend—which they were compelled, indeed, endlessly to attack and condemn—and who yet spoke out the most passionate love, hoping to make the kingdom new, to make it honorable and worthy of life" (194).

Historically, then, Baldwin bears out his old contention that both black and white citizens on this continent are destined to live together on the same street and determine their own future.

No Name in the Street, however, ends on a dark note, as some critics have suggested,[15] precisely because Baldwin had not yet discovered the true name for American people. The most painful episode in the book that influences his outlook on the racial question is his journey into the deep South. There he discovered not only a sense of alienation between black and white people, who had lived together over the generations, but an alienation within the white man himself. While a Southerner was conceived in Baldwin's mind as a man of honor and human feeling like a northern liberal, he struck Baldwin as a man necessarily wanting in "any viable, organic connection between his public stance and his private life" (53-54). Baldwin was in fact conscious that white people in the South always loved their black friends, but they never admitted it. This is why Baldwin characterizes the South as "a riddle which could be read only in the light, or the darkness, of the unbelievable disasters which had overtaken the private life" (55).

But Baldwin's search for a national identity in the name of brotherhood and love does not end in the South. Baldwin returns to the streets of the North. In the eyes of a middle-aged black writer, the potential for a truly American identity and understanding emerges in the city of the North through the black and white coalition with the radical students, and even in the black and white confrontation in the labor unions. Moving to Chicago in the thirties, Wright witnessed a coalition that existed between black men and white underground politicians, but this interracial cooperation, as he realized, did not arise out of the brotherhood on the part of the white men but out of their political and economic motives.[16] Such a white and black relationship as Baldwin envisioned in the sixties was a rallying cry for the black people who have seized the opportunity to make the once pejorative term *black* into what he calls "a badge of honor" (189). Although this encounter may entail hostile and dangerous reactions, it is, he asserts, a necessary crucible for black people to endure in achieving their identity. In the context of the late sixties, this is what he meant by the experience which a person, black or white, must face and acquire so that the person might attain identity. Baldwin hoped that the estrangement he witnessed in the South would not repeat itself in the North.

His most romantic quest in *No Name in the Street* involves the "flower children" he saw walking up and down the Haight-Ashbury section of San Francisco in the late sixties. Observing the young black men putting their trust not in flowers but in guns, he believed that the scene brought their true identity to the threshold of its maturity. The flower children, in his view, repudiated their fathers for failing to realize that black Americans were the descendants of white fathers; they treated the black children as their denied brothers as if in defiance of their elders. "They were in the streets," he says in allusion to the title of this work, "in the hope of becoming whole" (187). For Baldwin, the flower children were relying upon black people so that they could rid themselves of the myth of white supremacy. But he was undeniably a realist. He had no confidence in the black men who were putting their trust in guns, nor did he trust the flower children. In this episode he is quick to warn black listeners: "this troubled white person might suddenly decide not to be in trouble and go home—and when he went home, he would be the enemy" (188). In Baldwin's judgment, the flower children of the city in America became neither true rebels nor true lovers, either of whom would be worthy of their name in their quest for a national identity. In either case, he says to chide himself, "to mistake a fever for a passion can destroy one's life" (189).

The spectacle of the flower children thus figures as one of the saddest motifs in *No Name in the Street*. Although the vision of the young Baldwin was centered in love and brotherhood, the sensibility of the older Baldwin here smacks of shrewdness and prudence. Idealism is replaced by pragmatism, and honesty and sincerity clearly mark the essential attitude he takes to the problem of identity in America. His skeptical admiration for the flower children casts a sad note, for the encounter symbolizes the closest point to which black and white Americans had ever come in their search for love and understanding.

But at heart Baldwin was scarcely a pessimist. These pages, filled with love and tenderness, vividly express his feeling that, through these children, black Americans have learned the truth about themselves. And this conviction, however ephemeral it may have been, contributes to his wishfulness and optimism of the seventies. He has come to know the truth, stated before,[17] that black Americans can free themselves as they learn more about white Americans and that "the truth which frees black people will also free white people" (129). Baldwin's quest continues in *If Beale Street Could Talk*, for the novel is the catalyst for disseminating the truth. Even though Baldwin stresses the human bondage that exists within the black community, he also recognizes, in his imagination at least, the deep, universal bonds of emotion that tie the hearts of people regardless of their color of skin.

For Baldwin, the bondage that exists on Beale Street is hardly visible from outside. City life, as depicted by American realists from Stephen Crane and Theodore Dreiser down to James T. Farrell and Richard Wright, often brings out isolation and loneliness to the residents. The city is a noisy, crowded place, yet people scarcely talk to one another. New York City, Baldwin's home town, also struck Baldwin as emblematic of the impersonality and indifference that plagued city life in America. On his way to the South on a writing assignment, he stopped by the city to rest and to readjust his life, spent on foreign soil for nearly a decade. But all he heard was "beneath the nearly invincible and despairing noise, the sound of many tongues, all struggling for dominance" (*No Name* 51). The scene is reminiscent of what Crane, in the guise of a tramp, faces at the end of "An Experiment in Misery": "The roar of the city in his ear was to him the confusion of strange tongues, babbling heedlessly; it was the clink of coin, the voice of the city's hopes, which were to him no hopes."[18]

Unlike an existentialist in search of individual autonomy in the face of the void, chaotic, and meaningless universe, Baldwin seeks order, meaning, and dream in one's relation to others. A critic has dismissed *If Beale Street Could Talk* as "pretentious and cloying with goodwill and loving kindness and humble fortitude and generalized honorableness."[19] But because Baldwin is a confirmed romantic, his concept of love and honor is expressed with a sense of idealism. Neither the turbulence that embroils the urban ghetto nor the indifference that sweeps over it can disperse his dream.

It is ironic that the impersonality and estrangement which permeate Beale Street compel its residents to seek a stronger and more meaningful relationship with others. Tish, separated from her fiancé in jail, reflects on her happy childhood days, "when Daddy used to bring me and Sis here and we'd watch the people and the buildings and Daddy would point out different sights to us and we might stop in Battery Park and have ice cream and hot dogs."[20] Later in the story, Baldwin portrays the crowded subway, an epitome of city life, and suggests the notion that city inhabitants are forced to protect themselves. When a crowded train arrives at the platform, Tish notices her father instinctively puts his arm around her as if to shield her from danger. Tish recalls:

> I suddenly looked up into his face. No one can describe this, I really shouldn't try. His face was bigger than the world, his eyes deeper than the sun, more vast than the desert, all that had ever happened since time began was in his face. He smiled: a little smile. I saw his teeth: I saw exactly where the missing tooth had been, that day he spat in my mouth. The train rocked, he held me closer, and a kind of sigh I'd never heard before stifled itself in him. (52)

This motif of human bondage also appears as a faint noise coming from Tish and Fonny's unborn child. Tish hears it in the loud bar where she and her sister Ernestine talk about their strategy to get Fonny out of jail:

> Then, we are silent. . . . And I look around me. It's actually a terrible place and I realize that the people here can only suppose that Ernestine and I are tired whores, or a Lesbian couple, or both. Well. We are certainly in it now, and it might get worse. I will, certainly—and now something almost as hard to catch as a whisper in a crowded place, as light and as definite as a spider's web, strikes below my ribs, stunning and astonishing my heart—get worse. But that light tap, that kick, that signal, announces to me that what can get worse can get better. (122)

The bondage of black and white people in *If Beale Street Could Talk* could also be solidified, as could the black kinship, if the relationship were based upon a mutual understanding of others as individual human beings rather than as blacks who have typically been victimized by white society, or as whites who have habitually oppressed blacks under the banner of racial supremacy. No sooner does one treat another human being for an economic or political purpose than such a relationship ceases to exist. To show the possibility of a prosperous relationship between black and white people in the city, Baldwin has created many sympathetic portraits of white people. The Jewish lawyer the black families hire to defend Fonny is initially an ambitious man bent on advancing his career but later becomes an altruistic individual. The Italian woman who owns a vegetable stand informs the police of a racial harassment committed by a white hoodlum, thereby helping Fonny to be exonerated of his action to protect Tish, a victim of the white man's insult. The owner of a Spanish restaurant willingly allows Tish and Fonny to have dinner on credit out of his compassion for their unjust plight.

For Baldwin, black people in the North, in contrast to those in the South, can move freely and talk frequently with fellow residents. His white characters, unlike those in Wright's fiction, are seldom stereotyped. Whether they are prejudiced or fair-minded, materialistic or humanistic, they are always individuals capable of making their own judgments. It seems as though the spirit of individualism in which they have grown up becomes, in turn, contagious among the black people. In *No Name in the Street*, Baldwin shows why black men living in Paris were treated as individuals as Algerians were not. "Four hundred years in the West," he argues, "had certainly turned me into a Westerner—there was no way around that. But four hundred years in the West had also failed to bleach me—there was no way around *that*, either" (42).

The westernization of black people in America, as Baldwin would have agreed with Wright, has taken place by far at a swifter pace in the North than in the South. Southern life for black people, as vividly portrayed in *No Name in the Street*, was not only stagnant and dark, but it created terror. Baldwin traveled down the Southland at the time of the racial turmoil in Little Rock, Arkansas, in the late fifties, when black children attempted to go to school in front of a hostile army and citizenry to face the white past, let alone the white present. During his stay he encountered one of the most powerful politicians in the South, who made himself "sweating drunk" to humiliate another human being. Baldwin distinctly recalls the abjectness of this incident: "With his wet eyes staring up at my face, and his wet hand groping for my cock, we were both, abruptly, in history's ass-pocket." To Baldwin, those who had power in the South still lived with the mentality of slave owners. The experience convinced him that a black man's identity in the South was defined by the power to which such white men tried to cling, and that a black man's humanity was placed at the service of their fantasies. "If the lives of those children," he reflects, "were in those wet, despairing hands, if their future was to be read in those wet, blind eyes, there was reason to tremble" (61-62). It is characteristic of his narrative that the height of terror, as just described, is set against the height of love the child Baldwin felt when his life was saved by his stepbrother. His narrative thus moves back and forth with greater intensity between the author's feelings of abjectness and exaltation, of isolation and affinity.

Baldwin's style becomes even more effective as his tendency toward rhetorical fastenings and outbursts is replaced by brief, tense images that indicate a control of the narrative voice. For instance, one summer night in Birmingham, Baldwin met in a motel room one Rev. Shuttlesworth, as marked a man as Martin Luther King, Jr. Gravely concerned with Shuttlesworth's safety for fear that his car might be bombed, Baldwin wanted to bring it to his attention as Shuttlesworth was about to leave the room. But the minister would not let him. At first, there was only a smile on Shuttlesworth's face; upon a closer observation, he detected that "a shade of sorrow crossed his face, deep, impatient, dark; then it was gone. It was the most impersonal anguish I had ever seen on a man's face." Only later did he come to realize that the minister was then "wrestling with the mighty fact that the danger in which he stood was as nothing compared to the spiritual horror which drove those who were trying to destroy him" (*No Name* 67). A few pages later, this shade of dark and sorrow is compensated for by that of light and joy. Baldwin now reminisces about his Paris days—how little he had missed ice cream, hot dogs, Coney Island, the Statue of Liberty, the Empire State Building, but how much he had missed his brothers, sisters, and mother: "I missed the way the dark face closes, the way dark eyes watch, and the way, when a dark face opens, a light seems to go on everywhere" (71).

Unlike W. E. B. Du Bois and Jean Toomer, who viewed the South with deep nostalgia, Baldwin, like Richard Wright and John A. Williams, was repulsed by it. Even though at times he felt an affinity with the black people in the South and found his home there, he also found, as does Richard Henry in *Blues for Mister Charlie*, that once he had lived in the North he could not go home again. Baldwin's quest for humanity in *If Beale Street Could Talk* is not merely to seek out affinity with black people; it is to search the interior of city life. He is in search of a human bond in the hearts and souls of people. It stresses the conventional and yet universal bondage innate in man, a human affinity that can grow between man and woman, members of a family, relatives, friends—any group of individuals united in the name of love and understanding.

Fundamental to Baldwin's concept of human bondage is the relationship of love between a man and a woman that yields posterity. What saves Fonny and Tish from loneliness and despair is their expecting the child in her womb. Every time she visits him in jail, they focus their talk on the unborn baby. Whenever he sees her face during the visit, he knows not only does she love him, but "that others love him, too. . . . He is not alone; we are not alone." When she looks ashamed of her ever expanding waistline, he is elated, saying, "Here she come! Big as *two* houses! You sure it ain't twins? or triplets? Shit, we *might* make history" (162). While at home, she is comforted by Ray Charles's voice and piano, the sounds and smells of the kitchen, the sounds and "blurred human voices rising from the street." Only then does she realize that "out of this rage and a steady, somehow triumphant sorrow, my baby was slowly being formed" (41).

However crowded, noisy, and chaotic Baldwin's city may be, one can always discover order, meaning, and hope in one's life. The street talks as though conflict and estrangement among the residents compel them to seek their ties with smaller human units. Not only does the birth of a child, the impending birth of Tish and Fonny's baby, constitute the familial bond, but it also signals the birth of new America. Baldwin has earlier conceived this idea in *No Name in the Street*, in which the first half of the book, "Take Me to the Water," depicts the turmoil of American society in the sixties and the second, "To Be Baptized," prophesies the rebirth of a nation. In the epilogue he writes: "An old world is dying, and a new one, kicking in the belly of its mother, time, announces that it is ready to be born." Alluding to the heavy burden falling upon American people, he remarks with a bit of humor: "This birth will not be easy, and many of us are doomed to discover that we are exceedingly clumsy midwives. No matter, so long as we accept that our responsibility is to the new born: the acceptance of responsibility contains the key to the necessarily evolving skill" (196).

Baldwin's extolment of the relationship between Tish and Fonny also suggests that the interracial relationships of love and sex as seen in *Another Country* are often destroyed by the forces of society beyond their control. In such a relationship, genuine love often falls a victim of society, a larger human unit. Baldwin's love story in *If Beale Street Could Talk* also suggests that a homosexual relationship is an antithesis to the idea of rebirth. Levy, Fonny's landlord, is a personable, happily married young man. Being Jewish, he values the closeness in family life and the offspring marriage can produce. He willingly rents his loft to Fonny, who needs the space to work on his sculptures, because he is aware of his own happiness in raising children and wants his tenants to share the same joy. "Hell," Levy tells Fonny, "drag out the blankets and sleep on it. . . . Make babies on it. That's how *I* got here. . . . You two should have some beautiful babies . . . and, take it from me, kids, the world damn sure needs them." Out of sympathy for Fonny's situation, he even forgoes payment of the rent while Fonny is in jail, saying, "I want you kids to have your babies. I'm funny that way" (133-34).

As urban society disintegrates because of its indifference and impersonality, the love and understanding that can unite smaller communities, couples, families, relatives, and friends become essential to the pursuit of happiness. Those who are deprived of such relationships cannot survive. Daniel Carty, Fonny's childhood friend, who is also arrested by the D.A.'s office, is a loner. Without ties to his family and relatives, he is doomed.

Tony Maynard, Baldwin's former bodyguard, who appears in *No Name in the Street*, is reminiscent of Daniel Carty. Tony is imprisoned on a murder charge arising from a mistaken identity.[21] Since the title "To Be Baptized" in *No Name in the Street* suggests the idea of rebirth, Baldwin's motif of alienation, which Tony's episode illustrates in the latter portion of the book, seems incongruous. In any event, Tony is treated as a victim of the indifference and hatred that exists in society; like Daniel, he is without the protection of his family and relatives. Ironically, he is a professional bodyguard for a man but no one else can guard him.

While Baldwin often evokes the idea of rebirth in *No Name in the Street* by biblical references, he has a penchant to assail, in *If Beale*

Street Could Talk, those who find their haven in the church. To him, a long history of the Christian church has partly resulted in the enslavement of black people in this country, and the black people "who were given the church and nothing else"[22] have learned to be obedient to the law of God and the land but failed to be independent thinkers.[23] Mrs. Hunt, Fonny's mother, like Cross Damon's mother in *The Outsider*, has a blind trust in Christ. She even believes that Fonny's imprisonment is "the *Lord's* way of making my boy think on his sins and surrender his soul to Jesus" (64). Her doctor convinces Mrs. Hunt, who has a heart problem, that her health is more important than her son's freedom. By contrast, Fonny's father Frank is a defiant disbeliever. "I don't know," Frank tells his wife, "how God expects a man to act when his son is in trouble. *Your* God crucified *His* son and was probably glad to get rid of him, but I ain't like that. I ain't hardly going out in the street and kiss the first white cop I see" (65). Although it is tragic that Frank commits suicide when he is caught stealing money to raise funds to defend his son, Frank's action suggests the genuine feeling of love and tenderness a father can have for his son.

Baldwin ends *If Beale Street Could Talk* on a triumphant note. Fonny is out of jail, however temporary it may be, because of the efforts by those who are genuinely concerned about his welfare. Not only has he been able to endure his ordeal, but his experience in jail has renewed his human spirit. The last time Tish visits him in jail, he tells her: "Listen, I'll soon be out. I'm coming home because I'm glad I came, can you dig that?" (193). The final scene once again echoes the voice that conveys Baldwin's idea of love and rebirth. Fonny is now a sculptor at work in his studio: "Fonny is working on the wood, on the stone, whistling, smiling. And, from far away, but coming near, the baby cries and cries and cries and cries and cries and cries and cries and cries, cries like it means to wake the dead" (197).

Baldwin completed this scene of freedom and rebirth on Columbus Day, 12 October, as indicated at the end of the book. The reference to Columbus Day may easily remind one of Pudd'nhead Wilson's calendar note for that day in the conclusion of Mark Twain's classic novel of racial prejudice: "October 12, *the Discovery. It was wonderful to find America, but it would have been more wonderful to miss it.*"[24] While Twain's intention in the book is a satire on American society and on slavery in particular, Baldwin's in *If Beale Street Could Talk* is to discover a new America. When Baldwin declares in the epilogue for *No Name in the Street* that "the Western party is over, and the white man's sun has set. Period" (197), one can be puzzled. The question remains whether or not Baldwin had come away from the turbulent sixties as a disillusioned American. Throughout *No Name in the Street* he has fluctuated between his feelings of love and hatred as his episodes betray. From the perspective of his hatred and resignation, the book clearly bodes ill; from the perspective of his love and understanding, though avowedly less frequent, it nevertheless suggests its author remains hopeful. But in *If Beale Street Could Talk* Baldwin's ambivalence has largely disappeared, and the book tells that the sun will also rise in America, this time for black citizens as well as for white citizens.

Notes

1. Joyce Carol Oates, "A Quite Moving and Very Traditional Celebration of Love," *New York Times Book Review*, 26 May 1974, 1-2.

2. I agree with Kichung Kim, who advances the theory that the difference between Wright and Baldwin arises from the two different concepts of man. Kim argues that the weakness Baldwin sees in Wright and other protest writers "is not so much that they had failed to give a faithful account of the actual conditions of man but rather that they had failed to be steadfast in their devotion . . . to what man might and ought to be. Such a man . . . will not only survive oppression but will be strengthened by it." See Kim, "Wright, the Protest Novel, and Baldwin's Faith," *CLA Journal* 17 (March 1974): 387-96.

3. James Baldwin, "Alas, Poor Richard," *Nobody Knows My Name* (New York: Dial, 1961), 151.

4. Richard Wright, "How 'Bigger' Was Born," *Native Son* (New York: Harper, 1966), xxvii.

5. James Baldwin, *Notes of a Native Son* (New York: Bantam Books, 1968), 27-28.

6. See Saul Bellow, *Seize the Day* (New York: Viking, 1956), 25. Tish in *If Beale Street Could Talk* often wonders if their baby would inherit Fonny's narrow, slanted, "Chinese" eyes.

7. Richard Wright, *The Outsider* (New York: Harper, 1953), 23.

8. Albert Camus, *The Stranger*, trans. Stuart Gilbert (New York: Vintage Books, 1942).

9. James Baldwin, *No Name in the Street* (New York: Dell, 1972), 59.

10. See Granville Hicks, "Outcasts in a Caldron of Hate," *Saturday Review* 45 (1962): 21.

11. Saunders Redding observed that Wright, who paid homage to Africa, failed to find home there. See Redding, "Reflections on Richard Wright: A Symposium on an Exiled Native Son," *Anger and Beyond: The Negro Writer in the United States*, ed. Herbert Hill (New York: Harper, 1966), 204. Like Wright, John A. Williams, who hailed from Mississippi, has said, "I have been to Africa and know that it is not my home. America is." See Williams, *This Is My Country Too* (New York: New American Library, 1956), 169.

12. To reveal this kind of malady in society as Baldwin attempts to do in *No Name in the Street* requires an artist's skills. The juror's response is reminiscent of Aunt Sally's to Huck Finn, who reports that a steamboat has just blown up a cylinder-head down the river:

> "Good gracious! Anybody hurt?"
> "No'm. Killed a nigger."
> "Well, it's lucky; because sometimes people do get hurt."

See Mark Twain, *Adventures of Huckleberry Finn*, ed. Henry Nash Smith (Boston: Houghton, 1958), 185. What Twain and Baldwin share is the genuine feeling an intense individualist possesses; both writers feel their own great powers and yet recognize the hopelessness of trying to change the world overnight.

13. *Prose and Poetry from the Old Testament*, ed. James F. Fullington (New York: Appleton, 1950), 77.

14. In a later volume of essays, Baldwin makes a similar assertion about black Americans' somber realization of themselves: "This is why blacks can be heard to say, *I ain't got to be nothing but stay black, and die!*: which is, after all, a far more affirmative apprehension than *I'm free, white and twenty-one*." See *The Devil Finds Work* (New York: Dial, 1976), 115.

15. See, for example, Benjamin DeMott, "James Baldwin on the Sixties: Acts and Revelations," in *James Baldwin: A Collection of Critical Essays*, ed. Keneth Kinnamon (Englewood Cliffs, N.J.: Prentice-Hall, 1974), 158.

16. See Richard Wright, *12 Million Black Voices* (New York: Viking, 1941), 121-22.

17. In 1961 Baldwin wrote in his essay "In Search of a Majority": "Whether I like it or not, or whether you like it or not, we are bound together. We are part of each other.

What is happening to every Negro in the country at any time is also happening to you. There is no way around this. I am suggesting that these walls—these artificial walls—which have been up so long to protect us from something we fear, must come down" (*Nobody Knows My Name*, 136-37). In 1962 he wrote in "My Dungeon Shook": "Well, the black man has functioned in the white man's world as a fixed star, as an immovable pillar: and as he moves out of his place, heaven and earth are shaken to their foundations. . . . But these men are your brothers—your lost, younger brothers. And if the word *integration* means anything, this is what it means: that we, with love, shall force our brothers to see themselves as they are, to cease fleeing from reality and begin to change it." See *The Fire Next Time* (New York: Dial, 1963), 23-24.

18. See *Great Short Works of Stephen Crane* (New York: Harper, 1968), 258.

19. John Aldridge, "The Fire Next Time?" *Saturday Review*, 15 June 1974: 24-25.

20. James Baldwin, *If Beale Street Could Talk* (New York: Dial, 1974), 9.

21. I agree with Benjamin DeMott, who regards Tony Maynard as an undeveloped character despite much space given for that purpose, but the weakness of Baldwin's characterization results from his use of a sterile man in the context of creation and rebirth (DeMott, "James Baldwin on the Sixties," 158).

22. See Baldwin's interview by Kalamu ya Salaam, "James Baldwin: Looking towards the Eighties," *Critical Essays on James Baldwin*, ed. Fred L. Standley and Nancy V. Burt (Boston: Hall, 1988), 40.

23. Sondra A. O'Neale observes in her essay "Fathers, Gods, and Religion: Perceptions of Christianity and Ethnic Faith in James Baldwin" that "more than the heritage of any other Black American writer, Baldwin's works illustrate the schizophrenia of the Black American experience with Christianity." Black people, she argues, needed a distinction "between Christianity as they knew it to be and Christianity as it was practiced in the white world." See *Critical Essays on James Baldwin*, 125-43.

24. Mark Twain, *Pudd'nhead Wilson* and *Those Extraordinary Twins*, ed. Sidney E. Berger (New York: Norton, 1980), 113.

Bearing the Burden of the Blues: *If Beale Street Could Talk*

Trudier Harris

In *If Beale Street Could Talk* (1974), Baldwin completes the inversion he hinted at in "The Outing." The novel moves its focus away from characters who are inside the church, or who have grown up in it, to characters who have consistently rejected its influence on their lives. In the dichotomy that Baldwin has set up with insiders and outsiders, with church members being insiders, the symbolism is now reversed; those within the church are "outside" the realm of human caring. The church has degenerated into a haven for people who do not wish to deal with their family problems or face the realistic pressures of the world. Tolerance, the ability to forgive, charitable sacrifice, self-effacing love—virtues traditionally associated with the church—are assigned to characters who have no history of commitment to the church. Earlier characters, such as Gabriel, might have laid claim to these virtues, but rarely did they show them; now Baldwin has stripped away the facade. People who remain in the church are publicly and privately intolerant, selfish, destructively fanatical; especially the women, who, in previous works, had retained some of the attributes of goodness even when they were repressed within the church.

Baldwin's progression away from the church is due in part to his witnessing of the many failures it has produced over the years; his characters in early works are living monuments to those failures. He concluded at one point that "there was no love in the church. It was a mask for hatred and self-hatred and despair,"[1] The church has especially failed in its ability to support characters in the secular realm of their existence beyond the home—as far as Baldwin is concerned, it has provided no way of dealing with the political and social environments. Many of the tenets it has espoused have been so perverted by the Gabriels of the world that the very concept of religion needs to be redefined. *If Beale Street Could Talk* is an effort at such redefinition.

Those in the novel who are inside the church, like Mrs. Hunt, are no longer saved, or even waging serious soul-searching battles; they are buffoons. In Baldwin's scheme of redefinition, those outside the church are the individuals who truly espouse the tenets of Christianity as exemplified by Christ. To an extent, therefore, Baldwin's vision has become paradoxically more secular even as it becomes more religious; the most positive characters are those Christlike ones who exist outside the church.

In contrast to *Go Tell It on the Mountain*, where the nuclear family and security were centered upon having a strong connection to the church, in *If Beale Street Could Talk*, being outside the church means having a nuclear family and potential security. It also means having the will to fight problems that arise instead of simply praying to God that those problems might be removed. Being inside the church means waiting for that pie in the sky and refusing to get involved with the police and jails, even for the sake of saving a loved one. Consequently, being inside the church means destruction of the family in fundamental ways. Certainly we can say that Gabriel had a detrimental effect upon his family, but we were left to imagine the specifics of those futuristic consequences; in *If Beale Street Could Talk*, we see the fanatical church sister Mrs. Hunt ignoring her jailed son, and we get testimony of his beatings and of his constant degradation. We do not have to speculate on what will happen to him; therefore, a harsher judgment is passed upon Mrs. Hunt and her clinging to the destructive church connection she has.

Initially, then, Baldwin moves the positive black women characters in *If Beale Street Could Talk* beyond active participation in the church. Second, he redefines the tenets of Christianity as practiced by his characters (or at least reclaims what previous characters have perverted), and he thereby releases Christianity from the storefront and post office buildings with which it has been associated previously. This reversal in order to recapture the basic tenets of morality is a literary manifestation of an idea that Baldwin presented many years earlier in *The Fire Next Time*:

> It is not too much to say that whoever wishes to become a truly moral human being (and let us not ask whether or not this is possible; I think we must believe that it is possible) must first divorce himself from all the prohibitions, crimes, and hypocrisies of the Christian church. If the concept of God has any validity or any use, it can only be to make us larger, freer, and more loving. If God cannot do this, then it is time we got rid of Him. (p. 67)

The characters in *Beale Street* have progressed to that divorce and to the reclamation of the true love of God.

This progression certainly provides another level of discussion of the treatment of black women in Baldwin's works. Still, the images have not been completely changed; they have only been reworked. Those very positive characters—Tish, her mother, and her sister—must still be judged as either good or bad primarily in relation to how far they are removed from the negative image of the church as represented by Mrs. Hunt. The discussion of the women can move to new levels, but only because Baldwin has been willing to recast his approach to an image that has appeared throughout his fiction.

The majority of the black female characters in *If Beale Street Could Talk* are women who are not tied down by their own notions of guilt about their actions. They are women for whom morality is a much more flexible concept than it has been in any of the previous works. If John had been jailed in *Go Tell It on the Mountain*, for example, Elizabeth would not conceivably have condoned stealing from a warehouse to raise the money for his bail; but that is precisely what some of the women in *Beale Street* accept as a natural part of their existence. Questions of morality are no longer simplistically two-sided; for these women, more complexity develops, and there is ample room for extenuating circumstances. By rejecting the morality of the fundamentalist black church, they represent characters who no longer believe themselves guilty beyond redemption. Theirs is a morality of action, which demands that the individual do what he or she can to further the case of a loved one and to see the will of God manifested on earth; there is no philosophy of sitting around waiting for the Lord's will to be done. These women have no time to wallow in guilt over imaginary crimes; they act and judge their actions only in terms of effectiveness for accomplishing their purposes. They do not assume that they are forever in the position of praying to be excused for their mere existence on earth; their self-conceptions are larger than that of the Elizabeths of the world, and their consciences are more lenient than that of the Florences.

The neatness with which the black women characters in the novel fit into Baldwin's schema has not been matched by any more detailed treatment of their place in his fiction. Critics have been divided in their response to the novel, those who damn it being especially vigorous. William Edward Farrison is dismissing, even condescending in his commentary; he complains about everything from the title to the way in which the novel is told. He offers further: "Neither in numbers nor in kinds do the characters in *If Beale Street Could Talk* command the reader's highest regards. None of them are especially admirable for either good or bad qualities, except perhaps a wealth of amorality and the aplomb with which most of them revel in four-letter vulgarities and their derivatives." John Aldridge is saddened "to see a writer of Baldwin's large gifts producing, in all seriousness, such junk." On the other hand, John McCluskey finds the supportive father image attractive, especially since so many of Baldwin's earlier works revolve around destructive relationships between fathers and sons. He also applauds the general mood of optimism that pervades the novel. Finally, he maintains that the characters are realistic, not "super-folk" (a position I disagree with later in this chapter).[2] None of these critics focuses particularly on the role of the women in the novel.

The women, clearly presented and sharply drawn in opposition to each other, range from Mrs. Hunt, a sanctified, aloof, pitiful excuse for a mother, to Sharon Rivers, a glorified, long-suffering one, and to her daughter Tish (Clementine), Fonny's devoted lover and narrator of the story. Images of Sharon and Mrs. Hunt are shaped by their reactions to their children, Tish and Fonny (Alonzo), during the crisis when Fonny is wrongly jailed for rape and when nineteen-year-old Tish, pregnant with Fonny's child, works to get her baby's father out of jail. Ernestine, Tish's sister, is equally committed to saving Fonny; she provides a pleasant contrast to Adrienne and Sheila, who are Fonny's noncaring sisters. The black women are drawn at two poles: good and bad, the bad ones truly villainous in their negligence and apathy and the good ones altruistic and Christlike in their dedication and commitment. The best women in the novel are the most Christlike because they truly understand New Testament teachings about love. The worst women, such as Mrs. Hunt, have little or no understanding of the loving sacrifices of Jesus; they are more interested in the church in its secular connotations—as ritual, show, and performance. They are different from Elizabeth in *Go Tell It on the Mountain* in that they believe the very act of going to church constitutes righteousness; Elizabeth, who goes to church frequently, nevertheless recognizes her own shortcomings. To the women outside the church, God, as He is traditionally conceived by churchgoers, is out of New York. They work, therefore, to put into practice for themselves the miracles of love and sacrifice of the New Testament; they do not wait to be lifted by invisible hands or buoyed up by the clouds of faith. Tish, her mother, and her sister, the representatives of this more-religious-than-church category of religion, are the most attractive female characters in the novel.[3]

Tish, who narrates the story, succeeds fairly early in getting us to sympathize with her position even if, later, we might not be inclined to trust completely her evaluations of scenes at which she is not physically present. It is important initially, though, that we do believe in her and sympathize with her predicament as a nineteen-year-old, unmarried, pregnant black woman who may never get married if her lover is kept in jail (for a rape he did not commit). Tish's plight offers the necessary verisimilitude to capture our attention and for us to follow willingly where she leads us as narrator. Where she leads us is to a disturbing family relationship with the Hunts, Fonny's family, and to a supportive, idealized family relationship with the Riverses, her own family. Dialogue interspersed with the narration reinforces Tish's evaluation that the Hunt women do not care for their son and brother, and that the father, Frank, will be the only familial help the Riverses can expect in their efforts to get Fonny out of jail. The Riverses, Sharon, Ernestine, and Joseph, are ideally supportive of Tish and Fonny, and provide a fortress of warmth in which Tish finds the strength to keep on keeping on. Her family is easily a foil for the Hunts, and the women in her family are the models against whom the Hunt women look like social monsters.

* * *

Mrs. Hunt, whose separation from her family and from reality is indicated by the fact that she is seldom referred to by her first name (comparable to Mrs. Breedlove in Toni Morrison's *The Bluest Eye*), is a woman who cannot be forgiven because she hates her boychild, Fonny.[4] Any mother may have a preference for one child over another for a variety of reasons, but Mrs. Hunt has rejected Fonny, her youngest child, because he is not light-skinned and does not have good hair (Adrienne and Sheila are and do); nor has he come into the bosom of the church she values so deeply. The rejection puts Mrs. Hunt and her daughters outside the range of sympathy within the black community that would have characterized the aftermath of the sixties decade of black awareness. Blacks who were still praising mulattoes in 1974, after such an intense problack fervor, could be dismissed from racial and cultural sympathy more readily than their counterparts of decades earlier. We are not inclined, therefore, to suffer Mrs. Hunt gladly, and we see her more as a buffoon than as a serious mother image.

First of all, she is a hypocrite. She pretends that she loves Jesus and the church and that she is concerned about her family coming into the religious fold, but she is reluctant to take the time to get young Fonny ready for Sunday school and to ensure that he actually arrives at church when she sends him in that direction. The tone of Tish's evaluation of these traits is condemnatory, especially when she maintains the truth is that Mrs. Hunt is "lazy and didn't really like getting up that early" because "there wasn't anybody to admire her" in Sunday school.[5] Still, "sighing deeply and praising the Lord," she would get up, dress Fonny, and send him off, never certain that he would be in church when she arrived. "And, many times," Tish adds, "that woman fell out happy in church without knowing the whereabouts of her only son: 'Whatever Alice don't feel like being bothered with,' Frank was to say to me, much later, 'she leaves in the hands of the Lord'" (p. 26). What truly religious mother could possibly have such an irreligious attitude toward her son? And what husband, if his wife is truly converted, could possibly have such a sarcastic attitude toward her actions? Frank's comment, therefore, reinforces the portrait of Mrs. Hunt's character and solidifies the negative evaluation of her as mother and as professing Christian.

This scene, although early in the novel, is not the first glimpse we get of Mrs. Hunt. That view also shows her hypocrisy, but paints her too as somewhat of a sexual deviate. The scene is made even uglier because Fonny playfully relates it to Tish. What should be one of the most private occurrences between two people is shared with a third party, and it is that sharing that intensifies its deviancy. The tale, set against Tish's comment that Fonny *had* to go to church because Mrs. Hunt was determined to save him when she couldn't save Frank, is evoked by Tish's questions concerning the Hunts' sex life. Fonny describes what passes for making love between his parents:

> "Yeah. But not like you and me. I used to hear them. She'd come home from church, wringing wet and funky. She'd act like she was so tired she could hardly move and she'd just fall across the bed with her clothes on—she'd maybe had enough strength to take off her shoes. And her hat. And she'd always lay her handbag down someplace. I can still hear that sound, like something heavy, with silver inside it, dropping heavy wherever she laid it down. I'd hear her say, The Lord sure blessed my soul this evening. Honey, when you going to give your life to the Lord? And, baby, he'd say,

and I swear to you he was lying there with his dick getting hard, and, excuse me, baby, but her condition weren't no better, because this, you dig? was like the game you hear two alley cats playing in the alley. Shit. She going to whelp and *mee-e-ow* till times get better, she going to get that cat, she going to run him all *over* the alley, she going run him till he bite her by the neck—by this time he just want to get some sleep really, but she got her chorus going, he's going to stop the music and ain't but one way to do it—he going to bite her by the neck and then she got him. So, my Daddy just lay there, didn't have no clothes on, with his dick getting harder and harder, and my Daddy would say, About the time, I reckon, that the Lord gives *his* life to me. And she'd say, Oh, Frank, let me bring you to the Lord. And he'd say, Shit, woman, I'm going to bring the Lord to *you. I'm* the Lord. And she'd start to crying, and she'd moan, Lord, help me help this man. You give him to me. I can't do nothing about it. Oh, Lord, help me. And he'd say, The Lord's going to help you, sugar, just as soon as you get to be a little child again, naked, like a little child. Come on, come to the Lord. And she'd start to crying and calling on Jesus while he started taking all her clothes off—I could hear them kind of rustling and whistling and tearing and falling to the floor and sometimes I'd get my foot caught in one of them things when I was coming through their room in the morning on my way to school—and when he got her naked and got on top of her and she was still crying, Jesus! help me, Lord! my Daddy would say, You got the Lord now, right here. Where you want your blessing? Where do it hurt? Where you want the Lord's hands to touch you? here? here? or here? Where you want his tongue? Where you want the Lord to enter you, you dirty, dumb black bitch? You bitch. You bitch. You bitch. And he'd slap her, hard, loud. And she'd say, Oh, Lord, help me to bear my burden. And he'd say, Here it is, baby, you going to bear it all right, I know it. You got a friend in Jesus, and I'm going to tell you when he comes. The first time. We don't know nothing about the second coming. Yet. And the bed would shake and she would moan and moan and moan. And, in the morning, was just like nothing never happened. She was just like she had been. She still belonged to Jesus and he went off down the street, to the shop." (pp. 18-21)

Presumably, Tish is merely recording Fonny's story, and it should be looked upon as his evaluation, not hers. Even so, his sharing of unpleasantness about his mother extends some of Tish's earlier impressions of Mrs. Hunt. The woman's hypocrisy ranges to physical possessions (also exemplified later when Tish attends church with her) as well as it is maintained in the holy facade that allows her to cover up animal passion. The church service is her sexual inspiration. The pure and cleansing emotion she had started to release in church is transformed into a degrading wallowing in the dirt of the flesh. Her holiness will not allow her to admit that, so she plays the game like the cats Fonny uses to describe her. Her passion is made the rawer because she cannot confront it as such; it must be made to seem as if she is overpowered, taken against her will. That way, she can enjoy thoroughly the sins of the flesh, a symbolic rape in terms of wish fulfillment, and yet remain without guilt, somehow suspended above the baseness that is the true nature of her passion; she attributes the baseness to someone else.

The role her husband plays as a foil for Jesus suggests again that Alice Hunt can submit to the sexual degradation without lowering herself. Frank takes her unto himself in the same way that Jesus takes sinners to His bosom. Jesus washes away their troubles, as Frank overpowers Mrs. Hunt's objections, and He makes them anew (rebirth in Christ, baptism), as the peaceful start of a new week indicates Frank has done with Mrs. Hunt. The double entendre meanings in burden bearing and the second coming tie the secular and the sacred even more clearly in their perverse connection, with the effect that what was presumed to be holy is lowered instead of the base being elevated.

Frank calling Mrs. Hunt a black bitch also increases the lowering effect and the drop back to the reality from which she tries to escape. High yellow like her daughters, the once beautiful Mrs. Hunt doubtless believes that she has married below her station. She probably thought she would be compensated by having the dark and thankful Frank dotingly provide for her in one of those mythical darker-skinned/

lighter-skinned liaisons, and Frank's tailor shop business does provide a stable life for the family until he goes out of business (about the time Fonny is jailed). Calling the woman black forces her from the unreality of the church to the reality of the bedroom, where, like a bitch in heat, she enjoys the funkiness of making love as much as the husband enjoys lowering her from her holiness. Both husband and wife have allowed their relationship to degenerate to the ugliness that Fonny makes public and that serves to show what a negative image of black womanhood Baldwin considers Mrs. Hunt to be.

That ugliness also serves as a contrast later on to the lovemaking that goes on between Fonny and Tish. Fonny tells Tish that Frank and Alice do not make love "like you and me," and that is quite true. With Frank and Alice, lovemaking represents a dismantling of religion. It is only by throwing out Jesus and replacing him with a perversion that Frank and his wife can approach each other sexually. With Fonny and Tish, who have been to church but who do not believe, their lovemaking is the creation of a new form of religion.[6] It represents a coming together for commitment to and preservation of their love in spite of all obstacles, especially those represented by laws and courts. For Tish and Fonny, God is out of New York, and their only salvation is through nurturing, comforting, and helping each other.

Almost parallel sexual scenes—that between Frank and Mrs. Hunt and that between Fonny and Tish—are used for drastically different purposes in the novel. Baldwin uses what happens between Frank and Mrs. Hunt as another way of rejecting the faulty, hypocritical practice of religion that is at the center of his thematic concerns in the novel. It is questionable if any sexual experience Mrs. Hunt could engage in would be considered positive. Her perversion of sex is equal to her perversion of religion; she is hypocritical about both, and both are ugly. However, as Baldwin uses the same symbolism grounded in the church to show that women connected with it no longer have to feel guilty about their connection or lack of it, so he uses sex for a dual purpose. The same symbolism is used sexually to change the meaning of what human beings can do to each other with their bodies just as the symbolism of the church can be used simultaneously to suggest that people are both inside and outside the traditional church. There is no contradiction in viewing the sexual experiences in two drastically different ways, an evaluation with which Donald Gibson concurs:

> The scenes describing sexual relations between Mr. and Mrs. Hunt contrast sharply with those describing sexual relations between Tish and Fonny. For the Hunts, sex is a grim and sadistic parody of a religious rite and as ugly as the relation between them. For Tish and Fonny the contrary prevails. Their sexual relations are perfect, without ugliness or pain, even to the point of being highly romanticized. Although Tish is sexually innocent, a virgin, her initiation is perfectly achieved, so perfectly that the couple experience mutual orgasm.[7]

The two sexual rites parallel the distinctions in the two religious characters as best represented by Mrs. Hunt and Sharon Rivers.

Fonny's recounting of the sexual battle between his father and mother comes before the scene in which Tish recalls going to church with Mrs. Hunt and Fonny as a child. The effect is to paint the pious woman as a sanctified hypocrite not only in church, but out of it. We are prepared, therefore, for some unchristian action on Mrs. Hunt's part on that churchgoing Sunday. Fair-skinned Mrs. Hunt, who "had been a very beautiful girl down there in Atlanta" (p. 23), must escort the freshly scrubbed brown-skinned Fonny and the black Tish to church. Fonny is presented for church "looking absolutely miserable, with his hair all slicked and shining, with the part in his hair so cruel that it looked like it had been put there with a tomahawk or a razor, wearing his blue suit" (pp. 21-22). Tish, who is "dark" and has hair that is "just plain hair," and who is not attractive by most people's standards, is made to feel her unattractiveness in the tone in which Mrs. Hunt greets her. And the three parade down the street, with Mrs. Hunt cloaking herself in the expectations of Sunday morning; she guides the youngsters to their destination "like a queen making great strides into the kingdom" (p. 25). Tish will later think of walking into the church when she walks into the Tombs to visit Fonny in jail (p. 32).

Mrs. Hunt is aware of performance and show, and their parade through the streets reminds Tish of a fair. The secular context anticipates the arrival at church, where Tish points out that

> the church had been a post office. . . . They had knocked down some walls and put in some benches and put up the church signs and the church schedules; but the ceiling was that awful kind of wrinkled tin, and they had either painted it brown or they had left it unpainted. When you came in, the pulpit looked a mighty long ways off. To tell the truth, I think the people in the church were just proud that their church was so big and that they had somehow got their hands on it. (p. 27)

Size allows for show, and the secular/performance context is again emphasized over the sacred. Baldwin underscores that tendency to hypocrisy in many of his churchgoers by allowing them to worship in buildings not originally designed for church purposes. Here, the building is a post office; in *Go Tell It on the Mountain*, it had once been an abandoned store and is considered a theater by one of the characters.[8] When Baldwin was preaching, he had noted the connection between the church and the theater, and it was partly because of that recognition that he gave up preaching. He says in *The Devil Finds Work*: "When I entered the church, I ceased going to the theater. It took me awhile to realize that I was working in one."[9] The theatricality inherent in hypocritical churchgoers is what defines Mrs. Hunt.

Initially, the size of the church enables her to display her Christian responsibility by parading Tish and Fonny down the aisle and to show off her fancy dress in the process.

> We entered that church and Mrs. Hunt led us straight down the aisle which was farthest to the left, so that everybody from two aisles over had to turn

and watch us. And—frankly—we were something to watch. . . . Mrs. Hunt, who, somehow, I don't know how, from the moment we walked through the church doors, became filled with a stern love for her two little heathens and marched us before her to the mercy seat. She was wearing something pink or beige, I'm not quite sure now, but in all that gloom, it showed. And she was wearing one of those awful hats women used to wear which have a veil on them which stops at about the level of the eyebrow or the nose and which always makes you look like you have some disease. And she wore high heels, too, which made a certain sound, something like pistols, and she carried her head very high and noble. She was saved the moment she entered the church, she was Sanctified holy, and I even remember until today how much she made me tremble, all of a sudden, deep inside. It was like there was nothing, nothing, nothing you could ever hope to say to her unless you wanted to pass through the hands of the living God: and He would check it out with her before He answered you. The mercy seat: she led us to the front row and sat us down before it. She made us sit but she knelt, on her knees, I mean, in front of her seat, and bowed her head and covered her eyes, making sure she didn't fuck with that veil. I stole a look at Fonny, but Fonny wouldn't look at me. Mrs. Hunt rose, she faced the entire congregation for a moment and then she, modestly, sat down. (pp. 28-29)

The dress and the veil are important because Mrs. Hunt will shortly enter into a singing and shouting competition with a fellow worshiper, the sole purpose of which seems to be to show off their holiness and their clothing; they are "trying to outdo each other" (p. 30). During the singing of "Blessed Quietness, Holy Quietness," the women call and respond to each other with alternating lines of the song, and the singing interlude leads to the shouting competition:

I guess I'll remember until I die that black lady's white rose. Suddenly, it seemed to stand straight up, in that awful place, and I grabbed Fonny's hand—I didn't know I'd grabbed it; and, on either side of us, all of a sudden, the two women were dancing—shouting: the holy dance. The lady with the rose had her head forward and the rose moved like lightning around her head, our heads, and the lady with the veil had her head back: the veil which was now far above her forehead, which framed that forehead, seemed like the sprinkling of black water, baptizing us and sprinkling her. People moved around us, to give them room, and they danced into the middle aisle. Both of them held their handbags. Both of them wore high heels. (p. 32)

The details that would stick in a child's mind—the flashing rose, the swaying veil, the handbags and the high-heeled shoes—embody the contrasts in professed belief and action that drive Fonny and Tish away from the church; they never go again. Any claim Mrs. Hunt can make to being truly religious has been undercut by her performance and hypocrisy, by her refusal to separate the secular and the sacred.

Her vindictive response to Tish's pregnancy is in keeping with the personality that has been shown to us previously; her piety has already been ridiculed. She would rather "trust in God" than fight to get Fonny out of jail, and, somewhat paradoxically, she would rather believe that Tish is a slut than think her son has voluntarily made love with Tish. She calls it a "lustful action" and maintains that the Holy Ghost will cause the child to "shrivel" in Tish's womb (p. 84). In her assertion that Tish will suffer but Fonny will be forgiven, Mrs. Hunt holds the traditional sanctimonious view that pregnancy before marriage is always the girl's fault. Her rejection of the grandchild Frank has just said he would be "mighty glad" to receive provokes him beyond endurance; he knocks her down. This is another in a series of events in which his wife and daughters will refuse to offer support in family crises. Such attitudes are part of the reason Frank commits suicide later in the novel.[10] Neither her professed Christianity nor her weak heart causes Mrs. Hunt to relent when the men leave the women alone to reconcile their hard feelings. She continues to deny kinship to the child and to see her own daughters as models of behavior over Sharon's daughters: "These girls won't be bringing *me* no bastards to feed," she proclaims, "I can guarantee you that" (p. 89). She is seriously deluded about her daughters' sex lives, for, although Adrienne and Sheila are presented as self-righteously superior little snobs for whom no man would be good enough, their scandalous sexual habits (titillation, but not copulation) are known to the streetwise Ernestine. The fact that Mrs. Hunt fails to see the truth about her daughters is but another measure of her blindness about her own sexual habits and her refusal to confront the reality of Fonny's incarceration.

Mrs. Hunt disappears from the novel after this scene because she is not involved in and does not particularly care about the tangible efforts to get her son out of jail; she is content to pray. Her pernicious influence, however, is always felt when Tish talks about Frank and how Fonny's incarceration works such a destructive influence upon him. It is Frank with whom we sympathize even when he knocks his wife down, because he is on the side of life, innocence, parenthood, and reality. Mrs. Hunt sits prissily by and waits for unseen hands to work miracles.

The woman is physically and philosophically ugly to us. As Baldwin's representative of everything that is wrong with the church and with the hypocritical professors of Christianity, she serves well. In another ironic reversal, she has removed herself from the guilt earlier church women have felt by removing herself emotionally from the world around her. She has sacrificed all for her version of Christ, so there is no need for her to feel guilty about what she does on earth. She is completely one-dimensional in her philosophy, completely without participation in the secular/sacred clash that caused so many of the women in earlier works to feel guilty about their actions. Mrs. Hunt believes she is totally wedded to Christ; consequently, there is no ambiguity in her actions, at least not from her point of view. Unlike Florence, who left her mother and induced an inordinate amount of guilt for not having fulfilled her Christian duty, Mrs. Hunt is able to reject her son precisely in the name of Christianity and the idea of being dutiful. ("If thy right eye offend thee, pluck it out." "One should reject father, mother, husband, and children for the sake of God.")

* * *

Mrs. Hunt's daughters have rejected their brother as surely as their mother has; they join her at the end of the spectrum of women defined by aloofness and detachment from the crisis that should bring the two families together. In their attitudes toward Fonny, in their dress, in their mutual support of their mother's position against Fonny, Adrienne and Sheila are like Siamese twins, two misplaced configurations in a world that no longer puts special value on their particular brand of virtue. The two girls could never bring their mother any bastards because they could never find any man good enough, that is, light-skinned and middle class enough, for whom they would consider having children. They are too superior to touch their "nappy-headed" brother to get him dressed for Sunday school and too condescending in their parlor room manners to make Fonny's trouble their own.

If Adrienne and Sheila had appeared in a work at the turn of the century, they would have been tragic mulattoes or members of a blue-vein society, probably the latter. They are superficially concerned about manners and clothing and education, but not about deeper questions of morality and the political nature of the society in which they live. They are willing to believe that Fonny's incarceration is his own fault, which shows the level of their perception. Their attitudes are made clear in the scene of the announcement of Tish's pregnancy, which is a central (if not *the* central) one in the novel, the only time all members of the two families get together and discuss Fonny's and Tish's situation. The girls arrive with their noses in the air, quietly superior to the "trash" they believe they have been forced to call upon. "They smiled at an invisible host of stricken lovers as they entered our living room, and Adrienne, the oldest, who was twenty-seven, and Sheila, who was twenty-four, went out of their way to be very sweet with raggedy-assed me, just like the missionaries had told them" (pp. 76-77).

Aloofness and parlor room manners allow the sisters to keep their distance from trouble and the reality of Tish's and Fonny's predicament. Tish chides Adrienne for not visiting Fonny in jail, for preferring to be out with "some half-honky chump" instead of attending the family meeting. Adrienne says nothing in response, but her silence says to Tish that Adrienne "would never again, for *any* reason, allow herself to be trapped among people so unspeakably inferior to herself" (p. 82). Silence and aloofness soon give way to the confusion when Frank strikes Mrs. Hunt. The two sisters assist their mother as the men leave, Sheila accusing the Riverses of "sneering" at her mother's faith and Adrienne referring to them as "funky niggers" who have overreacted simply because her mother asked who was going to take care of the baby.

Class consciousness clearly separates the women. Yet Tish can transcend their hatred of Fonny to feel sorry for these advocates of such a fleeting pretentiousness. She notices that Adrienne is "too old" for what she is wearing, and that Sheila is "too young" (p. 77). She sees that flashy clothing does not make Sheila secure and that the makeup Adrienne wears does not hide the fact that her "skin was rejecting the makeup by denying it any moisture" and that "the face and the body would coarsen and thicken with time" (p. 88). Though they have tried to escape Harlem by going to City College and to escape sympathy for their brother by maintaining he would not be in jail if he had stuck to reading and studying, they will forever be two black women who are basically plain in spite of their light skin.

The Hunt women leave the Riverses, whom they consider "foul-mouthed people," and step out of any further concern about Fonny. Tish, Sharon, and Ernestine have "to look squarely in the face the fact that Fonny's family didn't give a shit about him and were not going to do a thing to help him. *We* were his family now, the only family he had: and now everything was up to us" (p. 92). Alice Hunt recedes into religion; Adrienne and Sheila disappear into activities they consider suitable to the images they have of themselves. There is little substance to the sisters and little that we have to consider beyond the announcement scene. They serve to show how uncaring Fonny's family is about him, but, as individuals, they elicit very little interest from us. We do not care about them or about what may happen to them; indeed, Tish, who has little reason for being sympathetic toward them, is perhaps more so than we are. The women are cultural and racial anachronisms whose tragedy is that they do not realize how far out of time and place they really are.

* * *

The blandness and boredom surrounding Fonny's sisters is counteracted by the vivacity surrounding Tish's sister Ernestine, who represents an evolved stage of black womanhood. She has moved from the primping of early years to commitment to black community health, especially that of children; she is at this stage at the time of Fonny's and Tish's trouble. Ernestine is an activist, an untiring worker who commands attention and action of most people with whom she comes into contact. She is Tish's supporter and a source of strength. Unlike the Hunt sisters, whom we cannot imagine even walking the streets of Harlem, let alone maneuvering in them, Ernestine is streetwise and politically conscious. She knows the possibilities for life-stifling activities in the legal system that Adrienne and Sheila prefer never to encounter and that Mrs. Hunt leaves in the hands of the Lord, and she knows how to offset some of the destructive activities. How she arrived at this state will clarify later on how she thinks in assisting Tish and Fonny. She has gone from being "vain," from having her "hair curled and her dresses . . . always clean," to "wearing slacks and tying up her hair and . . . reading books like books were going out of style." She resolves to take "no more of the white man's lying shit" (p. 47) and begins to work in a hospital, where one of her first experiences is to see a twelve-year-old Puerto Rican girl die from drugs.

Her appearance during the confrontation with the Hunt clan reflects her politics ("She was wearing gray slacks and an old blouse and her hair was untidy on her head and she wore no makeup" [p. 88]). She is not interested in the superficial outside, for her mind and heart reflect the commitment that guides her life. She is outspoken in her indictment of the women and in expressions of anger evoked by their indifference and their hypocrisy. To Sheila's complaint that Sharon is sneering at her mother's faith, Ernestine responds: "Oh, don't give me that bullshit. . . . You so shamed you got a Holy Roller for a mother, you don't know what to do. You don't sneer. You just say it shows she's got 'soul,' so other people won't think it's catching—and also so they'll see what a bright, bright girl *you* are. You make me sick" (p. 86). She threatens to tear out Adrienne's Adam's apple with her fingers or carve it out with a knife if she so much as touches Tish. In an atmosphere that has degenerated into insult and hatred, Ernestine can play the role that will subdue the Hunts. Her street language and dramatic gestures reinforce her point. Again, since sympathies have been created in favor of the Riverses instead of the Hunts, we are willing to tolerate the limits to which Ernestine goes. She is in pain at witnessing the lack of caring the Hunt women show even as she is in the process of insulting them.

For women who are so timid about sex, and who would reduce lovemaking between Fonny and Tish to something ugly, they find their timidity turned against them as Ernestine hurls sexual insults at them. When Sheila says, "I knew we shouldn't have come," Ernestine stares at her, laughs, and replies: "My. I must have a dirty mind, Sheila. I didn't know that you could even *say* that word" (pp. 87, 88). The women are more than ready to go, but Ernestine's insults follow them out the door and to the elevator:

> "Ladies," she said, and moved to the elevator and pressed the button. She was past a certain fury now. . . . "Don't worry. We'll never tell the baby about you. There's no way to tell a baby how obscene human beings can be!" And, in another tone of voice, a tone I'd never heard before, she said, to Mrs. Hunt, "Blessed be the next fruit of thy womb. I hope it turns out to be uterine cancer. And I mean that." And, to the sisters, "If you come anywhere near this house again in life, *I will kill you*. . . . You just cursed the

> child in my sister's womb. Don't you *never* let me see you again, you broken down half-white bride of Christ!" And she spat in Mrs. Hunt's face, and then let the elevator door close. And she yelled down the shaft. "That's your flesh and blood you were cursing, you sick, filthy, dried-up cunt!" (pp. 90-91)

The words are ugly in the mouth of any human being, but especially from one woman to another. Ernestine becomes the heavy in this scene in her threats of physical violence and in the intensity of the insults. Interestingly, she uses the word "cunt" in referring to Mrs. Hunt (as Tish uses it earlier referring to Adrienne). The word is not one that women frequently use to insult other women; it is a word men use to insult women. Consider the context in which Baldwin uses the word in *Another Country.* Richard and Cass argue in front of Eric about writers, and Richard implies that Cass would prefer a guy like Vivaldo to himself. "And you know why? You want to know why? . . . Because you're just like all the other American cunts. You want a guy you can feel sorry for, you love him as long as he's helpless" (p. 208). And again, in anger, several pages later, Richard calls Cass a cunt when he discovers her affair with Eric (p. 316). In the language they use, therefore, Ernestine and Tish are identified with males. Even the virtuous qualities Ernestine espouses in helping Fonny and Tish, then, are tied in some ways to the masculine qualities Baldwin prefers at times over feminine ones. Ernestine's language identifies her with such traits, as it identifies Tish with some of Baldwin's male narrators.

Ernestine's angry words heap a reality upon the Hunt women that they consistently refuse to face. Since we have already seen Mrs. Hunt in an act of what passes for lovemaking, her pristine response to Tish's pregnancy is permeated with hypocrisy. Since we have already seen her degraded in her own marital bed, we know that her hopes for her daughters are grounded in fantasy; Ernestine's words and actions could force her to reflect upon her own sexual situation. It is only because Ernestine comes back from the elevator in tears, and trembling, that we are willing to accept that her outburst has caused her perhaps as much suffering as it will cause the recently departed Hunt women.

Still, it is precisely because Ernestine is a woman of action that help will come to Fonny and Tish. It is through her work with children that Ernestine is able to locate a lawyer, Hayward, to take Fonny's case. It is Ernestine who discovers that Bell, the white cop who is behind all of Fonny's troubles, killed a twelve-year-old black boy a few years before; how that information can be used in court is not yet clear, but at least Ernestine is a person who believes in gathering all the ammunition she can, and she has a thorough file on Bell. It is Ernestine, too, who consistently forces Tish to see the ugliest possibilities in the war they have to fight so Tish will not be surprised and perhaps have a miscarriage if those things become reality later on.

Ernestine acts as a nurturer and a protector for Tish, a kind of mother image. She makes Tish see that whether or not Mrs. Rogers, the woman who has been urged by Bell to accuse Fonny of raping her, has indeed been raped is irrelevant. They must plan as if she had been and as if she believes her story about Fonny. Their course of action must be to discredit Bell and to show that he was out to get Fonny for another incident. It is Ernestine who makes Tish realize that Sharon is the only person who can follow Mrs. Rogers to Puerto Rico and try to get her to change her testimony. It is Ernestine who looks after Tish when Sharon is in Puerto Rico and who insists, with Joseph, that Tish quit her job. And it is Ernestine who cultivates the actress for whom she works in order to get enough money for Fonny's bail. Ernestine, then, combines the virtues of the Elizabeths and Florences of the world with a new trait: action uninhibited by external forces or inner doubts. She is understanding and loving, but she refuses to stand by and hope that things will get better. She takes matters into her own hands as often as she can.

The role Ernestine plays in relation to Tish offers a glimpse at another idealized bond in the Baldwin canon—that between two sisters. No sisters in any of Baldwin's works prior to this point have been old enough to have a real relationship (remember the children in *Go Tell It on the Mountain* and in the stories); Elizabeth, Florence, Deborah, Esther, and Ida have all been the only females in their families. Baldwin has created many families—in "Sonny's Blues," in *Tell Me How Long the Train's Been Gone*—in which no female siblings are present. To have two young black women who share their heartaches and hopes in *If Beale Street Could Talk* is quite a different presentation. Tish has in Ernestine the confidante and big sister that Elizabeth found in Florence and that Deborah so desperately needed. With the character of Ernestine, Tish is buttressed on all sides in her distressing time during Fonny's arrest; she has a supportive mother and father, a lover, and a caring sister. She and Ernestine form another bond in that little world Baldwin creates to withstand all outside pressures.

Ernestine and Tish join with their parents, Sharon and Joseph Rivers, in forming the idealistic, fairy-tale family structure that is the core of *If Beale Street Could Talk*. Sharon and Joseph are unmatched in parental concern, caring, duty, tolerance, responsibility, and support. Some critics, such as John McCluskey, maintain that, in the creation of this family, Baldwin was finally able to achieve in familial relationships what he had been working toward since *Go Tell It on the Mountain*. Joseph, unlike Gabriel Grimes, truly loves his offspring.[11] He resorts to stealing from the docks where he works (Frank steals from the garment center) and selling the goods to help raise money for Fonny's bail (Fonny has become the son for whom no sacrifice is too great).[12]

* * *

Just as the father image is idealized in *If Beale Street Could Talk*, so is that of the mother. Sharon is perhaps unlike any black mother, in fiction or in reality. She is equally as supportive as Joseph, but she also has qualities that sometimes stretch credibility. Still, unlike the women in *Go Tell It on the Mountain* and "Sonny's Blues," whose long-suffering Christian patience is their dominant virtue, Sharon is outside the church, the antithesis of Mrs. Hunt. In a novel that derides the form of

Christianity practiced as irrelevant and stymying, Sharon's position is a plus, just as Mrs. Hunt's is a minus.

Sharon Rivers is the active culmination of all the portraits of black mothers who have appeared in Baldwin's fiction to this point, and she anticipates those who will appear in *Just Above My Head*. I emphasize *active*; the many mothers prior to Sharon may have wanted to do the same things that she does, but they were unable to. For example, Elizabeth may have wanted to help John in his battles, both silent and verbal, against Gabriel, but she lacked both the strength and the position of support for offering such active assistance. The mother in "Sonny's Blues" may have wanted to explain things to Sonny just as the mother in "Come Out the Wilderness" may have wanted to take her daughter's side against her husband, but neither woman could do more than hope for the best in their passively supportive roles. The shadowy Mrs. Scott, Rufus' and Ida's mother in *Another Country*, wended her way along passively instead of trying to assist her troubled son and her wayward daughter; indeed, this mother simply disappears from the novel in the same way that the mother is equally diminished in *Tell Me How Long the Train's Been Gone*. In both cases, the glimpses of them we do get suggest that they are further developments of the Elizabeth tradition. With Sharon Hunt, Baldwin takes that tradition out of the closet and makes it a viable, though idealized, concept again. Sharon is the quintessential mother whose very presentation evokes memories of those earlier mothers who were so ineffectual, but whose desires to assist their children may have been just as strong as hers. Sharon has the advantage of a supportive husband who is not in conflict with either of his children and who would stand by her, with them, through any crisis. She becomes MOTHER to highlight all the earlier portraits of mothers; her very idealization is the source of all the problems we have with her.

Sharon's reaction to Tish's pregnancy is perhaps the most questionable scene in which she appears, and the one in which her role as idealized mother is most clearly presented. Tish comes home, exhausted, knowing the time has come to share her news with someone. When Tish tries to tell Sharon the news, but breaks into tears instead, Sharon already knows what the problem is (as does Ernestine). In a way, then, it is Tish who is in for a surprise because the tolerant Sharon has bided her time and not pressed her to verbalize what is already known. Sharon's reaction once the news is out is calm, controlled, almost proud.

> She said, "Tish, I declare. I don't think you got nothing to cry about." She moved a little. "You tell Fonny?" . . .
>
> "What you crying about?"
>
> Then she did touch me, she took me in her arms and she rocked me and I cried.
>
> She got me a handkerchief and I blew my nose. She walked to the window and she blew hers.
>
> "Now, listen," she said, "you got enough on your mind without worrying about being a bad girl and all that jive-ass shit. I sure hope I raised you better than that. If you was a bad girl, you wouldn't be sitting on that bed, you'd long been turning tricks for the warden." . . .
>
> "Tish," she said, "when we was first brought here, the white man he didn't give us no preachers to say words over us before we had our babies. And you and Fonny be together right now, married or not, wasn't for that same damn white man. So, let me tell you what you got to do. You got to think about that baby. You got to hold on to that baby, don't care what else happens or don't happen. *You* got to do that. Can't nobody else do that for you. And the rest of us, well, we going to hold on to you. And we going to get Fonny out. Don't you worry. I know it's hard—but don't you worry. And that baby be the best thing that ever happened to Fonny. He needs that baby. It going to give him a whole lot of courage." (pp. 40-41)

It is a wonderfully encouraging scene that borders on fantasy. First of all, Sharon has given Tish the space she needed by refusing to confront her with the suspicion of pregnancy. Second, she refuses to make an issue of marriage, which would have been the reaction of Florence's mother or Elizabeth's aunt. And she defends her daughter's action in the face of the harsh, uncompromising world around them. Fonny's incarceration is also important to Sharon's reaction, as well as the fact that Sharon, who is outside the church, is not as harsh in her judgment of presumed moral lapses as more conventional black mothers would be. Still, the tone of the scene is so extremely positive that it overshadows those considerations and suggests that the reaction is solely due to Sharon's personality as mother.

In the scene quoted, Baldwin has eradicated the tension that is usually present between parents and their children in his fiction. A different kind of tension will return in *Just Above My Head* between Julia and her father, but the majority of the siblings and their parents from this point on in Baldwin's fiction at least manage a peaceful coexistence. Here, with Tish and her mother, the peacefulness extends into a blissful, ideal relationship. The daughter, unlike Florence, has nothing to fear from her mother and nothing to feel guilty about for the actions she has committed. There is a sharing, a freedom in the relationship that never could have existed between John and Elizabeth, between Elizabeth and her aunt, or between Florence and her mother. That space to grow, which John so desperately needed from Gabriel in *Go Tell It on the Mountain*, is cheerfully granted to Tish by her mother as well as her father. The limits of parental authority have been relaxed, and the child has been endowed with a trusting confidence in the parents that enables her to consider sharing her most secret of secrets with them. Tish is four years older than John, but the comparison between them is no less valid. From the way his character is set up, one can easily imagine John being under the influence of Gabriel for a long period beyond his fourteen years. In contrast, the freedom Tish feels and the support she is given show the openness of the relationship Baldwin may have desired in the earlier work and that he can now imaginatively claim.

Sharon sees Tish's pregnancy as a cause for celebration; nothing is allowed to detract from that context.[13] Sharon considers the occasion so special that she takes out a bottle of "very old French brandy," which she has had for years, to formalize the announcement to Joseph and Ernestine: "Daddy poured and Mama gave us each a glass. She looked at Joseph, then at Ernestine, then at me—she smiled at me. 'This is a sacrament,' she said, 'and, no, I ain't gone crazy. We're drinking to a new life. Tish is going to have Fonny's baby.' She touched Joseph. 'Drink,' she said" (p. 54). Joseph is equally as encouraging and supportive as Sharon, Ernestine stands with tears in her eyes, and the sacrament is truly considered holy.[14]

This scene is perhaps one of many that led John Aldridge to consider the novel larger than life, a position I share. Aldridge complains that Baldwin "has produced another fantasy of rather large social implications, this time one in which the characters of black people living in contemporary Harlem are shown to be so noble and courageous that one is constrained to wonder how we ever imagined that conditions in the black urban ghetto are anything other than idyllic."[15] The good vibes continue to flow within the Rivers family until the mood is destroyed by the arrival of the Hunts; meanwhile, Sharon is one of the major keepers of the good vibes. The brandy is her idea; she decides to elevate Tish's pregnancy to something glorious and wonderful. That is her privilege as the idealized mother.

Her unorthodox behavior, as mentioned, can be explained partly in the nontraditional attitude she holds toward the church. It is only on holiday occasions, Tish tells us, that her family goes to church. Sharon's identity is secure in her family and work; she does not need the religious source in the way that Mrs. Hunt finds identity in it. Just as Fonny and Tish make a religion out of romantic love, Sharon makes hers out of familial love. Tish comments on her family's lack of regular religious habits: "We were Baptists. But we didn't go to church very often—maybe Christmas or Easter, days like that. Mama didn't dig the church sisters, who didn't dig her, and Sis kind of takes after Mama, and Daddy didn't see any point in running after the Lord and he didn't seem to have very much respect for him" (pp. 25-26). The comment, which is made on the occasion Tish goes to church with Fonny and Mrs. Hunt, shows the contrast between the Riverses and the Hunts. Sharon, like Ernestine, believes in human action, not in waiting on the Lord. If God helps those who help themselves, then that is fine, but Sharon and her family do not believe in praying for miracles that they can bring about for themselves.

Sharon's unorthodox behavior as mother is also partly explained by her own unorthodox behavior as a young woman. She had been daring enough to run away from home with a drummer to pursue a singing career and, when they parted and the career possibility failed, to fall in love with and marry Joseph after knowing him only a week. She is still "young" enough, therefore, to empathize with young love and the unpredictable circumstances it can create. She had met Joseph at a bus station in Albany where she sat "trying to look tough and careless" (p. 35), but conveying only her fright. Joseph had fallen for her and pursued her to New York, where "within a week, he had married her and gone back to sea" and Sharon, "a little stunned, settled down to live" (p. 37). Sharon had been twenty when she married Joseph. She had trusted him enough and believed in the love enough to respond favorably to him, and her faith has been rewarded, for at the time of Tish's pregnancy, she and Joseph have been married about twenty-five years. Her personal history, therefore, could account for her tolerant behavior toward Tish and Fonny, for the young people *would* be married if Fonny had not been jailed.

Sharon's levelheaded approach to life also serves well in the scene with the Hunts. She controls Tish by her mere presence and prevents her from saying things to Mrs. Hunt that would be as harsh as what Ernestine says. She urges Mrs. Hunt to understand Frank's intense feelings for the welfare of his son; failure to heed the admonition is what makes Frank knock his wife down. Sharon thinks of Mrs. Hunt's weak heart when the woman falls, insists that the men get out of the way and allow the women to handle the situation, and explains the seriousness of Mrs. Hunt cursing the child. In addition to Mrs. Hunt's weak heart, Sharon maintains:

> "She got a weak head. . . . The Holy Ghost done softened your brain, child. Did you forget it was Frank's grandchild you was cursing? And of course it's *my* grandchild, too. I know some men and some women would have cut that weak heart out of your body and gladly gone to hell to pay for it. You want some tea, or something? You really ought to have some brandy, but I reckon you too holy for that." (p. 86)

And she peacefully pleads with Mrs. Hunt to accept the child: "But the child that's coming . . . is your grandchild. I don't understand you. It's your *grandchild*. What difference does it make how it gets here? The child ain't got nothing to do with that—don't none of us have nothing to do with *that*!" (p. 89). She is never vindictive toward the Hunts, but she does not attempt to prevent Ernestine from being so. Perhaps Sharon feels they deserve to be made a little uncomfortable.

Just as Sharon has been ideal in accepting Tish's pregnancy, she also has an ideal response to Fonny bringing Tish home early on the morning following the night of Tish's loss of virginity. The scene in which Fonny and Tish first make love comes immediately after the ugly scene with the Hunt women. Structurally, it serves to counteract the effect of the Hunt women's presence, if not blot it out completely, and to consecrate what has happened between Fonny and Tish. Sharon does not get excited when Fonny and Tish show up; she merely asks where they have been. In the face of Fonny mentioning marriage to explain the night out, Sharon's paltry objections quickly dissolve. Joseph enters the room and anything else to be said is between him and Fonny. "We, the women," Tish says, "were out of it now, and we knew it" (p. 106). So they wait patiently while Fonny and Joseph go into another room; they return shortly, and the entire family agrees about the marriage. Sharon is there as a silent, supportive force in the scene, but she has no large critical part to play in objecting to her daughter's decision at such an early age (Tish is eighteen), or in objecting to Fonny, or in squarely confronting what they all know has happened a few hours earlier between Fonny and Tish.

In contrast to the background role she plays in the proposal scene, Sharon is outspokenly supportive of Tish in Hayward's office when he tells them how complicated the case has become as a result of Mrs. Rogers' disappearance. Tish bursts into tears, and Sharon counters with:

> "Tish . . . you a woman now. You *got* to be a woman. We are in a rough situation—but, if you really want to think about it, ain't nothing new about that. That's just exactly, daughter, when *you do not give up*. You *can't* give up. We got to get Fonny out of there. *I don't care what we have to do to do it*—you understand me, daughter? This shit has been going on long enough. *Now. You* start thinking about it any other way, you just going to make yourself sick. *You* can't get sick now—you know that—I'd rather for the state to kill him than for *you* to kill him. So, come on, now—we going to get him *out*." (p. 118)

The tone and language of Sharon's speech could very easily be in the mouth of Joseph, or other of Baldwin's male characters, especially in expressions like "we are in a rough situation" and "This shit has been going on long enough." Rufus' repeated refrain before he commits suicide in *Another Country* is "This shit has got to stop" (p. 61). Sharon's urgent outburst convinces Tish that they must steel their nerves and prepare for the fact that someone has to pursue Mrs. Rogers to Puerto Rico. That someone, as Tish and Ernestine later agree, has to be Sharon.

For a middle-aged expectant grandmother, whose traveling experiences range from Birmingham to Albany to Harlem, to undertake a trip to Puerto Rico in pursuit of a woman whom she has never seen requires no small stretch of the imagination. Yet it is a measure of Sharon's idealized portrait as mother that allows her not only to undertake the task, but actually to go and find Mrs. Rogers. This working-class black woman, who lives in a housing project and who has perhaps never even fantasized an island vacation, manages her task with competency and with a finesse that, if not incredible, at least forces us to view her in a different light. She plans for her trip with a strategy comparable to that of Ernestine's. Of the two snapshots Tish has of Fonny, Sharon takes the one in which he appears with his arm around Tish, smiling into the camera. The sympathetic intent is to get Mrs. Rogers to realize that such a smiling young man, so obviously in love with Tish, could not possibly be the young man who has raped her. Sharon also chooses clothing to portray herself as a concerned mother, not as a forceful, inconsiderate gringo who has come to strong-arm a change of testimony from Mrs. Rogers. It is a testament to her ideal image as mother that Sharon, who is afraid of flying, takes to the air to help her offspring, for indeed Fonny is as much hers as Tish is.

Sharon's trip to Puerto Rico allows Baldwin to develop some of the ideas he has hinted at of the political connections between American blacks and other Third World peoples. They need to form a sympathetic bond against the forces that oppress them. Sharon's sympathetic young cab driver senses that need. He attaches himself to her for the duration of her stay, adopting her in the best sense of that word. He and the Spanish family who own the restaurant where Fonny and Tish have eaten frequently are the positive images of Spanish-speaking people in the novel. They join forces with the blacks and the Italians against Bell, the cop who would divide blacks and Puerto Ricans and conquer both by having them fight each other. That political implication pervades Tish's relation of Sharon's trip to Puerto Rico as well as other parts of her narration.[16] And Sharon capitalizes on that connection as well. When she meets Mrs. Rogers, she emphasizes that they must help each other because they are both black.

Too unstable to accept that argument or to believe in its ultimate truth, Mrs. Rogers screams Sharon out of her life and, two days later, collapses into a miscarriage and insanity. Pietro, the father of the child, understandably refuses to ask Mrs. Rogers to rethink the testimony she has given, and Sharon has gone to visit the woman alone. Before she resorted to the appeal to common color, she had appealed to Mrs. Rogers as a mother (Mrs. Rogers has other children) and, recognizing the vulnerability and fear the girl feels, as a daughter. But the mother image that is so idealized in New York has no appeal in Puerto Rico. Sharon must return to New York without having accomplished her goal, and the D.A. now has an additional excuse to keep Fonny in jail until the deranged Mrs. Rogers is well enough to testify against him (the potentially hopeless case Bell would love to see).

Nonetheless, Sharon's going to Puerto Rico represents the ultimate contrast to images of womanhood embodied in Mrs. Hunt and her daughters. Her commitment to family is unquestionable, and her sacrificial ability to *do* immortalizes her among black mother images in Baldwin's fiction. She recognizes no limitations that could be placed on her by church and society, and it is that freedom of thinking and action that makes her an unusual image of black woman to this point in Baldwin's fiction. Certainly Ida is a woman of activity, but she is by no means as psychologically free of external influences as Sharon is.

* * *

The most important image of black womanhood we see in *If Beale Street Could Talk* is Tish, primarily because Tish is the first black woman Baldwin allows to tell her own story. He had used a third-person limited point of view with Ruth in "Come Out the Wilderness," but he had never trusted a black woman to relate her own story, or trusted himself enough to dare adopt that pose. Sylvander comments briefly on Baldwin's ambivalence about using Tish as narrator; she quotes Baldwin: "To try to tell a story from the point of view of a pregnant woman is something of a hazard. I tried to avoid it, but she's the only one who can tell the story."[17] Baldwin's decision may reflect his sensitivity to criticism that he had not given black women a truly enviable and integrated place in his fiction.[18]

Tish's first-person narration is recognizably different in its major stylistic features from Baldwin's omniscient point of view in *Go Tell It on the Mountain* and from a male's first-person narration in, for example, *Tell Me How Long the Train's Been Gone* (1968). The typical descriptive sentence below from *Go Tell It on the Mountain* contains a wealth of metaphorical language. It is consciously designed to carry the theme of the novel in terms of the conditions of sin and guilt (the grime of life) that exist within the Grimes family. Dust and dirt pervade their apartment just as surely as they pervade the distortions Gabriel has made of religion.

> Dirt was in the walls and the floorboards, and triumphed beneath the sink where roaches spawned; was in the fine ridges of the pots and pans, scoured daily, burnt black on the bottom, hanging above the stove; was in the wall against which they hung, and revealed itself where the paint had cracked and leaned outward in stiff squares and fragments, the paper-thin underside webbed with black. (pp. 21-22)

Sin lives in the lives of the characters in the same way the dirt clings to the walls and appliances. The omniscient narration, by its very nature, is depersonalized even when it carries images of almost living things. The sentence itself is very complex, with ideas just as embedded in it as the dirt is in the walls and the floorboards. In the novel, language carries theme, and metaphor and subject are synonymous.

Omniscient narration can allow for the plays on language that Baldwin develops in *Go Tell It on the Mountain* and would account for some of the differences in narration there and in *If Beale Street Could Talk*, but there are also some differences in comparing Tish's first-person voice with that of Leo Proudhammer's in *Tell Me How Long the Train's Been Gone*. Leo's voice has overtones of the metaphorical language Baldwin uses in *Go Tell It on the Mountain*, and the sentence structure is sometimes equally as complex.

> When Caleb, my older brother, was taken from me and sent to prison, I watched, from the fire escape of our East Harlem tenement, the walls of an old and massive building, far, far away and set on a hill, and with green vines running up and down the walls, and with windows flashing like signals in the sunlight, I watched that building, I say, with a child's helpless and stricken attention, waiting for my brother to come out of there. (p. 8)

The windows become a beacon of the bond between the two brothers, and the hilly setting emphasizes the distance between them. The sentence conveys the notion that the child Leo is just as imprisoned as is his brother Caleb.

We can see some conscious differences when we consider a descriptive sentence from *If Beale Street Could Talk*. The language operates upon a single level, with Tish stating explicitly the secondary meaning instead of leaving that to be inferred by the reader.

> Her hair is turning gray, but only way down on the nape of her neck, in what her generation called the "kitchen," and in the very center of her head—so she's gray, visibly, only if she bows her head or turns her back, and God knows she doesn't often do either. (p. 33)

For sheer number of words, Tish's description of her mother's hair is an unusually long sentence for *If Beale Street Could Talk*, which is not the case with the sentences quoted from *Tell Me How Long the Train's Been Gone* and *Go Tell It on the Mountain*. Tish usually narrates in spurts of choppy sentences or choppy phrases within longer sentences. Although she and Leo Proudhammer relate experiences from about the same ages in their lives, Tish's narration is always simpler. Yet the simplicity is not merely a matter of typography; her language is consciously less metaphorical than narrators in other Baldwin works, and her diction is less abstract. Her images are invariably concrete (going to the Tombs is like crossing the Sahara, Fonny's face looks as though it is plunging into water, a piano player's hands are beating the brains out of a piano, tears are like orgasms, skin is like raw, wet potato rinds), and she works to make concrete those that are abstract by nature:

> Being in trouble can have a funny effect on the mind. I don't know if I can explain this. You go through some days and you seem to be hearing people and you seem to be talking to them and you seem to be doing your work, or, at least, your work gets done; but you haven't seen or heard a soul and if someone asked you what you have done that day you'd have to think awhile before you could answer. But, at the same time, and even on the self-same day—and this is what is hard to explain—you see people like you never saw them before. They shine as bright as a razor. (pp. 8-9)

Like narrators before her, however, Tish is very critical in unveiling the "shit" of the political and legal system in America.[19]

Tish is also far more conscious of audience than the previous narrators (as Hall Montana will be in *Just Above My Head*). It is important to her that the audience know and sympathize with her social situation and use it in evaluating or responding to the legal hassles she and Fonny are having. She is careful to reveal information for its strategic advantage. She begins her narration with a visit to Fonny in jail, remarking by the way: "I hope that nobody has ever had to look at anybody they love through glass" (p. 4), a comment deliberately meant for us as readers. A few lines later, she gets more familiar by saying, "You see: I know him." Then she announces her pregnancy to Fonny, then she tells us they are not married, *then* she tells us their ages. The effect is sympathy, first of all, for separated lovers, then especially for expectant parents who are separated. When we discover that the child is illegitimate, and that the parents are little more than children, our sympathy is total. It will be many, many pages before we know why Fonny is in jail, but we *feel* at this point that whatever the reason is, it is unjust. As Tish rides home on the bus, she continues the sympathetic second-person references and draws them out to a dramatic appeal: "—Can you imagine what anybody on this bus would say to me if they knew, from my mouth, that I love somebody in jail? . . . Can you imagine what anybody on this bus would say? What would *you* say?" (p. 9). We would say that there is something inherently wrong with a system that creates such suffering and that causes so much pain between lovers, for, after all, *we* believe in love.

I contend that Baldwin allows Tish's femininity to make the public appeal for sympathy. Who could possibly blame this hurt young woman for bringing all her defenses to bear in helping her lover? It is like crying when all else fails; it is a permissible action for women, but not for men. It can be argued that there is an implied male audience that Tish appeals to for approval (the "you" of the narration), one that will identify with Fonny's plight *as male*. In this sense, the narrative voice itself is subservient as it appeals to the implied audience, and that subservience is grounded in femininity. Even when Hall cries out almost as loudly in *Just Above My Head*, and at times even louder, the effect is not the same. His is the inconsolable pain of one brother crying out for the loss of another in that age-old respectable union of male/male liaisons; Tish's cry is the potentially consolable lament of the individual who has been wronged and believes that wrong can and should be righted.

Tish is a new breed of narrator for Baldwin, one who can relate complex emotions and issues in the simple style that is designed to reflect her age and her predicament as well as her educational level. She is intelligent, analytical, and politically cognizant of events happening around her. Although Tish can deal with complex issues, she does not have the complex voice that is often the case with Hall Montana and some of the other Baldwin narrators; consequently, the characters she presents are idealized and one-dimensional. For her portraits of the female characters, this means that the types that lead from Elizabeth and Deborah continue through Sharon Rivers and Ernestine (they will culminate in the presentation of Ruth and Mama Montana in *Just Above My Head*). Tish's narration, even when she assumes an omniscient stance, falls short of allowing Sharon or Mrs. Hunt or any of the other women to wrestle with the kinds of questions that consumed Elizabeth. There is no other side to Mrs. Hunt, no mechanism to allow us to see if she really feels differently about her church activities than the scenes in which we find her would suggest. There is no other side to Sharon Rivers, no reflection to detract from the idealized portrait we get of her as a committed, sensitive, caring mother. With the narration in her hands, Tish keeps complexity out of the family situation and locates it in the legal and social system that is presented as the enemy of all the idealized characters who are revealed to us; it is evil, and the family, with the exception of Mrs. Hunt and her daughters, is good. A similar dichotomy is set up in *Go Tell It on the Mountain* between the saved and the sinners, but there Baldwin manages to give much more depth and substance to the either/or situation; in *If Beale Street Could Talk*, substance and shades of gray give way to celebration of goodness and its possible triumph over the forces of evil. In some ways, a fairy tale of hope has replaced a genuine effort to live in this world as realistically as possible, though certainly the issues being confronted are real ones.

The unusual features in Tish's narration do not point to a similar unusualness in her character. In her relationship to Fonny, she is a very traditional black woman character. Her raison d'être comes from her man; she is very little without him. Her attitudes toward sex, the baby, and general male/female relationships have been shaped by Fonny. It is Fonny who makes the story what it is; Tish is only as alive, as suffering, as in pain as Fonny's predicament demands that she be. From their very earliest encounters, Tish's reality is shaped by Fonny's reality.

In fighting for Fonny, in making his pain our pain, his reality our reality, Tish's role resembles the one Ida plays for Rufus in *Another Country*. Without her need to avenge Rufus' death, Ida would have a far less complex reason for appearing in *Another Country*. Without Fonny and his predicament, there would not be a story to relate in *If Beale Street Could Talk*. In this comparative sense, therefore, *If Beale Street Could Talk* is just as male oriented as *Another Country* is. Somewhat surprisingly, Tish's growth is not as measurable as Ida's, nor is there ever the final separation of the male and female psyches in *If Beale Street Could Talk* that is implied in *Another Country.* Tish and Fonny are one; or rather, Fonny is the center of the circle and Tish revolves around him.

From the time they had a childhood fight and made up, they had been the Romeo and Juliet of the neighborhood, a little island of caring and concern against the uncaring streets in which they had met. They had known, Tish maintains, long before they had any knowledge of or sexual interest in each other, that they would always be together. Their togetherness means, though, that Fonny is primary and Tish is secondary; and she willingly accepts that state of affairs. It means that Fonny's evaluation of Tish *as woman* takes precedence over her own thoughts. In fact, she almost always agrees with Fonny.

Initially, Tish accepts Fonny's evaluation that she is not very pretty. About herself, she says: "Well, I'm dark and my hair is just plain hair and there is nothing very outstanding about me and not even Fonny bothers to pretend I'm pretty, he just says that pretty girls are a terrible drag" (p. 22). She excuses Fonny's judgment by saying that he is really thinking of his mother when he makes the comment about her. Intended to show a preference based on substance rather than superficiality, the comment simultaneously conveys a chauvinism that Fonny retains on other occasions. When Daniel, an old friend of Fonny, visits the couple in Fonny's rented room, Fonny teasingly remarks: "Tish ain't very good looking, but she can sure get the pots together" (p. 129), and Tish is happy that she and her man are together and all is right with the world. And indeed there is no reason for complaint built into her character; as far as we know, she has no ambition beyond being wife to Fonny and mother to his children. She works at a perfume counter in a department store, and no mention is ever made of her wanting to go to school or otherwise change her status. While comments like Fonny's can be used to suggest that the relationship between Fonny and Tish is grounded in reality, they nevertheless suggest that

that reality must judge itself by something external to it. How can someone be considered *not* pretty unless there is a standard of prettiness against which she is being judged? What Tish fails to see in herself, in her voluntary blindness, she can comment on much more analytically in another context. Of her mother, she says: "I think she's a beautiful woman. She may not be beautiful to look at—whatever the fuck *that* means, in this kingdom of the blind" (p. 33), yet she refuses to lift her own blinders when Fonny makes such references to her.

In addition, this woman who is able to relate her story with perception, humor, and imagination accepts Fonny's evaluation that she is not very bright. In explaining to Daniel why he would like to escape with Tish from New York, Fonny says that he is "scared of what might happen to both of us—without each other. Like Tish ain't got no sense at all, man—she trusts everybody. She walk down the street, swinging that little behind of hers, and she's *surprised*, man, when some cat tries to jump her. She don't see what I see" (p. 125). Later, when Tish finds herself in a situation where Fonny's evaluation seems accurate, she says: "Fonny is right about me when he says I'm not very bright" (p. 167). She has just been approached by the young hoodlum who is ultimately responsible for Fonny's trouble with Bell. She had felt a hand on her hip and thought it was Fonny until it dawned on her "that Fonny would never, never touch" her that way in public. Fonny returns, beats the guy up, and is almost arrested by Bell. The cop must relent when the shopowner testifies on Fonny's behalf, and thwarting of Bell's power causes him to stalk Fonny until he gets him in jail. And Tish partly blames her lack of gray matter in bringing about the whole situation.

In the priorities in Fonny's life, Tish fits into a comfortable second place position. She does not have to worry about competition from other women, but Fonny's art is first in his life. On the night he and Tish first make love and when he pledges his commitment to her, he explains his position:

"I live with wood and stone. I got stone in the basement and I'm working up here all the time and I'm looking for a loft where I can really work. So, all I'm trying to tell you, Tish, is I ain't offering you much. I ain't got no money and I work at odd jobs—just for bread, because I ain't about to go for none of their jive-ass okey-doke—and that means that you going to have to work, too, and when you come home most likely I'll just grunt and keep on with my chisels and shit and maybe sometimes you'll think I don't even know you're there. But don't ever think that, ever. You're with one all the time, all the time, without you I don't know if I could make it at all, baby, and when I put down the chisel, I'll always come to you. I'll always come to you. I need you. I love you. . . . Is that all right, Tish?" (pp. 95-96)

And Tish responds, "Of course it's all right with me." Later, when Fonny is talking with Daniel, he emphasizes the same point: "I got two things in my life, man—I got my wood and stone and I got Tish. If I lose them, I'm lost" (p. 125). Again, the wood and stone come first, and Tish accepts the order of things, the place and worth that Fonny has assigned to her; that role is the source of her fulfillment and underscores Tish's urgency in getting Fonny out of jail.

Tish believes that things happen between men and men, as between Frank and Fonny, Joseph and Frank, Joseph and Fonny, and Fonny and Daniel, that can never happen between women. At those times, such as the morning Fonny asks Joseph for his daughter's hand in marriage, women should recede into the background; they should simply trust their men to make everything turn out all right. Women, Tish says, "must watch and guide," but men "must lead" and they "will always appear to be giving far more of [their] real attention to [their] comrades" (pp. 72-73) than they give to women. Woman must trust that her place is secure.

The religion of love that Fonny and Tish create depends upon Fonny being in the role of Lord and Master. He guides Tish through sexual initiation, and he is responsible for the change she undergoes, the religious conversion in the creation of their love religion. He initiates the action, calms her fears, baptizes her, and brings her forth anew. He is her Lord, and he calls her by the thunder of the sexual explosion they create. Henceforth, she is his. A song they laughingly sing with Daniel is revealing in its content:

> When he takes me in his arms,
> The world is bright, all right.
> What's the difference if I say
> I'll go away
> When I know I'll come back
> On my knees someday
> For, whatever my man is
> I am his,
> Forevermore!
>
> (p. 129)

Being his forevermore means accepting what he has to offer, a relevant context in which to place Tish's pregnancy. She views the conception of the baby as the giving of a portion of Fonny's life to her, a sacred trust comparable to that of God and the Virgin Mary. Tish says: "And when he started to pull out, I would not let him, I held on to him as tightly as I could, crying and moaning and shaking with him, and felt life, life, his life, inundating me, entrusting itself to me" (p. 177). She is sure that this is the moment the baby was conceived, the giving of the trust she also accepts. The many scenes in which Sharon, Joseph, and Ernestine admonish Tish to get the baby here safe and sound are symbolic reminders to save Fonny's life from Bell and others in the legal system who would kill him by turning him into a bowing and scraping "nigger." The time Tish spends waiting for the baby to be born, especially near the end of the novel, is intricately intertwined with the time Fonny has spent in jail. The baby waits to be born; Fonny waits to be released. Both lives must be saved.

Tish's position in relation to Fonny represents the position of all the women in the novel in relation to all the men. No woman in the novel is complete without the intellectual or emotional support of a man or a male figure, on either a real level or a symbolic one. Tish is essentially an appendage to Fonny and to Baldwin's notions of masculine superiority. Whether it is a matter of judging beauty or being guided through daily life, Tish believes she cannot function without Fonny.[20] For Sharon, Joseph is the Lord and Master. His approval of Tish's pregnancy makes everything all right, just as his approval of the marriage proposal has done earlier. The women may make up their minds before he does, but his stamp of approval is needed before they can experience true peace of mind. For all her independence and going off from Birmingham to Albany, Sharon's life is only stabilized and she finds purpose only after she meets Joseph. Never once does she find reason for complaint against him, and never once does she disagree with a decision he makes. Remember, too, she admonishes Tish to save the baby for Fonny, for what it will mean to him; she does not mention what it will mean to Tish.

Mrs. Hunt is as much an appendage to her masculine God as Sharon and Tish are to the men in their lives. God is suitor and Mrs. Hunt sacrifices all for Him, even her son. Frank expresses this view of his wife's perverted relationship with God in the scene in the Rivers home. He threatens to blow off some heads if his son is not soon out of jail, then says to his wife: "And if you say a word to me about that Jesus you been making it with all these years, I'll blow your head off first. You was making it with that white Jew bastard when you should have been with your son" (p. 81). Ernestine has also referred to Mrs. Hunt as a "half-white bride of Christ" (p. 91). By submitting herself totally to a spiritual master, Mrs. Hunt has deprived her family of maternal affection. In the physical realm, however, especially the sexual, Frank is her lord. She calls on the Lord during the sexual encounter Fonny describes and Frank assumes that role for her by saying things such as "I'm the Lord," "The Lord's going to help you, sugar," and "You got the Lord now, right here" (pp. 19, 20). Frank is her sexual master in an ugly context just as powerfully as Fonny is Tish's sexual master in what to her is a beautiful one.

Even Ernestine, in her aggressive, streetwise independence, must seek masculine advice and help in getting Fonny out of jail. She must defer to Hayward's skills in spite of her gathering information about Bell's prejudiced policing habits (no one would think of getting a female lawyer for Fonny). Though Ernestine anticipates Julia Miller in that she remains without a lover at the conclusion of the novel, she is not as healthy as that absence would suggest in a schema of progression. She spends her time serving and helping others instead of focusing on her own future; she has almost become asexual, which makes the absence of male lovers in her life less significant than it seems initially (and she still serves Fonny). Finally, Adrienne and Sheila have little identity beyond looking for light-complexioned black men to rescue them from the sordid future lives they envision in Harlem. Without their male rescuers, the sisters are in "terrible trouble" (p. 45), so they take out their frustration and anger on their "nappy-headed" brother.

More is seen of women in active, decisive positions in *If Beale Street Could Talk*, and certainly Tish's role as narrator is a new departure. Those who are active are clear in their denial of any church influence over their actions. Their characters are consistently free of the guilt earlier black women would have felt for their actions. The only possible feelings of guilt Tish or Sharon or Ernestine could have can only result from failure in their attempts to get Fonny out of jail, and even if that possibility should develop, it would not have a church-based morality as its source. Though free of guilt, the women are not free of the basic position of woman in Baldwin's works as inferior to and in need of man. Though most are free of the masculine God, they are ultimately not truly free of domination, because their happiness and fulfillment are tied to their lives with male figures. It is a limitation in their conception that they seek for no more and ask no questions about the way things are. Good they do and good feelings they inspire are short-circuited by the fact that they have never heard of freedom from men and never desired to know of it.

Notes

1. James Baldwin, *The Fire Next Time* (New York: Dell, 1963), pp. 57-58. Further references to this source will be parenthesized in the text.

2. William Edward Farrison, "If Baldwin's Train Has Not Gone," in Therman B. O'Daniel, *James Baldwin: A Critical Evaluation* (Washington, D.C.: Howard Univ. Press, 1977), p. 79. Farrison's comment must be put in the context of his general approach to Baldwin in the article; he is offended by Baldwin's "greatly overworked four-letter words" and by the "plethora" of sexual acts in which a novel like *Tell Me How Long the Train's Been Gone* "needlessly abounds." Farrison superimposes a rather straitlaced morality onto Baldwin's novels and sees *If Beale Street Could Talk* not as a culmination of the writer's talent to that point, but as a diminution. John W. Aldridge, "The Fire Next Time?" *Saturday Review/World* (June 1974): 25; John McCluskey, essay review of *If Beale Street Could Talk* in *Black World* (December 1974): 51-52, 88-91.

3. Perhaps the most serious and detailed treatment of women in a Baldwin novel is that offered by Hortense Spillers on *If Beale Street Could Talk*. See "The Politics of Intimacy," in *Sturdy Black Bridges*, ed. Roseann P. Bell, Bettye J. Parker, and Beverly Guy-Sheftall (Garden City, N.Y.: Doubleday, 1979), pp. 87-106.

4. Baldwin apparently had firsthand knowledge of this kind of parental separation. One of his friends recalled Baldwin's mother addressing his father, David Baldwin, as *Mr.* Baldwin; Fern Marja Eckman, *The Furious Passage of James Baldwin* (New York: Evans, 1966) p. 72. Mrs. Hunt and David Baldwin have in common the religious fanaticism that separates them from their offspring.

5. James Baldwin, *If Beale Street Could Talk* (New York: Signet, 1975), p. 26. Further references to this source will be parenthesized in the text.

6. Trudier Harris, "The Eye as Weapon in *If Beale Street Could Talk*," *MELUS* 5 (Fall 1978): 54-66 refers to the act as a form of religion.

7. Donald B. Gibson, *The Politics of Literary Expression: A Study of Major Black Writers* (Westport, Conn.: Greenwood Press, 1981), p. 120.

8. James Baldwin, *Go Tell It on the Mountain* (Knopf, 1953; rpt. New York: Dell, 1974), p. 121. Leo Proudhammer, in *Tell Me How Long the Train's Been Gone* (Dial Press, 1968; rpt. New York: Dell, 1970), says that "the theater began in the church," p. 323. Further references to this source will be parenthesized in the text.

9. James Baldwin, *The Devil Finds Work* (New York: Dial, 1970), p. 29. Eckman quotes Baldwin as saying: "Being in the pulpit was like being in the theater. . . . I was

behind the scenes and knew how the illusion worked" (pp. 72-73). Baldwin also refers to his role in the church as a "gimmick" and to the church business as a "racket"; see *The Fire Next Time* (New York: Dial, 1963), pp. 38, 44.

10. Critics who suggest that Frank commits suicide because he is despondent over the loss of his job fail to consider the negative effect of his wife and daughters upon his mental attitude. (Frank has been fired for stealing items to sell to help meet Fonny's bail.) Since they are so unconcerned about Fonny, Frank realizes that losing his job possibly means that Fonny will remain in jail. The lost job is therefore the catalyst to suicide, not the cause. Fonny has emphasized that Frank stayed with Mrs. Hunt only because of him; when it seems to Frank that his one reason for staying will be forever out of his reach, he kills himself. McCluskey calls Frank's suicide "one of the least convincing acts of the entire novel," asserting that it goes against the optimistic current. *Black World*: 89.

11. Perhaps the relationship between the parent and the child works so well because the offspring are female, not male. The counterpart in the idealized male parent/male offspring relationship is suggested in Frank and Fonny, but the focus of the novel does not provide for much concentration on them as parent and child.

12. Craig Werner provides interesting commentary on the economics at work in the novel. He sees it in part as a culmination of Baldwin's attitude toward the society in which black people constantly come in in second place. Baldwin offers in *If Beale Street Could Talk*, Craig Werner suggests, a "concrete tactical suggestion" for those who are economically deprived; "the oppressed" should "*use* the system whenever possible, play on its built-in weaknesses," as Joseph and Frank obviously do. Werner, "The Economic Evolution of James Baldwin," *College Language Association Journal* 23 (September 1979): 27.

13. The impending birth is considered to be the most important issue here. It ties to Baldwin's belief about saving the children and to the Mary, Joseph, Jesus analogy that permeates the story. See Louis H. Pratt, *James Baldwin* (Boston: Twayne, 1978), pp. 28-29.

14. The sacrament here ties in with the imagery of a holy conception between Fonny and Tish, with Joseph, like the biblical Joseph, serving as surrogate father to the child in the absence of Fonny, its real, holy father.

15. Aldridge, pp. 24-25.

16. Baldwin discusses this connection between blacks, Puerto Ricans, and other minorities in *No Name in the Street* (New York: Dial, 1972), p. 149. Remember, it was a little Puerto Rican girl who sparked Ernestine's commitment, and it is Puerto Ricans Tish imagines being in the same predicament as Fonny.

17. Carolyn Wedin Sylvander, *James Baldwin* (New York: Ungar, 1980), p. 84.

18. Pratt discusses in detail Baldwin's conflict with the Black Aesthetic nationalist critics such as Amiri Baraka and Eldridge Cleaver. They insisted, in the 1960s, that Baldwin hated himself and other blacks. The excessively positive images of the prominent black characters in *If Beale Street Could Talk* could be in part a bowing to that criticism; see pp. 23-27, 125-129. It could also be a result of the extended conversation on black men and women that Baldwin had with Nikki Giovanni in November of 1971; see James Baldwin and Nikki Giovanni, *A Dialogue* (London: Michael Joseph, 1975).

19. Tish as narrator is one of the things John McCluskey finds attractive about the novel; he likes "the simplicity and authenticity of the voice" but recognizes "it cracks on occasion." See McCluskey's essay review of the novel in *Black World* 24 (December 1974): 90.

20. Most importantly, she is the *body* through which Fonny's baby will be brought into the world.

The Fire Last Time

Henry Louis Gates, Jr.

"I am *not* in paradise," James Baldwin assured readers of the *Black Scholar* in 1973. "It rains down here too." Maybe it did. But it seemed like paradise to me. In 1973 I was 22 years old, an eager young black American journalist doing a story for *Time*, visiting Baldwin at his home just outside the tiny, ancient walled village of St. Paul de Vence, nestled in the alpine foothills that rise from the Mediterranean Sea. The air carried the smells of wild thyme and pine and centuries-old olive trees. The light of the region, prized by painters and vacationers, at once intensifies and subdues the colors, so that the terra-cotta tile roofs of the buildings are by turns rosy pink, rust brown, or deep red.

Baldwin's house was situated among shoulder-high rosemary hedges, grape arbors, acres of peach and almond orchards, and fields of wild asparagus and strawberries; it had been built in the eighteenth century and retained its frescoed walls and rough-hewn beams. And yet he seemed to have made of it his own Greenwich Village café. Always there were guests, an entourage of friends and hangers-on, and always there was drinking and conviviality. The grape arbors sheltered tables, and it was under one such grape arbor, at one of the long harvest tables, that we dined. The line from the old gospel song, a line that Baldwin had quoted toward the end of his then latest novel, suggested itself: "I'm going to feast at the welcome table." And we did—Baldwin, and Josephine Baker, well into her 60s but still with a lean dancer's body and the smooth skin that the French called "café-au-lait," and Cecil Brown, author of *The Life and Lovers of Mister Jiveass Nigger* and one of the great hopes of black fiction, my fiancée, Sharon Adams, and I.

At that long welcome table under the arbor, the wine flowed, food was served and taken away, and Baldwin and Baker traded stories, gossiped about everyone they knew and many people they didn't know, and remembered their lives. They had both been hurt and disillusioned by the United States and had chosen to live in France. They never forgot or forgave. At the table that long, warm night they recollected the events that led to their decisions to leave their country of birth, and the consequences of those decisions: the difficulty of living away from home and family, of always feeling apart in their chosen homes; the pleasure of choosing a new life, the possibilities of the untried. A sense of nostalgia pervaded the evening. For all their misgivings, they shared a sense, curiously, of being on the winning side of history.

People said Baldwin was ugly; he himself said so. But he was not ugly to me. There are faces that we cannot see simply as faces because they are so familiar, so iconic, and his face was one of them. And as I sat there, in a growing haze of awe and alcohol, studying his lined visage, I realized that neither the Baldwin I was meeting—mischievous, alert, funny—nor the Baldwin I might come to know could ever mean as much to me as James Baldwin, my own personal oracle, the gimlet-eyed figure who stared at me out of a fuzzy dust jacket photograph when I was 14. For that was when I first met Baldwin, and discovered that black people, too, wrote books.

It was the summer of 1965, and I was attending an Episcopal church camp in eastern West Virginia, high in the Allegheny Mountains. This was no ordinary church camp. Our themes that year were "Is God dead?" and "Can you love two people at once?" (Episcopalians were never ones to let grass grow under their feet.) After a solid week of complete isolation, a delivery man, bringing milk and bread to the camp, told the head counselor that "all hell had broken loose in Los Angeles," and that the "colored people had gone crazy." Then he handed him a Sunday paper, screaming the news that Negroes were rioting in some place called Watts. I, for one, was bewildered. I didn't understand what a riot was. Were colored people being killed by white people, or were they killing white people? Watching myself being watched by all of the white campers—there were only three black kids among the hundreds of campers—I experienced that strange combination of power and powerlessness that you feel when the actions of another black person affect your own life, simply because both of you are black.

Sensing my mixture of pride and discomfiture, an Episcopal priest from New England handed me a book. *Notes of a Native Son*, it was called. Was this man the author, I wondered to myself, this man with a closely cropped "natural," brown skin, splayed nostrils, and wide lips, so very Negro, so comfortable to be so? This was the first time I had heard a voice capturing the terrible exhilaration and anxiety of being a person of African descent in this country. From the book's first few sentences, I was caught up thoroughly in the sensibility of another person, a black person. Coming from a tiny and segregated black community in a white village, I knew that "black culture" had a texture, a logic, of its own, *and* that it was inextricable from "white" culture. That was the paradox that Baldwin identified and negotiated, and that is why I say his prose shaped my identity as an Afro-American, as much by the questions he raised as by the answers he provided.

I could not put the book down. I raced through it, then others, filling my commonplace book with his marvelously long sentences that bristled with commas and qualifications. The biblical cadences spoke to me with a special immediacy, for I, too, was to be a minister, having been "saved" in a small evangelical church at the age of 12. (From this fate the Episcopalians—and also Baldwin—diverted me.) Eventually I began to imitate Baldwin's style of writing, using dependent clauses whenever and wherever I could. Consider a passage from *Nobody Knows My Name*:

> And a really cohesive society, one of the attributes, perhaps, of what is taken to be a "healthy" culture, has, generally, and I suspect, necessarily, a much lower level of tolerance for the maverick, the dissenter, the man who steals the fire, than have societies in which, the common ground of belief having all but vanished, each man, in awful and brutal isolation, is for himself, to flower or to perish.

There are sixteen commas in that sentence. And so in my essays at school I was busy trying to cram as many commas into my sentences as I could, until my high school English teacher forbade me.

Of course, I was not alone in my enthrallment. When Baldwin wrote *The Fire Next Time* in 1963, he was exalted as *the* voice of black America; and it was not long before he was spoken of as a contender for the Nobel Prize. ("Opportunity and duty are sometimes born together," he wrote later.) Perhaps not since Booker T. Washington had one man been taken to embody the voice of "the Negro." By the early '60s his authority seemed nearly unchallengeable. What did the Negro want? Ask James Baldwin.

The puzzle was that his arguments, richly nuanced and self-consciously ambivalent, were far too complex to serve straightforwardly political ends. Thus he would argue in *Notes of a Native Son* that

> the question of color, especially in this country, operates to hide the graver question of the self. That is precisely why what we like to call "the Negro problem" is so tenacious in American life, and so dangerous. But my own experience proves to me that the connection between American whites and blacks is far deeper and more passionate than any of us like to think. . . . The questions which one asks oneself begin, at last, to illuminate the world, and become one's key to the experience of others. One can only face in others what one can face in oneself. On this confrontation depends the measure of our wisdom and compassion. This energy is all that one finds in the rubble of vanished civilizations, and the only hope for ours.

One does not read such a passage without a double take. By proclaiming that the color question conceals the graver questions of the self, Baldwin leads you to expect a transcendence of the contingencies of race, in the name of a deeper artistic or psychological truth. But instead, with an abrupt swerve, he returns you precisely to those questions:

> In America, the color of my skin had stood between myself and me; in Europe, that barrier was down. Nothing is more desirable than to be released from an affliction, but nothing is more frightening than to be divested of a crutch. It turned out that the question of who I was was not solved because I had removed myself from the social forces which menaced me—anyway, these forces had become interior, and I had dragged them across the ocean with me. The question of who I was had at last become a personal question, and the answer was to be found in me.
>
> I think there is always something frightening about this realization. I know it frightened me.

Again, these words are easily misread. For Baldwin was proposing not that politics is merely a projection of private neuroses, but that our private neuroses are shaped by quite public ones. The retreat to subjectivity, the "graver questions of the self," would lead not to an escape from the "racial drama," but—and this was the alarming prospect that Baldwin wanted to announce—a rediscovery of it.

That traditional liberal dream of a non-racial self, unconstrained by epidermal contingencies, was hopefully entertained and at last, for him, reluctantly dismissed. "There are," he observed,

> few things on earth more attractive than the idea of the unspeakable liberty which is allowed the unredeemed. When, beneath the black mask, a human being begins to make himself felt one cannot escape a certain awful wonder as to what kind of human being it is. What one's imagination makes of other people is dictated, of course, by the laws of one's own personality and it is one of the ironies of black-white relations that, by means of what the white man imagines the black man to be, the black man is enabled to know who the white man is.

This is not a call for "racial understanding." On the contrary, we understand each other all too well, for we have invented one another, derived our identities from the ghostly projections of our alter egos. If

Baldwin had a central political argument, it was that the destinies of black America and white were profoundly and irreversibly intertwined. Each created the other, each defined itself in relation to the other, each could destroy the other.

For Baldwin, America's "interracial drama" had "not only created a new black man, it has created a new white man, too." In that sense, he could argue, "The history of the American Negro problem is not merely shameful, it is also something of an achievement. For even when the worst has been said, it must also be added that the perpetual challenge posed by this problem was always, somehow, perpetually met." These were not words to speed along a cause. They certainly did not mesh with the rhetoric of self-affirmation that liberation movements, including those masquerading as a newly "Afrocentric" science of man, require. Yet couldn't his sense of the vagaries of identity serve the ends of a still broader, braver politics?

As an intellectual, Baldwin was at his best when he explored his own equivocal sympathies and clashing allegiances. He was here to "bear witness," he insisted, not to be a spokesman. And he was right to insist on the distinction. But who had time for such niceties? The spokesman role was assigned him inevitably. The result was to complicate further his curious position as an Afro-American intellectual. In those days, on the populist left, the favored model of the oppositional spokesman was what Gramsci called the "organic intellectual," who participated in, and was part of, the community, which he would not only analyze but also uplift. And yet Baldwin's basic conception of himself was formed by the older but still well-entrenched ideal of the alienated artist or intellectual, whose advanced sensibility entailed his estrangement from the very people he would represent.

Baldwin could dramatize the tension between these two models, especially in his fiction, but he was never to resolve it. A spokesman must have a firm grasp on his role and an unambiguous message to articulate. Baldwin had neither, and when this was discovered a few short years later, he was relieved of his duties, summarily retired, shunted aside as an elder statesman. Indeed, by the time I met him, on that magical afternoon in St. Paul de Vence, he had become (as my own editor subsequently admonished me) passé. Anyone who was aware of the ferment in black America was familiar with the attacks. And nothing ages a young Turk faster than still younger Turks; the cruel irony was that Baldwin may never have fully recovered from this demotion from a status that he had always disavowed.

If Baldwin had once served as a shadow delegate for black America in the congress of culture, his term had expired. Soldiers, not delegates, were what was wanted these days. "Pulling rank," Eldridge Cleaver wrote in his essay on Baldwin, "is a very dangerous business, especially when the troops have mutinied and the basis of one's authority, or rank, is devoid of that interdictive power and has become suspect." He found in Baldwin's work "the most grueling, agonizing, total hatred of the blacks, particularly of himself, and the most shameful, fanatical, fawning, sycophantic love of the whites that one can find in any black American writer of note in our time." According to Amiri Baraka, the new star of the Black Arts Movement, Baldwin was "Joan of Arc of the cocktail party." His "spavined whine and plea" was "sickening beyond belief." In the eyes of the young Ishmael Reed, he was "a hustler who comes on like Job."

Cleaver attacked Baldwin on more than racial grounds. For the heated new apostle of black machismo, Baldwin's sexuality, that is, his homosexuality, also represented treason: "Many Negro homosexuals, acquiescing in this racial death-wish, are outraged because in their sickness they are unable to have a baby by a white man." Baldwin was thus engaged in "a despicable underground guerrilla war, waged on paper, against black masculinity." Young militants referred to Baldwin, unsmilingly, as Martin Luther Queen. Baldwin, of course, was hardly a stranger to the sexual battlefield. "On every street corner," Baldwin would later recall of his early days in the Village, "I was called a faggot." What was different this time was a newly sexualized black nationalism that could stigmatize homosexuality as a capitulation to alien white norms, and in that way accredit homophobia as a progressive political act.

A new generation, so it seemed, was determined to define itself by everything Baldwin was not. By the late '60s Baldwin-bashing was almost a rite of initiation. And yet Baldwin would not return fire, at least not in public. He responded with a pose of wounded passivity. And then, with a kind of capitulation: the shift of political climate forced him to simplify his rhetoric or risk internal exile.

As his old admirers recognized, Baldwin was now chasing, with unseemly alacrity, after a new vanguard, one that esteemed rage, not compassion, as our noblest emotion. "It is not necessary for a black man to hate a white man, or to have particular feelings about him at all, in order to realize that he must kill him," he wrote in *No Name in the Street*, a book he began in 1967 but did not publish until 1972. "Yes, we have come, or are coming, to this, and there is no point in flinching before the prospect of this exceedingly cool species of fratricide." That same year he told *The New York Times* of his belated realization that "our destinies are in our hands, black hands, and no one else's."

It is a stirring sentiment—and a sentiment that the earlier Baldwin would have been the first to see through. How far he had come from the author of *The Fire Next Time*, who had forecast the rise of black power and yet was certain that

> we, the black and the white, deeply need each other here if we are really to become a nation—if we are really, that is, to achieve our identity, our maturity, as men and women. To create one nation has proved to be a hideously difficult task: there is certainly no need now to create two, one black and one white.

All such qualms were irrelevant now. In an offhanded but calculated manner, Baldwin affected to dismiss his earlier positions: "I was, in some way, in those years, without entirely realizing it, the Great Black Hope of the Great White Father." If there was something ominous about this public display of self-criticism, it was because we could not forget that the forced recantation had no value that does not purport to be freely given.

In an impossible gambit, the author of *No Name in the Street* sought to reclaim his lost authority by signaling his willingness to be instructed by those who had inherited it. Contradicting his own greatest achievements, he feebly borrowed the populist slogans of the day, and returned them with the beautiful Baldwinian polish. "The powerless, by definition, can never be 'racists,'" he writes, "for they can never make the world pay for what they feel or fear except by the suicidal endeavor that makes them fanatics or revolutionaries, or both; whereas those in power can be urbane and charming and invite you to those houses which they know you will never own." This view—that blacks cannot be racist—is today a familiar one, a platitude of much of the contemporary debate. The key phrase, of course, is "by definition." For this is not only, or even largely, an empirical claim. It is a rhetorical and psychological move, an unfortunate but unsurprising attempt by the victim to forever exempt himself from guilt.

The term "racism" is here redefined by Baldwin, as it has been redefined by certain prominent Afro-American artists and intellectuals today, to refer to a reified system of power relations, to a social order in which one race is essentially and forever subordinated to another. (A parallel move is common in much feminist theory, where "patriarchy"—naming a social order to which Man and Woman have a fixed and opposed relation—contrasts with "sexism," which characterizes the particular acts of particular people.) To be sure, it does express, in an abstract and extreme manner, a widely accepted truth: that the asymmetries of power mean that not all racial insult is equal. (Not even a Florida jury is much concerned when a black captive calls his arresting officer a "cracker.") Still, it represents a grave political error.

For black America needs allies more than it needs absolution. And the slogan—a definition masquerading as an idea—would all too quickly serve as a blanket amnesty for our own dankest suspicions and bigotries. It is a slogan that Baldwin once would have debunked with his devastating mock-detachment. He would have repudiated it not for the sake of white America—for white America, he would have argued, the display of black prejudice could only provide a reassuring confirmation of its own—but for the sake of black America. The Baldwin who knew that the fates of black and white America were one also knew that if racism was to be deplored, it was to be deplored *tout court*, without exemption clauses for the oppressed.

Wasn't it this conviction, above all, that explained Baldwin's own repudiation of Malcolm X? I should be clear. His reverence for Malcolm was real, but it was posthumous. In a conversation with Kenneth Clark recorded in 1963, a year and a half before Malcolm's assassination, Baldwin ventured that by preaching black supremacy, "what [Malcolm] does is destroy a truth and invent a myth." Compared with King's appeal, he said, Malcolm's appeal was

> much more sinister because it is much more effective. It is much more effective, because it is, after all, comparatively easy to invest a population with false morale by giving them a false sense of superiority, and it will always break down in a crisis. That is the history of Europe simply—it's one of the reasons that we are in this terrible place.

Still, he cautioned, the country "shouldn't be worried about the Muslim movement, that's not the problem. The problem is to eliminate the conditions which breed the Muslim movement." (Five years later, under contract with Columbia Pictures, Baldwin began the task of adapting Malcolm to the screen.)

That ethnic scapegoating was an unaffordable luxury, moreover, had been another of Baldwin's own lessons. "Georgia has the Negro," he once pithily wrote, slicing through the thickets of rationalization, "and Harlem has the Jew." We have grimly seen where the failure of this more truthful vision has led: to the surreal spectacle of urban activists who would rather picket Korean grocery stores than crack houses, on the assumption that sullen shopkeepers with their pricey tomatoes, and not smiley drug dealers with their discount glass vials, are the true threat to black dignity.

As I say, by 1973 the times had changed; and they have stayed changed. That, I suppose, is our problem. But Baldwin wanted to change with them. That was his problem. And so we lost his skepticism, his critical independence. Baldwin's belated public response to Cleaver's charges was heartbreaking, and all too symptomatic. Now he would turn the other cheek and insist, in *No Name in the Street*, that he actually admired Cleaver's book. Cleaver's attack on him was explained away as a regrettable if naive misunderstanding: the revolutionary had simply been misled by Baldwin's public reputation. Beyond that, he wrote,

> I also felt that I was confused in his mind with the unutterable debasement of the male—with all those faggots, punks, and sissies, the sight and sound of whom, in prison, must have made him vomit more than once. Well, I certainly hope I know more about myself, and the intention of my work than that, but I *am* an odd quantity. So is Eldridge, so are we all. It is a pity that we won't, probably, ever have the time to attempt to define once more the relationship of the odd and disreputable artist to odd and disreputable revolutionary. . . . And I think we need each other, and have much to learn from each other, and, more than ever, now.

It was an exercise in perverse and willed magnanimity, and it was meant, no doubt, to suggest unruffled strength. Instead it showed weakness, the ill-disguised appeasement of the creature whose day had come and gone.

Did Baldwin know what was happening to him? His essays give no clue; increasingly they came to represent his official voice. But his fiction became the refuge of his growing self-doubts. In 1968 he published *Tell Me How Long the Train's Been Gone*. Formally speaking, it was his least successful work, but in its protagonist, Leo Proudhammer, Baldwin created a perfectly Baldwinian alter ego, a celebrated black artist who, in diction that matched the eloquence of Baldwin's essays, could express the quandaries that came increasingly to trouble his creator. "The day came," he reflects at one point, "when I wished to break my silence and found that I could not speak: the actor could no longer be distinguished from his role." Thus did Baldwin, our elder statesman, who knew better than anyone how a mask could deform the face beneath, chafe beneath his own.

Called to speak before a civil rights rally. Proudhammer ruminates on the contradictions of his position:

> I did not want others to endure my estrangement, that was why I was on the platform; yet was it not, at the least, paradoxical that it was only my estrangement which had placed me there? . . . It was our privilege, to say nothing of our hope, to attempt to make the world a human dwelling place for us all; and yet—yet—was it not possible that the mighty gentlemen, my honorable and invaluable confreres, by being unable to imagine such a journey as my own, were leaving something of the utmost importance out of their aspirations?

These are not unpolitical reflections, but they are not the reflections of a politician. Contrast LeRoi Jones's unflappable conviction, in an essay called "Reflections of Two Hotshots" published in 1963, that "a writer must have a point of view, or he cannot be a good writer. He must be standing somewhere in the world, or else he is not one of *us*, and his commentary then is of little value." It was a carefully aimed arrow, and it would pierce Baldwin's heart.

The threat of being deemed obsolete, or "not one of *us*," is a fearful thing. *Tell Me How Long* depicts a black artist's growing sense that (in a recurrent phrase) he no longer belongs to himself, that his public role may have depleted the rest of him. Of course, "the burden of representation," as Baldwin once called it, is a common affliction in Afro-American literature, an unfair condition of hardship that black writers frequently face; but few black writers have measured its costs—the price of this particular ticket to ride—as trenchantly as Baldwin. He risked the fate, and in some ways finally succumbed to the fate, that Leo Proudhammer most feared, which was to be "a Jeremiah without convictions."

Desperate to be "one of us," to be loved by his own, Baldwin allowed himself to mouth a script that was not his own. The connoisseur of complexity tried his hand at being an ideologue. To be sure, he could still do anything he wanted with the English essay. The problem was that he no longer knew quite what he wanted, and he cared too much about what others wanted from him. For a generation had arrived that didn't want anything from him—except, perhaps, that he lie down and die. And this, too, has been a consistent dynamic of race and representation in Afro-America. If someone has anointed a black intellectual, be assured that someone else is busily constructing his tumbril.

We stayed in touch, on and off, through the intervening years, often dining at the Ginger Man when he was in New York. Sometimes he would introduce me to his current lover, or speak of his upcoming projects. I did not return to St. Paul de Vence until shortly after his death four-and-a-half years ago at the age of 63. This time I came to meet his brother David. The place had changed remarkably in the twenty or so years since Baldwin settled there. The grape arbors are now strung with electric lights. Luxury homes dot the landscape on quarter-acre plots, and in the midst of this congestion stands Baldwin's ten-acre oasis, the only undivided farm acreage left in St. Paul.

When I recounted for David Baldwin the circumstances of my meeting his brother for the first time, his wide eyes grew wider. He rose from the table, went downstairs into the study—where a wall of works by and about Henry James faces you as you enter—and emerged with a manuscript in hand. "This is for you," he said. He handed me a play. It was the last work that James Baldwin completed as he suffered through his final illness, and it was called "The Welcome Table." It was set in the Riviera, at a house much like his own, and among the principal characters were "Edith, an actress-singer/star: Creole, from New Orleans," "Daniel, ex-Black Panther, fledgling playwright" with more than a passing resemblance to Cecil Brown, and "Peter Davis, Black American journalist." Peter Davis—who has come to interview a famous star, and whose prodding questions lead to the play's revelations—was, I should say, a far better and more aggressive interviewer than I was; Baldwin, being Baldwin, had transmuted the occasion into a searching drama of revelation and crisis.

Narratives of decline have the appeal of simplicity, but Baldwin's career will not fit that mold. "Unless a writer is extremely old when he dies, in which case he has probably become a neglected institution, his death must always seem untimely," he wrote in 1961, giving us fair warning. "This is because a real writer is always shifting and changing and searching." Reading his late essays, I would like to imagine him embarking on a period of intellectual resurgence. Despite the unfortunate pronouncements of his later years, I believe that he was finding his course again, and exploring the instability of all the categories that divide us. As he wrote in "Here Be Monsters," an essay published two years before his death, and with which he chose to conclude *The Price of the Ticket*, his collected nonfiction: "Each of us, helplessly and forever, contains the other—male in female, female in male, white in black, and black in white. We are part of each other. Many of my countrymen appear to find this fact exceedingly inconvenient and even unfair, and so, very often, do I. But none of us can do anything about it." We needed to hear those words two decades ago, and we especially need to hear them now.

Now we are struggling in this country to fathom the rage in Los Angeles; and slowly we are realizing how intertwined, as Baldwin insisted, are the destinies of black and white America, and how easily one can lay waste to the other in the fury of interracial fratricide. Thirty years ago, Baldwin believed that an effort by the handful of "relatively conscious" blacks and whites might be able to avert the prophecy of the old spiritual: "God gave Noah the rainbow sign, No more water, the fire next time!" The belief proved difficult to sustain. Good intentions—increasingly scarce these days—seem easily defeated by the cycles of poverty, the structural as well as the cultural determinants of urban decay, alienation, and hopelessness. Today, as black intellectuals try to sort outrage from opportunism, political protest from simple criminality, they may wonder if the sense of mutuality that Baldwin promoted can long survive, or if his "elegant despair" alone will endure.

But perhaps times are due to change again. An influential black intellectual avant-garde in Britain has resurrected Baldwin as a patron saint, and a new generation of readers has come to value just those qualities of ambivalence and equivocality, just that sense of the contingency of identity, that made him useless to the ideologues of liberation and anathema to so many black nationalists. Even Baldwin's fiercest antagonists seem now to have welcomed him back to the fold. Like everyone else, I guess, we like our heroes dead.

The Magic of James Baldwin

Darryl Pinckney

The draining away of James Baldwin's magic was a drama much discussed in the years leading up to his death in 1987 at the age of sixty-three. There had been the first act of waif in Harlem, literary vagabond in Paris, and avenging angel of the Freedom Summer, when his exalted voice captured the tension of a nation confronted by what looked like a choice between honoring and betraying its ideals of social justice. The essays, novels, and short stories had come with all the authority of purpose and brilliance of language any young writer could hope for. Then followed the last act of weary old believer riding the transcontinental winds, when the social strife to which he had committed himself as a witness seemed to frustrate his gift for describing what was going on in mad America and in his midnight self.

In the late 1960s Baldwin the panelist was roughly treated in some black militant quarters, which blotted out the occasions when he had been sharply interrogated by white commentators. Baldwin repudiated the status he worried he'd been given as the "Great Black Hope of the Great White Father," and found a way to keep on going. Seven of his twenty-two books were published between 1971 and 1976.

Baldwin minded the drama of apostolic succession others tended to cast him in. He did not consider himself written-out or irrelevant, in much the same way that Langston Hughes and then Richard Wright had felt that no one was going to sideline them before their time. However, his later essays and his last, very pro-family novels failed to convince a large part of his audience that his work still held the revelatory subtleties so long associated with his name. Because of the Pauline obstinacy with which he stuck to his subjects, these later works were unfavorably compared to the earlier ones that had made him a star.[1]

Three years ago the Modern Library brought out a new hardcover edition of *The Fire Next Time* and this bold essay which first riveted the public mind more than thirty years ago has returned, properly enshrined with much else in two Library of America editions. One volume gathers together his essays, the other his early novels and stories.

1

The Lord may not be there when you want Him, but when He gets there He's right on time, church people used to say. A sense of timely intervention surrounds the publication of Baldwin's work in such a distinguished series, because so many hundreds of his pages coming all at once urge us to concentrate our attention on what he actually wrote. Though Baldwin's books have long been in circulation, cultural memory has not been fair to his toughness. The image has grown of this improbable duckling with a swan's sensibilities persecuted by fortune's magpies. Perhaps we like our dead black heroes a little on the fabulous victim side.

Perhaps also the sheer elegance of his prose style has upstaged the fierceness of his message. Baldwin was a deeply civilized man, but he refused to become middle class, and he maintained a streetwise distrust of the poses of deracination and alienation, including his own, and of the bohemian escapes available mostly to white people and to the privileged in general. He did not subscribe to the romance of exile; he had little patience with the cries the Beats and their student admirers made about being oppressed. He was obsessed with defining freedom, but he did not present himself as a free spirit. Most of the time in his writing he tried to subdue the certainty of divine election that raged around the nation's flinty moral core.

It hardly seems possible that the voice of Baldwin's early essays has become historical, that fifty years have gone by since he first announced himself on the scene. Baldwin wrote about the racial situation in the US largely in terms of Anglo-Saxon and Afro-Saxon that William Dean Howells would have understood. But maybe one of the reasons he gets escorted down the catwalk of contemporary identity politics as a martyr to Difference is that much of what he had to say about race came in the form of autobiographical reflection. The sympathy-sucking, almighty "I" is everywhere these days.

Baldwin laced his writings with explicit warnings against the chill of self-exposure. However, it is not just because of his self-restraint that he remains a powerful tutelary presence in the uses of the first person. Though he found in his writing a permanence of self that the insecurity of his social condition could not threaten, his own experience interested him mostly for what it told him about the larger world. "The Negro in extremis," F. W. Dupee called him, pointing out that if Baldwin's skin color constituted his fate then he made of it an existentialist virtue.[2]

Baldwin said he was born with his subject matter and he meant it—but not at first. He published more than two dozen reviews and essays before his first novel, *Go Tell It on the Mountain* (1953). He counted his apprenticeship as a reviewer of books by and about blacks—being black supposedly made him an expert, he said—among the reasons he packed his bags and went to France at the age of twenty-four. The majority of the ten pieces that make up his first essay collection, *Notes of a Native Son* (1955), are also from those postwar years.

In an elliptical preface of daring assertions, Baldwin defines his relationship to his subject matter. He argues that "the Negro problem" was nearly inaccessible from any profound point of view, because it had been written about so widely and "so badly." A Negro risks becoming articulate only "to find himself . . . with nothing to be articulate about." His past led to Africa, not Europe, which meant that he, Baldwin, "a kind of bastard of the West," brought to "Shakespeare, Bach, Rembrandt, to the stones of Paris, to the cathedral at Chartres, and to the Empire State Building, a special attitude." These monuments did not contain his history; they offered him no reflection of himself. "I was an interloper." However, he had no other heritage, having been "unfitted for the jungle or the tribe." He would therefore have to "appropriate these white centuries" and accept his "special attitude."

He had hated and feared white people; had despised black people, "possibly because they failed to produce Rembrandt" and in so doing had given the world a "murderous power" over him. This "self-destroying limbo" explains, he feels, why "prose written by Negroes has been generally speaking so pallid and so harsh." He does not expect the Negro problem to be his only subject, but it was the gate he had to unlock before he could write about anything else. Meanwhile, he sees in Faulkner and in passages of Robert Penn Warren the beginnings of "something better," and, for him, Ralph Ellison is the first Negro writer to use in language "some of the ambiguity and irony of Negro life." Baldwin thus places himself on the side of serious literature, a position he elaborates on in two essays that follow.

In "Everybody's Protest Novel," he examines *Uncle Tom's Cabin* as the cornerstone of American protest fiction. Baldwin condemns Stowe's anti-slavery novel as a self-righteous "catalogue of violence." Stowe was "an impassioned pamphleteer" interested in man's relationship to God, not in relationships between humans. She could not embrace Uncle Tom without first purifying him of sin, robbing him of his humanity, and divesting him of sex. Her work is animated by a "terror of damnation."

Yet because the supposed aim of protest novels is to bring freedom to the oppressed,

> they are forgiven, on the strength of these good intentions, whatever violence they do to language, whatever excessive demands they make of credibility. . . . One is told to put first things first, the good of society coming before niceties of style or characterization. Even if this were incontestable—for what exactly is the "good" of society?—it argues an insuperable confusion, since literature and sociology are not one and the same.

The curses in Wright's *Native Son* as an answer to the exhortations in *Uncle Tom's Cabin*, Baldwin says, are a continuation of the impossible heritage of the Negro in America, that "country devoted to the death of the paradox." Bigger Thomas's sulfurous hate makes him submissive Uncle Tom's descendant.

In "Many Thousands Gone" Baldwin again turns an unforgiving eye on *Native Son*. He describes how its mere publication in 1940 was written about as a triumph for American democracy, even though it was really just "one of the last of those angry productions" of the 1920s and 1930s. Baldwin contends that Wright assumed a false responsibility when he allowed himself to be cast as the representative of black people. But in recording his rage "as no Negro before him had ever done," Wright captured the fearful image white people have in mind when they speak of the Negro.

Baldwin's main objection to *Native Son* is that Wright attempted to redeem a monster on social grounds. Bigger's force comes from his being "an incarnation of a myth." The novel reflects, but does not interpret,

> the isolation of the Negro within his own group and the resulting fury of impatient scorn. It is this which creates its climate of anarchy and unmotivated and unapprehended disaster; and it is this climate, common to most Negro protest novels, which has led us all to believe that in Negro life there exists no tradition, no field of manners, no possibility of ritual or intercourse, such as may, for example, sustain the Jew even after he has left his father's house. But the fact is not that the Negro has no tradition but that there has as yet arrived no sensibility sufficiently profound and tough to make this tradition articulate.

Bigger, meanwhile, satisfies the national taste for the sensational. He may through his crimes oblige people to see the results of oppression, but white people don't really fear someone like him so much as they do ordinary Negroes who give no cause for complaint. Bigger remains a monster and this, Baldwin argues, supports the notion that Negro life is indeed "as debased and impoverished as our theology claims" and leads back to the assumption that to become truly human the black man "must first become like us."

Stowe's novel about a slave whose passivity made him a better

Christian than whites and Wright's work about a black boy whose environment made him reject his family and commit murder dealt with the most familiar parts of Baldwin's heritage that he was trying to get away from: his church upbringing and his Harlem background. But it is also clear from the popular fiction with which he equates protest novels—*Little Women*, the novels of James M. Cain—that his reservations about *Uncle Tom's Cabin* and *Native Son* as famous examples of a category of American literature to which he as a black writer was expected to contribute stem from his doubt that such books could earn lasting prestige as art. Protest fiction was just another ghetto, a proletarian literature in blackface. These essays are a declaration of Baldwin's critical independence, as well as of his physical distance.

Baldwin did not come from a literary movement or from the uptown leftist groups of his generation such as the Committee for Negroes in the Arts and the Harlem Writers' Club. Though Baldwin found downtown Trotskyite periodicals open to him in his early days, he came of age in an era when psychoanalysis was replacing Marxism in New York intellectual life. Through his writing he acted out an exploration of consciousness, beginning with the question of who is speaking to or for whom when James Baldwin talks about race.

> Our dehumanization of the Negro then is indivisible from our dehumanization of ourselves: the loss of our own identity is the price we pay for our annulment of his.

Baldwin does this everywhere in *Notes of a Native Son*. If such a passage were to read "Your dehumanization of us," "Your dehumanization of the Negro," or "White people's dehumanization of the Negro people," then its tone would be immediately accusatory. As it is, he disarms the defensiveness whites then had when talking to blacks about the racial situation. He is not speaking as a white, but he imposes a communal identity on whites which, as Murray Kempton noted, was alien to their speech at the time, but not to that of blacks. As a rhetorical refinement the plural lends his voice a jurist's or referee's impartiality. It is the American in him speaking, his projection of the American conscience. The ambiguity of point of view could be taken as a restatement of the historical problem of the dual consciousness of blacks. Whether or not this American had to be not-Negro was the question Baldwin asked of a dichotomy between race and citizenship that seemed fixed.

Stowe and Wright provide the only literary occasions in *Notes of a Native Son*. Three essays are accounts of American locations, Harlem and the South, places just the mention of which conjures up the subject of race. "The Harlem Ghetto" presents a congested, dispirited urban landscape unchanged since Baldwin's childhood, except for the added insult of housing projects. He judges the Negro leader to be in a hopeless situation and observes that the Negro press is so narrow because it is a faithful imitation of mainstream tabloids. Baldwin's Harlem is completely empty of the glamorous elements of its past, but the churches remain, as does the Harlem resident's ambivalence toward Jewish people as the identifiable shop owners, landlords, foreigners, and white people among them. "Georgia has the Negro and Harlem has the Jew."

The trip Baldwin describes in "Journey to Atlanta" was made by his brother as a member of a Harlem gospel group contracted to entertain at rallies for Henry Wallace's campaign for president in 1948. Baldwin uses his brother's report to argue that blacks are pawns in the electoral process, regardless of political party. He is proud that blacks have low expectations of politicians, because the cynicism makes the ghetto doctrine, that of not being taken in, look like political sophistication after all.

These two essays sketch some of the reasons for his not wanting to be in the US. The title essay comes like a last look back. In "Notes of a Native Son" Baldwin remembers his embittered storefront preacher father who had been suspicious of his son's bookish inclinations. On the summer day in 1943 when Baldwin's father died, his father's last child was born. Not long before there had been a bloody riot in Detroit. After his father's funeral, held on the day that was also Baldwin's nineteenth birthday, a race riot broke out in Harlem. From this convergence of public and private upheaval, Baldwin weaves an extraordinary tale of captivity and flight. The journey out of Egypt was his great theme.

Baldwin had been away from home for a year discovering in the defense plants, bars, and restaurants of New Jersey "the weight of white people in the world." One scene of his trying to get served nearly ended in mob violence. He saw that his life was in danger, as much from what he carried in his own heart as from what other people might do. He returned to Harlem to wait for his father's death. All of Harlem seemed to be "infected by waiting," "violently still." The racial tension of the war years had churchly women and prostitutes together on the stoops, united by their distrust of policemen "on horseback, on corners, everywhere, always two by two." A rumor ignited the rage—"I had declined to believe in that apocalypse which had been central to my father's vision"—and after the night of rioting, Baldwin, passing looted shops on his way to the cemetery, and looking at the avenues strewn with everything from cornflakes to beer, was left with an "impression of waste" as difficult to face as the lessons of his father's burdened life.

> It began to seem that one would have to hold in the mind forever two ideas which seemed to be in opposition. The first idea was acceptance, the acceptance, totally without rancor, of life as it is, and men as they are: in the light of this idea, it goes without saying that injustice is a commonplace. But this did not mean that one could be complacent, for the second idea was of equal power: that one must never, in one's own life, accept these injustices as commonplace but must fight them with all one's strength. This fight begins, however, in the heart and it now had been laid to my charge to keep my own heart free of hatred and despair. This intimation made my heart heavy and, now that my father was irrecoverable, I wished that he had been beside me so that I could have searched his face for the answers which only the future would give me now.

This is very moving, transparent, and real. The riot may not have crossed beyond ghetto lines, but Baldwin makes something transcendent of the emotions behind it. The elevated language throughout the essay concentrates on the dignity at stake in the lives of the people he was writing about. "Choose you this day whom you will serve," his father's favorite biblical text went. Baldwin places his heightened voice in the service of people who had reason to think of themselves as unheard. The lyricism of his despair doesn't condescend to them or exploit them, because the expressiveness of their church is his, his claustrophobia of spirit is theirs. But at the same time he tells a story of belonging and not belonging, of rejection and coming back, but not staying. Even as he honors his subject he claims something back for himself, just by having such a defiantly lucid style at his command.

In the remaining essays of *Notes of a Native Son*, Baldwin's reflections on race come from observing a different society and himself in it. He describes the relation of American Negroes to Africans in Paris; his wrongful arrest for theft and his brief Christmas imprisonment in a Paris jail; and what went unspoken between himself and the residents of a Swiss village because of their perception of him as a black man and the corrective feelings he both did and did not want to have in response. These essays are faultlessly rendered, as if to prove his point that individual experience is the only real concern of the artist. The entire book is also a sort of hymn to the divided consciousness, and to the consolation he found in being able to talk about the social prison he had escaped. In Baldwin's determination not to be what whites thought he should be or what his background predicted he would be, in his will to become a writer, there was always the atmosphere that he had committed an act of civil disobedience.

2

Nobody Knows My Name (1961) came out five years after *Giovanni's Room*—a novel that was controversial not only because it concerns a love affair between two men but also because all of its characters are white—and just before *Another Country*, the book that was to make him a best-selling novelist. He characterizes this second collection as "a private logbook," because questions of color hid graver questions about the self. But the book is also intended to have the front-line quality of his return to the US to see the growing protest movement there for himself. Baldwin says the essays were written in a period when he realized that his first youth and exile were both coming to an end.

The "complex fate" of being an American, he declares, freed him of the illusion that he hated America. In a report from the historic 1956 Paris Congress of Negro-African Writers and Artists, a conference of black intellectuals from Africa, Europe, the Caribbean, and the US, organized by the Negritude journal *Présence Africaine*,[3] Baldwin argues that, however limited their possibilities, blacks in the US were not as interested in overthrowing oppressors as they were in getting the existing machinery to work for them. The US State Department had refused Du Bois a passport to attend the conference; nevertheless the US was "home" to millions of blacks who could be considered "the connecting link between Africa and the West."

Baldwin displays some unease with the ideas put forward by the elders of Negritude, Alioune Diop, Aimé Cesaire, and Leopold Senghor. He understands the post-Bandung Conference solemnity among delegates as owing to their common political subjugation to Europe and to "the European vision of the world." However, he is not convinced that alternative cultural perspectives can really be what they claim, because the histories of colonial peoples can't be eradicated. Since the literature of American Negroes is written in a language from Europe, Baldwin doubts Senghor's claim that literature by American Negroes has recognizable African sources. When Senghor finds traces of an African heritage in the writings of Wright that Wright himself was unaware of, perhaps, Baldwin says, he robs Wright of the individualism he had won for himself as a writer who had survived the American South.

The desire to diminish the importance of European culture by reconstructing a lost African past is just as restrictive of black artists and intellectuals, Baldwin feels. His intellectual tradition and temperament led him to question rather than to commune with social symbols. Senghor's society "did not seem to need the lonely activity of the singular intelligence." Nor is a cohesive society necessarily tolerant of the dissenter. Men like Senghor and Cesaire were themselves products of the collision of cultures and thus already stood outside the cohesive society whose culture they both lament and champion.

This essay, as the first formal encounter in Baldwin's writing with what would now be called the debate over Eurocentrism, would, like so much else of his early work, one day come back to haunt him. At the time it reflected the tensions among black intellectuals in their exile and the consequences for them of political ferment back home. In Baldwin's view, US society was something new, still in formation, and therefore salvageable. The intimation that blacks and whites in the US weren't isolated and that Europe and Africa are not abstract places carries over into the next two essays, in which Baldwin's intense gaze once again takes in New York and Harlem. But the main point of *Nobody Knows My Name* comes from Baldwin's first trips to that seemingly cut-off place, the South.

The idea of "the Old Country" had always frightened him, Baldwin says, but the poet Sterling Brown, identified in "A Fly in Buttermilk" as "an older Negro friend" in Washington, reminds Baldwin that he, Baldwin, is only one generation away from the South. He would discover that what had been to him books, headlines, and music could be a real part of his heritage, his identity. He shields those he spoke to, because their views could put them in danger, or because he didn't want to embarrass them. A black educator seizes on the facts that Baldwin had never been to college and couldn't drive a car. Baldwin suspects that the man is defensive about being a Southern Negro because of his anxiety that change might threaten his place in the segregated school system. The future down South, Baldwin says, is like heaven: everyone talks about it but no one wants to go there just yet.

However, at least one student in the vanguard of integration at a white high school could look forward. He tells Baldwin that his old school symbolized a "dead end" for black teachers as much as it represented the grim future that black students faced. Of his former classmates, several girls had left school because they were pregnant and just days before Baldwin arrived eighteen boys were taken away to the chain gang. The bewildered young white principal of the youth's new high school assures Baldwin that he has a job to do, though he never dreamed of "a mingling of the races" and has no reason to think black schools aren't as good as white ones. Baldwin reflects that segregation has worked so well it has allowed white people "to *create*, in every generation, only the Negro they wished to see."

In the title essay, originally published in 1959, Baldwin, as a Northern Negro in the South, sees that his ancestry is both black and white, a closeness he thinks may explain why whites hate blacks. Integration had worked well after the sun went down, Baldwin is told. The South's official segregation differed little from unofficial segregation in the North, except in its baffling etiquette. After visiting Charlotte, North Carolina, and Atlanta, Georgia, Baldwin suspects that the argument over whether black children had the right or capacity to learn in white schools was "criminally frivolous," given the country's general lack of respect for intellectual life. The hidden dispute was about power and sex, and Baldwin predicts a stiffening of the already "implacable Negro resistance."

Baldwin watches black men on the streets, on buses, trying to imagine what he would be like had his family never left the South. A guilty feeling that the boycotts and test cases have been for his sake and for that of every Negro in the North awakens in him a need to bestow as much moral advantage as possible on the Negroes going into what he saw as the field of battle. The old black men whom white Southerners love dislike even well-meaning paternalism because they do not want to depend on others. "Men do not like to be protected, it emasculates them." Black men have always known this while white men have denied it, which Baldwin says gave rise to a "dreadful paradox": "The black men were stronger than the white. I do not know how they did it, but it certainly has something to do with that as yet unwritten history of the Negro woman."

Black people in the South were experiencing the 1950s as a period of impending turbulence. But Baldwin was just passing through. Too much was happening and the reasons for it went back too far for Baldwin's quick intelligence to do more than survey a surface that only suggested the depths. The South would always have a more convincing presence in his work as a metaphor than as a region he could make a pilgrimage to. His real and troubling roots were elsewhere—uptown, in Harlem, in the dreams he had sitting on a windowsill reading Dickens.

Much of Baldwin's regretful tone and his effectiveness as an emerging spokesman—a term he disliked—came from what he presented as his bewilderment that whites apparently had never seriously considered what the race problem had done to themselves. Baldwin was restating an argument that went back to the days when abolitionists cautioned slaveholders about their eternal souls. But also important to the persuasiveness of his social views, to his imagination, to his insistence that change in racial attitudes be included among signs of progress, were the years he lived in Europe when Germany had officially repented and set out to reconstruct itself as a society. The New Deal and the Marshall Plan told blacks how fast social remedies could be deployed when there was enough political will.

The second part of *Nobody Knows My Name* contains a portrait of Norman Mailer, who in *Advertisements for Myself* calls Baldwin's prose "perfumed," "too charming to be major," suggesting that Baldwin hadn't his own street credibility. Baldwin is sympathetic in reply and, because of his fine Negro manners, he turns in a performance of behaving better than the other person. But he slyly breaches good manners by repeating in print what others have said about Mailer, such as, according to Baldwin, the jazz musicians whom Mailer thought he was so down with. They didn't think him hip. They said he was "sweet."

Time has obscured what Mailer and Baldwin once had in common. Mailer's essay "The White Negro" is a protest against the threat of mass destruction during the early part of the cold war. It was absurd, the feeling went, to behave as though life were normal or society rational when human beings faced daily the potential for total extinction. Some white writers, Mailer among them, allied themselves with blacks in calling for society to recreate itself, for people to cultivate values that went beyond the concerns of middle-class comfort. Mailer felt a connection with black men as US society's genuine dissenters.[4]

Nobody Knows My Name, which became something of a best seller, also includes Baldwin's memoir, "Alas, Poor Richard." Written after Wright's death in 1960, it is treated by Baldwin's biographers as being eerily foreshadowing, as though he had predicted his own fate in his worry that he might become as isolated and uncertain in exile as Wright, his early mentor, had seemed to him. Wright's hurt reaction to Baldwin's criticisms of *Native Son* surprised him, Baldwin says, but he admits to something resembling symbolic patricide. In retrospect Baldwin praises Wright's work for its dry, savage folkloric humor and for how deeply it conveys what life was like on Chicago's South Side. The climate that had once made Wright's work read like a racial manifesto had gone. Baldwin found when reading Wright again that he did not think of the 1930s or even of Negroes, because Wright's characters and situations had universal meanings. Wright was not, finally, the polemical writer "he took himself to be." Yet Baldwin still minded the "gratuitous" violence in Wright's work, seeing it as the consequence of the internal censorship of black writers, which put violence in the place where sex ought to have been.

Nevertheless, Wright, snubbed in the Paris cafés by American Negroes and Africans who had once been his friends, wandering "in no-man's land between white and black," became, Baldwin says, an object lesson for him in the hazards of expatriation. He was suspicious of Wright's friendships with Sartre and de Beauvoir, and doubted that Wright's new friends in his "adopted country" could appreciate him, the mischievous, cunning "Mississippi pickaninny." Wright paid for his illusion of safety by renouncing the sources of his inspiration and giving up his knowledge of "the powers of darkness." Baldwin says he defended Wright when other blacks said Wright had severed himself from his roots, because he knew how easy it was to charge him with the same thing.

Baldwin hints that Wright's problem was with other blacks, whereas his own problem was being black in the US. But he could not have taken the view of Wright that he did were he not congratulating himself for going back to the US. Though he says that at the time of his death Wright had found himself again as a writer, he pities Wright his years of paralyzing distance from the struggle. Because of the gulf—created either by education or by the mysteries of talent—between their circumstances and those of the blacks they could be made to feel they had left behind, black writers in Baldwin's day paid a guilt tax in piety, and took loyalty oaths to the cause, pledging that they would not forget. Perhaps that is what Baldwin meant when he said that Europe had prepared him for America.

In relation to Wright, Baldwin sets himself up as a sort of patriot, rather like Larkin claiming in the early 1960s that literature had replaced life as Auden's subject, meaning that Auden's work had suffered because of expatriatism. Baldwin was also asserting his generation's immunity from what he regarded as the mistakes of its immediate predecessors. He had written mostly about race and the same "powers of darkness" he said Wright had risked losing touch with. But if Wright turned out not to be such a polemical writer, then Baldwin was no longer bound by his promise to break the confines of the protest tradition in his own work.

3

Another Country was competing with *Lord of the Flies* at the top of the paperback best-seller lists when *The Fire Next Time*, actually two essays, appeared in 1963. The main essay was originally published in *The New Yorker* as "Letter from a Region of My Mind," and was so widely discussed it became a news item, taking Baldwin's face onto the cover of *Time* magazine.

The Fire Next Time is a refutation of those articles hostile to the Nation of Islam that came out at around the same time, just as it seems to call out to Martin Luther King's lament about the cup of endurance running over in "Letter from a Birmingham Jail," also of that year. But Baldwin's language overshadows or preempts his context, which is maybe why, even today, no thought comes up when reading Baldwin of social scientists like Kenneth Clark or Erik Erikson, whose work in the same period also stressed the legacy of psychological damage handed on by racism. Every scar in Harlem seems to breathe on its own in this intense recapitulation of themes from Baldwin's earlier autobiographical writings.

> Every effort made by the child's elders to prepare him for a fate from which they cannot protect him causes him secretly, in terror, to begin to await, without knowing that he is doing so, his mysterious and inexorable punishment. He must be "good" not only in order to please his parents and not only to avoid being punished by them; behind their authority stands another, nameless and impersonal, infinitely harder to please, and bottomlessly cruel. And this filters into the child's consciousness through his parents' tone of voice as he is being exhorted, punished, or loved; in the sudden, uncontrollable note of fear in his mother's or his father's voice when he has strayed beyond some particular boundary.

In *The Fire Next Time* Baldwin explores his religious conversion at the age of fourteen and the terrified refuge he found in being a performer in the pulpit until his faith crumbled three years later, because he had been reading again, starting "fatally" with Dostoevsky, which fueled his resentment of Christian hypocrisy. As a former child preacher in Harlem, Baldwin appreciated why blacks were increasingly attracted to the Nation of Islam's creed that God was black. He understands the Black Muslims as followers drawn from a depressed population that doesn't have "the time or energy" to read, and for whom hope elsewhere has died:

> For the horrors of the American Negro's life there has been almost no language. The privacy of his experience, which is only beginning to be recognized in language, and which is dented or ignored in official or popular speech—hence the Negro idiom—lends credibility to any system that pretends to clarify it.

Baldwin recounts a visit to Elijah Muhammad's strange Chicago mansion headquarters, where he sees Muhammad's appeal as a father figure, but remains ruefully skeptical. The Muslim movement was a dream of power, offering an invented past. African-Americans had no future anywhere without a real past.

Consequently, white Americans were themselves deluded if they supposed Negroes expected anyone to "give" them anything. When whites held out the possibility that Negroes could become their equals, Baldwin was reminded of North Africans in 1956 asking if the French were ready to be civilized. At bottom, he says, the Negro problem was really the white man's wish not to be judged by people who aren't white, the desire to be released from "the tyranny of the mirror."

Baldwin's "I" summons "them," white Americans; "him," the Negro; and "one," the Negro observing whites; but the voice that once searched for "our" America is absent. His "we" doesn't appear when talking about the US; only when speaking of humanity in general, of creatures cringing before God. In taking up truth's cause, Baldwin had chosen sides. *The Fire Next Time* derives its force from precisely the same "theological terror" he had previously criticized Harriet Beecher Stowe for. It also contains a dilemma that Baldwin, the apostle of paradox, was ill prepared to meet. It sounds like a paradox for him to warn that blacks were of two minds about being integrated into a burning house. But it also seems a paradox for him to think that his influence—the power of a minority to threaten a majority with moral collapse—depended on how much that majority cared about its moral vocabulary as well as his.

4

Baldwin became more of a spokesman than Wright had ever been, partly because his moment coincided with the age of television. He was soon under FBI surveillance, just as Wright had been, but Wright was never invited to advise the US attorney general, as Baldwin was to be. In "The Dangerous Road Before Martin Luther King," an essay Baldwin wrote after he traveled with the civil rights leader in 1961, he admires King as the first black leader who said to whites what he said to Negroes and vice versa.

In Baldwin's view, King was different from but not entirely free of what he calls the official black leadership, whose members he assumed came from "the most unlucky bourgeoisie in the world's entire history." They were trapped "between black humiliation and white power" and were more loyal to their class than to the black masses they supposedly represented. Baldwin sees a gap between this official leadership and the young, "who have begun nothing less than a moral revolution." Because of King's middle-class background Baldwin wonders if King, whom he first met in 1958, can meet the expectations blacks have of visionary leaders while also resisting the pressures white people in power put on an official black leadership schooled in the politics of concession.

Baldwin was a luminous presence on the literary scene, but to key figures in mainstream civil rights organizations he was not altogether respectable. Adam Clayton Powell forced King to drop Bayard Rustin from the SCLC because he considered Rustin's sexuality a liability.[5] King maintained a certain distance from Baldwin for the same reason. Though part of the celebrity contingent of the March on Washington, with Marlon Brando's arm around him, Baldwin had not been asked to speak.

After reading *The Fire Next Time*, Hannah Arendt warned him that in politics love was a stranger. In any case, love began to play less of a part in his rhetoric. He was more attuned to the confrontational mood of the country. In *Nothing Personal* (1964) he noted that many people in Texas were passing out handbills accusing President Kennedy of treason. Perhaps this was his way of showing that there was something behind Malcolm X's infamous remark about Kennedy's murder being a case of the chickens coming home to roost.

Baldwin liked Malcolm X right away, because he knew all about the sad correlation in a black urban youth's experience between a life of petty crime and a life as one of the saved.[6] He respected his mocking attitude and retaliatory incisiveness about white power. While not relinquishing King's ideal of racial justice as a path toward national redemption, Baldwin agreed with Malcolm X that the history of racism in the US had to be acknowledged before any meaningful change could take place. Malcolm X, on the other hand, chafing under the Nation of Islam's restrictions on his political activities, said while traveling in Africa that he wanted a "real" revolution, not the "pseudo revolt" of people like James Baldwin.

It was a time when every day seemed loaded with tragic turning points. Baldwin was often on hand, speaking, observing. He spoke at a Manhattan rally to protest the deaths of four black children in a church bombing in Birmingham, Alabama.[7] The racial struggle had spread from the South, where Baldwin was an outsider, to the North and his native ground of tenements and garbage dumps. He was still able to find that American "we" in his velvet sack of rhetorical devices. In "The American Dream and the American Negro," Baldwin's contribution to a debate with William F. Buckley, Jr., at Cambridge University in 1965, he warns that there is little hope that "we, the Americans," accept that his ancestors are both black and white, and that black people are just like everybody else.

The darkening of the civil rights struggle coincided with a fall in Baldwin's overall critical fortunes. A terribly earnest play, *Blues for Mr. Charlie*, opened on Broadway in 1964 to mixed reviews. Then his collection of short stories, *Going to Meet the Man* (1965), failed to win the acclaim that had greeted his previous works of fiction. Because some critics at the time wondered if Baldwin hadn't gone anti-white, later on he would too easily say that he lost favor with white critics because his message had become difficult for them to accept.

When he dealt with concrete issues, he was unanswerable. In an article published in 1966, "A Report from Occupied Territory," Baldwin is chilling about the "arrogant autonomy" of the police, the part they played in the Harlem riot of 1964 and in the murder charges brought against the Harlem Six, the black men arrested for defending themselves. He calls his report a "plea for the recognition of our common humanity," but hints that although "we" in Harlem weren't so much at the mercy of cops and landlords anymore, patient explanation and background-seeking calls from officials in Washington when the weather began to warm up belonged to the power relationships of the past. As the Sixties intensified, Baldwin published few essays, many of them immediate reactions to events or the texts of speeches, nothing like his considered essays.

The era of praying with your feet, as the saying went, was drawing to a close, and something in Baldwin's tone was beginning to change as well. He stopped trying to answer the question whites frequently asked of blacks during this volatile period: What does the Negro want? Instead, his mission was to hold up the mirror that he believed whites were fearful of. Because he was sure that whites minded being judged by nonwhites, his intention had elements of temerity and revenge. He argued that when a white person looked at a black that white person saw and then wanted to deny the bloody history reflected in the black person's skin. He often said that blacks knew more about whites than whites knew about blacks. Increasingly, whites became an abstraction in his discussions, just as the Negro habitually had been to most white observers. In any case, white, Baldwin said repeatedly, was an attitude, not a color, and black was a condition.

While Baldwin had become scornful of white liberals because, he said, they believed themselves to be already saved, he was nevertheless attacked by black militants as a beneficiary of liberalism. The rise of black consciousness led some blacks to question black writers' relation to their audience and the makeup of Baldwin's in particular. Ishmael Reed categorized Baldwin as a black writer who spoke to whites as a guide to black feeling. He wasn't really addressing blacks in his work, Reed claimed, because he was only saying what blacks already knew.[8]

In 1966, the year Stokely Carmichael cried "Black Power" on television after the attempt on James Meredith's life, Amiri Baraka reprinted in *Home: Social Essays* a vitriolic article in which he says that Baldwin's writing presents a "Joan of Arc of the cocktail party." Baraka denounces the emphasis on individual experience in Baldwin's writings as a "spavined whine and plea" that was "sickening past belief." Baraka implies that what he takes as Baldwin's conciliatory attitude toward whites wasn't that of a "real" black man anyway.[9]

Baldwin's militant black critics seemed to link what they considered his cultural elitism to the open treatment of homosexuality in his work as well as to his reputation among whites. A straight black male writer once complained that queer black male writers enjoyed an unfair social advantage because they were not a threat to straight white men in the same way that straight black men were. The history of tokenism also had something to do with the lurking resentment toward Baldwin and with the punitive feeling that he should be left to his white-created reputation, history having moved on.

Baraka confines himself to Baldwin's writing, to the persona of the essays. However, Eldridge Cleaver's first published article, which appeared in *Ramparts* in 1966 and was later reprinted in his first-person celebration of his badness, *Soul on Ice* (1968), starts off by talking about Baldwin's work, but quickly degenerates into a grisly polemic equating homosexuality in black men with what Cleaver calls "a racial death-wish."

Norman Mailer had been among the group of white editors and writers who encouraged Cleaver to write while he was serving a fourteen-year sentence in Soledad Prison for assault with intent to commit murder. In his article Cleaver says that *Another Country*, together with the "literary crime" of Baldwin's "arrogant repudiation" of "The White Negro" in *Nobody Knows My Name*, led him to revise his opinion of Baldwin, whose books he once eagerly awaited. Cleaver says that Baldwin attacked Mailer, a white opponent of white supremacy, because of Baldwin's "total hatred of blacks, particularly of himself."

Baldwin's "interpretation" of the Paris Conference of Negro-African Artists and Writers in 1956, Cleaver goes on to claim, makes his "antipathy" toward blacks "shockingly clear." Baldwin felt "revulsion" for the advocates of Negritude, who were "rejuvenating" the "shattered psyches and cultures of black people," whereas Baldwin was just defending "his first love—the white man." Cleaver says this was the reason Baldwin plunged the "blade of Brutus into the corpse of Richard Wright," a giant, rebel, and "heterosexual."

Jeremiah downtown, Job uptown, Baldwin was no more acceptable to macho Black Power advocates than he was to mainstream black leaders. He had already questioned the acceptable images of masculinity as narrow social constructions, like racial classifications. He had talked about the "American white man's lack of sexual security" and the Negro as a "phallic symbol." He claimed that when a Negro was present, white people would not talk about sex, because sex was right there, in the middle of the room, "drinking a dry martini."[10] However, blacks militarized by Vietnam taunted white authority by impugning the masculinity of white men. At a time when blacks were debating the limitations of King's nonviolence and the Negro family's "matriarchal structure," black militants were more interested in deciding who the real men were than they were in redefining that manhood.

Baldwin had written about the price black men in the South had been made to pay just for walking in a manner that suggested they had any pride. Because the negative reactions of whites to Black Power sometimes seemed like the old fear of black men, Baldwin would not criticize the militants' macho postures, especially not in the context of a society where definitions of what a man was he regarded as misguided to begin with.

Baldwin was also dismissed for not knowing enough about economic and political issues to be on speakers' platforms.[11] He'd worked with Bertrand Russell's War Crimes Tribunal, helped the NAACP in Mississippi conduct a murder inquiry, been involved with CORE, SNCC, and an organization that aided striking black longshoremen in San Francisco. But the fashion for what passed as ideological rigor and the demand that collectivism be valued over individualism made Baldwin's approach look obsolete.

5

> When more time stretches behind than stretches before one, some assessments, however reluctantly and incompletely, begin to be made. Between what one wished to become and what one *has* become there is a momentous gap, which will now never be closed. And this gap seems to operate as one's final margin, one's last opportunity, for creation. And between the self as it is and the self as one sees it, there is also a distance, even harder to gauge. Some of us are compelled, around the middle of our lives, to make a study of this baffling geography, less in the hope of conquering these distances than in the determination that the distances shall not become any greater.[12]

Up until the late Sixties Baldwin had always talked of his public commitments as being worthwhile, but not the main purpose of his life. His writing and his speaking both may have been acts of witnessing, but they were not the same, he said. He recognized how useful his participation in public events was for him as someone given to avoiding his private life, by which he meant his writing desk. A great deal of Baldwin's domestic and writing life in the 1960s took place in Istanbul, a city he stepped in and out of, like a parallel universe, but he never referred in his work to his life there. All the strangers called "Jimmy Baldwin," he once said, meaning the many roles he felt his life obliged him to play.

By the late 1960s, Baldwin was saying that he had no choice but to be a part of the civil rights struggle. He never let anyone draw him out about whether violence was ever justified, a question put with some persistence in the 1960s, as if the answer would indicate which blacks could be reasoned with. Instead, he turned such discussions back to what blacks suffered in the US, holding to his mission of showing whites what it was like to be judged by strangers, and to his gospel that the race problem was, at bottom, a moral problem for whites. I will maintain my ways before Him.

Baldwin's fame may have been enhanced by the resurgence of interest in books by blacks, but civil rights also gave him the chance to pay the "dues" he was so haunted by, to do penance for a reputation associated with his exile. He was wanted because black celebrities had become a regular part of civil rights rallies. Show business fascinated him anyway and he wrote about famous blacks in the arts as though they knew one another, because they had been through similar experiences to get where they were. He was excitedly offhand when describing how he once walked up to Sidney Poitier in an airport on his way to a "gig."[13]

When Baldwin thought about himself in relation to blacks who had not escaped the ghetto, he, for a long time, no doubt had in mind his family still in Harlem. As the eldest of nine children, he said that he couldn't change his habits of telling others what to do, no more than he could shed the "egotism" and "rigidity" of being an eldest sibling. He had felt protective toward the black youths of the early sit-ins who, in their "adolescent dark," were deciding on an undreamed-of future for themselves by facing down the law and the lawless. After the deaths of

Malcolm X and then Martin Luther King, he said more than once that Malcolm X had been like a little brother to him or that he had looked upon King as a younger brother, though they were both his age.

His expressions of solidarity may have been a kind of romantic appropriation, but when it came to dealing with the Black Panthers, whom Baldwin met in 1967, his habit of projecting an immediate kinship between himself and other people working in the movement meant something in addition to the convention of speaking of blacks as one big family. Coming across as a big brother said that his interest in them, streetwise young black men, was social, not sexual. Jean Genet could eroticize the Panthers all he wanted, because, though queer, he was white and a foreigner, an ex-convict and famous for it. But Baldwin, a black man, had to neutralize what branded him an outcast among outlaws. Also, it is difficult to patronize a youngish man who insists on declaring himself old in relation to everybody else.

Then yonder came the blues in the form of Nixon's Southern election strategy. Everything seemed to go haywire in the backlash. Between 1968 and 1970, twenty-eight Panther leaders were killed. Baldwin told interviewers that it was difficult to write between assassinations. Racism had come to occupy the place original sin had had in his Pentecostal upbringing. In a conversation taped in 1970, Margaret Mead was startled by Baldwin's remark that because he had done nothing to prevent it he was responsible for the murder of the black girls in the Alabama church in 1964.[14]

His persona had aged dramatically, though he was not yet fifty. The swiftness with which the promise of the Freedom Summers had deteriorated into seasons of riot and backlash had altered the nature of time, he said. In his mournful "An Open Letter to My Sister, Miss Angela Davis,"[15] Baldwin seizes on the hope that although he was no different from his father, taught, like him, to despise himself as a "nigger," Angela Davis was already different from her father's generation. A year later he told the poet Nikki Giovanni the "absolute reaction" of Black Power had come too late for his generation, but black children at least would no longer grow up internalizing the propaganda of race inferiority.[16]

In *No Name in the Street* (1972) Baldwin seems to study every drop of his rage at the failure of white Americans to realize the harm their power had done to others and ultimately to themselves. He writes as an anguished survivor of the 1960s, but the "self-destroying limbo" he once risked has been replaced by a need to cover up how deeply white America had hurt him by being wounding in return. He'd said before that the relationship between blacks and whites in the US was like a marriage, a way of emphasizing how tied together they were, though segregated. In this, his divorce petition, he is the abandoned spouse who insists that he'd never been taken in by the wedding vows.

In the beginning of *No Name in the Street*, Baldwin recalls that when he was to appear with King at Carnegie Hall he got fitted for a dark suit. Two weeks later, he writes, he wore the same suit to King's funeral. He remarked to a columnist that he would never be able to wear it again. A friend of Baldwin's, a US postal worker whom he rarely saw, had seen the newspaper story and, because they were the same size, asked for the suit that to Baldwin was "drenched in the blood of all the crimes of my country." Baldwin went up to Harlem in a hired "Cadillac limousine" in order to avoid the humiliation of watching taxis not stop for him, a black man. His life came into the "unspeakably respectable" apartment of his friend like "the roar of champagne and the odor of brimstone." He characterizes himself as he assumes he must have appeared to his friend's family: "an aging, lonely, sexually dubious, politically outrageous, unspeakably erratic freak."

His friend had also "made it"—holder of a civil-service job; builder of a house next to his mother's on Long Island. Baldwin was incredulous that his friend had no interest in the civil rights struggle. They got into an argument about Vietnam. Baldwin says he realized then that the suit belonged to his friend and to his friend's family. "The blood in which the fabric of that suit was stiffening was theirs," and the distance between him and them was that they did not know this.

The story is tortured and yet, regardless of Baldwin's outrage at indifference or his identification with slain civil rights leaders, there is something wrongly insinuating about his depicting his scarcely worn suit as drenched and stiffening with blood, even metaphorical blood. People still remember what Jesse Jackson's shirt looked like after King was shot.

Baldwin gives the impression in *No Name in the Street* that when first in Paris, in the late Forties, his true friends during this uncertain period had been Algerian. He says that when he returned to Paris in the summer of 1952, after having observed the "foul, ignoble time" of McCarthyism in the US, most of the Algerian cafés were closed and his Algerian friends had disappeared. After Dien Bien Phu fell the police became even more "snide and vindictive" toward nonwhites. Baldwin would have been keenly aware of the French government's hostility toward foreign residents in France who were too vocal in their support of the Algerian revolution. He once told Philip Rahv that the effects of the Algerian war made Paris seem more like home. He'd always been critical of Camus's position on Algeria in *Combat*. But either Baldwin had suppressed his closeness to Algerians, had never gotten around to writing about it before, or he was blacking up his past in order to make it more political. His early essays about his expatriate life suggest that he inhabited a Left Bank of bad hotels and hospitable cafés and that most of his friends were white. Moreover, where Baldwin once thought to "appropriate" Western cultural heritage, he now contends that "the South African coal miner" or "the Algerian mason" had "no reason to bow down before Shakespeare" and no "honorable access" to the cathedral at Chartres.

Baldwin then turns his attention to 1956 and the International Conference of Black Writers and Artists. He doesn't discuss the article he wrote about the conference that had so inflamed Cleaver, or retract what he'd said then, because he now writes as if he'd always been a pan-Africanist. Instead, he remembers that outside the Sorbonne every newspaper kiosk he saw featured the face of Dorothy Counts trying to make her way through a North Carolina mob to get to school. "Some one of us should have been there with her!" It made him furious and ashamed, he says. He knew then that he could "no longer sit around in Paris discussing the Algerian and the black American problem. Everybody else was paying their dues, and it was time I went home and paid mine."

In looking back on his tour of the South in 1957, Baldwin reveals that afterward he experienced a kind of collapse, the paralysis of "retrospective terror." He calls what he had already written about the South "more or less impersonal." For example, he left out his shock when during one meeting he was "groped by one of the most powerful men in one of the states I visited." Baldwin remembers the billboards, rotting automobiles, pint bottles, and the "strident and invincible melancholy" of the Deep South's music, but there the chronological structure of *No Name in the Street* breaks off.

In the second section of his book Baldwin returns to 1968. When King was murdered, Baldwin tells us, he was living in Hollywood, or at the Beverly Hills Hotel, or in Palm Springs, working on a screen version of *The Autobiography of Malcolm X*. He dropped everything to fly to Atlanta to squeeze into the funeral. "I had been in London when Malcolm was murdered." And he had been in Puerto Rico, he remembers, working on the last act of a play, when Medgar Evers was murdered. There was no "away," but there were plenty of places where he could go to remind himself that he felt trapped.

Interspersed with his memories of shattering long-distance bulletins are two stories that Baldwin relates to his loss of faith in the possibility of the US becoming what he would call a just society. The Malcolm X film project ended because of the conflict he felt between being a writer and being a "public witness to the situation of black people" in what he wrote. Then a casual friend was arrested in Hamburg to stand trial for murder in New York, which began the nightmare of trying to help someone with limited resources fight the machinery of the US justice system.

The experience leads Baldwin to recall campaigns in aid of the Black Panther leadership. Where he was sympathetic but probing in his analysis of the Nation of Islam in *The Fire Next Time*, he is unreservedly on the side of the Panthers in *No Name in the Street*. They would have been just another street gang, he observes, had it not been for their broad community support. They stood for the liberation of the ghetto, that "rehearsal for concentration camps," and established schools and breakfast programs. They announced themselves as a "force for the rehabilitation of the young" who were wasting away in prisons, in the army, or on drugs. The Panthers made themselves targets, Baldwin says, but armed themselves in a spirit different from that of whites who feared their neighbors. People in the ghetto loathed the police as some of the worst-trained and most poorly educated whites in US society.

Baldwin says that he responded to the Panthers as young black men who had been "singled out" for "repression" and made victims of "a reign of terror." Huey Newton, who was twenty-five years old when Baldwin met him, struck him as "old fashioned." He could almost imagine Newton one day "working quietly in a law firm" and living in the suburbs, except that something always went wrong when he tried to picture it. He hadn't read *Soul on Ice* when he met Cleaver, he says, but he was aware of a constraint between them. When he did read it, he said with a calculated mildness that he of course didn't like what Cleaver said about him, but he perhaps could understand that Cleaver felt "impelled to issue what was, in fact, a warning." Cleaver must have regarded him as of "too much use to the Establishment to be trusted by blacks." But Cleaver had used his reputation against him "naively and unjustly" and had confused him with the "unutterable debasement of the male" he must have seen in prison.[17] This and the other fragmentary reflections in the book end as bleakly as they began. In an epilogue Attica has happened, George Jackson is dead, and Angela Davis is still in jail.

Not even Baldwin could resist taking advantage of the license to lash out that black people had never had before those days of rage. Historically the limitations on what could be said publicly were as definite as any other dangerous barrier in a segregated society. Reprisals of one kind or another for going too far occur in every period of the history of blacks in the US. The mass character of the civil rights movement in the 1960s, however, provided the sense of being protected by unprecedented numbers.

Those who talk of a falling off in Baldwin's work sometimes point to *No Name in the Street.* The notion goes that because of what he had been through, he abdicated as a writer and resorted to preaching; that in the kingdom of the first person, few in American letters had so harnessed the language; but that he threw away his incantatory subtlety, gave it up from moral fatigue, or got conned out of it by the pressure black nationalism put on the idiom.

But those who interpret Baldwin's work after *The Fire Next Time* as a coming home to the folk refer to *No Name in the Street* as evidence that he had, indeed, turned a corner. As his record of the 1960s, however, *No Name in the Street* isn't any less "impersonal" than his earlier reports from the South or Harlem, though he struggled to make it otherwise. "Something has altered in me; something has gone away." He wants to make plain his rejection of those who he feels have rejected him, and his warnings, and therefore all black people. Baldwin proclaims that Western nations have been caught "in the lie of their pretended humanism," that "the white man's sun has set." But in concluding that black people would never be free in the US as it was, Baldwin tried to do more than once again threaten white people with the prospect that the nation might remain unsaved.

To turn his hurt into an asset he gave his message a last-testament mood. His argument for socialism in the final paragraphs brings to mind Du Bois's embrace of Marxism toward the end of his life, which was also his announcement that he had given up on the US. *No Name in the Street* differs from Baldwin's earlier works of nonfiction in its attempts to put the racial situation in the US in a global perspective. In the early Seventies blacks who felt powerless in the US reached out for the consolations that insurgencies abroad offered them. Baldwin seems to be saying that white people in the US would one day experience for themselves the isolation he was then feeling, given the nonwhite majority worldwide.

The Sixties never faded for Baldwin, which is perhaps why his later nonfiction is like an extended coda to what he'd already written. He maybe thought of himself as starting over when he revised his autobiography yet again in *The Devil Finds Work* (1976), in which he retells the story of his formative years through reflections on some fifty films, from Bette Davis movies to *Lady Sings the Blues*. Blacks were beginning to have an impact in Hollywood in the early 1970s and some of the first major studies of blacks in US cinema had recently come out. Some of the films that Baldwin covers evoke memories of his avid reading as a youngster—*Treasure Island*, *A Tale of Two Cities*. He is interested in film as both an archive of the country's popular attitudes and a seductive medium of more influence than books when it comes to inculcating and spreading ideas about race and national innocence.

Baldwin's new impotent aggression toward white America erupts sporadically in *The Devil Finds Work*, and he returns to his problems with the Malcolm X film project. But the book is really a work of nostalgia. He remembers people like the white schoolteacher who didn't pity him. She stubbornly faced down his father's disapproval and took her obviously gifted pupil to the theater and the movies. He counts her among the reasons he never managed to hate white people completely. He connects his sentimental education as an audience member with the problems of his developing consciousness as a black. But the film industry's distortions of history and evasion of reality are too easy a target.

"And of all this, I think to myself, will be only a page in history." The pages turned, the miscarriages of justice went by, the Harlem Six of 1964 had become the Wilmington Ten of 1977. By this time he assumed every topic had been politicized. He didn't seem to care how convenient it might be for those who were against radicalism for other reasons to be able to say that his writing went downhill when his rhetoric became conventionally radical. The time and distance necessary to distill experience had, he suggested, been taken away by the continued urgency of his times. In his late pieces his reliance on illuminating simplicities is unchanged whether his argument is going anywhere or not, but his prose can still be vivid and exciting.

From the start Baldwin's voice cast a spell because he declined overt expression of that bitterness black people can feel they have a right to. Instead, he offered the menace of forgiveness and redemption. Though he was hardly the first black writer to challenge the US with its moral rhetoric, his persona, as an astonishingly mature young writer, was that he was self-created, unique, radical in his ambivalence. His arguments from that early time are difficult to summarize, because one sentence speedily pursues the implications of the sentence before it. The velocity of his clauses is a part of their beauty. His phrases almost leap beyond their content, the arresting testimony of a skeptical young black man who has come through to tell us that all versions of the self are hopelessly, humanly provisional.

In his last years he published tellingly few essays, and these aren't so much about issues of the day as they are revisions yet again of his existing story.[18] "My diaspora continues." Somewhere Baldwin says that by the time he was seventeen everything about being black in the US had happened to him, that he hadn't needed to go through anything else to guess what lay in store for him. But the memory of having had a series of menial jobs as a black teenager is not the same as not having had one since. He didn't go on, he went back, recalling that he had hit the streets at the age of seven or that he was sixteen when a Harlem racketeer fell in love with and protected him.

The news in his late essays is in his mood of supposed candor. He is correcting, refusing to moderate his negativism about the US, and therefore neither betraying nor being betrayed anymore. It is as though he were settling accounts, criticizing, by being more damning, an earlier self for having mastered such a blameless voice. Perhaps he was being Malcolm X to his own Reverend King. But he is filling out scenes he'd already turned over to the public domain. The rest of his wilderness is hidden. Except for mention of classroom discussions when he was a visiting instructor, little of Baldwin's direct experience as a middle-aged adult figures in his nonfiction writings. His voice had two stops: the young man who thought about his forlorn early years and then the knowing man who vouched for that young man's baroque sense of grievance.

In one of his last published essays, "The Price of the Ticket," Baldwin says that in the church he came from "we" were counseled "to do our first works over," to go back and reconsider our deeds. His "we" has become "black people in this country" and his family, "living and dead." Toward the end of his life he accepted that he was often in the pulpit in his essays, as though that were—more than anyone knew—a natural place for him to speak from. "Lord, teach me to write so well that I shall no longer want to," Auden said.

Notes

1. See David Leeming, *James Baldwin: A Biography* (Henry Holt, 1994); Randall Kenan, *James Baldwin* (Chelsea House, 1994); James Campbell, *Talking at the Gates: A Life of James Baldwin* (Viking, 1991); Horace A. Porter, *Stealing the Fire: The Art and Protest of James Baldwin* (Wesleyan University Press, 1989); W. G. Weatherby, Jr. *James Baldwin:Artist on Fire* (Donald I. Fine, 1989); and Caryl Phillips, "Dinner at Jimmy's," in *The European Tribe* (Farrar, Straus and Giroux, 1987). I am grateful to Mr. Campbell and to Mr. Phillips for sharing with me their files and thoughts on Baldwin.

2. F.W. Dupee, *'King of the Cats' and Other Remarks on Writers and Writing* (Farrar, Straus and Giroux, 1965; University of Chicago Press, 1984).

3. For a description of the conference see Michel Fabre, *The Unfinished Quest of Richard Wright* (Morrow, 1973). See also Stephen Howe, *Afrocentrism: Mythical Pasts and Imagined Homes* (Verso, 1998).

4. In "My Negro Problem—and Ours" (*Commentary*, February 1963), Norman Podhoretz remembers the sort of blacks Mailer cast as natural dissenters as the "bad boys" who persecuted him when he was growing up in Brooklyn in the 1930s. Italians and Jews feared the Negro youths who embodied "the values of the street—free, independent, reckless, brave, masculine, erotic." The qualities he envied and feared in the Negro, Podhoretz says, made the Negro "faceless" to him. But he was as faceless to them, he says, as Baldwin claims blacks are to whites in general.

5. Rustin had been arrested on a morals charge in California in 1953 and the *Los Angeles Times* got hold of the story. Powell threatened that unless King broke with Rustin he would announce that King and Rustin were having a sexual relationship. Rustin was then organizing the protests at the Democratic convention in Los Angeles in 1960, and Powell didn't want Kennedy embarrassed by them. See Jervis Anderson, *Bayard Rustin: Troubles I've Seen* (HarperCollins, 1997).

6. See Kenneth B. Clark's interviews with Baldwin, Malcolm X, and Martin Luther King in *The Negro Protest* (Beacon Press, 1963).

7. Baldwin's remarks were reprinted in *Seeds of Liberation*, edited by Paul Goodman (Braziller, 1964). He starts off by reminding his audience that "we can change the country," meaning blacks and whites together. As he goes on he lectures the whites in audience, or whites in general, as in "Because I am not what you said I was." Baldwin's "I," in this case, is standing in for all other blacks.

8. See William M. Banks, *Black Intellectuals: Race and Responsibility in American Life* (Norton, 1996). Kenneth B. Clark tried to defend Baldwin, saying in *Dark Ghetto* (Harper and Row, 1965) that Baldwin was a black artist whom blacks in the ghetto identified with, because although he'd left the ghetto physically, he was still there psychologically.

9. As a student at Howard University in 1955, Baraka defended Baldwin's play, *The Amen Corner*, when not everyone at Howard wanted the university's theater department to stage it. Baraka was among the speakers at Baldwin's funeral, which suggests that his dismissal of Baldwin in the 1960s had been act of defining himself against a famous, older black writer, just as Baldwin in his youth had taken on Wright. For Baraka's eulogy see Quincy Troupe, editor, *James Baldwin: The Legacy* (Simon and Schuster, 1989).

10. In an interview with Eve Auchincloss and Nancy Lynch Handy, reprinted in Bradford Daniel, editor, *Black, White and Gray: Twenty-one Points of View on the Race Question* (Sheed and Ward, 1964).

11. See Harold Cruse, *The Crisis of the Negro Intellectual* (Morrow, 1967).

12. James Baldwin, "God's Country," *The New York Review*, March 23, 1967, p. 17.

13. "Sidney Poitier," *Look*, July 23, 1968. See also Caryl Phillips, "James Baldwin and Hollywood," *The Guardian*, January 11, 1991.

14. *Margaret Mead/James Baldwin: A Rap on Race* (Lippincott, 1971).

15. *The New York Review*, January 7, 1971, pp. 15-16.

16. *James Baldwin/Nikki Giovanni: A Dialogue* (Lippincott, 1973).

17. Leeming says that Baldwin was more cautious about his association with the Panthers than he suggests in *No Name in the Street*, particularly after gunfire broke out at a rally in LA. In his biography, Campbell notes that although Baldwin declined to be

critical of Cleaver in public, he was scathing about him in private. As late as 1984, Baldwin was telling interviewers that he spent much of the late 1960s trying to "undo the damage" Cleaver had done him among militant audiences.

18. *The Price of the Ticket: Collected Nonfiction, 1948-1985* (St. Martin's, 1985) showed where Baldwin had been and where he could yet go were it not for the "if onlys" of life. *The Evidence of Things Not Seen* (Holt, Rinehart, and Winston, 1985) bleakly affirmed the principle that writers must be allowed to make their own mistakes.

James Baldwin: The Risks of Love

Darryl Pinckney

1

James Baldwin had a way of sometimes signing off at the end of his books—"Istanbul, Dec. 10, 1961," "New York, Istanbul, San Francisco, 1965-1967," or "Oct. 12, 1973, St. Paul de Vence." Maybe the words spoke to Baldwin about the labor of composition, suggesting rooms where he'd worked, nights when he'd struggled. Think of "Dublin 1904/Trieste 1914." As a way of signing off along the road Baldwin was traveling, such markers also said something about the glamour and cosmopolitanism that being a writer had always meant to him.

Baldwin said that throughout his adolescence, hemmed in at home and hemmed in by Harlem, he'd "read books like they were some kind of weird food." But when he told Richard Wright he'd been dreaming of France since he was twelve years old, maybe he was tugging at an older person's heartstrings a little. He doesn't seem to have had any special feeling for French culture or for legends of the Lost Generation, though traces of Hemingway have been detected in his earliest stories. Similarly, Harlem Renaissance lore about Countee Cullen taking classes at the Sorbonne or Langston Hughes waiting tables in Montmartre doesn't seem to have played much part in Baldwin's dream of France either. Paris, as the capital of Baldwin's personal and literary freedom, existed in the future that Wright suddenly projected for him. He followed Wright in 1948, determined to prevent himself from "becoming *merely* a Negro; or, even, merely a Negro writer." That was the language of universalism before people accepted that black writers had been speaking it all along.

Around the time that Baldwin left Harlem's churches, New Jersey's industrial marshes, and Greenwich Village's bars for Paris, Henry James was returning to Europe in the luggage of a new generation of American expatriates. Otto Friedrich, a young recent Harvard graduate writing a novel in Paris, remembered that at Christmas in 1949 Baldwin gave him a copy of F. O. Matthiessen's edition of James's *Notebooks* inscribed with lines from *The Middle Years* that he himself had first quoted to Baldwin.[1]

Matthiessen challenged the position, made popular by Van Wyck Brooks in the Twenties, that James made a fatal mistake when he became an expatriate, because he cut himself off from his material and produced tempests in "exquisite teapots."[2] Matthiessen argued that James offered a robust examination of American values and the American character, raising themes about "the eternal outsider" and "the passionate pilgrim" that were pertinent to Baldwin. For Baldwin, James's Americans, searching for experience, transcended their backgrounds in "deep and dark" Europe.

Toward the end of his life Baldwin recalled the isolation of not knowing French his first year in Paris. He was thrown back onto his own speech, which was closer to that of Bessie Smith than it was to that of Henry James, he said.[3] But in his hunt for a model, it's not hard to see the appeal that an American martyr to sensibility would have had for Baldwin, a deracinated young black writer seeking to ally himself with an aesthetic that held the protest tradition to be confining. And yet, for all that, too much romantic emphasis can be given to James's influence on Baldwin's work.

In the beginning Baldwin set the bar very high, and maybe one of the reasons his fiction generally doesn't give off the effortless authority of his essays is that he was somewhat inhibited by how much he felt he needed to achieve as a novelist in order to consider himself validated as a writer. He came of age in the days of the quest for the Great American Novel, the definitions of which can seem old-fashioned or middlebrow in the present era. But the conventional literary novel, with its responsibility to reflect something profound about society, was Baldwin's ennobling venture, his chosen form.

As a first novel worked on and worked on, *Go Tell It on the Mountain* (1953) hung over Baldwin's head for as long as *Invisible Man*

(1952) had over Ralph Ellison's. But Baldwin was working with a third-person voice that was much less liberated than Ellison's on-the-edge first-person narrator. For Baldwin, whose fictional imagination answered to a jealous creed of being true to experience, the autobiographical elements of *Go Tell It on the Mountain* were perhaps less than a blessing for a first novelist.

Go Tell It on the Mountain is about a religious family in Harlem so clearly based on Baldwin's own that he no doubt had to think about appeasing or failing to appease the shadows of the real people that fell across his characters. By becoming a writer he meant to make the home folks proud, but grime in the remembered, then disguised, shabby living room can be wounding to a working mother and to siblings still calling that living room home. Baldwin's mother was said to have been especially worried about how her husband was depicted in her son's work. In the title essay of *Notes of A Native Son* (1955), Baldwin talks about his fraught relationship with his father, but gives no indication that Baldwin senior was not his natural father. In *Go Tell It on the Mountain*, the youthful main character is illegitimate, but hasn't been told that the father who hates him is really his stepfather.

Go Tell It on the Mountain has a self-conscious, guarded formality that Baldwin didn't need after this attempt to make peace with the ghosts in his father's house. He tells a sadistic story, but there is an underlying gentleness in his farewell to the Harlem he came from. Kindness to his own sympathy is in the exculpatory psychology and also in the tone that announces the wish to make Lenox Avenue the setting for high art, to credit people who are socially marginal with being as capable of refined inner dramas and complex feelings about the ordering principles of their lives as any bourgeois family in fiction. The careful texture of Baldwin's realism may explain why Langston Hughes concluded that Baldwin had written "a low-down story in a velvet bag." Hughes's criticism showed how little attuned to the black church the ear of the blues poet could be. Baldwin's first novel is saturated with Scripture and the rhetoric about Judgment Day as a settling of earthly accounts that still has a special meaning for black congregations.

Baldwin wanted *Go Tell It on the Mountain* to be about black people, not about the race problem. The tender age of his protagonist helps to distance his Harlem story from the protest fiction he had criticized Wright and Chester Himes for writing. The novel opens in 1935, on the fourteenth birthday of Johnny Grimes, who has been marked by his family and their Pentecostal church to be a preacher. His severe father is a deacon, a "holy handyman." Johnny faces an evening "tarry service" at the storefront church, Temple of the Fire Baptized, at which he is expected to "come through" to the Lord, to rise from "the threshing floor" as one of God's anointed. The rituals of the all-night service will signal not only Johnny's surrender to God, but also his submission to his father's authority, after which his destiny in the church will be, so he fears, "irrevocable."

Johnny's father, Gabriel, once had a mighty reputation as an evangelist, but his work on the preaching circuit has long since been curtailed by the factory job he needs to support his family. Gabriel is consumed with hatred for whites and looks forward to the day when whites will show Johnny that to them he also is just another "nigger." As interpreter of the Lord's Word, Gabriel slaps Johnny's long-suffering mother and savagely whips his rebellious, street-inclined younger brother. Johnny recognizes that his intelligence is a shield from, if not a weapon against, his father.

The question of Johnny's place in US society is off in the future, but he knows enough to have decided that he will not be like his father, "or his father's fathers." There are libraries downtown that he hasn't yet the confidence to enter, but he believes that if he can conquer the world his father has failed in, then he can put in place of the love his father denies him the approval of white people who despise black men like his father. He excels in school and has been told by white teachers that he "might become a Great Leader of His People," though he has no interest in his people or in "leading them anywhere." His father only tells him that he's "ugly" and that he has "the face of Satan."

Johnny can't reconcile his attraction to the larger world with what his family has taught him is the will of God. The path to the experiences he craves seems to lead to sin's precipice, which can mean the movies, not to mention his sexual awakening. His memories of going to church on Sunday include seeing people still in their Saturday night clothes and being curious about what the "muddy-eyed" men and harsh-voiced women did in the cathouses. The eldest of four children, Johnny has heard his parents in their bedroom "over the sound of rats' feet," and remembers the first time his mother disappeared and returned with a little stranger. A fifth child is on the way. Johnny is also preoccupied with the reason for his confusion in the presence of his new Sunday school teacher, the pastor's seventeen-year-old sinewy nephew from Georgia who has already been censured for the sin that is waiting in his flesh.

The biblical-sounding vocabulary of "lewdness" and "loins" may be corny now, in the way that sexual terminology dates faster than most other things in fiction, but it isn't coy. The attempt not to be shy about the "trembling," "moaning," and "mewing" is very much in character with the familiar-with-the-low but high-minded realism in that era of the daring but sober Problem Novel. A woman's vagina is "her secrecy," this being Baldwin, and she may find herself in the act of "uncovering some black boy's hanging curse" for the same reason.

Sin, not racism, is the subject most discussed in *Go Tell It on the Mountain*, though the novel makes it clear that the people who debate the nature of sin have frustrated and brutal lives because they are black and poor. Their fear of sin is an expression of their having internalized the social controls that afflict blacks in segregated US society, which is why the seemingly arbitrary renunciations of the "holy life" offend Johnny in a way he cannot yet articulate. Church doctrine takes over from and embellishes the larger society's rules. At the same time temptations to sin represent the limited chances blacks have to make choices as individuals. Sin presents itself to Johnny's mind as a form of human potential.

Baldwin gathers his main characters at the tarry service where Johnny is to enter into the communion of the saints. While the elders watch Johnny go into a deep trance of prayer and emotion at the altar, Baldwin interrupts the action to give chapters to Johnny's Aunt Florence, to his father, Gabriel, and then to his mother, Elizabeth. Their thoughts travel away from the church service and back to the South of the turn of the century and World War I. They remember their own journeys to the Lord and the blighted promises of their youth. They are only one generation away from slavery. Their memories show that Baldwin's Harlem of the Great Depression is still an insecure migrant community.

Baldwin had not yet visited the South when he was writing *Go Tell It on the Mountain*. Perhaps that is why this region, as Johnny's relatives remember it, is a generalized place of sketchy interiors, frosty yards, weeping gates, anonymous fields, starry nights, unspecified taverns, and roads that lead to nowhere. However, for Baldwin's purposes, in his novel he almost didn't need to have been South. The contrast with the descriptions of the everyday urban environment reinforces the message that a legacy of confinement was fading for Johnny's generation. His uptown streets are quick with sensation and possibility while the South is the landscape of the dimly remembered, although ultimately inescapable.

Memories of devastated love and transgressions yet to be atoned for make the grown-ups in Johnny's family somewhat like lifers eyeballing a short-timer on his way to his parole hearing. Even when Baldwin shows the congregation on a boat ride and at a picnic, the sanctified church is as isolated and hierarchical as a prison. But the Bible gives the generations a common language. The longings of the present and the sorrows of the past find steady distillation in the metaphors of the gospel songs, spirituals, and hymns that either come up within each chapter or stand as epigrams for chapters. Baldwin assigns his characters a sharp theological awareness and liturgical fluency. They know the Books of Deuteronomy, Luke, or Matthew as coldly as he did. Johnny himself hasn't much private language or kid slang. Instead, phrases borrowed from passionate seekers after the City on the Hill supply fuel for what the unquenchable fire of adolescence wants to say.

> And still, on the summit of that hill he paused. He remembered the people he had seen in that city, whose eyes held no love for him. And he thought of their feet so swift and brutal, and the dark gray clothes they wore, and how when they passed they did not see him, or, if they saw him, they smirked. And how their lights, unceasing, crashed on and off above him, and how he was a stranger there. Then he remembered his father and his mother, and all the arms stretched out to hold him back, to save him from this city where, they said, his soul would find perdition.

In the end Johnny is saved. He has a fleeting vision of God. After much weeping and raging, "the Lord laid him out."

The story Baldwin tells in *The Fire Next Time* (1963) of how he left the church when he was seventeen makes it tempting to regard flight from the church as the eventual outcome for Johnny, too, regardless of the note of acceptance with which *Go Tell It on the Mountain* ends. Johnny's rebellion can only have been postponed, because in most development-of-a-sensibility novels individual freedom is a secular dream. Some commentators have argued that in his novel Baldwin views the church as a form of escapism, like sex and drugs, and that the novel's religious aspects are just part of its larger culture. But where Baldwin's portrayal of his church was once spoken of as an expression of migration's trauma and the adaptability of urban blacks, now it is just as likely to be taken as proof of continuity with the Southern past, especially since rediscovered nineteenth-century spiritual narratives about the conversion experience have provided a literature for the history of the religion of blacks.[4]

Baldwin's solemnity about the black church leading a supplicant from the bondage of sin into the blessings of sanctification hadn't been seen in fiction by blacks for some time. The piety of African-American literature was a constraint that Harlem Renaissance writers had thrown off. Countee Cullen's *One Way to Heaven* (1932) turns on the falseness of the con artist hero's conversion. "A Christian must learn to lap water like a dog." Zora Neale Hurston steps aside to explain the social anthropology of the raucous back-country services and the visions of heaven, "the rim bone of nothing," that accompany the conversion of the womanizing preacher-hero in her first novel, *Jonah's Gourd Vine* (1934). But Baldwin never cracks a smile at the expense of his church, as if to say that by his time black people had been laughed at enough on stage and in movies for being on their knees. Then, too, maybe humor did not seem sufficiently literary to Baldwin. In any case Baldwin's realism reasserts the dignity of the African-American religious idiom. It was as though, in France, Baldwin had contracted an existential seriousness about rebellion against God.

2

The sad conclusion of Baldwin's second novel, *Giovanni's Room* (1956), finds God still on the side of the narrator, David, a white American expatriate telling, in a series of extended flashbacks, the story of his passionate affair with Giovanni, an Italian youth who had tried to survive in the after-hours economy of Paris. Baldwin's gutsiness, considering the 1950s and the hidden risks to his name as a writer, is apparent in the premise of queer love between white characters who are not sorry in the expected way for that love. Though Giovanni commits a murder and is condemned to the guillotine, David doesn't think that just because he fell in love with Giovanni he has sacrificed the "heavy grace of God." Rather, he blames himself for having failed Giovanni, for abandoning him to the life in which violence between the hustling and the hustled is not unknown.

Boys are more afraid of affection than they are of lust, Baldwin has David observe at one point: an example of how, when dealing with the category "homosexuality," Baldwin usually ends up being more concerned with masculine desire and ideas of masculinity in general. In an essay published in *Zero*, a small Paris magazine in 1949, Baldwin goes beyond his wintry Protestantism to declare that homosexuality was not condemned by nature so much as it was a crime in the sight of God, "man's most intense creation." He suggests that those who abhor it judge their own morality instead, in much the same way that in his essays on race he refused to let the subject put him on the defensive and threw the need to explain back onto whites. He ridicules American novels that unwittingly present the queer as someone who could "wear down the resistance of a normal man," pointing out that such novels are concerned not with homosexuality but with "the ever-present danger of sexual activity between men."

However, in a much less bold essay, published in 1954,[5] Baldwin raises the themes that *Giovanni's Room* elaborates on: the rigid concepts that make masculinity a prison; the woman as fact in male life and warden of doubtful reform; the sexual underworld as a trap. At the beginning of their affair Giovanni asks David why he doesn't accommodate both sexes. But bisexuality isn't an option for David. He is fixed instead on what he sees as the miserable social destiny that openly expressed love for a man would impose on him.

David begins his story in the south of France, where he is waiting for Giovanni's execution and preparing to go back to the US. Hella, the girl he nearly married, is already on the high seas homeward. David regrets that he once lied to Giovanni, saying he'd never slept with a man before. He is moved to relate the history of his "self-contempt," starting with a boy on Coney Island and the anguish after they'd been together that he had done something monstrous. Unwanted knowledge of himself sat in his mind like a "decomposing corpse." In San Francisco, living with his father and aunt, he sank into a life of weary drinking, unhappy women, and low-level jobs. He managed his routine of ordinariness by refusing to admit what “shamed and frightened” him. In his heart, however, he knew why he left for France.

His second year in Paris, broke and aimless, he meets the dark and “leonine” Giovanni. David, good-looking and blond, sometimes gets dinner invitations from an older businessman who has introduced him to an ill-lit bar that has too “emphatic” a reputation. Giovanni enters the scene along the same lines, given work papers by the bar’s predatory patron alert to the value of a beautiful barman. David and Giovanni accept favors without being obligated or defining themselves outright, using men who would exploit them if given the chance, maybe even humiliate them in retaliation for wanting young men who have no desire for them.

Giovanni’s Room is mean to the middle-aged and even meaner to its male characters who aren’t butch. As David and Giovanni slide in an evening from being regular guys to being boys with a “vocation,” they are closely watched by “*les folles*,” the bar’s habitués who resent that their own youthful discoveries are long past. Baldwin presents the doomed love of Giovanni and David sympathetically, but David as a first-person narrator is also a guide to the supposedly unhappy sexual underworld. He encounters the sort of painted customers who filled Gustav von Aschenbach with foreboding.

David says in retrospect that he was unable to resist the storm of his instant connection with Giovanni, after which the metaphor of Giovanni being dangerous water develops quickly. Giovanni’s squalid maid’s room, far from the city center and smelling of an alcohol-burning stove, becomes their retreat. David feels that life there is taking place beneath the sea. He waits a month before he tells Giovanni about Hella. A late winter and an entire spring of improvised life with Giovanni brings about the dreaded change in David. The day comes when they are out walking and David is attracted to a passing youth who likes the attention. But another day, when by himself, David stares at a sailor and is intimidated by the answering sneer. Once he was a guy whose contempt put in their place guys like the one he has become.

Giovanni loses his job because of the patron's jealousy, and increasingly David feels as though he is being dragged to the bottom of their private sea. He begins to resist Giovanni's spell, to reject their apparent future of talks, cigarettes, walks, and cognac. The relationship of stumbling home drunk together becomes a power struggle. David accuses Giovanni of wanting to make him into a housewife because, he says, Giovanni lacks the nerve to find a real one. In the early summer David gets word of Hella's return to Paris. He walks out of the room without telling Giovanni where he is going. Three days later he comes across Giovanni by chance and Hella doesn't understand his rudeness to a friend who'd taken him in, so he told her, when he could no longer afford his hotel. Though David says he'd come to regard women as solid ground and Hella as a post he could moor himself to, throughout Baldwin's novel women come off as clueless in a male world of covert signals and shaded conversations, unless they are shrewd crones keeping watch over the cash register.

When David goes back for his things, the discarded Giovanni, having little left to fight for and no longer interested in the moral upper hand, reveals that he left his village and vineyard for Paris the day he buried his stillborn child and made his woman and mother scream by spitting on the family crucifix. In Paris, he, the blasphemer, was suffering God's punishment. David closes the door on Giovanni's tears and reproaches. After that, whenever he runs into him, David notes that Giovanni's clothes are shabbier and his mannerisms off-putting in their camp theatricality. Finally, a hostile look before a newsstand is the only communication between them.

David has no identity apart from being an American, a child of conformity, abroad in that very American sense of being in flight from himself. Travel, as a form of breakdown and recuperation, permits the shattering, then restorative liaison that must be renounced upon reentering the adult world. As he looks back he sees Giovanni as a street kid whom he could not save.

Time goes by; the stones of Paris turn gray again; and a face comes back to haunt David. Giovanni is wanted for the murder of the patron. David imagines Giovanni's desperate act, his stored-up rage that made him lash out at the patron who, David speculates, coerced Giovanni into sex, debased him, and then laughingly refused to give him his job back. Baldwin sacrifices the patron so that the story doesn't have to have a predictable suicide—not that a queer murder isn't also predictable in what was at the time a literary tradition of inevitably tragic heroes. Perhaps Baldwin decided that attacking an exploiter and being executed by the state gave Giovanni more masculine nobility than would dying by his own hand from a broken heart.

Giovanni's Room has a fast-moving plot—rare in Baldwin's fiction. The compression of its prose conveys a sense that the best lines about love have behind them two or more about the pain of love. There is some period scenery, showing a city slowly emerging from postwar austerity, but mostly the stone-softening mist, scalding sun, or lightless gray of Paris has a function like that of a soundtrack, indicating the moods of David's deteriorating affair. He has been in love with the city and has got sick of it. Moreover, because it is a story retold, Baldwin is free to move immediately into the elegiac and valedictory, the tone that gives his personality as a writer the most command:

> Until I die there will be those moments, moments seeming to rise up out of the ground like Macbeth's witches, when his face will come before me, that face in all its changes, when the exact timbre of his voice and tricks of his speech will nearly burst my ears, when his smell will overpower my nostrils. Sometimes, in the days which are coming—God grant me the grace to live them: in the glare of the grey morning, sour-mouthed, eyelids raw and red, hair tangled and damp from my stormy sleep, facing, over coffee and cigarette smoke, last night's impenetrable, meaningless boy who will shortly rise and vanish like the smoke, I will see Giovanni again, as he was that night, so vivid, so winning, all of the light of that gloomy tunnel trapped around his head.

This is the fatalism of first love—after the apprenticeship to love is over, so is love itself.

Of all Baldwin's novels, *Giovanni's Room*, with its theme of the failure of innocence, offers the most straightforward connection to his reading of Henry James. David's Americanness, as a cultural impediment, Baldwin likened to Lambert Strether's New England heritage in *The Ambassadors*. As though he had heard Strether's advice, "Live!," David admits that his difficulty was in saying "Yes" to life. His affair with Giovanni even covers the same span of seasons, from winter to summer, as Strether's rescue mission of young Chad Newsome. David's being white further intensifies the connection to James. His Americanness can be set against the Old World without the complications of race.

Baldwin's all-white cast also seemed a factor in the novel's bravery when it was first published, though Leslie Fiedler pointed out at the time how weird it was that there was not a single black in David's Paris, their presence being one of the things the city had long been known for among Americans.[6] The exclusion of blacks from *Giovanni's Room* may be the result of the trouble Baldwin had with editors over early drafts of *Go Tell It on the Mountain*, when they objected to Johnny's recognizing his homosexuality. Perhaps Baldwin told himself he could do either blacks or queers, but not both. Moreover, David's whiteness gave Baldwin the camouflage he needed in order to let David speak out about homosexuality.

There were notable precedents of blacks using whites as protagonists. For black writers at the turn of the century, such as Charles Chesnutt and Paul Laurence Dunbar, the "non-racial" or "raceless" novel was a commercial venture, usually a love story. Later, in the 1930s, novels by blacks that feature whites as main characters were influenced by the works of naturalism that had brought the ethnic working class into American literature, which meant that they were not "raceless" in the old-fashioned sense. William Attaway's first novel, *Let Me Breathe Thunder* (1937), about two train-hopping hoboes in the

American Northwest, has a homoerotic element in the devotion of the first-person narrator to his feckless buddy. Chester Himes's first novel, finished in 1937, *Yesterday Will Make You Cry,*[7] is an autobiographical account of his prison life, which makes it surprising that the college-educated narrator, stifling his love for a fellow inmate, is white. Willard Motley's first novel, *Knock on Any Door* (1947), follows the son of Italian immigrants, from altar boy in Denver to a life of crime and the execution chamber in Chicago.[8] It is telling that these novels are about whites who have lost caste.

The strictly "raceless" novel returned with Richard Wright's *Savage Holiday* (1954), one of the failures of his exile. Wright's portrait of a New York insurance executive having a murderous breakdown was greeted in some quarters with the argument that in dealing exclusively with white characters Wright had denied himself what gave his work its ferocious animation. To a certain extent, criticism of Wright for being too abstract was an attack on his literary ambition. The raceless novel, in any case, or the novel with whites as main characters, figures, at least as an experiment, in the careers of the best-known expatriate black writers.[9] They were, in effect, questioning the definitions of the black writer, if not of African-American literature itself, rather as black science fiction writers of the next generation would do in the 1960s.

In the Fifties black writers had few chances to demonstrate that they had any knowledge of life that did not have something to do with being black. Blacks did not impinge on the raceless novel written by blacks in the way that the white world suffuses the atmosphere of all-black novels. It's easy to forget that in *Go Tell It on the Mountain* no whites really come into the picture, apart from a man Johnny bumps into on his way home from Central Park, which gives Baldwin the opportunity to rewrite the scene from Ellison's *Invisible Man* where the narrator throttles the white man who jostled him because he didn't see him. In Baldwin, the black youth and the elderly white are polite as they go their separate ways.

3

Giovanni's Room was as much Baldwin's goodbye to Paris as *Go Tell It on the Mountain* had been to Harlem. His experience of the old Modernist capital as a milieu made him bold once he got back to the US. He introduced his Harlem to his Paris in the Greenwich Village of *Another Country* (1962), which he began in Paris but apparently didn't get far with until he returned to the US for an extended period in 1957. It is a dialogue-driven work about various kinds of love, particularly the interracial love affair kind. Baldwin is aggressive in depicting sexual relations between blacks and whites, as if to make up for the gentle metaphors that bridged the sexual waters in his first two novels.

He writes here as though he were dragging the subject of mixed-race romance from its traditional clandestine atmosphere. Sex scenes previously associated with dime-store novels or the avant-garde had been gradually making their way into the literary mainstream. Nevertheless, Baldwin was still trading in stereotypes, almost the only language then available with which to speak of the sexual fear of social equality and race mixing.

Baldwin never says so directly, but it can be worked out that *Another Country* opens in 1955, in the months after the murder of Emmett Till, a fourteen-year-old black youth with a speech impediment who had allegedly whistled at a white store owner's wife in Money, Mississippi. Though weighted with a cotton gin chain, Till's body rose to the surface of the Tallahatchie River. During the trial that became one of the most notorious of the decade, the defendants ate ice cream cones in court. Baldwin would base his play, *Blues for Mr. Charlie* (1964), on Till's murder. In *Another Country* the case is a scandal his characters would have been aware of. It is important, however, as part of Baldwin's social context, a background that says his novel's theme is serious, not exotic. The anxieties of freedom that his black and white characters brood on are set in a time when whites could still pretend that a black man accused of wanting to have sex with a white woman gave a jury sufficient grounds to acquit the white men who had killed him.

New York City is not America, many would have thought back then, but as Baldwin portrays it, Greenwich Village, with its hostile landlords and adolescent gangs, was far from being a haven for blacks and queers. He sometimes places a resentful white policeman on the pavement, looking in at the mixed bar crowd. The interracial couples and same-sex partners rage a great deal about how strangers react to their anticonventional relationships. As Baldwin's people of the sexual vanguard ride uptown and downtown, on subways and in taxis, in the company of their lovers or alone with their thoughts, they are like members of a resistance group or a political underground, alert that people who may not be on their side can read their minds.

Blacks and whites alike are victims of the country's clotted sexual attitudes, Baldwin perhaps means to show, because his characters all carry such a punitive burden of assumptions about the sexual characteristics of blacks and whites. Baldwin's people see themselves as living in a society in the process of breaking down, which leaves them individually responsible for setting and upholding new rules of behavior. This responsibility depends on scorching honesty about the Self and a humble belief in the redemptive power of Love. Much like the Christianity it is somehow intended to replace, Love, for Baldwin's defeated hipsters and defensive bohemians, is a revelatory faith.

The realization that love matters more than race revenge has come too late for Rufus Scott, a black jazz drummer who reviews his descent into the hopelessness that has him trying to sell himself to men in Times Square for the promise of a warm bed. With Rufus, the novel enters the first of its many sprawling flashbacks and flashbacks within flashbacks. Seven months earlier: Rufus meets Leona, a Southern white girl, at a Harlem club. He takes her to a party of Charlie Parker music and marijuana. They have sex on the balcony overlooking Riverside Drive and Rufus forgets the tenderness inspired by her story of divorce, estrangement from family, and the removal of her child from her care. "Under his breath he cursed the milk-white bitch and groaned and rode his weapon between her thighs." The "venom" shoots out of him, "enough for a hundred black-white babies." She goes home with him to his Village apartment, to a relationship of booze, misunderstandings, violence, and more sex that is close to rape in his mind.

Rufus's friends watch helplessly as he scourges Leona and thus destroys himself. When Rufus's best friend, Vivaldo, meets Leona, Rufus suspects him of flirting, of thinking that because Leona is with him, a black man, she is available to any man. Then he frets that Vivaldo might not think Leona attractive enough for white men. Rufus also resents the freedom to misbehave that Vivaldo has because he's white, an "Irish wop" from the depths of Brooklyn. Vivaldo's women can make drunken scenes because his presence protects them, whereas Leona is that much more vulnerable when out with Rufus. The racial sensitivities of white lovers and white friends have a period quality in the novel, as much as the hep lingo of cats, squares, you dig, dads, kicks, and pads. "I know—a lot of things hurt you that I can't really understand," the earnest Vivaldo admits to Rufus, who doesn't like to be called "boy."

One of Rufus's fights with Leona starts when she, "a hard up white lady," tries to tell him that there is nothing wrong in being "colored." She knows that Rufus doesn't think he's good enough, even for her. She can't compete with his unhappiness; she can only hurt along with him. She loses her waitress job and can't get another, her appearance has so deteriorated. Rufus also stops working, has nothing left to pawn, and picks fights with white men. Apparently, this is his first affair with a white woman. Until he was with Leona he hadn't thought about "the big world" and its power to hate. He feels that he is suddenly visible to whites because he is with a white woman. Still, it's never entirely clear why this relationship should send a member of the sophisticated jazz scene into a frenzy of self-hate, racial fear, and sexual rage.

In the days before his death Rufus's urban world becomes brutally eroticized; even subways seem to him to enter tunnels with "phallic abandon." Perhaps it is enough for Baldwin to suggest that Leona is the fuse to an explosion that had been building in Rufus for some time.

Battered by him, Leona is taken to Bellevue. In a paroxysm of guilt, Rufus leaps to his death from the George Washington Bridge.

Rufus's suicide comes early on in the novel. He is the one black character depicted largely through an internal point of view. After his funeral, the emotional emphasis of the novel shifts from how blacks feel in the white world to how the experiences of the white characters with and among blacks affect their feelings about the white world. Vivaldo will fall in love with Rufus's sister, Ida, and she, the black woman, is to be observed from the outside, her thoughts guessed at by Rufus's white friends, who scrutinize her intensely. The white characters in Baldwin's novel become anxious over how they really feel about blacks when it comes to holding hands with a black person on the street and how they hope the blacks they know will see and judge them nevertheless.

Vivaldo is no stranger to uptown. He's been rolled while trying to pick up women in Harlem. Even so, he persists in thinking that he belongs in those "dark streets . . . precisely because the history written in the color of his skin contested his right to be there." For Vivaldo, associating with black people expresses his sense of escape from the "unexamined" life that he imagines is the lot of the multitudes around him. It is as though he is visible to himself when he's with Ida, his portable Harlem. He is not uncritical of her, of her haughty and free manner. Vivaldo is proud of her in that "overt, male way," but soon it is his turn to wonder, much as Rufus did, if white men are looking at Ida as a whore, if they regard him as having made nothing more than a back-alley conquest.

As a bohemian, Vivaldo looks down on television and takes an instant dislike to the agent and producer Ellis, whom he and Ida meet at a book party. However, he is threatened by Ellis's power, especially when Ida responds too readily to Ellis's offer to help her should she decide to pursue a career as a singer. Vivaldo, the bookstore clerk, believes that the possibility of becoming a true artist still exists for him, if he could only buckle down to the novel that Ida keeps him from working on when she's at his Village apartment, turning up "the carnal heat." Vivaldo's chief literary ideal is Dostoevsky—and feverish Dostoevsky more than circuitous Henry James seems to have been in Baldwin's mind for the hot-tempered talkathon about forgiveness that is *Another Country.*

Into the story of Vivaldo's insecurity and Ida's hurt, of bared teeth and bellies grinding "cruelly," of whinnying, clinging, galloping, and bucking either like "an infuriated horse" or a "beached fish," comes Eric, who has been living in France for three years, not getting far as an actor. Eric is an Alabama white boy with a history of loving black men. He is first seen in *Another Country* in the south of France, where *Giovanni's Room* ends. But not for him David's unhappy fate. Eric has Yves, a rent boy who reminds him of Rufus in his "brave, tough vulnerability." He also has a decision to make: whether to return to New York to be in a Broadway play or to allow his sojourn in Europe to turn into "exile."

Baldwin renders the sex between Eric and Yves as a matter of whispers and heartbeats like "the far-off pounding of the sea." The romantic modesty contrasts sharply with the mattress-thrashing between men and women in the novel. Eric's role is to be therapeutic, a layer-on of hands for the officially straight but emotionally weary. However, his importance in Baldwin's scheme of black man-white woman/white man-black woman is symbolic. In a novel of such committed psychological realism, where Baldwin piles assertion upon assertion about his characters' states of mind, that Eric appears as an artificial presence has less to do with his sexuality than with his being unmixed as a character, unlike the others, who are a mess. Then, too, the ghost of Rufus keeps upstaging him, stealing his function as a prompter of self-examination in others.

Ida has been working as a waitress, but is pcrhaps on her way as an artist after her debut in a Village jazz bar, arranged by Ellis. The occasion is marred by Vivaldo's jealousy. Ida and Ellis may be having an affair. As if tracing Rufus's footsteps, Vivaldo pitches around Manhattan:

> And summer came, the New York summer, which is like no summer anywhere. The heat and the noise began their destruction of nerves and sanity and private lives and love affairs. The air was full of baseball scores and bad news and treacly songs; and the streets and the bars were full of hostile people, made more hostile by the heat. . . . It was a city without oases, run entirely, insofar, at least, as human perception could tell, for money; and its citizens seemed to have lost entirely any sense of their right to renew themselves. Whoever, in New York, attempted to cling to this right, lived in New York in exile—in exile from life around him; and this, paradoxically, had the effect of placing him in perpetual danger of being forever banished from any real sense of himself.

The story begins to accelerate. The drinking also picks up. Baldwin's people put away as much as any Village denizen in a Dawn Powell novel. The Brandy Alexanders and highballs of that time and place are never far from needing hands as secrets come out. Baldwin inserts Bessie Smith and Billie Holiday lyrics throughout *Another Country*, hymns carrying the gospel that people tear one another limb from limb in the name of "that love jive."

Ida turns out to be very conscious of herself as the agent of her brother's retribution. She admits that revenge for what happened to Rufus just because he was black guides her dealings with Ellis and Vivaldo as white men. Black men uptown who could be of use to her in her vague plan to get back at the world don't want her because she is too dark. They see women like her on Seventh Avenue every day. So, like Rufus, she has hit the A train for downtown:

> I used to see the way white men watched me, like dogs. And I thought about what I could do to them. How I hated them, the way they looked, and the things they'd say, all dressed up in their damn white skin, and their clothes just so, and their little weak, white pricks jumping in their drawers.

Sometimes Vivaldo suspects that the black male musicians she works with aren't offended by Ellis's presence, because they can assume that Ida is using him. But Vivaldo, who can do nothing for her professionally, is therefore obviously her lover, and the black musicians show their hostility to him by ignoring him at her gigs. Black men are made uncomfortable by the couple or they accuse Ida of betraying and castrating them. However, as Ida reveals to Vivaldo, they are free to insult her, a black woman, even on stage. Reverse exploitation—a black woman using a white man—doesn't work here. Ellis grins from the sidelines at Ida's public humiliations and it suits him, married himself, that she, his girlfriend, always has to go home too.

Vivaldo tells Ida that suffering has no color. But she has made him suffer because of his color, even if she only has the power to do so because he is the more loving. Baldwin was too interested in the concreteness of racial experience to mean that love transcends race. Ida recognizes that she is being vengeful toward the wrong white guy, but he's the only sort of white guy who would care why. Baldwin shows Ida in the act of "stroking" away Vivaldo's "innocence," but Vivaldo's asking Ida to be more trusting of and less defensive with him is not the same thing as Ida's teaching him what it's like for her to be with a white guy or the cost for him of being with her. He must renounce his whiteness, even its hip version. But the racial conversion, so to speak, doesn't work both ways. What is there for him if she gives up blackness? The sheer edginess of the situation is part of her attractiveness to him in the first place.

"I am Baudelaire and I love my brown mistress," the narrator in Jack Kerouac's *The Subterraneans*, published four years before *Another Country*, exclaims of his lost "half Indian half Negro" love. Leo, as Kerouac dubs himself, first sees Mardou sitting on a car one night in San Francisco in 1953. The possibility of immersing his "lonely being" in the "warm bath and salvation of her thighs" inspires his crusade to overcome her distrust. Soon he is the "big gleeful hoodlum" proud to have a "nice strong little beauty to cut along the street with," proud of her "thongs of sandals, dark eyes, little soft brown face," her "part Negro highclass" and "bop generation" way of speaking, and especially pleased that the bop king himself, Charlie Parker, is "distinctly digging" her from the stage and noting that she is with him.

Leo worries what his mother, her sister, and her Southern in-laws would make of Mardou. During bouts of paranoia he is sure that all black women are thieves and that Mardou will steal his "white soul." The love binge ends when, after three months of drinking, smoking, and yapping until dawn, he is careless with her once too often. Leo had hoped she would bring clarity to his tragic vision of himself and America, but she moves on instead. As a story of love gone wrong, Kerouac's evocative novel demonstrates how racial images filtered through sexual desire—very much like those in Baldwin's novel—can take on tender meanings when the intention of a work is self-criticism rather than social criticism.

Another Country has both a deliberate emphasis on the sexual images of blacks in the white mind as well as an unreflective endorsement of the image of blacks as being more passionate than most whites. Such images have a long history in the US. That black women were said to be wanton helped to justify the coercive practices of slavery; after the Civil War the image of black men as rapists of white women formed part of the campaign to disenfranchise black male voters. By the Jazz Age, when the tom-toms were beckoning, the cult of the primitive had transformed many low-down qualities that were supposedly innate in blacks into cultural virtues. One of the legacies of the Harlem Renaissance was the take-over and literary embrace of "being loud," that thing many black people had been taught to be ashamed of. In time, celebrating the earthiness of blacks became a measure of a black person's self-acceptance and pride in black culture. In Baldwin's day, the insisted-upon sensuality of blacks was seen as a cultural advantage, something whites could be mocked for wanting. Nobody urges Ida to give up her sexual capital.

In US fiction up until Baldwin's time, white men who take up with black women may renounce their inheritances or find themselves disinherited, but they are not automatically cast out in the way that Becky in Jean Toomer's *Cane* (1921), who has long been living by the train tracks with her two black sons, is. Or such white women tend to be nowhere on the country's social scale to begin with. Leona can only take without protest the beatings Rufus gives her, which may be partly why Baldwin made the white woman in the life of his bisexual black hero in his next novel, *Tell Me How Long the Train's Been Gone* (1968), rich enough in her own right to defy convention.

That Ida is dark and poor lets Baldwin bypass the complications to black identity of class, light skin, and education that figure so importantly in much of the fiction since the 1920s about black women being with white men. Though black women in novels about interracial love affairs are often shown having to deal with either family and community disapproval or the internal disquiet of feeling that they have deserted the cause of black freedom, seldom are they portrayed as women who have fallen to the lowest depths because of their romances. There is always the suggestion that these women may be trying to escape the black condition through whatever status they can derive from a connection with a white man. Significantly, no novels about a black woman going off with a white man who is poor come to mind before *Another Country.*

4

A black woman character in Baldwin's short-story collection, *Going to Meet the Man* (1965), is mindful of slavery's legacy when she tells her white boyfriend that they're not on the plantation and he's not the master's son. In the title story, a white sheriff taunts a jailed black protester, saying that black people were lucky white men had pumped some white blood into the black race. He then realizes that he has given himself an erection. In his fiction about human relations between people of different races Baldwin had to take into account the closeness of sex to violence. As a young critic he had complained that in fiction by blacks violence occupied the place where sex ought to have been. Part of the appeal of *Another Country* when it was published was that it showed emotional intimacy between people of different races as well as sexual intimacy. It captured the mood of a special, unrepeatable time, those discussions inspired by the Freedom Summers of cooperation and listening, when blacks and whites could sit down in an equality of self-consciousness and say the most sincere and helpless things to one another. Baldwin's tone promised them an absence of ridicule, which was a new variation on an old theme.

Chester Himes was the first black writer to take the sexual image of the black man and shove it back into America's face. In *The Primitive* (1952), he offers a bitter anatomy of the affair between Jesse Robinson, a black writer, and the financially secure Kriss Cummings. Most of the novel takes place in Kriss's apartment. The telephone summons deliveries of food that goes bad and bottles of Scotch that quickly empty. In the mounting chaos Kriss screams, "Niggers! niggers! niggers! That's all you niggers talk about." Jesse hates himself for sleeping with a white woman, but at the same time he tells himself that it is good therapy: "White man kick his ass until he gets sick; get some white woman ass and get well. Good for her too. White man kick her ass till she gets sick; screw some black niggers and get even." The hysteria ends when Jesse stumbles blind drunk into her bedroom with a kitchen knife. He phones the police the next morning. "I'm a nigger, and I've just killed a white woman." As Himes would later explain,

> To describe a black man, the blackness of his skin, black sexual organs, black shanks, the thickness of his lips, the aphrodisiacal texture of his kinky hair, alongside the white breasts, pink nipples, white thighs and silky pubic hair of a white woman, no matter how seriously intended, is unavoidably pornographic in American society.[10]

"All love is white," the failed black law student tells the white girl who becomes his wife and his ruin in Eugene O'Neill's *All God's Chillun Got Wings* (1924). But the notion that whiteness represents purity is left far behind in Amiri Baraka's *The Dutchman* (1964). The silent, smiling white girl stabs the black student whom she has invited to come on to her on the subway. Interracial sex has been firmly politicized. Baraka's warning to black men about white women is unequivocal: don't trust them. In this charged cultural climate, a controversy erupted over William Styron's novel, *The Confessions of Nat Turner* (1967). Styron, well aware of how the black man had been characterized as a "sexual carnivore of superhuman capacities" with "mythical powers of eroticism," took a historical figure as his protagonist, a married Virginia slave preacher who in 1831 led the most serious slave revolt in US history. Moreover, he chose to write in the first person, made Turner celibate, and then imagined an obsession with a white woman as the decisive drama of his black hero's inner life.[11]

Years later, when looking back on the fury of his black critics, Styron remembered that he was encouraged by Baldwin in his effort to get inside his black character's skin, to find the "sense of withinness"[12] of a black character that Faulkner had not found. Turner, Styron decided, was a madman animated by Old Testament revenge. But for all of Turner's biblical flights in Styron's "meditation," his Turner is really Rufus Scott. What Styron has Turner say about filling a white girl with his "milky spurts of desecration" is very like Rufus's revenge fantasies, as though Styron had consulted Baldwin's novel about how far he could go.

Meanwhile, the black man's involvement with white women as a theme continued to attract black writers who wanted to stress how liberated young blacks were. In Cecil Brown's *The Life and Loves of Mr. Jive Ass Nigger* (1969), George, a young black teller of tales on the loose in Vietnam War-era Copenhagen, embarks on a series of conquests of white women. Like the other expatriate black men he hangs out with, George regards the black lover as a warrior. He rejects the masochistic guilt of Wright's Bigger Thomas, whose fear of the white man was so great that a "mere kiss stolen from a white woman's breath" had to be "smothered in a fiery furnace." Instead, he relates to the outcasts of life and literature, among them "James Baldwin." But suspecting that he's become what whites expect, George concludes that for him to see the black gigolo as existential man is false. "Existentialism is a white man's attempt to get at blackness." "If you're black you don't need to get at anything. You're already there." This had been Baldwin's point all along.

Baldwin was always urging whites—and heterosexuals—to put themselves in the outsider's position, which was why, as the civil rights movement of the 1960s unfolded, his work supported the belief that at heart blackness was a purifying and refining aesthetic. At a time when blacks were being instructed to be more middle class—or white, as militants claimed—so that integration would appear less threatening, Baldwin was speculating that maybe whites could find their better selves and a truer vision of US society on the black side of national life. Come by me. This deep confidence in the morality of the black experience, as it was then called, is also why black identity itself is seldom the thing at stake in Baldwin's novels. However, a number of factors, including the growing influence in the late 1960s of Frantz Fanon—his reproachful language about the colonized mind and the interracial relationship as an expression of a black individual's unconscious desire to be white—would make Baldwin's argument for the necessity of something like a conversion experience on the part of white people seem to many blacks in his audience either too coddling of them or long beside the point for black people.

Baldwin also must have felt that he had exhausted intimate relations between blacks and whites as a subject. *If Beale Street Could Talk* (1974) represents his return to the Harlem family. Baldwin knew more than a few people who had landed in prison. He tries to show the impact that getting caught up in the US justice system has on ordinary people. In his scheme it simply makes them heroic. No other novelist since Balzac has hated the cops so much, but Baldwin wants to celebrate a black family's survival, to praise the bonds between sisters, between parents and child. Similarly, *Just Above My Head* (1979), a saga bringing in three decades of a family's history, meanders sentimentally and everyone is uniformly "caring." The hagiographic approach results in an all too neat symmetry: us versus them. Clearly, Baldwin considered portraying the black family as healthy and enduring, in spite of racism, to be sufficiently provocative, but the idealized family members in these novels suggest a loss in audacity of conception.

In the beginning Baldwin adapted Henry James's man of leisure to his own purposes. And just as James's main characters are usually bereft of immediate family, in Baldwin's early work his sensitive protagonists also are at liberty in "vast bright Babylon." But increasing disillusionment with racial politics may have led him to look for a way to address more directly the concerns of a wider black audience. His biographers tell that as Baldwin's years accumulated he became more dependent on his own family. His last two novels were perhaps his way of honoring what they stood for, of making up for his earlier writings in which he demonstrated that he had a far more complicated picture of family. *Tell Me How Long the Train's Been Gone* (1968) is about the fatigue of a world-class black actor, his search for a place to rest and people to trust. The novel seems very much about the loneliness of Baldwin's own international fame and his need to be taken care of. It is also the last time a rebel outcast speaks for himself in Baldwin's fiction.

Though Baldwin's best-known short story, "Sonny's Blues," about an addict who succumbs to the ravages of the street, is beautifully told by an algebra teacher, for the larger canvas of the novel he usually stayed with the life of the artist. His theater world in *Tell Me How Long the Train's Been Gone* is full of lines like "The flame demands you. The flame will have you." Sometimes Baldwin could analyze the situation of the artist better than he could dramatize it. Nevertheless, Baldwin is intensely associated with the idea of the artist as a witness of his time. The irony is that for all his literary sensibilities, Baldwin was not by temperament avant-garde. But he was both to profit and to suffer from the cultural tendency back then whereby a work by a black was greeted as if it were the latest from some experimental scene. It helped that his titles were at once biblical and bluesy.

Robert Louis Stevenson had been one of Baldwin's favorite writers as a youth, and his own novels subliminally try to reclaim the homoerotic innocence of the adventure story. They are replete with nostalgia for the protection of an older brother. The seventeen-year-old Elisha who wrestles with Johnny as they clean up the church in *Go Tell It on the Mountain*; the seventeen-year-old black youth who works as a porter at the town courthouse and whom Eric remembers as his first sexual encounter in *Another Country*; the fiery older brother that the actor Leo Proudhammer recalls nestling up next to in their childhood bed in *Tell Me How Long the Train's Been Gone*; Crunch, the eighteen-year-old repentant lady-killer whom Arthur, the young gospel star, falls in love with in *Just Above My Head*—perhaps these were messages to himself about what he had not forgotten and still hoped to find, someone like the son of his stepfather's previous marriage, who used to carry Baldwin on his shoulders at Jones Beach but never returned after his father, Baldwin's stepfather, drove him from the house.

But thought was also adventure—another James mantra. The sexual life that Baldwin rarely wrote about in depth in his essays he investigated in his earlier fiction, and that is why these novels were like news. They were on youth's side, though youth culture, as people have come to think of it, was only just beginning when Baldwin's reputation was at its height. Now his work has gone the way of Steinbeck's—into the curriculum, and as the province of ever younger readers. No matter. His was the voice that understood, the instructor and confessor of the young and forlorn. It was okay to see things differently, okay not to fit in. He leaves his young characters at their various crossroads, unashamed of vulnerability, with destinies to decide. Even as his main characters get older, their glance is always retrospective, looking back to the place where the road forked.

Baldwin once said that an abandoned novel could destroy a writer's life. But the huge success of *Another Country* put an unfortunate pressure on his life as a novelist. To justify the advances he needed from publishers in order to support his generosity to others, to stay in competition with the major white novelists of his day, Baldwin couldn't hand in the small, perfect work to which his lyrical gifts were most suited. He had to turn out another blockbuster, to reproduce somehow the winning formula of *Another Country.* The last novel, *Just Above My Head*, duly thickened. Baldwin had summoned it all from the interior before and was gambling on the arrival of another moment of daring that would let him tell "as much truth as one can bear, and then some." But in their rawness and denials, his novels after *Another Country* tell us little more than that life can be pretty bleak without metaphors.

Notes

1. Otto Friedrich, "Jimmy," in *The Grave of Alice B. Toklas and Other Reports from the Past* (Holt, 1989).

2. F. O. Matthiessen, *Henry James: The Major Phase* (Oxford University Press, 1944).

3. James Baldwin, "The Art of Fiction," *The Paris Review*, Vol. 26, No. 91 (1984); David Leeming, "An Interview with James Baldwin on Henry James," in *The Henry James Review*, Fall 1986.

4. In a fascinating collection of essays, *A Fire in the Bones: Reflections on African-American Religious History* (Beacon, 1995), Albert J. Raboteau, "an historian and believer," says that Baldwin's novel "offers one of the most profound depictions of the conversion experience." Johnny has entered a "spiritual aristocracy" where he is expected to accept the guidance of his elders.

5. "The Male Prison," reprinted in *Nobody Knows My Name* (1961).

6. In a letter to Baldwin written shortly after *Giovanni's Room* was published, Fiedler also expressed astonishment that no one had corrected the numerous mistakes in French grammar in the novel.

7. A version of Himes's first novel was published as *Cast the First Stone* in 1952.

Yesterday Will Make You Cry, as Himes wrote it, was finally published by Norton in 1998.

8. *Knock on Any Door* has sometimes been credited with starting a trend, but Ann Petry's *Country Place* (1947) was completed and Zora Neale Hurston's *Seraph on the Sewanee* (1948) was begun before Motley's novel became a best seller. As black women writers, Petry and Hurston use all-white casts to talk about the condition of women in general. If anything, Hurston's novel of white ruralism looks back to Julia Peterkin's all-black rural novel, *Black April* (1938).

9. Baldwin's contemporary and fellow expatriate, William Gardner Smith, published in 1950 *Anger at Innocence*, a novel about a timid white man who falls in love with a white girl pickpocket and then gets dragged down into the Philadelphia slums. In the same period Frank Yerby went from being a winner of Negro short-story contests to being an author of best-selling historical romances.

10. *The Quality of Hurt: The Autobiography of Chester Himes* (Thunder's Mouth Press, 1971). An unexpurgated version of *The Primitive* was published as *The End of a Primitive* (Alison and Busby, 1989). Sexual tensions between whites and blacks figure in most of Himes's early work. Similarly, three of William Gardner Smith's novels are about a black man's relationship with a white woman.

11. See *William Styron's Confessions of Nat Turner: Ten Black Writers Respond* (Beacon, 1968). Styron discussed some images of the black male in his review of *American Negro Slave Revolts* by Herbert Aptheker (International, 1963); see "Overcome," *The New York Review*, September 26, 1963.

12. Styron talked about his research and intentions in an essay published before his novel appeared. It is reprinted in *This Quiet Dust and Other Writings* (Random House, 1982). He looked back on the controversy surrounding his novel in "Nat Turner Revisited," *American Heritage* (October 1992). See also *Nat Turner Before the Bar of Judgment: Fictional Treatments of the Southampton Slave Insurrection* by Mary Kemp Davis (Louisiana State University Press, 1999).

RESOURCES

Chronology of James Baldwin's Life

1924	Emma Berdis Jones gives birth to a son, James, in New York City on August 2.
1927	Emma Jones marries David Baldwin, a clergyman and factory worker.
1935-1938	James Baldwin attends Frederick Douglass Junior High School. He meets Countee Cullen.
1938	Baldwin becomes a junior minister at Fireside Pentecostal Assembly and begins preaching.
1938-1942	Baldwin attends DeWitt Clinton High School.
1940	Baldwin leaves the church.
1942-1946	After graduating high school in January 1942, Baldwin works on a railroad in New Jersey and holds other odd jobs. He begins writing his first, unpublished novel, "In My Father's House."
1943	David Baldwin dies. Baldwin moves to Greenwich Village.
1944	Baldwin meets Richard Wright.
1945	Baldwin wins a Eugene F. Saxton Fellowship with Wright's help.
1946	Baldwin publishes first book review in *The Nation*. He sets aside "In My Father's House" and begins working on a second novel that will remain unpublished, "Ignorant Armies."
1948	Baldwin publishes first essay and first short story in *Commentary*. He wins a Rosenwald Foundation Fellowship and uses the money to move to Paris.
1949-1952	Baldwin lives in Paris and Switzerland.

1951–1952	Baldwin completes "In My Father's House" and retitles it *Go Tell It on the Mountain*. He returns to New York for the publication of *Go Tell It on the Mountain*.
1953	*Go Tell It on the Mountain* is published. Baldwin returns to Europe.
1954	Baldwin returns to New York in the summer. He finishes writing *Giovanni's Room*, *The Amen Corner*, and *Notes of a Native Son*.
1955	*Notes of a Native Son* is published. Howard University produces *The Amen Corner*.
1956	*Giovanni's Room* is published. Baldwin travels to Paris to cover a conference of black writers and artists, then returns to New York.
1957	Baldwin visits the South, where he meets Martin Luther King, Jr., and Rosa Parks, to research articles for *Harper's Magazine* and *Partisan Review*.
1959	Baldwin returns to Paris.
1960	Baldwin returns to the United States.
1961	*Nobody Knows My Name* is published. Baldwin returns to Europe.
1962	*Another Country* is published. Baldwin travels to Istanbul.
1963	*The Fire Next Time* is published. Baldwin appears on the cover of *Time* magazine on May 17. Along with other black leaders, he meets with Attorney General Robert Kennedy to discuss race relations. Medgar Evers, a civil rights activist, is assassinated on June 12.
1964	*Blues for Mister Charlie* opens on Broadway and is published. *The Amen Corner* is professionally produced for the first time, in Los Angeles. *Nothing Personal*, which features photography by Richard Avedon, is published. Baldwin is made a member of the National Institute of Arts and Letters.
1965	*Going to Meet the Man* is published. *The Amen Corner* opens on Broadway. Malcolm X is assassinated on February 21.

1967	Eldridge Cleaver attacks Baldwin in *Soul on Ice*.
1968	*Tell Me How Long the Train's Been Gone* is published. Martin Luther King, Jr., is assassinated on April 4.
1970	Baldwin returns to France and settles permanently at St. Paul de Vence, a village in southern France.
1971	Baldwin publishes *A Rap on Race* with Margaret Mead. *No Name in the Street* is published.
1972	The unproduced screenplay *One Day, When I Was Lost* is published.
1973	*A Dialogue*, based on the transcript of a conversation between Baldwin and Nikki Giovanni, is published.
1974	*If Beale Street Could Talk* is published.
1976	*The Devil Finds Work* and *Little Man, Little Man*, a children's book, are published.
1979	*Just Above My Head* is published and receives an American Book Award nomination.
1983	*Jimmy's Blues: Selected Poems* is published.
1985	*The Evidence of Things Not Seen* and *The Price of the Ticket: Collected Nonfiction, 1948-1985* are published.
1987	Baldwin dies in St. Paul de Vence. He is buried near the graves of Paul and Eslanda Goode Robeson at Ferncliff Cemetery, Ardsley, New York.
1998	*Early Novels and Stories* and *Collected Essays* are published.

Works by James Baldwin

Long Fiction

Go Tell It on the Mountain, 1953
Giovanni's Room, 1956
Another Country, 1962
Tell Me How Long the Train's Been Gone, 1968
If Beale Street Could Talk, 1974
Just Above My Head, 1979

Short Fiction

Going to Meet the Man, 1965

Nonfiction

Notes of a Native Son, 1955
Nobody Knows My Name: More Notes of a Native Son, 1961
The Fire Next Time, 1963
Nothing Personal, 1964 (with Richard Avedon)
No Name in the Street, 1971
A Rap on Race, 1971 (with Margaret Mead)
A Dialogue, 1973 (with Nikki Giovanni)
The Devil Finds Work, 1976
The Price of the Ticket, 1985
The Evidence of Things Not Seen, 1985
Conversations with James Baldwin, 1989
Collected Essays, 1998
Early Novels and Stories, 1998
Native Sons: A Friendship That Created One of the Greatest Works of the Twentieth Century—"Notes of a Native Son," 2004 (with Sol Stein)

Drama

The Amen Corner, pr. 1954, pb. 1968
Blues for Mister Charlie, pr., pb. 1964
A Deed from the King of Spain, pr. 1974

Poetry

Jimmy's Blues: Selected Poems, 1983

Screenplay

One Day, When I Was Lost: A Scenario Based on "The Autobiography of Malcolm X," 1972

Children's Literature

Little Man, Little Man, 1976

Bibliography

Allen, Brooke. "The Better James Baldwin." *New Criterion* 16.8 (April 1998): 29-36.

Als, Hilton. "The Enemy Within." *The New Yorker* 16 Feb. 1998: 72-80.

Baldwin, James. *Conversations with James Baldwin*. Ed. Fred L. Standley and Louis H. Pratt. Jackson: University Press of Mississippi, 1989.

Balfour, Lawrie Lawrence, and Katherine Lawrence Balfour. *The Evidence of Things Not Said: James Baldwin and the Promise of American Democracy*. Ithaca, NY: Cornell University Press, 2001.

Bloom, Harold, ed. *James Baldwin*. New York: Chelsea House, 2007.

Bobia, Rosa. *The Critical Reception of James Baldwin in France*. New York: Peter Lang, 1997.

Bone, Robert. *The Negro Novel in America*. 1958. New Haven, CT: Yale University Press, 1965.

Boyd, Herb. *Baldwin's Harlem*. New York: Atria, 2008.

Campbell, James. *Exiled in Paris: Richard Wright, James Baldwin, Samuel Beckett, and Others on the Left Bank*. Berkeley: University of California Press, 2003.

___________. *Talking at the Gates: A Life of James Baldwin*. New York: Viking Press, 1991.

Clark, Keith. *Black Manhood in James Baldwin, Ernest J. Gaines, and August Wilson*. Urbana: University of Illinois Press, 2002.

Davis, Ursula Broschke. *Paris Without Regret: James Baldwin, Kenny Clarke, Chester Himes, and Donald Byrd*. Iowa City: University of Iowa Press, 1986.

Dickstein, Morris. *Gates of Eden: American Culture in the Sixties*. New York: Basic Books, 1977.

Eckman, Fern Marja. *The Furious Passage of James Baldwin*. London: Michael Joseph, 1966.

Fabre, Michel. "James Baldwin in Paris: Love and Self-Discovery." *From Harlem to Paris: Black American Writers in France, 1840-1980*. Chicago: University of Illinois Press, 1991.

Field, Douglas, ed. *A Historical Guide to James Baldwin*. New York: Oxford University Press, 2009.

Hardy, Clarence E., III. *James Baldwin's God: Sex, Hope, and Crisis in Black Holiness Culture*. Knoxville: University of Tennessee Press, 2003.

Harris, Trudier, ed. *New Essays on "Go Tell It on the Mountain."* New York: Cambridge University Press, 1996.

Henderson, Carol E., ed. *James Baldwin's "Go Tell It on the Mountain" 50 Years Later*. Spec. issue of *MAWA Review* 19.1 (June 2004).

___________, ed. *James Baldwin's "Go Tell It on the Mountain": Historical and Critical Essays*. New York: Peter Lang, 2006.

King, Lovalerie, and Lynn Orilla Scott, eds. *James Baldwin and Toni Morrison: Comparative Critical and Theoretical Essays*. New York: Palgrave Macmillan, 2006.
Kinnamon, Keneth, ed. *James Baldwin: A Collection of Critical Essays*. Englewood Cliffs, NJ: Prentice-Hall, 1974.
Leeming, David. *James Baldwin: A Biography*. New York: Alfred A. Knopf, 1994.
McBride, Dwight A., ed. *James Baldwin Now*. New York: New York University Press, 1999.
Margolies, Edward. *Native Sons: A Critical Study of Twentieth-Century Negro American Authors*. Philadelphia: Lippincott, 1968.
Miller, D. Quentin, ed. *Re-Viewing James Baldwin: Things Not Seen*. Philadelphia: Temple University Press, 2000.
Nowlin, Michael. "Ralph Ellison, James Baldwin, and the Liberal Imagination." *Arizona Quarterly* 60 (Summer 2004): 117-40.
O'Daniel, Therman B., ed. *James Baldwin: A Critical Evaluation*. Washington, DC: Howard University Press, 1981.
Porter, Horace A. *Stealing the Fire: The Art and Protest of James Baldwin*. Middletown, CT: Wesleyan University Press, 1989.
Pratt, Louis H. *James Baldwin*. Boston: Twayne, 1978.
Romanet, Jerome de. "Revisiting *Madeleine* and 'The Outing:' James Baldwin's Revision of Gide's Sexual Politics." *MELUS* 22.1 (1997): 3-14.
Sanderson, Jim. "Grace in 'Sonny's Blues.'" *Short Story* 6 (Fall 1998): 85-95.
Scott, Lynn Orilla. *James Baldwin's Later Fiction: Witness to the Journey*. East Lansing: Michigan State University Press, 2002.
Sherard, Tracey. "Sonny's Bebop: Baldwin's 'Blues Text' as Intracultural Critique." *African American Review* 32.4 (Winter 1998): 691-705.
Standley, Fred L., and Nancy V. Burt, eds. *Critical Essays on James Baldwin*. Boston: G. K. Hall, 1988.
Sylvander, Carolyn Wedin. *James Baldwin*. New York: Frederick Ungar, 1980.
Tomlinson, Robert. "'Payin' One's Dues': Expatriation as Personal Experience and Paradigm in the Works of James Baldwin." *African American Review* 33.1 (Spring 1999): 135-48.
Troupe, Quincy, ed. *James Baldwin: The Legacy*. New York: Simon & Schuster, 1989.
Tsomondo, Thorell. "No Other Tale to Tell: 'Sonny's Blues' and 'Waiting for the Rain.'" *Critique: Studies in Contemporary Fiction* 36.3 (Spring 1995): 195-209.
Washington, Bryan R. *The Politics of Exile: Ideology in Henry James, F. Scott Fitzgerald, and James Baldwin*. Boston: Northeastern University Press, 1995.
Weatherby, W. J. *James Baldwin: Artist on Fire*. New York: Donald I. Fine, 1989.
Zaborowska, Magdalena J. *James Baldwin's Turkish Decade: Erotics of Exile*. Durham, NC: Duke University Press, 2009.

CRITICAL INSIGHTS

About the Editor

Morris Dickstein is Distinguished Professor of English at the Graduate Center of the City University of New York and senior fellow of the Center for the Humanities, which he founded in 1993 and directed for seven years. He is a widely published reviewer and critic, perhaps best known for his recent book on the 1930s, *Dancing in the Dark: A Cultural History of the Great Depression* (2009). His other books include *Gates of Eden: American Culture in the Sixties* (1977, 1997), *Leopards in the Temple: The Transformation of American Fiction, 1945-1970* (2002), *A Mirror in the Roadway: Literature and the Real World* (2005), and, as editor, *The Revival of Pragmatism* (1998). His essays and reviews have appeared in the *New York Times Book Review, Partisan Review, The American Scholar, Raritan, The Nation, Literary Imagination, Slate, Dissent*, the *Washington Post*, the *Chronicle of Higher Education, Bookforum*, and the *Times Literary Supplement* (London). He has served as film critic of the *Bennington Review* and *Partisan Review* and was an adviser for a documentary film about four leading New York intellectuals, Joseph Dorman's *Arguing the World*. He was a founder and board member (1983-89) of the National Book Critics Circle and Vice Chair of the New York Council for the Humanities from 1997 to 2001. He was a contributing editor of *Partisan Review* from 1972 to 2003 and served as president of the Association of Literary Scholars and Critics in 2006-07.

About *The Paris Review*

The Paris Review is America's preeminent literary quarterly, dedicated to discovering and publishing the best new voices in fiction, nonfiction, and poetry. The magazine was founded in Paris in 1953 by the young American writers Peter Matthiessen and Doc Humes, and edited there and in New York for its first fifty years by George Plimpton. Over the decades, the *Review* has introduced readers to the earliest writings of Jack Kerouac, Philip Roth, T. C. Boyle, V. S. Naipaul, Ha Jin, Ann Patchett, Jay McInerney, Mona Simpson, and Edward P. Jones, and published numerous now classic works, including Roth's *Goodbye, Columbus*, Donald Barthelme's *Alice*, Jim Carroll's *Basketball Diaries*, and selections from Samuel Beckett's *Molloy* (his first publication in English). The first chapter of Jeffrey Eugenides's *The Virgin Suicides* appeared in the *Review*'s pages, as well as stories by Rick Moody, David Foster Wallace, Denis Johnson, Jim Crace, Lorrie Moore, and Jeanette Winterson.

The Paris Review's renowned Writers at Work series of interviews, whose early installments include legendary conversations with E. M. Forster, William Faulkner, and Ernest Hemingway, is one of the landmarks of world literature. The interviews received a George Polk Award and were nominated for a Pulitzer Prize. Among the more than three hundred interviewees are Robert Frost, Marianne Moore, W. H. Auden, Elizabeth Bishop, Susan Sontag, and Toni Morrison. Recent issues feature conversations with Salman Rushdie, Joan Didion, Norman Mailer, Kazuo Ishiguro, Marilynne Robinson, Umberto Eco, Annie Proulx, and Gay Talese. In November 2009, Picador published the final volume of a four-volume series of anthologies of *Paris Review* interviews. *The New York Times* called the Writers at Work series "the most remarkable and extensive interviewing project we possess."

The Paris Review is edited by Philip Gourevitch, who was named to the post in 2005, following the death of George Plimpton two years earlier. A new editorial team has published fiction by André Aciman, Colum McCann, Damon Galgut, Mohsin Hamid, Uzodinma Iweala, Gish Jen, Stephen King, James Lasdun, Padgett Powell, Richard Price, and Sam Shepard. Poetry editors Charles Simic, Meghan O'Rourke, and Dan Chiasson have selected works by John Ashbery, Kay Ryan, Billy Collins, Tomaž Šalamun, Mary Jo Bang, Sharon Olds, Charles Wright, and Mary Karr. Writing published in the magazine has been anthologized in *Best American Short Stories* (2006, 2007, and 2008), *Best American Poetry*, *Best Creative Non-Fiction*, the Pushcart Prize anthology, and *O. Henry Prize Stories*.

The magazine presents two annual awards. The Hadada Award for lifelong contribution to literature has recently been given to Joan Didion, Norman Mailer, Peter Matthiessen, and, in 2009, John Ashbery. The Plimpton Prize for Fiction, awarded to a debut or emerging writer brought to national attention in the pages of *The Paris Review*, was presented in 2007 to Benjamin Percy, to Jesse Ball in 2008, and to Alistair Morgan in 2009.

The Paris Review was a finalist for the 2008 and 2009 National Magazine Awards in fiction, and it won the 2007 National Magazine Award in photojournalism. The *Los Angeles Times* recently called *The Paris Review* "an American treasure with true international reach."

Since 1999 *The Paris Review* has been published by The Paris Review Foundation, Inc., a not-for-profit 501(c)(3) organization.

The Paris Review is available in digital form to libraries worldwide in selected academic databases exclusively from EBSCO Publishing. Libraries can contact EBSCO at 1-800-653-2726 for details. For more information on *The Paris Review* or to subscribe, please visit: www.theparisreview.org.

Contributors

Morris Dickstein is Distinguished Professor of English at the Graduate Center of the City University of New York. He is a widely published reviewer and critic, perhaps best known for his recent book on the 1930s, *Dancing in the Dark: A Cultural History of the Great Depression* (2009). His other books include *Gates of Eden: American Culture in the Sixties* (1977, 1997), *Leopards in the Temple: The Transformation of American Fiction, 1945-1970* (2002), and *A Mirror in the Roadway: Literature and the Real World* (2005). In 2006-07 he served as president of the Association of Literary Scholars and Critics.

Barry Mann is an actor, writer, and educator based in Atlanta, Georgia. He has authored plays for adults and children, articles for the magazines *Storytelling* and *Dramatics*, and hundreds of essays on literary, historical, and social topics for various reference works.

Richard Beck is a writer living in New York City. He has written articles for *N+1*, *Bookforum*, and *The Boston Phoenix*.

Douglas Field is Senior Lecturer in English at Staffordshire University in England. He is the editor of *American Cold War Culture* (2005) and *A Historical Guide to James Baldwin* (2009). His work has been published in *African American Review*, *Callaloo*, the *Guardian* and the *Times Literary Supplement*.

James Campbell is a writer for the *Times Literary Supplement*, where he writes a weekly column. A frequent contributor to the *New York Times Book Review*, he is also the author of *Exiled in Paris* (2003), *Talking at the Gates: A Life of James Baldwin* (2002), *This Is the Beat Generation* (2001), and *Invisible Country: A Journey Through Scotland* (1990).

Horace A. Porter is F. Wendell Miller Professor of English and American Studies at the University of Iowa, where he focuses on African American fiction and autobiography. He is the author of *Stealing Fire: The Art and Protest of James Baldwin* (1990) and coeditor of *Call and Response: The Riverside Anthology of the African American Literary Tradition* (1998) and *Jazz Country: Ralph Ellison in America* (2001). His own memoir, *The Making of a Black Scholar* (2003), documents his journey from segregated schooling to collegiate educator.

Mildred R. Mickle is Assistant Professor of English and English Coordinator at Penn State Greater Allegheny. She is the author of several essays on Octavia E. Butler's works and has published essays on Lillian Allen and an interview with Jaki Shelton Green.

D. Quentin Miller is Associate Professor of English at Suffolk University in Boston. He is the author of *John Updike and the Cold War: Drawing the Iron Curtain* (2001) and editor of *Re-Viewing James Baldwin: Things Not Seen* (2000) and *Prose and Cons: Essays on Prison Literature in the United States* (2005). He is one of the editors of the

Heath Anthology of American Literature and of two composition textbooks, *The Generation of Ideas* and *Connections*. His articles have appeared in such journals as *American Literature*, *Forum for Modern Language Studies*, *Legacy*, *American Literary Realism*, and the *Hemingway Review* and in a variety of books and reference volumes. He is currently completing a manuscript on James Baldwin in the context of the law.

Charles Scruggs is Professor of English at the University of Arizona. His publications include *Jean Toomer and the Terrors of American History* (1998) and *Sweet Home: Invisible Cities in the Afro-American Novel*. His articles often focus on the works of Phillis Wheatley, Carl Van Vechten, Richard Wright, Ralph Ellison, James Baldwin, and Toni Morrison.

Peter Kerry Powers is Associate Professor and Chair of the Department of English at Messiah College in Pennsylvania. He is the author of *Recalling Religions: Resistance, Memory and Cultural Revision in Ethnic Women's Literature* (2001) and various academic essays and reviews that have appeared in such journals as *South Atlantic Review*, *Religion and American Culture*, and *American Literature*.

Geraldine Murphy was Professor of English at Wesleyan University and the first female faculty member there to be promoted to a tenured position. She is the author of *A Momentary Stay: A Short Story Collection* (1972) and *The Study of Literature in High School* (1968).

John M. Reilly is Professor of English and Director of the Graduate Program at Howard University. Focusing primarily on African American writers, he has been recognized for distinguished scholarship in ethnic literature with a citation from the Society for the Study of the Multi-Ethnic Literature of the United States (MELUS). He is editor of *The Oxford Companion to Crime and Mystery Writing* (1999) and author of *Tony Hillerman: A Critical Companion* (1996).

Tiffany Gilbert is Assistant Professor of English at the University of North Carolina Wilmington. She has published essays on the star image of Dorothy Dandridge in Otto Preminger's film *Carmen Jones*, on the diva politics in Douglas Sirk's film *Imitation of Life*, and on Giuseppe Verdi's opera *Otello*. Her current research projects range from exploring the relationship between consumption and masculinity in Patricia Highsmith's *The Talented Mr. Ripley* and Bram Stoker's *Dracula* to interrogating generic affinities and departures evident in Baldwin's *Notes of a Native Son* and Barack Obama's *Dreams from My Father*.

Lionel Trilling was Professor of English at Columbia University and a renowned American literary writer and critic. He was a member of the New York Intellectuals and a frequent contributor to the *Partisan Review*, and he is known for his criticism of a variety of canonical authors, including E. M. Forster, Isaac Babel, George Orwell, and John Keats. His publications include *Speaking of Literature and Society* (1980), *Of This Time, of That Place and Other Stories* (1979), and *The Opposing Self: Nine Essays in Criticism* (1955).

F. W. Dupee was Professor of English at Columbia University, a popular literary critic, and a renowned scholar of Henry James. His most famous collection of essays, *The King of the Cats*, was published in 1965.

C. W. E. Bigsby is Professor of American Studies at the University of East Anglia in Norwich, England. He is credited as the author or editor of more than forty books, the most recent being *One Hundred Days: One Hundred Nights* (2008) and *Arthur Miller: 1915-1962* (2008). An esteemed analyst of theater, he is considered the authoritative commentator on Arthur Miller, with whom he shared a thirty-year friendship.

Yoshinobu Hakutani is Professor of English and University Distinguished Scholar at Kent State University, where he teaches classes in American literature and African American literature as well as linguistics. His most recent book is titled *Cross-Cultural Visions in African American Modernism: From Spatial Narrative to Jazz Haiku* (2006), and he has published widely on Richard Wright and Theodore Dreiser.

Trudier Harris was J. Carlyle Sitterson Professor of English at the University of North Carolina at Chapel Hill for thirty years before her retirement in 2009. She is the author of many books, including *South of Tradition: Essays on African American Literature* (2002), *Saints, Sinners, Saviors: Strong Black Women in African American Literature* (2001), and *The Power of the Porch: The Storyteller's Craft in Zora Neale Hurston, Gloria Naylor, and Randall Kenan* (1996).

Henry Louis Gates, Jr., is Alphonse Fletcher University Professor at Harvard University and Director of the W. E. B. Du Bois Institute for African and African American Research. A prolific literary critic and theorist, he is recognized as one of America's leading scholars of African American literature and culture. Among his most prominent works is *The Signifying Monkey* (1988). Between 2006 and 2008, he hosted the PBS miniseries *African American Lives*.

Darryl Pinckney is an American novelist, playwright, and essayist. He is the author of the novel *High Cotton* (1992) and the collection of essays *Out There: Mavericks of Black Literature* (2002). He is a frequent contributor to *The New York Review of Books*.

Acknowledgments

"James Baldwin" by Barry Mann. From *Magill's Survey of American Literature*. Rev. ed. Copyright © 2007 by Salem Press, Inc. Reprinted with permission of Salem Press.

"The *Paris Review* Perspective" by Richard Beck. Copyright © 2011 by Richard Beck. Special appreciation goes to Christopher Cox, Nathaniel Rich, and David Wallace-Wells, editors at *The Paris Review.*

"Excerpt from *Exiled in Paris*" by James Campbell. From *Exiled in Paris: Richard Wright, James Baldwin, Samuel Beckett, and Others on the Left Bank* (2003), pp. 23-33. Copyright © 2003 by the Regents of the University of California. Reprinted with permission of the author.

"'This Web of Lust and Fury': Harriet Beecher Stowe, James Baldwin's Nineteenth--Century White Mother" by Horace A. Porter. From *Stealing the Fire: The Art and Protest of James Baldwin* (1989), pp. 39-66. Copyright © 1989 by Horace A. Porter. Reprinted by permission of Wesleyan University Press.

"Looking for Jimmy Baldwin: Sex, Privacy, and Black Nationalist Fervor" by Douglas Field. From *Callaloo* 27, no. 2 (2004): 457-480. Copyright © 2004 by The Johns Hopkins University Press. Reprinted with permission of The Johns Hopkins University Press.

"The Tale of Two Cities in James Baldwin's *Go Tell It on the Mountain*" by Charles Scruggs. From *American Literature* 52, no. 1 (March 1980): 1-17. Copyright © 1980 by Duke University Press. All rights reserved. Reprinted with permission of Duke University Press.

"The Treacherous Body: Isolation, Confession, and Community in James Baldwin" by Peter Kerry Powers. From *American Literature* 77, no. 4 (December 2005): 787-813. Copyright © 2005 by Duke University Press. All rights reserved. Reprinted with permission of Duke University Press.

"Subversive Anti-Stalinism: Race and Sexuality in the Early Essays of James Baldwin" by Geraldine Murphy. From *English Literary History* 63, no. 4 (1996): 1021-1046. Copyright © 1996 The Johns Hopkins University Press. Reprinted with permission of The Johns Hopkins University Press.

"'Sonny's Blues': James Baldwin's Image of Black Community" by John M. Reilly. From *Negro American Literature Forum* 4, no. 2 (July 1970): 56-60. Copyright © 1970 by African American Review. Reprinted with permission of African American Review.

"On James Baldwin's *Another Country*" by Lionel Trilling. From *A Company of Readers: Uncollected Writings of W. H. Auden, Jacques Barzun, and Lionel Trilling from The Readers' Subscription and Mid-Century Book Clubs*, edited by Arthur Krystal (2001), pp. 153-158. Copyright © 2001 by the Estate of Lionel Trilling, reprinted with permission of The Wylie Agency LLC.

"James Baldwin and the 'Man'" by F. W. Dupee. From *The New York Review of Books* 1, no. 1 (1963): 1-2. Copyright © 1963 by the New York Review, Inc. Reprinted with permission of the New York Review, Inc.

"The Committed Writer: James Baldwin as Dramatist" by C. W. E. Bigsby. From *Twentieth Century Literature* 13, no. 1 (April 1967): 39-48. Copyright © 1967 by *Twentieth Century Literature*. Reprinted with permission of *Twentieth Century Literature*.

"If the Street Could Talk: James Baldwin's Search for Love and Understanding" by Yoshinobu Hakutani. From *The City in African-American Literature*, edited by Yoshinobu Hakutani and Robert Butler (1995), pp. 150-167. Copyright © 1995 by Associated University Presses. Reprinted with permission of Associated University Presses.

"Bearing the Burden of the Blues: *If Beale Street Could Talk*" by Trudier Harris. From *Black Women in the Fiction of James Baldwin* (1985), pp. 128-163. Copyright © 1985 by The University of Tennessee Press. Reprinted with permission of the author.

"The Fire Last Time" by Henry Louis Gates, Jr. From *The New Republic* (June 1, 1992): 37-43. Copyright © 1992 by Henry Louis Gates, Jr. Reprinted with permission of the author.

"The Magic of James Baldwin" by Darryl Pinckney. From *The New York Review of Books* 45, no. 18 (November 19, 1998): 64-74. Copyright © 1998 by the New York Review, Inc. Reprinted with permission of the New York Review, Inc.

"James Baldwin: The Risks of Love" by Darryl Pinckney. From *The New York Review of Books* 47, no. 6 (April 13, 2000). Copyright © 2000 by the New York Review, Inc. Reprinted with permission of the New York Review, Inc.

Index